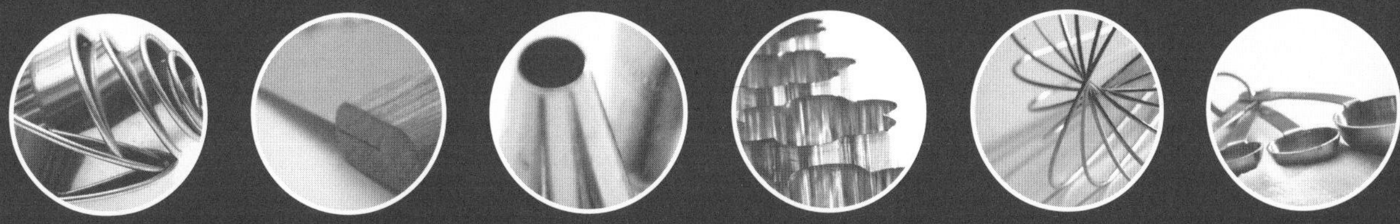

THE good cookie

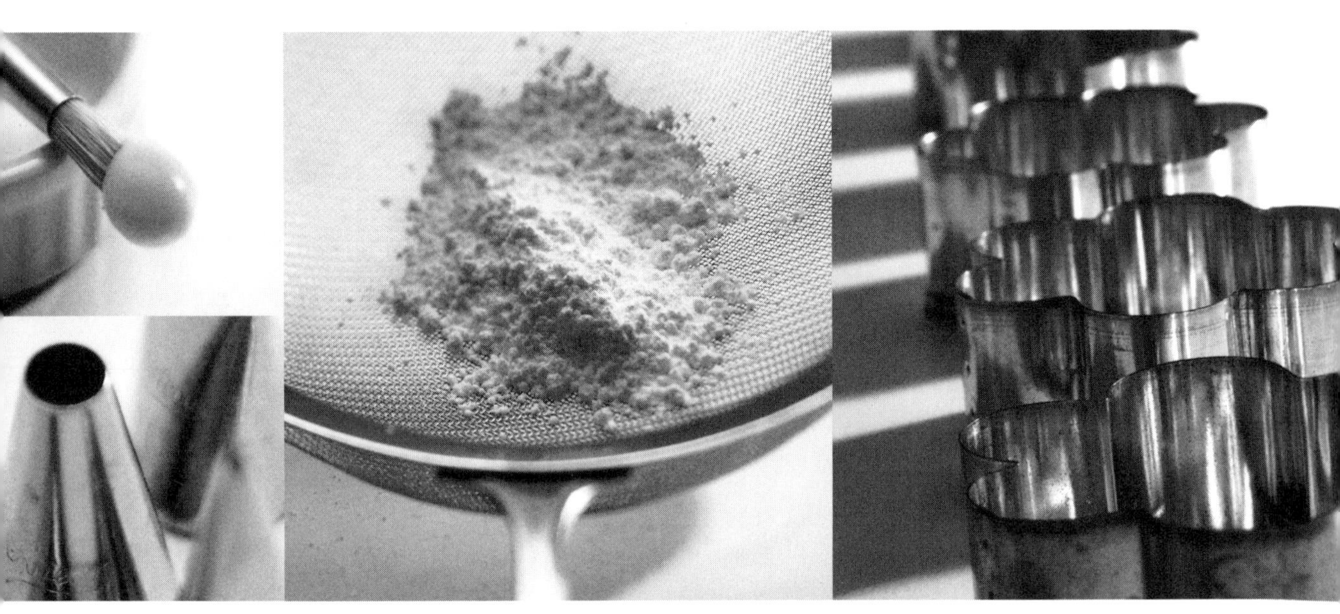

THE good cookie

TISH BOYLE

OVER 250 DELICIOUS RECIPES FROM SIMPLE TO SUBLIME

JOHN WILEY & SONS, INC.

This book is printed on acid-free paper.

Published by John Wiley & Sons, Inc., Hoboken, New Jersey
Published simultaneously in Canada

Library of Congress Cataloging-in-Publication Data

Boyle, Tish.
The Good Cookie : over 250 delicious recipes from simple to sublime / Tish Boyle.
p. cm.
Includes bibliographical references and index.
ISBN 0-471-38791-6 (cloth)
1. Cookies. I. Title.

TX772 .B69 2001
641.8'654–dc21

2001046888

Printed in the United States of America

DESIGNED BY VERTIGO DESIGN, NYC

10 9 8 7 6 5 4 3 2 1

To Dickie, the sweetest cookie of the batch

acknowledgments

While cookies are simple enough to make, cookbooks are not, and it is with the help and inspiration of many generous people that this one came to be. Thanks to Tim Moriarty, my good friend, former (and very much missed) colleague, and cookbook collaborator. Tim knows how to turn a phrase and contributed much to the text of this book. His dry wit and wacky outlook on life (and cookies) were greatly appreciated. Lisa Yockelson, my dear baking-obsessed friend, inspired me to write my first cookbook and continues to be my baking muse. I admire Lisa's dedication to the baking craft almost as much as her capacity for kindness. Lisa makes this world a sweeter place. Mickey Choate, my agent, makes things happen and then writes it all up in legalese. Thanks for pointing me in the right direction and giving me good ideas. At John Wiley & Sons, Inc., thanks to Pam Chirls, my editor, for offering me the opportunity to write this book and for her dedication to promoting the pastry and dessert world. To Andrea Johnson for her attention to detail and patience during the production phase. Much gratitude to the talented team at Vertigo Design for making this book look its best. To good friend Judith Sutton, whom I met years ago on my first day of cooking school in Paris, for painstakingly copyediting this book. Thanks to photographer John Uher, who not only takes delectable-looking photos, but makes every project an adventure of food, laughter, and fun. Thanks also to the rest of his team, Bob Piazza, another talented photographer, and Paul Williams, the Picasso of retouchers and all-around genius. To Michael Schneider for his generous support of my projects over the years. To Irina Brandler and Connie Banyez, who enthusiastically assisted with the cookie research. To all of the pastry chefs, friends, and colleagues who contributed wonderful cookie recipes: Ann Amernick, Stephanie Banyas, Amy Berg, Teaika Blocher, Chris Broberg, Carey Campbell, Lisa Cole, Pat Coston, Faith Fernbach, Marcy Goldman, Carole Harlam, Martin Howard, Denise Mondot, Jacquy Pfeiffer, Nicole Rees, Marshall Rosenthal, Denis Rufel, Richard Ruskell, Andrew Garrison Schotts, Biagio Settepani, Deborah Snyder, (again) Judith Sutton, Gerhard Wetzler, and (again) Lisa Yockelson. To my sister, Kathleen Bartoletti, for all her ideas, inspiration, and help with the Wicked Witch Candy Cottage. To all my critics, professional and otherwise, for keeping me on my toes. To all the men and women at a certain office of the Internal Revenue Service, for eating all those cookies. To my family, who have always supported my culinary career, even in the early years when it didn't seem all that promising. And finally, to any and all culinary adventurers who have ever attempted to bake from scratch—you are my greatest inspiration.

contents

introduction

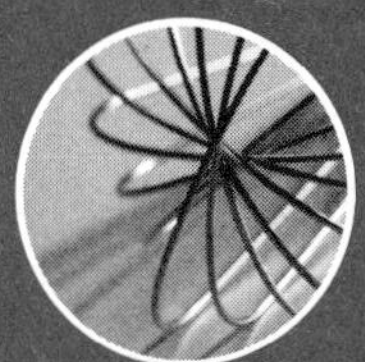

Everyone loves cookies. When you offer a plate of sweet, buttery cookies to a group of people, barriers break down, and formality fades away. Cookies have a universal appeal, a sort of magic quality that transcends age, background, and anything else that separates people.

Cookies are especially important to children. During my childhood, the certainty that a plateful of Oreos or Chips Ahoy was waiting for me at home along with a glass of cold milk helped create an oasis of calm in the face of elementary school anxieties. But while I loved packaged cookies, it was homemade cookies that I really craved—Toll House cookies loaded with chips, fudgy brownies, and Mom's rich little piped butter cookies topped with colorful sprinkles. I relished the yearly ritual of holiday baking that my two sisters and I shared with our mother: the measuring and mixing, the rolling and cutting, and then watching and waiting while the cookies baked. Then came the best part—decorating. It was something we could all do together, and when Dad came home, we would proudly show him something we had made ourselves, sure of his praise and approval. Mom stored the holiday cookies in tins, and for the remainder of the holiday season, the whole family was keenly aware of just where those tins were and what was in them.

Eventually, with encouragement from my perpetually hungry family, I began to bake on my own. The results were not always perfect (like the time I omitted the butter from a batch of chocolate chip cookies), but the cookies always vanished quickly—a good sign, I thought. Even imperfect cookies must be good. That was the beginning of my love affair with baking.

In recent years, I've attended numerous family and work-related festivities that featured home-baked cookies. After eating lots of cookies at these various venues, I was left with one prevailing observation: most of the home-baked cookies out there are pedestrian. In looking for cookie recipes, though, I found there is no shortage. There are thousands, maybe hundreds of thousands to choose from, in cookbooks and magazine articles, in newspaper food sections, and posted on web sites. Some of these recipes are good, but most are only average. Gradually the idea crystallized—why not revisit some of the cookie classics based on my experience as a professional in the baking field? While looking at ways of updating and improving upon the standards, why not also consider new creations that I'd been thinking about for some time? Writing *The Good Cookie* was less an attempt to build a new mousetrap than an effort to reexamine, add to, and improve on the existing body of cookie recipes.

Almost every culture in the world has a rich cookie tradition, the roots of which can be traced back for thousands of years. Cookies, or near relatives, existed in Asia, the Middle East, Central America, and Europe long before they flourished in North America. Cookies are continually evolving. Previous generations of Americans enjoyed fresh-made cookies straight from the oven. Then, starting in the '50s, and continuing through the end of the century, it seemed that no one had time to bake: it was the era of the packaged cookie. Now the pendulum is swinging back. More people are baking at home, sometimes from store-bought cookie doughs, it is true, sometimes from scratch. Heirloom recipes are being unpacked, and baking skills are re-emerging. Fresh-baked cookies are once again the only acceptable kind.

Cookies are textural and flavorful wonders, but it isn't until we grow up that we really understand the flip side of their magic: they are easy to make and usually require no special equipment. Cookie recipes run the gamut from chic and classic to simple, homespun, and familiar. Cookies are versatile: They can be huge or miniature, chewy or crisp, filled or frosted or plain, sweet or savory. They can be round, square, or rectangular or take the shape of animal, vegetable, or mineral. They can be kitschy or chic—or both at the same time. Many welcome variations.

At once one of the most satisfying and easiest of baking projects, cookies make great gifts. When you need a hostess gift, or something to contribute to the community bake sale, having a few great cookie recipes in your arsenal comes in handy. People remember, and they never grow tired of a great cookie.

A Bite-Sized History of the Cookie

Historically speaking, the cookie probably has two ancestors: the small cake and the biscuit. The earliest small cakes were doughs of flour and water baked on primitive versions of the hot plate: thin, flat stones on an open fire. Later, these simple doughs were baked in stone ovens. Ancient Egyptians used small cakes as part of important religious rituals. Other nearly contemporaneous cultures—including Assyrians and Babylonians—also made small cakes. A variety of Mesopotamian peoples, who were early bakers and consumers of products more closely resembling cookies, used dates as the core of small confections called sweetmeats. There is also evidence that the Greeks were enjoying spiced honey cakes in the fifth century B.C.

In addition to baking, the Romans used a combination of boiling followed by deep-frying to make their biscuit/cakes: a thick paste of wheat flour was boiled and spread on a hot pan or plate to bake. Once it cooled and hardened, the cake was cut into small portions and fried. The result was served with honey and pepper.

For the most part, however, the story of the cookie from earliest recorded time to the Middle Ages is the story of the biscuit. The word comes from the French *bis* ("twice") and *cuit* ("cooked"). Originally, biscuits were pieces of dough that were baked once, put in storage tins for a long time, and then baked again before being distributed to sailors on long sea voyages or soldiers on the march. Such biscuits would keep for years. "Hardtack" is another familiar word for these oven-baked, hard-as-a-brick staples. Soldiers under Louis XIV referred to them as "stone bread." At some point, fat was introduced into this hardtack dough. The addition of sugar was an essential precondition before the biscuit could evolve into the cookie. Persians were using sugar in baked goods as early as the seventh century B.C., but centuries elapsed before today's cookie emerged from the biscuit.

In England, the term "biscuit" is still used to mean "cookie" (in Spain, it's *galleta*; in Germany, *kek*). The word we use is taken from one brought to us by Dutch settlers: "cookie" derives from the word *koekje*, meaning "small cake." The term doesn't refer to those dry flour- and water-based items made on open fires or stone ovens; it refers to a practice common among cooks in medieval Europe, before the invention of the thermometer, for testing the heat of their ovens. They would drop little portions of dough onto pans and observe how long it took for them to harden. Once they'd served their purpose, these "little cakes" were supposedly given to children, as they were not substantial enough for adults. During the Middle Ages, both the methods and ingredients used for biscuits and small cakes began to diversify. Because so much was recorded and printed, we can now trace the origins of many of the cookies still enjoyed by Western cultures today. Gingerbread, cracknels, and meringue cookies are among the recipes that evolved during this time.

Craftsman bakers were common in large European towns from the sixth century onward. By the Middle Ages, these bakers were still primarily using hearth ovens and the boiling and frying methods of the Ancient Romans. These methods used to make cracknels, which were small, crisp, sweet biscuits, and simnels, which were thicker variations of cracknels.

During the Middle Ages, the methods and ingredients for biscuits and small cakes began to diversify. Eggs and ground nuts were introduced to many flour mixtures. Aeration was achieved through beaten egg whites and, later, beaten whole eggs. As sugar became more available and affordable, it was added to these mixtures, and the meringue and the sponge biscuit (also known as the "boudoir biscuit") were born. Spices were becoming more common, too. Many bakers by this time belonged to guilds. These guilds standardized recipes, and gave them names. As new cakes and biscuits were created, based on the introduction of new proportions, methods, and ingredients, names were given to them all: the Savoy biscuit; the shortcake (rich and buttery, leavened with yeast); the Italian biscuit (a meringue); the Lisbon, Naples, and Spanish biscuits; jumbles; croquants; and tuiles. A primitive gingerbread was born. Oatcakes were popular among Scottish soldiers. In Italy, they were enjoying "panis biscotus."

The transition from hearth baking and boiling and frying to the use of enclosed ovens was a gradual one. The ancient Romans did employ enclosed ovens—there is one in the ruins of Pompeii. But their simpler alternative, boiling and frying, along with open hearths and griddles, prevailed in Europe in the Middle Ages. Enclosed ovens were still costly and difficult to construct. And because most medieval dwellings were constructed of wood, wattle, and daub, ovens presented a fire hazard. A village would be fortunate to have one craftsman baker, whose bakehouse was located in a building far from the village, usually near a mill and a river or other water source. By the twelfth century, such ovens were common. In the mid- to late Middle Ages, noblemen were able to build stone dwellings of sufficient size to accommodate ovens, but it was not until the eighteenth century that ovens of stone or brick were commonplace in the homes of commoners, and that baking was preferred over frying in most of Europe. The frying tradition continued, however, in parts of Europe but especially in the Middle East and India.

Over time, various cultures adapted and shaped distinctive cookies according to taste, familiarity, tradition, and available ingredients. Think of the now familiar shortbread from Scotland, gingerbread from England, biscotti from Italy, macaroons and sablés from France, and butter and spice cookies from the Netherlands, Germany, and Russia. Springerle cookies from Germany represent the prime example of the early use of cookies: as part of rituals and ceremonies. Springerle cookies are embossed with an image, as were many "cookies" or "biscuits" of ancient times; it's conceivable that the cookies, with their images of people or animals, were eaten as a substitute for human or animal sacrifice. (*Springerle* means "little jumpers" in Dutch; historians thinks it refers to the imprinted image of a jumping horse.) Today, the springerle tradition continues, and these cookies are still formed using special rolling pins and plaques or molds that are imprinted with forms of humans, animals, flowers, and other commonplace objects.

In Colonial America, most small cakes (what we would think of as cookies, but called jumbles or apees at the time) were flavored with rose water, wine, caraway seeds, and nutmeg. It was Thomas Jefferson who introduced vanilla to the United States in 1789; he'd become familiar with it when he served as minister to France.

The Scotch were using the term "cookey" as early as the 1700s. It was employed, food historians think, to distinguish softer, chewier small baked goods from their crisper, durable biscuit cousins. The first recorded use of the term is in a 1796 cookbook published in Hartford, Connecticut by a woman named Amelia Simmons, who identified herself as "An American Orphan." She offers a recipe for a Christmas Cookey. The word turned up again as part of a recipe section in the 1896 Sears catalog, "Gingerbreads, Cookies, and Wafers."

The nineteenth century saw many advances in the evolution of the cookie. Nantes, the French seaport that was one of the busiest in the world at the time, was considered a center of the baking world too, since the basic biscuit was still a staple of the sailor's diet. Elegant variations, however, continued to emerge, in that country and throughout the world. In fact, the French claim credit for the first sandwich cookie—the *paille d'or*, two wafers enclosing raspberry jelly. As refined sugar, vanilla, and flour became more affordable, and chemical leavening agents like bicarbonate of soda encouraged experimentation, cookies as we know and love them really took off.

The first documented appearance of the word "brownie" was in the 1897 Sears catalog. Brownie recipes of the time, however, contained not a speck of chocolate; the "brown" in a Fannie Farmer cookbook brownie recipe of the same period came from molasses. Although some sources say that the brownie is named after its "inventor," a Maine woman named Brownie Shrumpf, she did not in fact invent the brownie: she named herself after the brownie—which makes perfect sense to me.

Legend has it that the brownie was "discovered" by an American in the nineteenth century whose defective oven had left her cake flat and heavy. She set it aside, hoping to salvage it, then discovered that it was moist and chewy and good enough to serve. Other versions have it that a baker forgot to add a leavening agent to her cake and found the dense unrisen result a delight. Legends like this abound in baking and pastry history, and they are often indiscriminately applied to many different recipes. In any case, the brownie slowly gained prominence for its ease of preparation, and by the 1930s, recipes for it could be found on many cocoa tins and chocolate wrappers.

The Commercial Cookie Explosion

In 1830, the first packaged cookies were sold in America. They were originally presented in tin boxes. By the 1870s, the wood-burning cast-iron range had become more common in American homes, and it was practical for people to bake at home. Packaged cookies, however, continued to roll off the line: the Fig Newton was born in 1891, when James Mitchell, owner of the Kennedy Biscuit Company, invented a machine that would pipe a hollow in a portion of cookie dough and fill it with jam. The company's first choice for a cookie filling was fig jam, and they named the resulting cookie after the nearby town of Newton, Massachusetts. Mitchell's company eventually became Nabisco. Today, more than a billion Fig Newtons are manufactured every year.

Barnum's Animal Crackers were introduced by Nabisco in 1902, complete with the string atop the box, which was to be used to hang it on the Christmas tree. In 1908, Hydrox Cookies were brought to market by the Sunshine Biscuit Company. Their name refers to hydrogen and oxygen, the elements that make up water; the company felt that sunshine and water were ideal emblems of purity and cleanliness.

Lorna Doones and Oreos were both introduced in 1912 by the National Biscuit Company. Lorna Doone was the heroine of a nineteenth century Scottish romance novel. The origin of the name "Oreo"? Even the people at Nabisco aren't sure, but it might be based on *or*, the French word for gold, which was the original package color. That ornate decoration on the Oreo is a wreath of posy-like flowers enclosing the symbol of Nabisco.

Ruth Wakefield created the Toll House cookie in 1933. Wakefield, who operated the Toll House Inn in Whitman, Massachusetts, was trying to make a chocolate cookie. In an attempt to save time, she simply cut up a chocolate bar and added the pieces to her brown sugar cookie dough, hoping they would completely melt as the cookies baked. They did not, and her mistake became a classic. It was originally called the Chocolate Crunch Cookie. As the cookie grew in popularity, the Nestle company asked permission to run the recipe on the wrapper of its semisweet bars. In 1942, they began to manufacture the chocolate morsels. The Toll House cookie is the official state cookie of Massachusetts.

Chocolate coating was not used on cookies until after World War II. "Distinctive Cookies," created by Pepperidge Farm in 1955, was one of the first commercial cookie lines made with butter.

The Girl Scouts began selling packaged cookies in 1936. In 1997, more than 182 million boxes were sold. The most popular? Thin Mints, every year since they first appeared in 1951.

Now it's time to write yourself into the cookie history book. Everything you need to know is in your hands.

How to Use This Book

If you're an experienced baker, this book will introduce you to new cookies. I've also collected what I think are the best recipes for familiar classic cookies. If you're a beginner, this book can act as "Baking 101": everything you need to know to get started to make these usually easy "little cakes." I've organized the "getting started" material on ingredients and equipment so that you won't be overwhelmed with too much too soon, but I've tried to include every bit of useful advice and cover every piece of equipment or ingredient you might ever need, so that you can take your own cookie obsession as far as you want to.

In the upfront and way-back sections you'll find:

- Descriptions and details on essential ingredients and equipment for making great cookies.
- Techniques, Tips, and Troubleshooting: if you wonder why a pan has to be greased, or why the oven racks must be positioned just so, you will find the answers here. If something goes wrong with a batch of cookies, you can find the reason here.
- Tips on decorating, wrapping, and shipping cookies for gift giving.
- A comprehensive list of sources for basic equipment, as well as harder-to-find equipment and ingredients.
- A special index of Cookies for Every Occasion. Whether you need to make a batch in a hurry, are looking for the perfect cookie to pair with coffee, are in the mood for something utterly decadent, or want an activity for the kids, here you'll find all sorts of choices.

Of course, the essence of this book is a collection of wonderful cookie recipes, organized according to common-sense, traditional categories.

Drop Cookies are the best-known, most popular, and easiest of cookies. They are made by dropping a soft dough onto a baking sheet from a spoon or small ice cream scoop. Many familiar cookies are found here, including the mighty chocolate chip, in many versions.

Rolled Cookies require some extra handling. The dough generally must be chilled, then rolled out and cut, usually with cookie cutters. The extra care results in beautifully shaped cookies, such as Classic Gingerbread Cookies.

Bar Cookies are made from a soft dough baked in a baking pan. After baking, the "cake" is cut into squares or rectangles.

Hand-Formed Cookies are defined, in part, by the technique and, in part, by their shape—everything from spheres and rectangles to more complex shapes such as pretzels.

Piped and Molded Cookies are formed by piping a rich, buttery dough out through a pastry bag or by placing it into special molds.

Refrigerator Cookies are make-ahead specialties. The dough is formed into a log, then refrigerated or frozen. When it's time to make cookies, disk-sized portions of dough are sliced off as needed and baked.

Filled and Sandwich Cookies are familiar to us all, through store-bought classics like the Oreo. Most people don't think of making these at home, but they're not at all difficult.

Decorator Cookies are for holidays and festive occasions such as weddings, for hostess gifts, or for extra-special bake sale items. They call for more sophisticated decorating procedures than most of the other cookies.

Savory Cookies and Crackers represent the "adults-only" section of the book. These are sophisticated unsweetened cookies and crackers that will be more at home paired with cheeses and spreads, or carry such nontraditional cookie flavors that they deserve their own section.

Basic Recipes include components that are used in some of the cookie recipes. You'll find a cookie dough that is the basis for a multitude of decorator cookies, plus icings, fillings, and buttercreams—in short, everything you need to make the recipes in this book and to go out on your own and create new ones.

If you're a beginner, I recommend you first read the chapters on equipment and ingredients, to be sure you have everything you will need. Then go on to read Chapter 4, Techniques, Tips, and Troubleshooting. You will then have a grounding in what to do, when to do it, and why. Once you're in the kitchen, ready to go, at first you may do some bouncing around, from the recipe you've chosen to a Basic Recipe to Ingredients or Equipment or the techniques and tips chapter, but soon enough it will all become second nature.

I'm sure I don't have to remind you to have fun. These are cookies. Fun—that goes without saying.

equipment

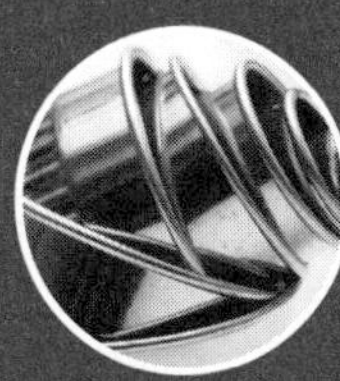

Baking cookies is much more of a pleasure when you have all the right equipment at hand, and it's all top quality. In the real world, of course, we make compromises—most people don't have the budget to buy every single pan, rack, whisk, and bowl they might ever need. Still, your experience of baking, and sometimes your final results, can turn on the slightest detail, so it does make sense to spend at least a little more for quality—you will probably save money in the long run.

Here's a rundown of the equipment you may need, depending on the recipe you're making. Don't be intimidated, though—you don't need it all to make most of the recipes in this book. Start with the basics, and add to your collection gradually, piece by piece.

Baking sheets and pans I recommend that you have at least four 11½ by 17½-inch heavy-duty aluminum baking sheets, also known as half sheet pans or jellyroll pans. These pans are perfect for baking all cookies, and they can comfortably hold fifteen regular-sized cookies. Aluminum is best, because it won't warp, and four is a good number because that way you can always have a sheet that is clean and cooled when your next batch of cookies is ready to be baked. I prefer these to the type called "cookie sheets," which tend to be smaller and less sturdy. If all you have are thin aluminum baking or cookie sheets, stack two of them together for extra insulation.

Nonstick baking sheets should be made of heavy-gauge metal, and the nonstick surface must be of good quality. Insulated baking sheets are another option. These have a layer of air sandwiched between two layers of aluminum, intended to ensure even baking and prevent burning the bottom of baked goods. I don't recommend that you use them for cookies that are intended to be crisp, though; the "insulation" tends to inhibit crisping. If you use insulated baking sheets, you will probably need to bake your cookies for the maximum time stated in the recipes.

Square or rectangular baking pans are usually used for bar cookies. The most useful are 8-inch square, 9-inch square, and 9 by 13-inch rectangular pans. Shiny metal pans are preferable to dark ones, because they reflect heat away from the bars, so they are less likely to overbake. Again, sturdy aluminum is the best choice, because of its good heat conduction. Use the size of baking pan called for in the recipe; if the pan is too big, the bars may overcook; if it is too small, the bars may not be completely done in the center.

Bar cookies can also be baked in glass baking pans. If you use either a glass baking pan or a dark metal nonstick pan for these recipes, reduce the oven temperature by 25 degrees and check for doneness at least 3 minutes earlier than indicated.

Bench scraper This is one of my favorite kitchen tools. A straight-edged metal device with a wooden or plastic handle, it is excellent for scraping dough off work surfaces and for cutting dough into portions. It is also called a dough scraper.

Bowls The best mixing bowls are made of Pyrex glass or stainless steel. Look for deep bowls with high sides, lips and spouts for pouring and handling. Buy a nested set in a variety of sizes. I don't recommend plastic; it's porous and will retain odors and oils, making it unsuitable for some uses, especially beating egg whites.

Box grater A box grater can be used to grate chocolate for decoration and for removing citrus zest (see Zester, page 19).

Cookie press A cookie press, also known as a cookie gun, is a hollow cylinder with a plunger at one end and a decorative tip at the other. A soft cookie dough is placed in the cylinder and then forced out via the plunger to make whatever form the tip is designed for. Many templates and tips are available for cookie presses.

Cookie scoop This is a small, trigger-style ice cream scoop which ensures perfect uniform half-spheres of dough. Cookie scoops are available in a variety of sizes.

Cookie stamp This is a round or square tool with an imprinted design and a short handle. When pressed down on a ball of cookie dough, the stamp flattens it to the desired thickness while creating a design in relief, which remains when the cookie is baked. Available in glass, ceramic, and wood, stamps come in a huge variety of designs. Naturally, this does not work with every type of dough (see Chapter 10, Piped and Molded Cookies); you need a firm dough that's not too rich and buttery, or the design will disappear as the cookie bakes.

Cookie cutters Made of tin-plated steel, stainless steel, plastic, or copper, cookie cutters are available in a variety of shapes and sizes, to cut cookie dough into specific forms.

Double boiler A double boiler consists of two pans that nest together. The smaller top pan holds the food to be melted, warmed, or cooked and sits in the larger pan, filled with an inch or two of water, which is heated to a simmer. It is used for ingredients like chocolate that need only gentle, indirect heat. Be sure that the bottom of the top pan does not touch the simmering water—it should only be warmed by the steam. A stainless steel bowl set over a pot of simmering water works well as an improvised double boiler.

Food processor The processor can be used to mix doughs and batters, blend icings, and chop nuts and other ingredients. One with a large capacity and a powerful motor is best, especially for mixing doughs.

Knives For the cookie baker, three are essential: A chef's knife, with a tapered blade ranging in length from 10 to 12 inches, is used for most cutting tasks, including slicing fruit, chopping nuts, and slicing dough from a roll. A long offset serrated knife with a 12- to 14-inch blade is excellent for chopping chocolate and cutting delicate cookies like biscotti. A paring knife, with a 2- to 3-inch blade, is easy to manipulate and can be used to peel fruit, split vanilla beans, create garnishes, and perform other tasks. I recommend stainless steel knives with sturdy handles.

Madeleine pans These elongated shell-shaped molds are available in two sizes. The larger, standard plaque has 12 depressions per pan, each 3 inches high. The miniature version has 20 depressions per pan, each 1¼ inches high.

Measuring equipment For accurate measurements, you should have:

- Heavy-duty 1-cup and 1-quart glass measuring cups made of heat-resistant glass (such as Pyrex), for measuring liquids; most have metric as well as cup and ounce measures.
- A set of nested metal measuring cups for dry ingredients in the following sizes: 1 cup, ¾ cup, ⅔ cup, ½ cup, ⅓ cup, and ¼ cup. These have straight rims for accurate leveling of ingredients.
- A set of metal graduated measuring spoons to measure smaller amounts of both dry and liquid ingredients. Include 1 tablespoon, 1 teaspoon, ½ teaspoon, and ¼ teaspoon sizes.

For information on how to measure ingredients accurately, see Chapter 4, Techniques, Tips, and Troubleshooting.

Mixers A *heavy-duty electric mixer* is not something that the novice baker needs to run out and buy right away, but if you enjoy baking you will find it indispensable for mixing doughs and batters. Choose a machine with a 4½- to 5-quart stainless steel bowl, a 325- to 350-watt motor (you need all that power for mixing stiff doughs), and at least three attachments: a whisk, a dough hook, and a paddle. A plastic splatter shield is a handy attachment that prevents dry ingredients and dough from flying out of the bowl. I recommend KitchenAid mixers.

A *hand-held electric mixer* is handy for making fillings, whipping egg whites, and mixing many doughs.

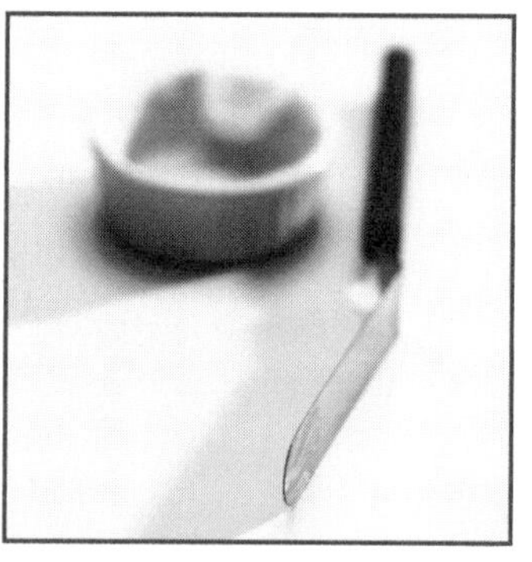

Offset metal spatula A small, angled metal spatula is the ideal tool for spreading tuile batter onto baking sheets, glazing cookies, and frosting brownies and bar cookies. It is also useful for smoothing bar cookie batter evenly in pans.

Oven The baking temperatures and times in this book are for a conventional home oven. If you are using a convection oven, reduce the temperatures by 25 to 50 degrees. If your cookies always seem to be over- or under-baked, your oven may need to be recalibrated. Test it with a high-quality oven thermometer. Some new models can be recalibrated digitally, just by following the instructions in the manual and pushing a few buttons. Otherwise, if it's off, you will need to call a service man.

Parchment paper Also called kitchen parchment, this is used for lining baking pans to provide a nonstick surface, making it easy to remove cookies. It's available in full professional-size sheets which can be cut in half to fit an 11½ by 17½-inch baking sheet, or rolls. Parchment paper can also be used to make disposable cones to be used for decorating cookies by piping icing, melted chocolate, etc.

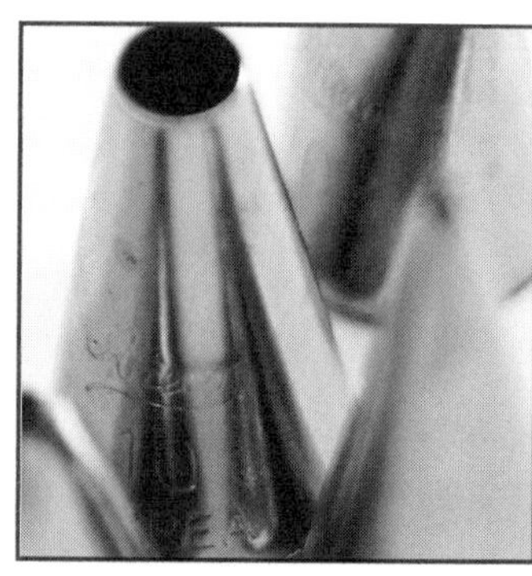

Pastry bags and tips Used to decorate cookies, pipe filling into sandwich cookies, and pipe out certain types of cookies, such as meringues. Pastry bags are available in nylon, polyester, and disposable plastic, and in a variety of sizes. 10- and 14-inch bags are the most practical for cookie making. Pastry tips are designed to create a variety of shapes including stars, leaves, roses, and

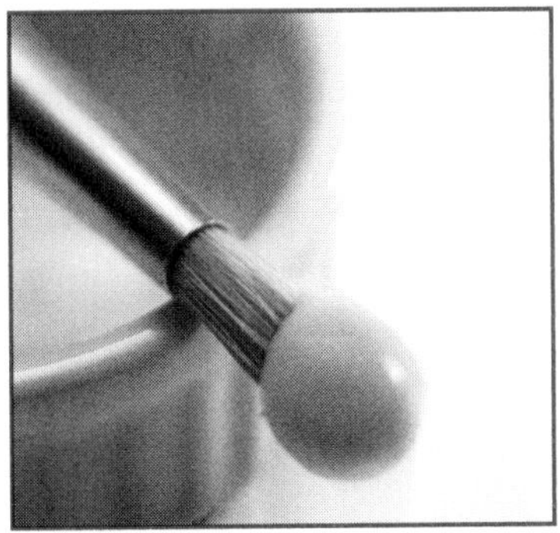

rosettes. Star and plain tips are frequently used to pipe out cookies. For delicate decorative work, use a small bag fitted with a plastic coupler, which allows you to change tips without emptying the bag each time. For filling or piping cookies, use a larger bag and the tip specified in the recipe.

Pastry brush This is a small flat brush from ½ to 2 inches wide which is used to apply egg wash or glaze to cookies. I prefer to use a 1½-inch wide brush for most cookie-making tasks.

Rolling pins Rolling pins are available in a wide range of sizes and materials: plastic, metal, glass, marble, and hardwood. I prefer hardwood, and find it useful to have two types in my cookie kitchen: the broom-handle type, often called a French rolling pin, which is a wooden cylinder 18 to 20 inches in length and 1¼ to 2 inches in diameter, and the type that has handles mounted on an axle. Long, heavy pins ease the task of rolling out doughs. If you go with wood, wipe it clean with a dry cloth rather than washing, or it may warp.

Sifter A sifter is used to aerate and remove lumps from flour and other dry ingredients. Turning the handle passes the ingredients through a fine-mesh screen, giving them a uniform consistency and/or blending them evenly.

Silicone baking mats Sold under the brand names Silpat and Exopat, these baking mats have recently become available to non-professionals. They are flexible sheets of a nonstick silicone that is strong enough to withstand very high heat. They are reusable—some up to 2000 times—and are available at good kitchen supply stores. Because they are a specialized, I do not call for using baking mats in these recipes, but if you have one, by all means use it instead of parchment paper when called for.

Spatulas A narrow metal spatula is useful for leveling off dry ingredients when you measure them and for releasing the stubbornly sticky edges of bar cookies from the pan. A wide flexible metal spatula, the type often known as a pancake turner, is ideal for picking up cookies from a baking sheet and transferring them to a wire rack or to storage containers; it's thin enough to get under the cookie without breaking it and wide enough to support it. A rubber spatula is used to scrape ingredients from the sides of a bowl or for spreading batter, and for many other tasks.

Thermometer An accurate oven thermometer is essential to ensure that your cookies will be properly baked. As an oven thermostat can often be inaccurate, use an oven thermometer every time you bake. A candy/deep fat thermometer which registers temperatures up to 500°F is essential for tasks such as making buttercream and frying doughnuts.

Timer A reliable timer is crucial for baking cookies. The timer built into your microwave, or your oven, should be sufficient if you stay in the kitchen, but I like to hang a stopwatch-type timer around my neck when I bake so I know that my cookies are done wherever I am.

Tins Airtight tins with tight-fitting lids will keep cookies fresh, and they're still the most decorative—and economical—way to present cookies as gifts.

Whisks Whisks are made in different sizes, suited to different functions. Large balloon-type whisks are for whipping ingredients when a lot of air must be incorporated (such as egg whites or cream) and for folding other ingredients into these delicate mixtures. Medium to small whisks are good for making egg- or starch-based mixtures and combining ingredients when you don't want a lot of air incorporated and want to avoid lumps. Look for a balloon whisk in the 12- to 14-inch size and two or three smaller sauce whisks in graduated sizes up to 10 inches.

Wire racks Wire mesh racks with small square grids are used to support cookies so that they cool properly after baking; the stubby legs and wire mesh allow air to circulate underneath the cookies so they cool evenly. Larger wire racks with parallel bars rather than grids can be used to support the baking sheets themselves or larger cookies. These racks can also be used for glazing or decorating cookies—the excess glaze drips off the cookies, creating a clean bottom edge and allowing you to collect the excess on a baking sheet underneath for reuse. Don't skimp on this purchase—properly cooling cookies prevents them from getting soggy from steam and condensation and is essential to their final texture; you should have a few on hand.

Wooden spoons Used to mix doughs and batters, liquids, sugars, and fats, wooden spoons are available flat or concave and slotted or unslotted. Wood is porous and will absorb odors; I suggest you keep a separate set for savory cooking.

Zester This handy tool consists of a handle and a blade with sharp-edged holes at its end; it is used to remove the zest from citrus fruits. A metal ginger grater or the fine side of a box grater (cover it with plastic wrap for easy removal of the zest from the grater) also works well. I highly recommend the Microplane Zester, a device that looks like a carpenter's rasp and is the perfect tool for zesting citrus fruits.

ingredients

Have you ever tasted a wonderful cookie and wondered what made it so great? Chances are, it wasn't an accident. Though cookies are considered a relatively simple sweet in the pastry world, there is still a wide margin for error in preparing them. A great recipe is a good start, but good ingredients, properly prepared, are also important to a cookie's success. Each ingredient, whether it's butter, eggs, or sugar, plays a key role in its flavor, texture, and appearance. So read each recipe carefully, and take ingredient descriptions literally. Should the butter be cold or softened? Should the eggs be at room temperature? Are the dry ingredients to be sifted together? Such details ensure that your cookies will be the best they can be. If you're unclear about the importance of any particular ingredient and its preparation, the following guide will explain it. Make ingredient substitutions only at your own risk!

Flours

Flour gives structure to baked goods. While the subject of flour can be confusing, it shouldn't be a problem if you remember one thing: always use the type of flour called for in the recipe, paying attention to terms such as "bleached" or "unbleached" and so forth. Flours vary in many ways, but the crucial difference is in protein content. Flours with a high protein content, such as unbleached flour, develop more gluten, which provides elasticity and strength to a dough. A cookie made from a high-protein flour will be relatively chewy, it will brown more readily, and it will spread more on the baking pan. Flours with lower protein levels—such as cake flour and whole-wheat flour—will result in tender cookies. Lower-protein flours absorb less liquid, so the cookies will spread less, but they will puff more, because there will be more steam. (The addition of eggs and the mixing methods also affect these factors.)

TYPES OF FLOUR

That's the big picture. Here are details on the flours called for in the recipes in this book.

All-purpose flour Made from a blend of hard (high-gluten) and soft (low-gluten) wheats, all-purpose flour is of medium strength with a protein content of 10.5 to 13 percent. There are two kinds: Bleached all-purpose flour has been chemically bleached. The bleaching agents used whiten the flour and make it easier to blend it with ingredients with higher percentages of fat and sugar. Bleached flour produces a more tender and buttery cookie. Unbleached all-purpose flour imparts a creamier color to baked goods, and it can yield crisper cookies. (Note: Avoid "self-rising" flours, which have added baking powder and salt.)

Bread flour This is an unbleached, hard-wheat flour that gives more structure to baked goods.

Cake flour This flour, made from soft winter wheats, contains very little protein; it is more refined than all-purpose flour. Cookies made with cake flour will have a delicate texture.

Whole wheat flour Milled from the whole wheat kernels, whole wheat flour is usually used in combination with other flours, to provide a nutty flavor and add texture to the finished cookie. It contains slightly more protein than cake flour. (By itself, whole wheat flour would produce heavy, dark cookies.)

STORING FLOUR

Most flours should be stored in airtight containers in a cool, dry place, because they can become rancid. Store whole wheat flour in an airtight container in the refrigerator. Use all-purpose, cake, bread, and whole wheat flour within two months of purchase. Flours can also be frozen, to extend their shelf life to up to a year. Double-wrap the flour and place in plastic containers and/or resealable bags.

MEASURING FLOUR

Measure flour by spooning it into the measuring cup and leveling the top with a knife; do not compress it. If you use too much flour, your cookies will be tough or crumbly and/or dry; too little, and the cookies will spread.

Fats

Fat provides cookies with flavor and makes them moist and tender. There are several types of fat, each with its own properties that result in particular flavors and textures.

Butter Its creaming abilities and flavor make butter the most important fat for baking. It is produced in salted and unsalted forms. Always use unsalted butter in baking, as it permits you to control the salt content of a recipe. Most of the recipes in this book specify the temperature the butter should be when used; pay close attention, and plan ahead, because butter temperature is crucial to the success of your cookies. Butter can be stored, wrapped in plastic, in the freezer for up to six months.

For cookies, I strongly recommend butter over butter-margarine blends or margarine; avoid reduced-calorie or low-fat butter or margarine. By law, U.S. butter must contain at least 80 percent butterfat. Recently, premium butters with a higher butterfat content—up to 86 percent—have shown up in gourmet food shops and some supermarkets. Use these butters for cookie recipes in which butter is the star (e.g., Classic Spritz Cookies, page 193), where the extra buttery flavor and texture make all the difference.

Solid vegetable shortening Vegetable shortening is 100 percent fat. It melts at a higher temperature than butter, so cookies made with it have more time to set in the oven and will not spread as much. Since it is flavorless, it should be used in combination with butter. Avoid the artificial butter-flavored shortening.

Sugar and Other Sweeteners

Sugar, in all its forms, is a carbohydrate that adds sweetness to cookies. It also makes cookies tender and moist, and makes them turn brown in the oven through the process of caramelization.

Brown sugar Brown sugar is granulated sugar with molasses added. There are two basic types: light and dark. Light brown sugar has a more delicate flavor and lighter color than its darker counterpart which contains more molasses. *Muscovado sugar* is a dark cane sugar with a fine, moist texture and a lingering molasses flavor. In the past few years, it has become available in many supermarkets, and it is worth seeking out. Because it has a tendency to dry out and become rock-hard, brown sugar should be stored tightly wrapped in a plastic bag inside an airtight container.

Coarse sugar This decorating sugar has granules that are much larger than granulated sugar. Also known as crystal sugar, it is available at cake-decorating supply stores.

Confectioners' sugar Also called powdered sugar, this is granulated sugar that has been processed to a powder. Although a small amount of cornstarch is added to prevent clumping, it should be sifted before use. Because it is less sweet and has a lighter texture than granulated sugar, it cannot be substituted in equal amounts for granulated sugar.

Corn syrup This thick, sweet syrup is made from cornstarch processed with enzymes or acids. It helps cookies to retain moisture and remain fresher longer. There are two types: light and dark. The dark has a richer flavor, but in general, they can be used interchangeably.

Granulated sugar Derived from sugarcane or sugar beets, this is the most common sweetener in cookie recipes.

Honey Honey is a golden syrup with a slightly greater sweetening power than sugar and a distinct flavor. Its flavor varies depending on the flowers the bees fed on. For a softer-textured cookie or bar, honey is a good sweetening agent because it attracts moisture; goods baked with honey will get even softer in storage. In most recipes, honey can be used in place of sugar in equal amounts, but reduce the amount of liquid in the recipe by ¼ cup for each cup of honey used.

Lyle's golden syrup Also known as refiner's syrup, this thick, delicious, golden syrup is a by-product of the sugar-refining process. It can be used interchangeably with light corn syrup and is available at gourmet food shops and many supermarkets.

Molasses A by-product of the sugar refining process, molasses is a thick, brownish-black syrup with a distinct, hearty flavor. It comes in three forms: unsulphured, sulphured, and blackstrap. Unsulphured has a relatively mild flavor; sulphured has a more pronounced flavor. Blackstrap molasses has the strongest flavor of the three, and would overwhelm the flavor of any cookie. Measure molasses with a liquid measuring cup.

Sanding sugar A fine granulated sugar that is available in a variety of textures and colors. Great for decorating cookies before or after baking, sanding sugar is available at cake-decorating supply stores.

Superfine sugar Also known as bar or castor sugar, superfine sugar is very fine grained and dissolves more easily than regular granulated sugar. It can be substituted for granulated sugar in equal amounts in recipes.

Turbinado sugar Sold under the brand name "Sugar in the Raw," this is a coarse-textured, pale blond raw sugar with a delicate molasses flavor. It is a great decorating sugar to be sprinkled on top of cookies just before baking.

Vanilla sugar This subtly flavored sugar can be substituted for plain granulated sugar in some recipes or lightly dusted over cookies before baking. To make vanilla sugar, split a vanilla bean lengthwise in half, place in a jar, and fill the jar with enough granulated sugar to cover bean. Cover and let stand for 24 hours; the sugar will absorb the vanilla flavor. The bean will be potent for up to a year; replenish the sugar as you remove it. If the seeds begin to mix with the sugar, strain the sugar through a fine-mesh sieve and return the seeds to the jar. This method can also be used with confectioners' sugar.

Cornstarch

Derived from corn, this powdery substance is most often used as a thickening agent. In the recipes in this book, however, it is used in place of a small amount of the flour in some doughs to make the cookies more tender.

Leaveners

Leaveners make cookies puff up by creating air bubbles in dough. It is important to store leaveners properly to maintain their activeness.

Baking powder This is composed of baking soda, cream of tartar, and cornstarch. When combined with a liquid, it releases carbon dioxide. Always use double-acting baking powder, the most common type, which releases some carbon dioxide when it is combined with a liquid and the rest when exposed to the oven's heat. Baking powder has a shelf life of about a year, after which it loses its strength. To test it, sprinkle a little over some hot water: if it fizzes, it is still active.

Baking soda Baking soda is a leavener that provides carbon dioxide bubbles when combined with an acid such as buttermilk or yogurt. It has an almost indefinite shelf life if stored in a dry place.

Yeast A living organism, yeast leavens doughs and batters through the process of fermentation. The recipes in this book call for active dry yeast. Do not substitute instant or rapid-rise (quick-rising) dry yeast. Store yeast in the refrigerator.

Eggs

According to a Russian proverb, "Love and eggs are best when they are fresh." Like many baking and pastry people, I love eggs in all their complex simplicity. Eggs bring richness and moisture, as well as structure, to cookies. Egg yolks, rich in fat, are generally used in baking as a thickener and binder; they make cookies tender. Egg whites, high in protein, are often used to add volume and air to cakes; they add strength and stability to cookies.

Eggs are graded for quality and freshness as AA, A, or B. Most eggs sold in supermarkets are either grade AA or A. Grade AA is best for baking; it has a thick white and strong yolk. Eggs should be stored in the coldest part of the refrigerator, in their original carton, with the more pointed end down. Because of the potential threat of salmonella poisoning, keep eggs refrigerated until shortly before using them, but for baking, eggs usually must be brought to room temperature. Do not use eggs with cracked shells.

If you can, buy organic, free-range eggs. Organic eggs are produced by hens whose feed is composed of ingredients that were grown with minimal use of pesticides, fungicides, herbicides, and commercial fertilizers. Free-range hens have daily access to the outdoors. The production costs of these eggs is higher, and the hens produce fewer eggs, so they're more expensive, but organic, free-range eggs generally have brighter yolks and better flavor. I think they are worth the extra price, especially in cookies where the egg flavor is particularly noticeable (e.g., White Chocolate Eggnog Bars, page 142).

Chocolate

There are many excellent chocolates available in supermarkets today. For cookie baking, there's no need to break the bank buying super-premium chocolate, but don't skimp on quality.

To store chocolate, wrap it first in plastic wrap, then in heavy-duty aluminum foil, and place it in an airtight container. Ideally, chocolate should be stored in a cool, dry place with a consistent temperature of around 65°F. White chocolate must be stored away from light because of the milk solids. Light will accelerate its oxidation, so that the chocolate can turn rancid overnight. Store, well wrapped, in a dark place. Properly stored, unsweetened and dark chocolate may keep for as long as several years. Milk chocolate will keep for one year and white chocolate for seven or eight months. See page 36 for instructions on melting chocolate and page 366 for a quick tempering method.

Unsweetened chocolate Also known as baking chocolate, this consists of pure chocolate liquor (ground cocoa nibs) and lecithin (a stabilizer). It does not contain sugar, and it cannot be used as a substitute for semisweet or bittersweet chocolate.

Bittersweet and semisweet chocolates These are the chocolates used most often in baking. Sugar, lecithin, vanilla, and more cocoa butter are added to unsweetened chocolate to create these chocolates, which are interchangeable (the FDA does not distinguish between the two categories). Both varieties must contain at least 35 percent chocolate liquor. Semisweet chocolate is generally sweeter than bittersweet chocolate, though this varies according to brand, and one company's semisweet chocolate may be comparable in sweetness to another's bittersweet chocolate. It is best to use your own taste as a guide in choosing between the two.

Milk chocolate Milk chocolate contains much less chocolate liquor than bittersweet (10 percent as compared to about 35 percent); it contains a minimum of 3.7 percent milk fat and 12 percent milk solids. Because of the milk component, it is sensitive to heat, and is therefore more difficult to cook and bake with.

White chocolate White chocolate contains no chocolate solids at all, just chocolate's natural fat, cocoa butter. Different products contain various proportions of cocoa butter, butterfat, sugar, milk solids, lecithin, and flavorings. Avoid the so-called "coating" products, which are made with vegetable fat instead of cocoa butter.

Chocolate morsels Chocolate morsels, or chips, are formulated especially to retain their shape when baked in cookies and other desserts. The manufacturers achieve this by substituting vegetable fat for some of the chocolate's natural fat, cocoa butter. Because of this, chocolate morsels should not be substituted for semisweet or bittersweet chocolate.

Cocoa powder Cocoa powder is the result of a hydraulic press operation in which virtually all of the cocoa butter is separated from the pure chocolate liquor. The "cake" that results is ground into a powder. There are two types of unsweetened cocoa powder: alkalized, or Dutch-processed, and nonalkalized. Dutch-processed cocoa powder has been treated with an alkali to neutralize its acidity, a process that creates a darker cocoa with less harshness. Nonalkalized cocoa powder tends to have more chocolate flavor. Instant cocoa mixes cannot be substituted for cocoa powder.

Nuts and Dried Fruits

Nuts are the centerpiece of many cookies, whether sprinkled on top, chopped and incorporated into the dough, or finely ground. Shelled nuts are available unblanched (raw, with skins intact; also referred to as "natural") or blanched (skins removed). Always buy whole nuts, and chop or grind them as necessary. Look for the freshest in specialty food markets and health food stores.

Almonds Almonds are grown in Australia, the Mediterranean, South Africa, and California. Their flavor is mellow and sweet. Almonds in their shells do not spoil as quickly as shelled. Once the package has been opened, store any leftover almonds in a tightly sealed container in a cool, dark space; under those conditions, shelled almonds can be stored for up to three months, or frozen for up to a year.

Cashews Buttery and slightly sweet, cashews are grown throughout the world, especially in India. Because they have a high fat content (48 percent), they can turn rancid quickly and should be stored in an airtight container in the refrigerator.

Hazelnuts Hazelnuts, also called filberts, are grown in Spain, France, and Turkey, but production is now thriving in Washington and Oregon as well. They are sweet and rich and pair beautifully with chocolate.

Macadamias Rich and buttery, this nut is grown primarily in Hawaii. Macadamias are expensive because they are labor-intensive to cultivate and process, and because they are relatively scarce—a 100-pound harvest yields a mere 15 pounds of edible nuts.

Peanuts Peanuts are grown throughout the Southern United States. Though there are several varieties, the most common ones are the Virginia and the Spanish peanut. Store shelled peanuts in an airtight container in the refrigerator for up to three months, or in the freezer for up to six months.

Pecans This sweet, rich nut is a member of the hickory family. The best pecans are from Georgia and Texas; their peak season is fall. For the sake of freshness, I recommend you buy them in the shell: 1½ pounds pecans in the shell will yield approximately 13½ ounces shelled. Be careful how you store them, as pecans will go rancid quickly. They can be refrigerated for up to three months or frozen for up to six months.

Pistachios This sweet nut originated in Turkey and is now grown in central Asia, the Near East, the Mediterranean, and California—a latecomer, as the first decent crop was not harvested there until 1978. Buy shelled pistachios if you can. If you can't find them shelled, look for pistachios in the shell that have not been dyed bright red, and buy twice as much, by weight, as you need for the recipe. Shelled, they will keep for three months in the refrigerator, or up to six months frozen. Unshelled, they can be refrigerated for six months or frozen for a year.

Walnuts This nut is grown in temperate areas throughout the world. American black walnuts have the richest flavor, which is faintly buttery and woodsy. The English, or Persian, variety is most common, and comes in three sizes: large, medium, and baby. Walnuts in the shell should not have any cracks or holes; out of the shell, they should look healthy, not shriveled. They can be stored in a cool, dry place for several months, in the refrigerator, tightly covered, for six months, or in the freezer, well wrapped, for up to a year.

For information on chopping, roasting, and blanching nuts, see Chapter 4, Techniques, Tips, and Troubleshooting.

Nut pastes Nut pastes are now available in many supermarkets, and you can find them in specialty food stores. The most commonly available nut paste, almond paste, is a close cousin to marzipan—which is a mixture of ground almonds, confectioners' sugar, and corn syrup—but it has a higher proportion of nuts and, unlike marzipan, is not cooked. Once you open a container of nut paste, it can be stored in the refrigerator for up to six months. Commercially

mixing it up with kids

Some cookies lend themselves to additional ingredients or toppings—especially bar cookies, but any cookie that you make with kids qualifies. One of my actor friends talks about how "process" is much more important than the final product. This is certainly true of baking with children.

Here's a list of suggested mix-ins. It includes the classic, the cutting edge, and the kind kids like.

Crunch!

- Chopped peanuts
- Chopped almonds
- Coated nuts
- Chopped macadamia nuts
- Chopped walnuts
- Chopped pecans

Chew!

- Dried cherries
- Dried apricots
- Glazed fruits
- Raisins
- Currants
- Candied orange peel

Sweet!

- Semisweet chocolate morsels
- White chocolate morsels
- Butterscotch morsels
- Peanut butter morsels
- Premium-quality bittersweet chocolate, cut into chunks
- Toffee, cut into chunks
- Candy bars, cut into chunks
- Shredded coconut
- Chocolate-drenched shredded coconut
- Chocolate-covered raisins
- Miniature marshmallows

Yuck!

- Gummy Bears
- Gummy Worms
- Swedish Fish, cut into pieces

prepared praline paste and hazelnut paste are also available. If you have trouble finding them, see Sources, page 376. Recipes for making your own praline and pistachio pastes are on pages 364 and 365.

Dried fruits Myriad fruits are available dried: apples, pears, apricots, cherries, cranberries, figs, and dates, to name a few. They are found in specialty food shops, health food stores, and the baking or produce sections of supermarkets. Stored in an airtight container in a cool, dry place, they will keep for six to twelve months. Some of these products contain sulfites, so check the labels if you're allergic. They also contain preservatives to keep them from hardening or discoloring and to inhibit mold and fungi. Dried fruit should be moist when you use it. If it has dried out, you may be able to bring it back by placing it in a steamer for a minute or two. See also: raisins.

Raisins These are grapes of a certain type, usually Thompson, that have been dried either in the sun or in a special dehydrating process. Golden raisins have been treated with sulfites to keep them from darkening.

Flavor Accents

Because they are used in small quantities, ingredients like salt and vanilla extract might seem almost optional in recipes. But flavor accents are critical to the success of the good cookie.

Salt Salt is an important ingredient in cookie doughs which acts as a flavor enhancer. Unless otherwise specified, use table salt for the recipes in this book. The larger crystals of kosher or coarse salt will make the measurements inaccurate.

Vanilla The sweet and mellow flavor and aroma of vanilla is irreplaceable. It finds its way into many cookie recipes, whether as the forward flavor or as a backnote. Vanilla is a pod fruit found on a vine that is in the orchid family. Two high-quality varieties of vanilla beans are Tahitian and Madagascar (or Bourbon). Most of the recipes in this book call for vanilla extract; always use pure vanilla extract, never imitation! When the vanilla flavor must be especially fresh and full of impact, the recipes call for vanilla beans. To use a vanilla bean, split it lengthwise and scrape out the seeds, then either add just the seeds or the seeds and the pod, depending on the recipe. Wrapped tightly in plastic, vanilla beans can be stored for up to three months in a cool, dry place or in the refrigerator. Never freeze vanilla beans, as this affects their subtle flavor.

techniques, tips, and troubleshooting

Cookies are fun, but baking is science. The recipes in this book tell you everything you need to know to make great cookies, but it is helpful to know why, for example, butter should be softened, dough should be chilled, baking sheets should be rotated, and so on. If you're unsure about how to perform a task that is mentioned in a recipe, you will find a full explanation here. Finally, if something has gone wrong with a batch, you will be able to find out why on these pages.

Preparing Ingredients

SOFTENING BUTTER

The temperature and consistency of the butter you use is crucial to the success of your cookies, as is the mixing method for incorporating the butter with the sugar. Follow the directions in each recipe. It takes about 45 minutes to bring cold butter to room temperature in a warm kitchen. (In a cold kitchen, it may take up to two hours.) I prefer to use the microwave to speed up the process. Unwrap the chilled butter, place it on a microwave-safe plate, and microwave on the defrost setting for 30 to 45 seconds, until the butter yields to your finger when gently pressed.

SEPARATING EGGS

Set out two bowls. Tap the egg against a flat surface to crack it and, holding the egg over one bowl, break the shell apart with your fingers, keeping the jagged edges somewhat close together. Allow the egg white to drip into the bowl. Then pour the contents of one half shell into the other, repeating the process until all of the white has dripped into the bowl. Pour the yolk into the other bowl. Continue with the number of eggs you need. If separating more than one egg, use three bowls instead of two: one to crack the egg over, one to pour the whites into, and one for the yolks. This will save you from contaminating all the whites if a yolk breaks.

BEATING EGGS

Eggs are beaten to incorporate air. They are either beaten whole—eggs and yolks together—or separately. Cream of tartar, an acid, is often added to egg whites before beating them to help stabilize them. Before beating egg whites, make sure the bowl is absolutely clean. Pay close attention to the cues given in the recipes; in general, beaten egg whites are ready when they are shiny and have reached the soft peak stage—if you dip a spoon into the whites and lift it out, soft, curved peaks form. For stiffly beaten whites, the peaks should stand straight up and not form a curl. Beating on medium rather than high speed helps prevent overbeating. Egg whites that are lumpy, dull, and dry-looking have been overbeaten.

MEASURING INGREDIENTS

To make a good cookie, it is absolutely crucial to measure all the ingredients accurately. Tough, dry, leaden cookies are most often the result of improperly measured flour.

To measure flour: Spoon the flour lightly into the measuring cup until it is mounded over the rim, then sweep a straight-edged knife or spatula across the cup to level it; do not tap the cup or pack the flour into it. Do not sift flour before measuring unless the recipe specifies so. If you feel your flour has been compacted in storage, stir it with a spoon prior to measuring. If sifted flour is called for in a recipe, pay attention to how it is described. The phrase "½ cup flour, sifted" means that you should measure the flour first, then sift it. The phrase "½ cup sifted flour" means that you should sift slightly more flour than you need (about ¾ cup), then measure out ½ cup.

To measure brown sugar and shortening: Spoon into a dry measuring cup and pack down firmly to fill the cup until it is level with the top of the cup.

To measure liquid ingredients: Pour into a liquid measuring cup, place on a flat surface, and inspect closely to be sure the liquid is at the mark you desire.

MELTING CHOCOLATE

The most important thing to remember about melting chocolate: moisture is the enemy of chocolate. Steam rising up from the bottom of a double-boiler, a drip from a saucepan, moisture from a spoon—any one of these can cause your chocolate to seize, which results in a clumpy mess. If your chocolate does seize, try whisking in 1 teaspoon of a neutral-tasting vegetable oil for each ounce of chocolate. This usually brings the chocolate to a workable state.

To melt chocolate in a double boiler: The easiest way to melt chocolate is in a double boiler. Place the coarsely chopped chocolate in the top of the double boiler over barely simmering water and heat, stirring frequently, until melted and smooth.

To melt chocolate in a microwave oven: Place the coarsely chopped chocolate in a microwave-safe container and microwave it at medium (50 percent) power for 1½ to 4 minutes, until the chocolate turns shiny. (Check often, because chocolate will retain its shape and look solid even though it has liquefied.) Stir milk and white chocolates after about 1½ minutes. On average, 6 ounces chopped semisweet chocolate will require 3 minutes to melt at medium power. (Strangely, chocolate actually melts faster at medium or low microwave heat than it does at high.)

Melting chocolate with a liquid: As mentioned above, melting chocolate will seize if it comes in contact with a small amount of liquid. In general,

2 ounces of chocolate can be safely melted with 1 tablespoon of a liquid such as milk, cream, liquor, or coffee—even water. Chocolate can be melted with a liquid, or butter, directly over low heat, but it must be watched very carefully.

PREPARING NUTS

To blanch almonds: Place them in a pot of simmering water for about 1 minute. Drain them in a strainer, then place them in a bowl of cold water. Pinch each nut: the skin will slide off. Let cool completely and dry before grinding.

Toasting nuts releases their natural oils and brings out their flavor.

To toast nuts: Position a rack in the center of the oven and preheat to the temperature called for below, depending on the type of nut. Place the nuts in a single layer on a baking sheet and toast, shaking the pan two or three times. After toasting, transfer the nuts to a room-temperature baking sheet to cool completely.

- Hazelnuts: Toast at 350°F for 8 to 12 minutes. After toasting, wrap the nuts in a clean towel and cool completely. Transfer the nuts to a large sieve and rub them back and forth against the mesh to remove the loose skins.
- Whole almonds: Toast at 350°F for 10 to 15 minutes. Blanched almonds will be golden when done, unblanched almonds when they are a light brown all the way through (cut one in half to check).
- Sliced or slivered almonds: Toast at 325°F for 5 to 10 minutes.
- Walnuts and pecans: Toast at 350°F for 5 to 10 minutes.

MAKING COOKIES

Plan ahead. Make sure you have all the ingredients you need. Nothing is worse than having to run to the grocery store for a missing item in the middle of a recipe. Unless otherwise specified, ingredients should be room temperature: this includes flour, butter, eggs, and nuts. Pay particular attention to the butter. "Softened" butter is not melted, nor is it firm. Butter that is not at the right temperature will not cream properly, and it may affect the baking time.

Distribute the mounds or cut-outs of dough evenly on the baking sheet, paying attention to the portioning and spacing directions in the recipe. Portioning the dough for your cookies uniformly and evenly will ensure proper baking and texture. If you decide to make the cookies larger or smaller than called for, you will need to adjust the baking time.

PREHEATING THE OVEN

Preheating the oven to the proper temperature generally takes about 15 minutes. Position the racks in the oven as directed in the recipe; this will affect the baking time and browning of your cookies.

ROLLING AND CUTTING OUT THE DOUGH

Dough that is to be rolled out should be firm but not hard. Don't allow it to get too soft either: roll out small portions at a time, keeping the yet-to-be-used dough in the refrigerator.

As you roll out the dough, you will need to lightly toss fairy-dust clouds of flour on the surface and/or on your rolling pin to prevent sticking. It's fun to toss flour, and it's a relief not to have sticky dough, but beware: the trick lies in using the least amount of flour possible. Too much flour will affect the texture of your cookies. You can roll sticky doughs between sheets of waxed paper; this will minimize your need for extra flour.

When cutting out cookies, stickiness again may become an issue. If the dough sticks to the cutter, dip it occasionally in a shallow bowl of flour or powdered sugar (or cocoa, for chocolate doughs) between cuts.

Baking Cookies

Unfortunately, baking cookies is not an exact science. Just as ingredients and kitchen equipment vary, so do oven temperatures and baking times. Consequently, my baking instructions should be viewed as suggestions, not scripture. Get to know your oven and adjust settings and baking times accordingly.

BAKING SHEETS

Some of these recipes call for greasing the baking sheets, others for lining them with parchment paper, or with either parchment or foil. These instructions are not arbitrary. When parchment paper is called for, it's necessary because the cookies may be particularly sticky, and parchment paper will make removing them easiest. Also, sometimes the parchment acts as an insulator so that the cookies don't overbrown; the baking time reflects the use of parchment paper.

The baking times in the recipes in this book are based on whether you are baking one or two sheets at a time, depending on the instructions in the specific recipe. If a recipe says "bake, two sheets at a time, for 10 to 12 minutes" and you bake only one sheet at a time, you should bake the cookies for less time, or they'll overbrown. Also keep in mind that if you use dark baking sheets or baking pans, the baking time will be less than if using stainless steel.

Make sure that the baking sheet is at room temperature, not still hot from the last batch, when you drop or place the dough on it. Having at least four baking sheets usually ensures that you won't have to reuse any sheets. (If necessary, however, you can, place portioned raw cookie segments on a sheet of foil or parchment and then place it on a still-hot baking sheet, as long as you immediately place the pan in the oven.)

troubleshooting guide

If the dough is dry and crumbly	Knead in 1 to 2 tablespoons of a liquid called for in the recipe, or milk or water.
If the dough is sticky, even after chilling	Mix in flour 1 tablespoon at a time until it is the proper texture.
If your cookies spread together during baking	Space the next batch at least 2 inches apart, and keep the dough chilled until ready to portion it on the baking sheet.
If your cookies spread and become too thin during baking	The butter may have been too soft. The baking sheets might be too warm if you are reusing them; cool them in the refrigerator between batches. You may have used too little flour; add a tablespoon or two to the remaining dough. The dough may need to chill for longer prior to portioning.
If your cookies are tough	You may have used too much flour; used the wrong type of flour or the wrong sugar (not fine enough); overworked the dough; used too much flour during rolling the dough; or baked the cookies for too long or at the wrong oven temperature (the oven may need to be recalibrated).
If your cookies are hard or dry	You probably either added too much flour, or other dry ingredient, or overbaked them. (Remember, when measuring flour, do not pack it into the measuring cup.) Your oven may be running hotter than the indicated temperature. Recalibrate your oven. When possible; for short term, reduce the baking time.
If your cookies are too soft	You may have measured the flour incorrectly and used too little; the butter may have been too soft (soft butter should just yield when gently pressed with your finger); or you may have added too much liquid. The cookies may simply be underbaked; increase the baking time by a minute or so.

For some recipes, I recommend placing a single baking sheet in the middle rack of the oven, because this ensures good air circulation. However, if you have a wide oven and can place two baking sheets side by side with at least an inch between them, do so, but reverse the positions of the baking sheets halfway through the baking time. Recipes that make a lot of cookies are generally baked two sheets at a time, with two racks positioned just above and below the center of the oven.

For cut-out cookies or other cookies with irregular shapes, place them on the baking sheet—and, later, on the cooling rack—in such a way that they alternate and fit together while leaving the specified amount of space between them (e.g., one row with the wide end facing you, the next with the wide end facing away). This way you can get more on the sheet at one time.

CHECKING FOR DONENESS

Always bake cookies for the minimum baking time given, then test for doneness. Watch them carefully after that, because overshooting by a minute, even seconds, can mean overdone cookies. One way to test for doneness is the visual check: most cookies will have begun to brown at the edges (of course, this won't apply to cookies made from a dark dough). When testing your cookies for doneness, keep the oven door open only for a short period of time; if it is a visual check, don't dawdle. If you must remove the baking sheet to test the cookies with a toothpick or lift to see the bottom, close the oven door while you test.

HIGH ALTITUDE BAKING ADJUSTMENTS

Generally speaking, if you are working in a kitchen at elevations 3,000 feet or more above sea level, you will need to reduce the oven temperatures in these recipes by 25 degrees and reduce the sugar amounts by 2 tablespoons per cup. At elevations above 5,000 feet, cut the baking powder in sweet and chocolate-rich doughs by half.

Cooling

Follow the specific directions in each recipe for cooling the cookies. Some are cooled briefly on the baking sheets, others are immediately transferred to cooling racks. (Cooling cookies on wire racks ensures even air circulation. Improperly cooled cookies will not have a good texture.) Generally, drop cookies and soft cookies should cool for 1 to 2 minutes on the baking sheet before you transfer them; thin, fragile cookies and dense cookies should be transferred immediately. Work quickly—the cookies may crisp too much if allowed to rest on a hot baking sheet. If cookies stick after the proper brief cooling interval, you can place the sheet in the oven for a few moments to loosen them. Use a thin spatula or pancake turner to transfer the cookies.

Bar cookies and brownies should be cooled in the baking pan on a wire rack. Some bar cookies and brownies are best cut when warm, but most should be allowed to cool prior to cutting. Follow the recipe directions. A sharp thin-bladed knife is best for cutting sticky bar cookies and brownies.

Decorating

Be sure that your decorations—chopped nuts, nonpareils, dragées, M&Ms, sprinkles, etc.—are not too heavy for the texture of the cookie. Thin wafer cookies and delicate sugar cookies can only take so much. You can press nonpareils and dragées firmly into the cookies before baking, or attach them to the cookies after baking with royal icing.

To make edible paint for application prior to baking: Whisk together 1 egg yolk, about ¼ teaspoon water, and a dab of paste or a dash of liquid food coloring. Be aware that the egg yolk will impart some color; start over, using an egg white instead if the color you want is not developing.

To make edible paint to be applied after baking: Combine several drops of liquid food coloring with 3 tablespoons water (this paint will only register well on sugar cookies and other light-colored cookies).

You can also use the powder known as "luster dust," which comes in a variety of colors. The powder can be blended with a small amount of vodka, or other clear spirit (start with ½ teaspoon powder to ¼ teaspoon vodka) and brushed onto unbaked or baked cookies.

If using stamps or other objects to create impressions in the surface of unbaked cookies, refrigerate the dough for about half an hour after stamping the cookies; the impressions will be more distinct.

To tint white chocolate, use a paste coloring; water-based food colorings will cause the chocolate to seize.

Melted white chocolate makes an excellent glue for lighter decorative elements like sprinkles, jimmies, and colored sugars. You can either pour the melted chocolate over the entire surface of the cookie or pipe out lines or swirls through a parchment paper cone. Spread the decorations on a plate and press the cookies into them—the decorations will adhere only to the areas coated with chocolate.

Be sure to allow decorated cookies to dry or cool completely before storing them.

making a parchment paper cone

A parchment paper cone is the best tool for creating dazzling hair-thin decorations on your cookies. To make a paper cone for piping:

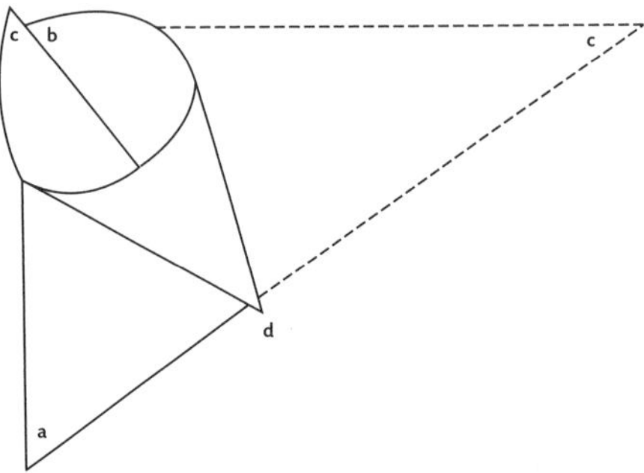

1. Cut a square of parchment paper in half diagonally, forming two triangles. Place one before you as shown.
2. Take right-hand Point C (longest side/furthest point) of the triangle and fold in up and toward Point B.

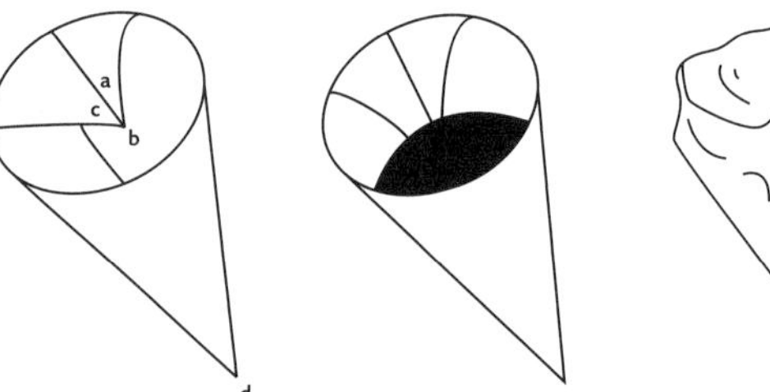

3. Take opposite Point A and fold up and around until it meets Points B and C at top to form the closed tip of the cone, Point D.
4. Fold Points A and C (at Point B) down (in the direction of Point D) to prevent the cone from unraveling.
5. To use, fill the cone halfway with filling and fold over the open end to seal and tighten. Snip off the tip of the cone to the desired size and pipe, using one hand to squeeze the cone and the other hand, near the tip, to guide it.

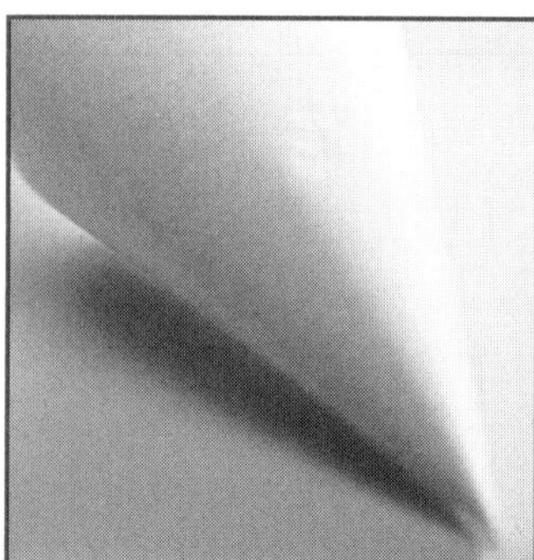

An alternative to a parchment cone
An easy, if less professional, alternative to a parchment cone is a small sealable plastic bag. Place the icing in the bag and seal it. Snip a tiny hole in one of the bottom corners of the bag, and squeeze the bag gently to drizzle the icing over cookies or bars.

storing, wrapping, and shipping cookies

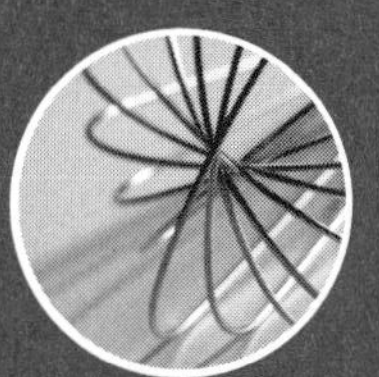

What you do with your cookies after you've baked them is just as important as what you do before that. No matter how good your cookies are right out of the oven, they won't be any good if they're stale. Plan in advance where and how you are going to store your cookies. Use the storing information in each recipe as a guide.

The Pillsbury Doughboy said it best: "Nothin' says lovin' like somethin' from the oven." A home-baked gift is the ultimate compliment. It shows that you cared enough to spend your own valuable time and effort. If you are sending cookies to friends or loved ones, whatever positive message you are trying to convey will be lost if you don't wrap and ship them properly. (I once sent a box of carefully decorated butter cookies to a boyfriend abroad; when he received it, it was a box of sweet-smelling crumbs.) To ensure the success of your edible gift, you must store your cookies properly so that they can be enjoyed at peak freshness. And when it comes time to giving cookies as gifts, proper protective wrapping combined with style and panache could make you a legend.

Storing

Follow the specific directions in each recipe for storage. In general:

- Let cookies cool completely before storing them, or the residual heat will produce steam that will soften the cookies and accelerate spoilage.
- Most cookies that are to be filled, glazed, or dusted with sugar should be finished as close to serving time as possible. Over time, filled cookies will soften, and powdered sugar and glazes will seep into the cookies.
- Store cookies in an airtight container, so moist cookies don't dry out, or crisp cookies don't absorb moisture from the air. Perfect are those locking plastic tubs, but resealable plastic bags are fine too. Cookie tins work as well—and have more charm. Separate layers of cookies with sheets of waxed paper—this is especially important for cookies that have been iced. Most cookies can be stored at room temperature for one week.
- Crisp cookies and cookies that contain chopped nuts, dried fruits, or alcohol will keep for a relatively long time (two weeks or more). A small piece of terra cotta that has been soaked in water will help keep cookies in the chewy family fresh. Place it in the tin of chewy cookies, and they will retain their texture longer. (A special terra cotta bear is available by mail-order; see Sources, page 376.)
- Do not store different types of cookies together, if possible. Dry, crisp cookies can absorb moisture from softer cookies, and butter cookies and other delicate cookies can take on the aromas, however pleasant they might be, of more strongly flavored cookies.
- Some cookies can be refrigerated, and these too should be tightly wrapped to prevent them from absorbing odors from neighboring items. Chocolate-coated cookies should be kept in a cool spot, but not refrigerated.
- Some cookies, such as butter-rich crisp ones, sugar cookies, brownies, and chocolate chip cookies, can be frozen for up to four months. Appropriate freezer wraps include freezer-weight plastic

bags, freezer paper, and—best, in my opinion—a plastic container lined with foil. Aluminum foil should not be used alone to wrap cookies to be frozen. The tiny holes that can form in foil when it is folded will allow moisture loss and freezer burn.

Cookies that are to be frosted or glazed are best frozen undecorated. They can, however, be frozen in their decorated state if they are "flash-frozen": place uncovered cookies in the freezer on a baking sheet. As soon as they are frozen hard, remove them, wrap, and return to the freezer.

To thaw frozen cookies, open the container a little bit to allow condensation to be released, and thaw at room temperature for 30 to 40 minutes. If you are glazing, frosting, or dusting them with sugar, be sure the cookies are completely thawed before decorating.

Shipping Cookies

Cushion the cookies when you pack them. The cookies should go in a durable container—again, a decorative tin is great for gift giving, but see Gift Wrapping Cookies, page 48, for other ideas. Line the container first with waxed paper, plastic wrap, or aluminum foil, as an added precaution against the cookies absorbing other odors.

Tightly pack the cookies in the container, making sure there is little space for the cookies to shift. You can individually wrap pairs of cookies, the flat sides facing, in foil or waxed paper, then lay them flat or stand them on end. Wrap crisp and soft cookies separately to preserve their texture.

For a tight seal, you can even do your own shrink-wrapping. Preheat the oven to 325°F. Line a baking sheet with two layers of paper towels. Wrap your cookies in clusters or in decorative stacks in good-quality plastic wrap (don't skimp on quality; cheap plastic wrap will melt). Cut away any excess plastic wrap. Place the paper-lined baking sheet in the oven for 5 minutes, then remove it from the oven and place the wrapped cookies at least 2 inches apart on it. Place the baking sheet in the oven and leave the door open slightly so you can watch it closely. In a matter of seconds, the plastic will collapse around the cookies. Remove, and allow to cool completely before packing.

Place the heaviest cookies on the bottom of the container. Separate layers with waxed paper and, if necessary, fill any spaces with crumpled waxed paper. When the container is almost full, place a sheet of colored cellophane or waxed paper over the top; it should be large enough so that, when you close the lid, it drapes over the rim; this will create an airtight seal.

Pack the container in a sturdy box with room for cushiony material such as packing peanuts, plastic bubble wrap, or plain old crumpled newspaper. Pack these into the bottom, add the cookie container, and fill the sides and top with more packing material. Don't forget the note, and seal the box with filament-reinforced tape.

Ship the package using priority mail, or overnight. It is usually best to ship early in the week; if you hand over a package on a Thursday or Friday, there's always the chance your cookies will sit in a warehouse over the weekend. Depending on the type of cookies you're sending, you might be able to freeze them in their tin (for at least 12 hours) prior to shipping to help ensure that they arrive fresh.

Cookies that ship well

- Moist cookies
- Bar cookies
- Drop cookies
- Crisp, buttery cookies
- Shortbread
- Some hand-molded and fruit-filled cookies

Cookies that do not ship well

- Thin, fragile cookies
- Brittle, tender, or crumbly cookies
- Cookies with sticky or very moist fillings or sticky glazes
- Cookies with a high proportion of egg whites, such as meringues

Gift Wrapping Cookies

Cookie tins, charmingly quaint, are still perfect for cookie giving; they're usually inexpensive too. But keep an eye out for items that will hold cookies with flair: baskets, antique containers, wooden boxes, pots and planters, even coffee cans, which can be decorated creatively. Get creative with the wrapping and cushioning; you can use colored tissue paper or festively colored cellophane wrap. You could arrange cookies on decorative plates, either ceramic or wood, in unusual shapes and colors, and then wrap. Line a basket with a cloth or paper napkin, colored plastic wrap, or wrapping paper. You can also arrange cookies in baking pans or molds that are appropriate to the cookies you are giving. Of course, there are also many festive, colorful shopping bags and special gift boxes available. Just remember that if the container itself is not airtight, you must wrap it in a plastic bag. Attach cookie-making tools or ingredients, such as whisks, wooden spoons, cookie cutters, jars of spices, vanilla beans, etc. Identify the wrapped cookies by affixing a label with decorative panache.

drop cookies

Drop cookies are the best known, most popular, and easiest of cookies to make. You will find crowd-pleasing classics in this chapter, and you should have no trouble achieving great results. Here too are many of the cookies of your childhood—chocolate chip, oatmeal, peanut butter, and other old-fashioned favorites.

These cookies are formed by dropping a soft dough onto the baking sheet. The most common way to "drop" the batter is to scoop up a portion with a tablespoon and scrape it onto the baking sheet using a second spoon. Some people prefer to use a spring-handled ice cream or cookie scoop, which ensures that your cookies will be a uniform size and shape. Be sure to space the cookies as directed in each recipe—these cookies spread during baking, how much depending on the butter content of the dough.

Some recipes in this chapter call for letting the dough stand, at room temperature or in the refrigerator, for a short period of time before baking. This allows the dough to firm up enough to hold a shape before and during baking.

soft-baked chocolate chunk cookies

MAKES ABOUT 18 COOKIES

These cookies are for those who love soft and chewy, rather than crisp, cookies. The secret is to use melted instead of softened butter, which gives them a soft texture and deep, nutty flavor. Overbaking will make them crisp, so watch carefully, and remove the cookies when they are just brown around the edges.

2½ cups all-purpose flour

½ teaspoon salt

½ teaspoon baking soda

¾ cup (1½ sticks) unsalted butter, melted

1 cup firmly packed light brown sugar

½ cup granulated sugar

2 large eggs

2 teaspoons vanilla extract

10 ounces bittersweet chocolate, cut into ¼-inch pieces

⅔ cup walnuts, chopped

1. Preheat the oven to 350°F. Line two baking sheets with parchment paper.
2. In a medium bowl, whisk together the flour, salt, and baking soda. Set aside.
3. In a large bowl, whisk together the melted butter and sugars. Whisk in the eggs one at a time, whisking until well blended. Whisk in the vanilla. Using a wooden spoon, stir in the dry ingredients until combined. Stir in the chocolate and walnuts. (The dough can be refrigerated, well wrapped, for up to 4 days or frozen for up to a month.)
4. Using a ¼-cup measure or ice cream scoop, drop the dough onto the prepared baking sheets, spacing them 2 inches apart. Bake, two sheets at a time, for 15 to 18 minutes, until the cookies are just brown around the edges; switch the position of the sheets halfway through baking. The centers of the cookies should be soft and slightly puffy. Let the cookies cool completely on the baking sheets or wire racks.

STORE IN AN AIRTIGHT CONTAINER AT ROOM TEMPERATURE FOR UP TO 2 DAYS.

Cookie Bite **Cooling the cookies on the baking sheets, thereby preventing air from circulating around them, keeps them from becoming crisp.**

sour cream chocolate chip cookies

MAKES **ABOUT 58 COOKIES**

The sour cream imparts a moist texture and subtle tang, and its flavor is nicely complemented by all the raisins, nuts, and chocolate. The end result? Crispy on the outside, moist on the inside, and delicious.

2 cups all-purpose flour

1 teaspoon baking soda

1 teaspoon salt

¾ cup (1½ sticks) unsalted butter, softened

1 cup granulated sugar

½ cup firmly packed dark brown sugar

1 tablespoon vanilla extract

2 large eggs

½ cup sour cream

1 cup raisins

1 cup coarsely chopped toasted walnuts

12 ounces bittersweet bar chocolate, chopped into ¼-inch or smaller pieces

1. Position two racks near the center of the oven and preheat the oven to 375°F. Line two baking sheets with parchment paper or foil.
2. Sift together the flour, baking soda, and salt into a medium bowl. Set aside.
3. In the bowl of an electric mixer, using the paddle attachment, beat the butter, sugars, and vanilla extract at medium speed until creamy, about 2 minutes. Beat in the eggs one at a time, beating well after each addition and scraping down the sides of the bowl as necessary. Add the sour cream, mixing until blended. At low speed, add the dry ingredients, mixing just until combined. Using a wooden spoon, stir in the raisins, nuts, and chopped chocolate.
4. Drop the dough by rounded tablespoonfuls onto the prepared baking sheets, spacing the cookies 2 inches apart. Bake, two sheets at a time, 12 to 15 minutes, until golden brown; switch the position of the sheets halfway through baking so that the cookies brown evenly. Transfer the cookies to wire racks and cool completely.

STORE **IN AN AIRTIGHT CONTAINER AT ROOM TEMPERATURE FOR UP TO A WEEK.**

milk chocolate macadamia nut cookies

MAKES **ABOUT 40 COOKIES**

The buttery flavor of macadamia nuts and the incomparable smoothness of milk chocolate are married in these sublime cookies. To ensure both consistent nutty flavor and crunch, some of the nuts are ground finely and the rest are coarsely chopped. I've added some bittersweet chocolate along with the milk chocolate so that both the chocolate and the nutty flavors have maximum punch.

2¼ cups all-purpose flour

1 teaspoon baking soda

½ teaspoon salt

1¼ cups salted macadamia nuts, divided

1 cup (2 sticks) unsalted butter

1 cup firmly packed light brown sugar

½ cup granulated sugar

2 large eggs

1 tablespoon vanilla extract

6 ounces Swiss milk bar chocolate, cut into ⅓-inch chunks

6 ounces bittersweet chocolate, cut into ⅓-inch chunks

1. Position a rack in the upper third of the oven and preheat the oven to 350°F. Spray two baking sheets with nonstick cooking spray.
2. In a medium bowl, whisk together the flour, baking soda, and salt. Set aside.
3. Coarsely chop ¾ cup of the macadamia nuts and set aside. Put the remaining ½ cup macadamia nuts and 2 tablespoons of the flour mixture in the bowl of a food processor and process until the nuts are finely ground, about 30 seconds. Add the ground nut mixture to the remaining flour mixture and stir until well combined; set aside.
4. In the bowl of an electric mixer, using the paddle attachment, beat the butter and brown and granulated sugars at medium speed until well blended. Add the eggs one at a time, beating well after each addition. Scrape down the sides of the bowl and beat in the vanilla extract. At low speed, beat in the dry ingredients. Using a wooden spoon, stir in the milk chocolate, bittersweet chocolate, and the coarsely chopped macadamia nuts. Cover the bowl and let the dough stand for 10 minutes. (The dough can be wrapped in plastic and stored in an airtight container in the refrigerator for up to 3 days or frozen, well wrapped, for up to a month.)
5. Drop the dough by 2-tablespoon mounds onto the prepared baking sheets, spacing them at least 2 inches apart. Bake the cookies, one sheet at a time, for 11 to 13 minutes, until golden around the edges. Cool the cookies on the baking sheet for 5 minutes, then transfer them to a wire rack and cool completely.

STORE **IN AN AIRTIGHT CONTAINER AT ROOM TEMPERATURE FOR UP TO A WEEK.**

gianduja chocolate chunk cookies

MAKES **ABOUT 33 COOKIES**

Gianduja (pronounced "jon-DOO-ya") is a creamy blend of pulverized hazelnuts and milk chocolate that is very popular in Italy. Since it has the same smoothness as chocolate, it is a wonderful addition to chocolate chip cookies, giving them the subtle flavor of milk chocolate and roasted hazelnuts. This recipe comes from Deborah Snyder, pastry chef at JUdson Grill in New York City. These wonderful cookies get their nutty texture from the addition of ground rolled oats. The recipe can easily be doubled.

¾ cup all-purpose flour

½ teaspoon baking soda

¼ teaspoon salt

1½ cups rolled oats (quick-cooking or old-fashioned)

4 tablespoons (½ stick) unsalted butter, softened

5 tablespoons solid vegetable shortening

½ cup firmly packed light brown sugar

6 tablespoons granulated sugar

1½ teaspoons light corn syrup

1 large egg

¾ teaspoon vanilla extract

7 ounces gianduja chocolate, cut into ½-inch pieces (Callebaut Gianduja is available from Dairy Fresh Chocolate; see Sources, page 377)

1. Position a rack in the center of the oven and preheat the oven to 350°F. Line two baking sheets with parchment paper or foil.
2. Sift together the flour, baking soda, and salt into a medium bowl. In the bowl of a food processor, process the rolled oats until finely ground, about 45 seconds. Stir the oats into the flour mixture and set aside.
3. In the bowl of an electric mixer, using the paddle attachment, beat the butter, vegetable shortening, sugars, and corn syrup at medium speed until creamy, about 2 minutes. Beat in the egg. Scrape down the sides of the bowl. Beat in the vanilla extract. At low speed, add the dry ingredients, mixing just until combined. Using a wooden spoon, stir in the gianduja chocolate.
4. Measure out rounded tablespoonfuls of the dough and, using wet hands, roll each portion into a ball. Arrange the balls 2 inches apart on the prepared baking sheets. Moisten your palm to prevent sticking, and flatten the balls into 1¾-inch disks. Bake the cookies, one sheet at a time, for 10 to 12 minutes, just until golden brown. Transfer the cookies to wire racks and cool completely.

STORE **IN AN AIRTIGHT CONTAINER AT ROOM TEMPERATURE FOR UP TO A WEEK.**

Cookie Bite **Shortening should be measured by pressing it into a dry measuring cup or measuring spoon and leveling it off with the back of a kitchen knife.**

PREVIOUS PAGE amy-oes 290

CLOCKWISE FROM TOP LEFT white chocolate key lime bars 126, snowflakes 318, wedding cake cookies 322

CLOCKWISE FROM LEFT whoopie pies 288, lemon lamb cookies 309, chocolate peppermint polka-dot pigs 312, colossal peanut butter cookies 70

FACING PAGE tangerine kumquat rounds 98

CLOCKWISE FROM LEFT almond raspberry tea cakes 213, chocolate hazelnut truffle squares 121, maple walnut leaves 90, caramel almond tiger cookies 286

CLOCKWISE FROM TOP LEFT pink plaid valentine hearts 320, ginger fortune cookies 176, miss kitty dog biscuits 95, chocolate-dipped almond crescents 168

FACING PAGE cinnamon animal crackers 79, ginger quakes 155, glazed lemon–poppy seed hearts 84

ABOVE wicked witch candy cottage 324

peanut butter chocolate chunk cookies

MAKES ABOUT 72 COOKIES

These cookies are for folks who love chunky peanut butter. They may not be as refined as some peanut butter cookies, but you're definitely getting your money's worth. Loaded with peanuts, cashews, and chunks of bittersweet chocolate, they showcase the pairing of chocolate and peanuts to perfection. The dough can be made ahead and frozen for up to a month, so if you get surprise guests, you can surprise them right back with an over-the-top treat.

1½ cups all-purpose flour

½ teaspoon baking soda

⅛ teaspoon salt

11 tablespoons unsalted butter, slightly softened

⅔ cup creamy peanut butter

⅔ cup firmly packed dark brown sugar

1 cup granulated sugar

2 large eggs

1½ teaspoons vanilla extract

½ cup unsalted peanuts, coarsely chopped

½ cup lightly salted roasted cashews, coarsely chopped

7 ounces bittersweet chocolate, cut into ¼-inch chunks

1. Position a rack in the center of the oven and preheat the oven to 350°F.
2. In a medium bowl, whisk together the flour, baking soda, and salt. Set aside.
3. In the bowl of an electric mixer, using the paddle attachment, beat the butter and peanut butter at medium-high speed until creamy, about 1 minute. Gradually add the brown and granulated sugars and beat at medium speed until well blended. Add the eggs one at a time, beating well after each addition. Scrape down the sides of the bowl and beat in the vanilla extract. At low speed, beat in the dry ingredients. Using a wooden spoon, stir in the peanuts, cashews, and bittersweet chocolate chunks. Cover the bowl and let the dough stand for 10 minutes. (The dough can be wrapped in plastic and stored in an airtight container in the refrigerator for up to 3 days, or frozen, well wrapped, for up to a month.)
4. Drop the dough by slightly rounded tablespoonfuls onto ungreased baking sheets, spacing the cookies at least 2 inches apart. Bake the cookies, one sheet at a time, for 11 to 13 minutes, until just starting to brown lightly around the edges; they should still be soft in the center. Cool the cookies on the baking sheets for 5 minutes, then transfer then to a wire rack and cool completely.

STORE IN AN AIRTIGHT CONTAINER AT ROOM TEMPERATURE FOR UP TO A WEEK.

rum-raisin chocolate chip cookies

MAKES ABOUT 72 COOKIES

The musky sweetness of rum-soaked raisins pairs well with chocolate. Dark rum not only carries deeper flavor than light rum, it's also not as piercingly sweet.

1 cup dark raisins

¼ cup dark rum

2½ cups all-purpose flour

1 teaspoon baking soda

½ teaspoon salt

1 cup (2 sticks) unsalted butter, slightly softened

1 cup firmly packed dark brown sugar

¾ cup granulated sugar

2 large eggs

1 tablespoon vanilla extract

¼ teaspoon rum extract

¾ cup pecans, coarsely chopped

2 cups (12 ounces) semisweet chocolate morsels

1. Combine the raisins with the rum in a small plastic container with a tight-fitting lid and let macerate at room temperature for at least 6 hours, or overnight.

2. Position a rack in the center of the oven and preheat the oven to 350°F. Spray two baking sheets with nonstick cooking spray.

3. In a medium bowl, whisk together the flour, baking soda, and salt. Set aside.

4. In the bowl of an electric mixer, using the paddle attachment, beat the butter and brown and granulated sugars at medium speed until well blended. Add the eggs one at a time, beating well after each addition. Scrape down the sides of the bowl and beat in the vanilla and rum extract. At low speed, beat in the dry ingredients. Using a wooden spoon, stir in the rum-soaked raisins, along with any remaining rum, and the semisweet morsels. Cover the bowl and let the dough stand for 10 minutes. (The dough can be wrapped in plastic and stored in an airtight container in the refrigerator for up to 3 days, or frozen, well wrapped, for up to a month.)

5. Drop the dough by 2-tablespoon mounds onto the prepared baking sheets, spacing them at least 2 inches apart. Bake the cookies, one sheet at a time, for 9 to 11 minutes, until the edges are brown but the cookies are still soft. Cool the cookies on the baking sheets for 5 minutes, then transfer them to a wire rack and cool completely.

STORE IN AN AIRTIGHT CONTAINER AT ROOM TEMPERATURE FOR UP TO A WEEK.

chocolate macadamia–peanut butter chip cookies

MAKES ABOUT 32 LARGE COOKIES

This recipe comes from Andrew Garrison Shotts, former pastry chef of the Russian Tea Room, among other fine places, and now a consultant for Guittard Chocolates. Drew has spent his entire professional life making elegant, restrained desserts and sleek showpieces of chocolate and sugar, but his cookies are the high-impact, "kitchen-sink" type, loaded with lots of goodies, such as macadamia nuts, bittersweet chocolate chunks, and peanut butter morsels.

2 cups all-purpose flour

1 teaspoon baking soda

1 teaspoon salt

1 cup (2 sticks) unsalted butter, slightly softened

¾ cup granulated sugar

⅔ cup firmly packed light brown sugar

3 large eggs

1 teaspoon vanilla extract

9 ounces bittersweet chocolate, cut into ¼-inch chunks

1 cup (6 ounces) Reese's peanut butter chips

1 cup unsalted macadamia nuts, coarsely chopped*

***Note:** If you can only find salted nuts, place them in a sieve and rinse under cold running water. Dry them thoroughly with paper towels.

1. Position a rack in the center of the oven and preheat the oven to 350°F.
2. In a medium bowl, whisk together the flour, baking soda, and salt. Set aside.
3. In the bowl of an electric mixer, using the paddle attachment, beat the butter at medium-high speed until creamy, about 1 minute. Gradually add the granulated and light brown sugars and beat until light and fluffy, about 2 minutes. Add the eggs one at a time, beating well after each addition and scraping down the sides of the bowl as necessary. Add the vanilla extract. At low speed, add the dry ingredients in three additions, mixing just until blended. Using a wooden spoon, stir in the bittersweet chocolate, peanut butter chips, and macadamia nuts just until blended.
4. Using a ¼-cup ice cream scoop or cup measure, drop the dough onto ungreased baking sheets, spacing them 3 inches apart. Bake the cookies, one sheet at a time, for 11 to 13 minutes, until golden brown around the edges. Transfer the cookies to a wire rack and cool completely.

STORE IN AN AIRTIGHT CONTAINER AT ROOM TEMPERATURE FOR UP TO A WEEK.

toffee pecan cookies

MAKES ABOUT 48 COOKIES

These cookies are loaded with English toffee bits and toasted pecans. They don't look elegant, but they are addictive.

2¼ cups all-purpose flour

1 teaspoon baking powder

¼ teaspoon baking soda

¾ teaspoon salt

¾ cup (1½ sticks) unsalted butter, softened

¾ cup granulated sugar

¾ cup firmly packed light brown sugar

3 large eggs

2 teaspoons vanilla extract

2 cups English toffee bits, such as Skor or Heath

1¾ cups pecans, toasted and chopped

1. Position a rack in the center of the oven and preheat the oven to 350°F. Line two baking sheets with aluminum foil and spray the foil with nonstick cooking spray.

2. Sift together the flour, baking powder, baking soda, and salt into a medium bowl. Set aside.

3. In the bowl of an electric mixer, using the paddle attachment, beat the butter and sugars at medium-high speed until light, about 2 minutes. Beat in the eggs one at a time, mixing well after each addition and scraping down the sides of the bowl as necessary. Beat in the vanilla extract. At this point the dough will look curdled. At low speed, add the flour mixture, mixing just until blended. Using a wooden spoon, stir in the toffee bits and pecans.

4. Drop the dough by rounded tablespoonfuls onto the prepared baking sheets, spacing the cookies 2 inches apart. Bake, one sheet at a time, for 14 to 16 minutes, until the cookies are starting to turn golden brown around the edges. Let the cookies cool on the baking sheets for 2 minutes, then carefully transfer them to a wire rack and cool completely.

STORE IN AN AIRTIGHT CONTAINER AT ROOM TEMPERATURE FOR UP TO A WEEK.

Cookie Bite **Toffee chips can sometimes turn rancid; always taste them before using them.**

sour cherry white chocolate chunk cookies

MAKES ABOUT 65 COOKIES

Even people who think white chocolate is tooth-achingly sweet will love these, as its sweetness is cut so winningly by the dried sour cherries. These cookies taste best when the cherries are cut into thin slivers, so that you get tiny bursts of tart cherry rather than an overwhelming flavor. It takes time to cut the little devils, but it makes a big difference.

2½ cups all-purpose flour

1 teaspoon baking soda

¼ teaspoon salt

1 cup (2 sticks) unsalted butter, softened

¾ cup granulated sugar

¾ cup firmly packed light brown sugar

2 large eggs

1 teaspoon vanilla extract

¼ teaspoon almond extract

¾ cup dried sour cherries, cut into thin slivers

1 cup slivered almonds, toasted and coarsely chopped

6 ounces good-quality white chocolate, cut into ¼-inch chunks

1. Position a rack in the center of the oven and preheat the oven to 350°F.
2. In a medium bowl, whisk together the flour, baking soda, and salt. Set aside.
3. In the bowl of an electric mixer, using the paddle attachment, beat the butter and sugars at medium speed until blended, about 1 minute. Add the eggs one at a time, beating well after each addition; scrape down the sides of the bowl. Mix in the vanilla and almond extracts. At low speed, add the dry ingredients and mix just until blended. Add the chopped cherries, almonds, and white chocolate chunks and mix at low speed just until blended.
4. Drop the dough by rounded tablespoonfuls onto ungreased baking sheets, spacing them 2 inches apart. Bake the cookies, one sheet at a time, for 11 to 13 minutes, until they are golden around the edges; do not overbake. Let the cookies cool on the baking sheets for 1 minute, then transfer them to a wire rack to cool completely.

STORE IN AN AIRTIGHT CONTAINER AT ROOM TEMPERATURE FOR UP TO A WEEK.

chocolate marble chunk cookies

MAKES ABOUT 60 COOKIES

This is the kind of cookie that people, especially kids, may stop and gawk at for, oh, about 2.3 seconds before they pounce: it's half dark chocolate dough, half light dough, marbled together into a cookie full of good stuff like pecans and chocolate chunks.

2¼ cups all-purpose flour

1 teaspoon baking soda

¾ teaspoon salt

1 cup (2 sticks) unsalted butter, softened

¾ cup firmly packed light brown sugar

¾ cup granulated sugar

2 teaspoons vanilla extract

2 large eggs

¼ cup Dutch-processed cocoa powder, sifted

12 ounces bittersweet or semisweet bar chocolate, cut into ½-inch pieces

1¾ cups pecan pieces

1. Position a rack in the center of the oven and preheat the oven to 375°F.
2. In a medium bowl, whisk together the flour, baking soda, and salt. Set aside.
3. In the bowl of an electric mixer, using the paddle attachment, beat the butter and sugars at medium-high speed until light, about 2 minutes. Beat in the vanilla extract and eggs one at a time, mixing well after each addition and scraping down the sides of the bowl as necessary. At low speed, add the flour mixture, mixing just until blended.
4. Transfer 1¾ cups of the dough to another bowl and set aside. Add the cocoa powder to the dough remaining in the mixer bowl and mix on low speed until blended. Add half of the chocolate and half of the pecans and mix until blended. Stir the remaining chocolate and pecans into the light-colored dough.
5. Fill one side of a 1-tablespoon measuring spoon with the light dough, making it well rounded, not level. Fill the remaining half with chocolate dough. Roll the doughs into a ball and place on an ungreased baking sheet. Moisten your palm to prevent sticking, and flatten the dough into a 1½-inch disk. Repeat with the remaining dough, spacing the cookies 2 inches apart. Bake, one sheet at a time, for 8 to 10 minutes, until the lighter dough just begins to color. Let the cookies cool on the baking sheets for 5 minutes, then transfer to a wire rack and cool completely.

STORE IN AN AIRTIGHT CONTAINER AT ROOM TEMPERATURE FOR UP TO A WEEK.

chocolate cranberry spice cookies

MAKES ABOUT 66 COOKIES

This recipe is courtesy of Tieaka Blocker, former pastry chef at the Hudson River Club in New York City. It's a spicy dark chocolate cookie with dried cranberries, chunks of white chocolate, and walnuts. Tart, sweet, spicy, and nutty—a lot of flavor in one cookie.

1½ cups all-purpose flour

6 tablespoons Dutch-processed cocoa powder

¼ teaspoon baking soda

1 teaspoon ground cinnamon

¼ teaspoon freshly grated nutmeg

⅛ teaspoon ground cloves

Pinch of salt

1 cup (2 sticks) unsalted butter, softened

¾ cup firmly packed light brown sugar

¾ cup plus 2 tablespoons granulated sugar

2 large eggs

1 tablespoon vanilla extract

¾ cup dried cranberries

7 ounces good-quality white chocolate, cut into ¼-inch pieces

¾ cup walnuts, toasted and coarsely chopped

1. Sift together the flour, cocoa powder, baking soda, cinnamon, nutmeg, cloves, and salt into a medium bowl. Set aside.
2. In the bowl of an electric mixer, using the paddle attachment, beat the butter and sugars at medium speed until light, about 2 minutes. Add the eggs one at a time, beating well after each addition and scraping down the sides of the bowl as necessary. Beat in the vanilla extract. Reduce the speed to low and add the dry ingredients in three additions, mixing just until combined. Using a wooden spoon, stir in the cranberries, white chocolate, and walnuts. Cover the bowl with plastic wrap and refrigerate the dough for at least 3 hours (or up to 3 days), until firm.
3. Position a rack in the center of the oven and preheat the oven to 350°F. Line two baking sheets with parchment paper or foil.
4. Pinch off pieces of the dough and shape into 1-inch balls. Arrange the balls on the prepared sheets, spacing them 2 inches apart. Bake the cookies, one sheet at a time, for 9 to 11 minutes, until just set but still very soft. Let the cookies cool on the baking sheets for 5 minutes, then transfer to a wire rack and cool completely.

STORE IN AN AIRTIGHT CONTAINER AT ROOM TEMPERATURE FOR UP TO A WEEK.

Cookie Bite **To keep brown sugar soft, store it in a sealed plastic bag within an airtight container. To soften hardened brown sugar, sprinkle it with a little water and heat it in a preheated 200°F oven for about 5 minutes. It can also be softened by storing it with a wedge of apple in an airtight container for a day.**

chocolate chocolate chip cookies

MAKES ABOUT 36 COOKIES

This cookie is made from a fudgy chocolate dough that is intensified with chunks of bittersweet chocolate and walnuts. The cookies have the texture of brownies, but are much more moist, placing them almost in the realm of candy.

¼ cup all-purpose flour

¼ teaspoon baking powder

14 ounces bittersweet chocolate, divided

2 tablespoons unsalted butter

2 large eggs, at room temperature

1 cup firmly packed light brown sugar

1 teaspoon vanilla extract

¾ cup coarsely chopped walnuts

1. In a small bowl, whisk together the flour and baking powder; set aside.
2. Chop 6 ounces of the chocolate into pieces between ¼ and ½ inch square; set aside.
3. Coarsely chop the remaining 8 ounces chocolate and place in the top of a double boiler with the butter. Melt the chocolate and butter over barely simmering water, stirring occasionally. Remove the pan from the heat; separate the top of the pan from the bottom and let the chocolate mixture cool for 10 minutes.
4. In the bowl of an electric mixer, using the whisk attachment, beat the eggs, brown sugar, and vanilla extract at high speed until doubled in volume, about 3 minutes. At low speed, blend in the melted chocolate mixture. Add the dry ingredients and mix just until combined. Using a wooden spoon, stir in the reserved chopped chocolate and the walnuts; the dough will be thin. Cover the bowl with plastic wrap and refrigerate for at least 1 hour (or up to 24 hours).
5. Position two oven racks near the center of the oven and preheat the oven to 350°F. Line two baking sheets with parchment paper or spray with nonstick cooking spray.
6. Drop the chilled dough by rounded tablespoons, 2 inches apart, onto the baking sheets. Moisten your palm to prevent sticking, and flatten each mound of dough slightly. Bake the cookies, two sheets at a time, for 9 to 11 minutes, until the cookies appear set; switch the position of the baking sheets halfway through baking. Do not overbake, or the cookies will be dry; the centers should not be completely set. Cool the cookies on the baking sheets for 10 minutes, then transfer them to wire racks to cool completely.

STORE IN AN AIRTIGHT CONTAINER AT ROOM TEMPERATURE FOR UP TO 1 WEEK.

monster fudge nut cookies

MAKES ABOUT 21 LARGE COOKIES

Like fudge in the round, these mega-cookies are packed with walnuts and jumbo chocolate chips (also known as miniature kisses), which are available in most supermarkets. Be careful not to overbake these cookies; they should be just set, and still moist on the inside.

12 ounces semisweet chocolate, chopped

6 tablespoons (3/4 stick) unsalted butter, cut into tablespoons

2/3 cup all-purpose flour

1 teaspoon baking powder

1/4 teaspoon salt

3 large eggs

1 cup granulated sugar

1 tablespoon vanilla extract

One 12-ounce bag Hershey's miniature semisweet kisses*

1½ cups coarsely chopped walnuts

***Note:** You can substitute 12 ounces semisweet chocolate, cut into ½-inch chunks.

1. Position a rack in the center of the oven and preheat the oven to 350°F. Grease two large baking sheets.
2. In the top of a double boiler, melt the chocolate and butter over barely simmering water, stirring occasionally, until smooth. Remove the top of the double boiler and allow the chocolate mixture to cool.
3. In a medium bowl, whisk together the flour, baking powder, and salt. Set aside.
4. In the bowl of an electric mixer, using the whisk attachment, beat the eggs at medium speed until blended. Gradually beat in the sugar. Increase the speed to high and continue beating until the mixture is thick and light, about 5 minutes. Stir the vanilla extract into the chocolate mixture and add it to the egg mixture, beating at medium speed until combined. At low speed, beat in the flour mixture, scraping down the sides of the bowl as necessary. Using a wooden spoon, stir in the miniature kisses and nuts. Chill the batter in the refrigerator for 10 minutes.
5. Using a ¼-cup ice cream scoop or cup measure, drop the dough onto the prepared baking sheets, leaving 2 inches between the cookies. Bake the cookies, one sheet at a time, for 10 to 12 minutes, until they are set on the outside but still moist on the inside. Cool the cookies on the baking sheets for 10 minutes, then transfer to a wire rack and cool completely.

STORE IN AN AIRTIGHT CONTAINER AT ROOM TEMPERATURE FOR UP TO 1 WEEK.

white chocolate chunk fudge cookies

MAKES ABOUT 36 COOKIES

This recipe is adapted from one that appeared in one of my previous books, *Chocolate Passion*. It was developed by my friend and colleague Nicole Rees, who combines a very dainty and lady-like demeanor with a ferocious, unbridled lust for sweets. Here is her wonderful fudgy dark chocolate cookie, touched with the earthy flavors of molasses and brown sugar and sweetened with chunks of white chocolate. Be sure to buy a high-quality white chocolate; it'll make all the difference.

3 ounces unsweetened chocolate, coarsely chopped

2 ounces semisweet chocolate, coarsely chopped

2 cups all-purpose flour

1 teaspoon baking soda

½ teaspoon salt

11 tablespoons unsalted butter, softened

1 cup firmly packed light brown sugar

¾ cup plus 2 tablespoons granulated sugar

1 tablespoon unsulphured molasses

1 tablespoon vanilla extract

2 large eggs, at room temperature

½ cup nonalkalized cocoa powder, sifted

9 ounces good-quality white chocolate, cut into ¼-inch chunks

1. Position a rack in the center of the oven and preheat the oven to 350°F. Line two baking sheets with parchment paper or foil.
2. Melt the unsweetened and semisweet chocolate together in a double boiler over simmering water, stirring until smooth. Set aside.
3. Sift together the flour, baking soda, and salt into a medium bowl. Set aside.
4. In the bowl of an electric mixer, using the paddle attachment, beat the butter at medium-high until creamy, about 1 minute. Gradually beat in the brown and granulated sugars and continue to beat for 1 minute, scraping down the sides of the bowl as necessary. Beat in the molasses and vanilla. Beat in the eggs one at a time. Beat in the cocoa powder. Add the melted chocolates and mix until blended. Reduce the speed to low and blend in half of the flour mixture, scraping the sides of the bowl as necessary. Using a wooden spoon, fold in the remaining flour, then the white chocolate pieces. Do not overmix.
5. Drop the dough in walnut-sized mounds, 2 inches apart, onto the baking sheets. Moisten your palm to prevent sticking, and flatten each mound slightly. Bake the cookies for 11 to 13 minutes, until the tops are puffed and cracked. Do not overbake, or the cookies will be dry. Cool the cookies on the baking sheets for 3 to 5 minutes, then transfer them to wire racks to cool completely.

STORE IN AN AIRTIGHT CONTAINER AT ROOM TEMPERATURE FOR UP TO 5 DAYS.

triple chocolate devil drops

MAKES **ABOUT 72 COOKIES**

Studded with chocolate chips and drizzled with white chocolate for a dramatic look, these cookies taste like devil's food cake. Don't overbake them or they will be hard and dry instead of moist and cakey, as they should be.

dark chocolate cookies

2 cups all-purpose flour

⅔ cup nonalkalized cocoa powder

1 teaspoon baking powder

½ teaspoon baking soda

⅛ teaspoon salt

¾ cup (1½ sticks) unsalted butter, softened

1⅓ cups granulated sugar

2 large eggs

1½ teaspoons vanilla extract

⅔ cup sour cream

1 cup (6 ounces) semisweet chocolate morsels

white chocolate drizzle

4 ounces good-quality white chocolate, chopped

make the cookies

1. Position a rack in the center of the oven and preheat the oven to 350°F. Lightly grease two baking sheets.
2. Sift together the flour, cocoa powder, baking powder, baking soda, and salt into a medium bowl. Gently whisk together to blend.
3. In the bowl of an electric mixer, using the paddle attachment, beat the butter and sugar at medium speed until light, about 2 minutes. Add the eggs one at a time, beating well after each addition and scraping down the sides of the bowl as necessary. Mix in the vanilla extract. At low speed, add the dry ingredients in three additions, alternating them with the sour cream in two additions, and mixing until just combined. Using a wooden spoon, stir in the chocolate chips.
4. Drop the dough by tablespoonfuls onto the prepared baking sheets, spacing the cookies 1 inch apart. Bake the cookies, one sheet at a time, for 12 to 15 minutes, or until no impression is left when you touch a cookie very lightly with a finger. Transfer the cookies to a wire rack and cool completely.

garnish the cookies

5. In a double boiler, melt the white chocolate over barely simmering water, stirring frequently. Scrape the melted chocolate into a small sealable plastic bag and seal the bag. Using scissors, cut a tiny hole in one of the bottom corners of the bag.
6. Arrange the cookies on a wire rack set over a baking sheet. Drizzle the white chocolate over the cookies in thin parallel lines. Refrigerate the cookies for 5 minutes, or just until the chocolate is set.

STORE **IN AN AIRTIGHT CONTAINER AT ROOM TEMPERATURE FOR UP TO 5 DAYS.**

oatmeal raisin cookies

MAKES **ABOUT 66 COOKIES**

This, the classic oatmeal cookie, represents the ideal marriage of sweet and nutty. The oatmeal gives the cookies their chewy texture and nutty flavor; chiming in are the raisins, ground pecans, shredded coconut, and the dark sweet note of light brown sugar.

2⅓ cups all-purpose flour

2 teaspoons baking powder

1½ teaspoons baking soda

1 teaspoon ground cinnamon

1 teaspoon salt

3½ cups quick-cooking rolled oats

1 cup (2 sticks) unsalted butter, slightly softened

1½ cups firmly packed light brown sugar

¼ cup granulated sugar

2½ teaspoons vanilla extract

2 large eggs

2 tablespoons whole milk

1 cup sweetened shredded coconut

1 cup pecans, coarsely chopped

1 cup raisins, coarsely chopped

1. Arrange two racks near the center of the oven and preheat the oven to 375°F. Grease two baking sheets.

2. Sift together the flour, baking powder, baking soda, cinnamon, and salt into a large bowl. Stir in the rolled oats.

3. In the bowl of an electric mixer, using the paddle attachment, beat the butter at medium speed until creamy, about 1 minute. Gradually beat in the brown sugar and beat at medium-high speed until well blended, about 2 minutes. Beat in the vanilla extract, then add the eggs one at a time, beating well after each addition and scraping down the sides of the bowl as necessary. Reduce the speed to low and add the dry ingredients, mixing just until combined. Add the milk, coconut, pecans, and raisins and mix just until combined.

4. Drop the dough by rounded tablespoonfuls onto the prepared sheets, spacing them at least 2 inches apart. Moisten your palm to prevent sticking, and flatten the mounds of dough slightly. Bake the cookies, two sheets at a time, for 12 to 14 minutes, until golden brown, switching the position of the sheets halfway through baking. Cool the cookies on the sheets for 5 minutes, then transfer them to wire racks and cool completely.

STORE **IN AN AIRTIGHT CONTAINER AT ROOM TEMPERATURE FOR UP TO 5 DAYS.**

Cookie Bite **To make chopping raisins easy, occasionally spray the blade of your knife lightly with nonstick cooking spray.**

apple spice oatmeal cookies

MAKES **ABOUT 52 COOKIES**

This is a sweet and spicy twist on the standard oatmeal cookie. Cubes of sautéed apple, intensified with apple juice concentrate, combine with spices, raisins, and walnuts in an oatmeal cookie base.

1¾ cups quick-cooking rolled oats

1½ cups all-purpose flour

2 teaspoons baking powder

¼ teaspoon baking soda

¾ teaspoon salt

1 teaspoon ground cinnamon

¼ teaspoon ground ginger

10 tablespoons (1¼ sticks) unsalted butter, divided, 1 stick softened

1 Granny Smith apple, peeled, cored, and cut into ¼-inch cubes

2 tablespoons frozen apple juice concentrate

1 cup firmly packed light brown sugar

½ cup granulated sugar

1 large egg

2 teaspoons vanilla extract

1 cup dark raisins

1 cup chopped walnuts

1. Position a rack in the center of the oven and preheat the oven to 375°F. Lightly grease two baking sheets.
2. In a medium bowl, combine the oats, flour, baking powder, baking soda, salt, cinnamon, and ginger. Set aside.
3. Heat 2 tablespoons of the butter in a medium skillet over medium heat until melted and foamy. Add the apple and cook, stirring occasionally, until softened, about 3 minutes. Stir in the apple juice concentrate and cook for another minute. Set aside to cool.
4. In the bowl of an electric mixer, using the paddle attachment, beat the remaining ½ cup (1 stick) butter and the sugars at medium speed until combined, about 1 minute. Add the egg and vanilla extract and beat until blended. At low speed, add the flour mixture one-third at a time, mixing just until blended. Using a wooden spoon, stir in the sautéed apple, raisins, and walnuts.
5. Drop the dough by rounded tablespoonfuls onto the prepared sheets, spacing the cookies 2 inches apart. Moisten your palm to prevent sticking, and flatten the mounds of dough slightly. Bake for 11 to 13 minutes, until the cookies are golden brown on the bottom. Transfer the cookies to a wire rack and cool completely.

STORE **IN AN AIRTIGHT CONTAINER AT ROOM TEMPERATURE FOR UP TO 5 DAYS.**

Cookie Bite **To core an apple neatly and easily, cut it in half and use a melon baller to remove the core from each half. Use a small paring knife to remove the stem, making two diagonal cuts in a V-shape on either side of it.**

banana-oatmeal chocolate chip cookies

MAKES **ABOUT 52 COOKIES**

Bananas are a natural with cereal, especially oatmeal. Chocolate, of course, is welcome everywhere. Start with oatmeal, add banana, chocolate, and a hint of cinnamon, and you really have a reason to get up in the morning.

1¾ cups quick-cooking rolled oats

1½ cups all-purpose flour

2 teaspoons baking powder

¼ teaspoon baking soda

¾ teaspoon salt

¾ teaspoon ground cinnamon

½ cup (1 stick) unsalted butter, softened

1 cup firmly packed light brown sugar

½ cup granulated sugar

1 large egg

2 teaspoons vanilla extract

1 cup (6 ounces) semisweet chocolate morsels

1 medium-sized ripe but firm banana, peeled and cut into ¼-inch pieces

1 cup coarsely chopped pecans

1. Position a rack in the center of the oven and preheat the oven to 375°F. Lightly grease two baking sheets.
2. In a medium bowl, combine the oats, flour, baking powder, baking soda, salt, and cinnamon. Set aside.
3. In the bowl of an electric mixer, using the paddle attachment, beat the butter and sugars at medium speed until combined, about 1 minute. Add the egg and vanilla extract and beat until blended. At low speed, add the flour mixture one-third at a time, mixing just until blended. Using a wooden spoon, stir in the semisweet morsels, banana, and pecans (it's all right if the banana pieces get a little mashed).
4. Drop the dough by rounded tablespoonfuls onto the prepared sheets, spacing the cookies 2 inches apart. Moisten your palm to prevent sticking, and flatten the mounds of dough slightly. Bake, one sheet at a time, for 11 to 13 minutes, until the cookies are golden brown on the bottom. Transfer the cookies to a wire rack and cool completely.

STORE **IN AN AIRTIGHT CONTAINER AT ROOM TEMPERATURE FOR UP TO 5 DAYS.**

Cookie Bite **For cooking and baking, use bananas that are beginning to turn brown and have few black spots. They have more flavor than bright yellow bananas.**

hermits

MAKES ABOUT 56 COOKIES

This spice cookie with an orange-scented drizzle glaze is a variation of a very old recipe, probably brought here in Colonial times, and now identified with New England. Hermits got their name because they keep so well; the wives of ship captains baked them for their husbands' long voyages. They are typically made with molasses, but I've substituted maple syrup, another New England favorite. Because they keep well, they're a perfect item to send to your kids at college, or make ahead of time for a holiday cookie tray.

hermits

2 cups all-purpose flour

½ teaspoon baking soda

1 teaspoon ground cinnamon

¾ teaspoon ground ginger

½ teaspoon ground cloves

¼ teaspoon freshly grated nutmeg

¼ teaspoon salt

¾ cup (1½ sticks) unsalted butter, softened

1 cup firmly packed dark brown sugar

2 large eggs

3 tablespoons pure maple syrup

1 tablespoon dark rum (optional)

1 teaspoon vanilla extract

1¼ cups dark raisins

1¼ cups coarsely chopped walnuts

orange icing

¾ cup confectioners' sugar, sifted

2 teaspoons freshly squeezed orange juice

2 to 3 teaspoons hot water

make the cookies

1. Position a rack in the center of the oven and preheat the oven to 350°F.
2. In a medium bowl, whisk together the flour, baking soda, cinnamon, ginger, cloves, nutmeg, and salt. Set aside.
3. In the bowl of an electric mixer, using the paddle attachment, beat the butter until creamy, about 30 seconds. Gradually add the dark brown sugar and continue to beat until the mixture is light in texture, 2 to 3 minutes. Add the eggs one at a time, beating well after each addition and scraping down the sides of the bowl as necessary. Beat in the maple syrup, rum, and vanilla extract. At low speed, beat in the flour mixture in two additions, mixing just until blended. Using a wooden spoon, stir in the raisins and walnuts.
4. Drop the dough by rounded tablespoonfuls onto ungreased baking sheets, spacing them at least 2 inches apart. Bake the cookies, one sheet at a time, for 9 to 12 minutes, until they are just set in the center and browned on the bottom. Transfer the cookies to wire racks and cool completely.

ice the cookies

5. In a medium bowl, whisk together the confectioners' sugar, orange juice, and just enough hot water to make an icing thin enough to drizzle. Scrape the icing into a small sealable plastic bag and seal the bag. Cut a small hole in one of the bottom corners of the bag, and drizzle the icing in parallel lines over the cookies. Let the icing set completely before storing the cookies.

STORE IN AN AIRTIGHT CONTAINER AT ROOM TEMPERATURE FOR UP TO 1 WEEK.

colossal peanut butter cookies

MAKES **ABOUT 23 JUMBO COOKIES**

These jumbo cookies represent nirvana for peanut butter lovers. Crispy on the outside and chewy on the inside, they are chock-full of chopped peanuts and peanut butter flavor. I recommend you bake these on an insulated baking sheet to ensure that the cookies don't overbrown on the bottom. If you don't have one, stack two heavy-gauge baking sheets together.

2½ cups all-purpose flour

2 teaspoons baking powder

½ teaspoon baking soda

¼ teaspoon salt

1 cup (2 sticks) unsalted butter, softened

1 cup creamy peanut butter, at room temperature

1 cup granulated sugar

1 cup firmly packed dark brown sugar

2 large eggs

1 tablespoon vanilla extract

¾ cup chopped unsalted peanuts

1. In a medium bowl, whisk together the flour, baking powder, baking soda, and salt; set aside.
2. In the bowl of an electric mixer, using the paddle attachment, beat the butter and peanut butter at medium speed until smooth. Gradually beat in the granulated and brown sugars. Beat in the eggs one at a time, beating well after each addition and scraping down the sides of the bowl as necessary. Beat in the vanilla extract. At low speed, gradually beat in the dry ingredients then chopped peanuts until blended. Cover the bowl with plastic wrap and refrigerate for 30 to 45 minutes, until the dough has firmed up.
3. Preheat the oven to 350°F. Lightly grease an insulated cookie sheet.
4. Using a ¼-cup ice cream scoop or cup measure, scoop 6 portions of the dough onto the cookie sheet, spacing them evenly. Moisten your palm to prevent sticking, and flatten each scoop into a 2½-inch disk. Using a fork, make a crosshatch indentation in the center of each cookie, sliding the fork across the cookie to continue the indentation all the way to the edges.
5. Bake the cookies for 18 to 20 minutes, until golden around the edges but still soft in the center; they will firm up as they cool. Transfer the cookies to a wire rack to cool completely.

STORE **IN AN AIRTIGHT CONTAINER AT ROOM TEMPERATURE FOR UP TO 5 DAYS.**

Cookie Bite **An unopened jar of peanut butter can be stored in a cool, dry place for at least a year. Once opened, it will stay fresh for about 3 months. For longer storage, keep it in the refrigerator to prevent it from turning rancid. Always use full-fat peanut butter in baking. Reduced-fat peanut butter will make the cookies tough and dry.**

coconut macaroons

MAKES **ABOUT 36 COOKIES**

These simple cookies are crispy on the outside, soft and moist on the inside. Their flavor reminds me of the wonderful, creamy coconut custard my mom baked when I was a kid. Don't overbake them, or they will be too firm when they cool.

2 large eggs

1 cup granulated sugar

⅛ teaspoon salt

⅓ cup all-purpose flour

1 teaspoon vanilla extract

3 cups (9 ounces) sweetened shredded coconut

1. Position a rack in the center of the oven and preheat the oven to 350°F. Grease an insulated baking sheet (or use two baking sheets, stacked on top of one another).
2. In a medium bowl, whisk together the eggs, sugar, salt, flour, and vanilla extract until well blended. Stir in the coconut.
3. Using a 1-tablespoon cookie scoop, melon baller, or measuring spoon, drop the dough into mounds on the prepared sheet, spacing them at least 2 inches apart. Bake the cookies for 14 to 16 minutes, until they are golden brown around the edges and a few strands of coconut on the tops of the cookies start to turn golden. Cool the cookies completely on the baking sheet on a wire rack. Repeat with the remaining dough.

STORE **IN AN AIRTIGHT CONTAINER AT ROOM TEMPERATURE FOR UP TO 2 DAYS, BUT THESE ARE BEST THE DAY THEY ARE MADE.**

new york black and white cookies

MAKES **ABOUT 14 LARGE COOKIES**

This cookie is a happy memory for anyone who grew up in the New York area—as long ago as Tammany Hall days—and Black and Whites are still found on every deli counter and in every pastry case in the city. As one who still succumbs to the temptation occasionally, I have to admit that many of those can be pretty awful. This version should restore the reputation of the Black and White, as it was in its heyday. This is a jumbo-sized sugar cookie that is glazed half and half with chocolate and vanilla. The cookie is puffy and delicately scented with vanilla, which mediates nicely with the twin glazes.

vanilla cookies

2 cups all-purpose flour

1 teaspoon baking powder

½ teaspoon baking soda

⅛ teaspoon salt

½ cup (1 stick) unsalted butter, softened

1 cup granulated sugar

1 large egg

2 teaspoons vanilla extract

½ cup sour cream

white glaze

1 cup confectioners' sugar

3½ tablespoons heavy cream

⅛ teaspoon vanilla extract

chocolate glaze

3 ounces semisweet chocolate, coarsely chopped

¼ cup heavy cream

1 tablespoon light corn syrup

make the cookies

1. Position a rack in the center of the oven and preheat the oven to 350°F. Grease two large baking sheets.

2. In a medium bowl, gently whisk together the flour, baking powder, baking soda, and salt. Set aside.

3. In an electric mixer, using the paddle attachment, beat the butter at medium speed until creamy, about 30 seconds. Gradually beat in the sugar, mixing until well combined. Add the egg and vanilla extract and mix until well blended. Scrape down the sides of the bowl. Alternately add the sour cream in two additions and the flour mixture in three additions, blending well after each.

4. Using a ¼ cup ice cream scoop or cup measure, scoop mounds of the dough onto the baking sheets, spacing them 3 inches apart. Moisten your palm to prevent sticking and pat the mounds into 2½-inch disks. Bake the cookies, one sheet at a time, for 15 to 17 minutes, until just beginning to turn light golden brown. Let the cookies cool on the baking sheet for 2 minutes, then transfer them to a wire rack to cool completely.

make the white glaze

5. In a small bowl, whisk together the confectioners' sugar, heavy cream, and vanilla extract until smooth. Cover the bowl and set aside.

make the chocolate glaze

6. Place the chocolate, heavy cream, and corn syrup in the top of a double boiler over barely simmering water. Heat, stirring occasionally, until the chocolate is melted and the glaze is smooth. Let the glaze cool until tepid, about 10 minutes.

ice the cookies

7. Using a small offset metal spatula, spread the white glaze on half of each cookie. Let the glaze set for 10 minutes.

8. Using the spatula, spread the chocolate glaze on the other half of each cookie. Let the cookies set at room temperature for at least 45 minutes.

STORE IN AN AIRTIGHT CONTAINER AT ROOM TEMPERATURE FOR UP TO 5 DAYS.

brutti ma buoni

MAKES ABOUT 48 COOKIES

Their name translates from the Italian as "ugly but good." They are in fact delicious—crunchy on the outside, soft on the inside, and loaded with nuts and chocolate. They will fill your kitchen with a wonderful orange-almond fragrance as they bake.

4 large egg whites, at room temperature

⅛ teaspoon cream of tartar

Pinch of salt

⅔ cup granulated sugar

2 teaspoons vanilla extract

½ teaspoon almond extract

1 teaspoon finely grated orange zest

½ cup hazelnuts, toasted and chopped

½ cup slivered almonds, toasted and chopped

2 ounces bittersweet chocolate, grated

1. Position two racks near the center of the oven and preheat the oven to 325°F. Lightly grease two baking sheets.
2. In the bowl of an electric mixer, using the whisk attachment, beat the egg whites at medium speed until foamy. Add the cream of tartar and salt, increase the speed to medium-high, and beat until soft peaks form. Gradually add the sugar and beat until stiff and glossy, about 2 minutes. Using a rubber spatula, gently fold in the vanilla extract, almond extract, orange zest, nuts, and chocolate.
3. Spoon the batter into 1¼-inch mounds on the prepared baking sheets, spacing the cookies at least 1 inch apart. Bake, two sheets at a time, for 25 to 30 minutes, switching the position of the sheets halfway through baking, until almost firm to the touch and lightly browned. Transfer the cookies to wire racks and cool completely.

STORE IN AN AIRTIGHT CONTAINER AT ROOM TEMPERATURE, IN A DRY ENVIRONMENT, FOR UP TO 3 DAYS. DON'T MAKE THIS COOKIE ON A HUMID DAY.

Cookie Bite To grate chocolate easily, place it in the freezer for about 5 minutes, and then grate it onto waxed paper.

rolled cookies

• classic gingerbread cookies • honey cinnamon graham cookies • cinnamon animal crackers • sablés • alsatian christmas stars • glazed lemon–poppy seed hearts • peanut butter shortbread rounds • almond java rounds • maple walnut leaves • pistachio shortbread cookies • chocolate-drizzled toasted coconut cookies • seafood cat cookies • miss kitty dog biscuits • sacristains • little crullers • tangerine kumquat rounds • welsh skillet cakes •

The dough for rolled cookies requires some special handling. First it must be rolled out, and then the cookies are shaped, usually with cutters. (For more on the rolling-out procedure, see page 38.) None of this is difficult, however, and the results are well worth it.

At one end of the rolled cookie spectrum, the key words are "elegance and subtlety": Sablés, Maple Walnut Leaves, Sacristains, and Little Crullers, not forgetting an unusual recipe from my family tree, Welsh Skillet Cakes. At the other, more whimsical end, you'll find Miss Kitty Dog Biscuits, Seafood Cat Cookies, and Cinnamon Animal Crackers. In between are the classics: gingerbread, molasses spice, and, of course, shortbread.

Basic cookie cutters can be found in many stores, and on page 376 I've listed companies that offer some wonderful cutters, to suit your every whim. You can also invent your own forms, creating templates out of cardboard or thin plastic. The dough scraps left after the cookies are cut out can be gathered together and rolled out again. In some recipes, however, the dough should be chilled for a short time before rerolling. Handling cookie dough multiple times may produce tough cookies. To avoid producing more scraps, use a large knife or pizza cutter to cut the rolled scraps into squares or rectangles instead of uneven shapes.

classic gingerbread cookies

MAKES **ABOUT 64 COOKIES**

This recipe is from Richard Ruskell, the owner of Pastry Maxine, a patisserie in North Scottsdale, Arizona. (Maxine, the real boss, is Richard's energetic Dalmatian.) The secret to Richard's incredible gingerbread cookies is simple: lots of ginger, a touch of molasses, dark brown sugar, and a hint of cinnamon.

3¼ cups bleached all-purpose flour

2 teaspoons ground cinnamon

1 tablespoon ground ginger

1 cup (2 sticks) unsalted butter, softened

¾ cup firmly packed dark brown sugar

¾ cup granulated sugar

1 large egg

2 tablespoons hot water

1½ teaspoons baking soda

1 tablespoon unsulphured (mild) molasses

Coarse sugar for sprinkling (optional)

special equipment

Assorted 2¾-inch cookie cutters

make the dough

1. In a large bowl, whisk together the flour, cinnamon, and ginger. Set aside.
2. In the bowl of an electric mixer, using the paddle attachment, beat the butter and sugars at medium speed until light, about 3 minutes. Beat in the egg.
3. In a small bowl, stir together the hot water, baking soda, and molasses until the baking soda is dissolved. At low speed, gradually add this mixture to the butter mixture. Increase the speed to medium and mix until blended. At low speed, add the dry ingredients in several additions, mixing just until combined. Scrape the dough onto a work surface and shape it into a disk. Wrap it in plastic wrap and refrigerate until firm, at least 2 hours (or up to 3 days).

cut and bake the cookies

4. Position a rack in the center of the oven and preheat the oven to 350°F. Grease two baking sheets.
5. Divide the chilled dough into quarters. Rewrap and refrigerate three of the quarters. On a lightly floured work surface, roll the dough out to a thickness of ⅛ inch, lightly flouring the dough and work surface as needed. Using 2¾-inch cookie cutters, cut out as many cookies as possible from the dough. Carefully transfer the cookies to one of the prepared baking sheets and sprinkle them with coarse sugar, if desired. Gather the scraps of dough together into a ball, flatten into a disk, wrap in plastic wrap, and refrigerate until firm enough to roll, about 30 minutes.
6. Bake the cookies until the tops are set, 8 to 10 minutes. Cool the cookies on the baking sheet on a wire rack for 2 minutes, then transfer to the wire rack to cool completely. Repeat the rolling, cutting, and baking procedure with the remaining dough. Reroll the scraps from each portion one time only to make more cookies.

STORE **IN AN AIRTIGHT CONTAINER AT ROOM TEMPERATURE FOR UP TO 1 MONTH.**

honey cinnamon graham cookies

MAKES ABOUT 56 COOKIES

These cookies are a cross between the "digestive biscuit," which is popular at teatime in Britain, and the American graham cracker. They're made with lots of honey and just a hint of cinnamon. The cookie crumbs also make a wonderful pie or cheesecake crust.

2⅓ cups all-purpose flour

½ cup whole wheat flour

1 teaspoon baking soda

1 teaspoon salt

½ teaspoon ground cinnamon

6 tablespoons (¾ stick) unsalted butter, softened

2 tablespoons solid vegetable shortening

⅓ cup granulated sugar

½ cup honey

1 teaspoon vanilla extract

⅓ cup water

special equipment

2-inch round cookie cutter

make the dough

1. In a medium bowl, whisk together the flours, baking soda, salt, and cinnamon. Set aside.

2. In the bowl of an electric mixer, using the paddle attachment, beat the butter, shortening, sugar, honey, and vanilla extract at medium speed until blended, about 1 minute. At low speed, add the flour mixture, mixing just until blended. Scrape the dough onto a work surface and, with floured hands, shape it into 2 disks (the dough will be sticky). Wrap each disk in plastic wrap and refrigerate for 2 hours, until chilled (or up to 3 days).

cut and bake the cookies

3. Position a rack in the center of the oven and preheat the oven to 325°F. Line two baking sheets with parchment paper.

4. Remove one of the dough disks from the refrigerator and place it on a floured work surface. Dust it lightly with flour and, using a rolling pin, roll it out to a thickness of ⅛ inch. Using a 2-inch round cookie cutter, cut out as many cookies as possible from the dough and arrange them 1 inch apart on the prepared baking sheets. Gather up the scraps, wrap in plastic, and freeze for 10 minutes before rerolling. Prick each cookie four times with a fork. Bake for 12 to 15 minutes, until the cookies are golden brown. Transfer them to a wire rack and cool completely.

5. Repeat the procedure with the remaining dough.

STORE IN AN AIRTIGHT CONTAINER AT ROOM TEMPERATURE FOR UP TO 5 DAYS.

Cookie Bite **Because whole wheat flour contains the wheat germ, it can become rancid, so it's best to store it in a sealable plastic bag in the refrigerator or freezer. Bring it to room temperature before using.**

cinnamon animal crackers

MAKES 76 TO 106 (DEPENDING ON SIZE) SMALL COOKIES

Although they are supposed to be childhood comfort food, adults will love these little treasures as well. It's traditional to call them crackers, even though everyone knows they're really mini cookies. The dough is made in the food processor in a matter of minutes, and then just needs to chill for 2 hours before rolling. For a sleeker finish, use brown sanding sugar (see Sources, page 376) instead of turbinado sugar.

1⅓ cups all-purpose flour

⅓ cup firmly packed dark brown sugar

¼ cup granulated sugar

½ teaspoon baking soda

¼ teaspoon ground cinnamon

¼ teaspoon salt

4 tablespoons (½ stick) unsalted butter, cut into ½-inch cubes and frozen

3 tablespoons whole milk

2 tablespoons honey

1 tablespoon vanilla extract

Turbinado sugar for sprinkling

special equipment

Assorted 1- to 1½-inch animal-shaped cookie cutters

make the dough

1. Place the flour, brown sugar, granulated sugar, baking soda, cinnamon, and salt in the bowl of a food processor and pulse a few times until blended. Add the butter and pulse until the mixture resembles coarse meal.

2. In a small bowl, whisk together the milk, honey, and vanilla. Add the flour mixture and pulse until the dough begins to come together. Scrape the dough out onto a floured work surface and pat it into a disk. Wrap the dough in plastic wrap and refrigerate until chilled, about 2 hours (or up to 3 days).

cut and bake the cookies

3. Position a rack in the center of the oven and preheat the oven to 350°F. Line two baking sheets with parchment paper or foil.

4. On a lightly floured work surface, using a rolling pin, roll out the chilled dough to a thickness of ⅛ inch, sprinkling it with flour as necessary to prevent sticking. Using assorted 1- to 1½-inch animal-shaped cookie cutters, cut out as many cookies as possible from the dough. Arrange the cookies on the prepared baking sheets, spacing them ½ inch apart. Repeat the process until all the dough is used.

5. Sprinkle the cookies with turbinado sugar. Bake the cookies, one sheet at a time, for 8 to 10 minutes, until slightly puffed and lightly browned; the cookies should still be soft—they will firm up as they cool. Transfer the cookies to a wire rack and cool completely.

STORE IN AN AIRTIGHT CONTAINER AT ROOM TEMPERATURE FOR UP TO 2 WEEKS.

sablés

MAKES ABOUT 50 COOKIES

***Sablé* means "sandy" in French, a reference to the texture of these cookies. They're buttery and a little crumbly, in a very appealing way. There are many different versions of sablés; this one is Breton. Brittany is famous for its salt, so these cookies have a healthy dose of it. That faint saltiness and texture make this the perfect choice if you like to crumble cookies over your ice cream or sorbet. The sablé is revered in France, much as the chocolate chip cookie is here. Unlike chocolate chip cookies, which are usually crammed with chips and nuts, sablés are understated, buttery numbers, in the Scottish shortbread vein. If you're underwhelmed by "understated," they make an excellent base for flavor variations, such as the lemon, walnut, and almond suggestions included here.**

2⅓ cups cake flour (not self-rising)

1 tablespoon baking powder

1 teaspoon fine sea salt

1 cup (2 sticks) unsalted butter, softened

¾ cup plus 2 tablespoons granulated sugar

1 teaspoon vanilla extract

4 large egg yolks

1 large egg, lightly beaten with 1 teaspoon water for egg wash

special equipment

1¾-inch round cookie cutter

make the dough

1. Sift together the cake flour, baking powder, and salt into a medium bowl. Gently whisk until well blended. Set aside.

2. In the bowl of an electric mixer, using the paddle attachment, beat the butter until creamy, about 30 seconds. Gradually beat in the sugar and salt and continue to beat until light in texture and color, about 2 minutes. Beat in the vanilla extract. Add the egg yolks one at a time, mixing well after each addition. Add the flour mixture at low speed, mixing just until blended and scraping down the sides of the bowl as necessary. Scrape the dough out onto a piece of plastic wrap and pat it into a disk. Wrap it in the plastic wrap and refrigerate for at least 3 hours, until firm (or up to 2 days).

cut and bake the cookies

3. Position a rack in the center of the oven and preheat the oven to 350°F. Line two baking sheets with parchment paper.

4. On a lightly floured work surface, roll out the dough with a rolling pin to a thickness of ¼ inch. Using a 1¾-inch round cookie cutter, cut out as many cookies as possible and arrange them ¾ inch apart on the prepared baking sheets. Gather up the scraps, wrap them in plastic wrap, and refrigerate them for at least 15 minutes before rerolling them and cutting out more cookies.

5. Brush the tops of the cookies with the egg wash, then brush them again. Bake the cookies, one sheet at a time, for 13 to 15 minutes, until they are lightly golden brown. Transfer the cookies to a wire rack and cool completely.

   Walnut Sablés: Process ½ cup walnuts, toasted, with ½ teaspoon ground cinnamon in a food processor until finely ground. Whisk into the sifted flour mixture in Step 1.

   Almond Sablés: Process ½ cup slivered almonds with 2 tablespoons of the sugar in a food processor until finely ground. Whisk this into the sifted flour mixture in Step 1. Add ¼ teaspoon almond extract with the vanilla extract.

   Lemon Sablés: Add 2 teaspoons finely grated lemon zest along with the vanilla extract in Step 2.

STORE IN AN AIRTIGHT CONTAINER AT ROOM TEMPERATURE FOR UP TO A WEEK.

alsatian christmas stars

MAKES **ABOUT 60 COOKIES**

Jacquy Pfeiffer is an award-winning pastry chef, culinary teacher, and co-owner of the French Pastry School in Chicago. He is from the Alsace region of France, and this is his mother's recipe. These Christmas stars, made with a cinnamon-scented almond butter dough that is rolled out, cut into star shapes, and topped with an egg glaze before being baked, are popular throughout Alsace and Germany. They keep well, so they are a good choice to make ahead for the holidays.

cinnamon cookies

1½ cups blanched almonds

2¾ cups cake flour (not self-rising)

2 teaspoons ground cinnamon

¼ teaspoon salt

1 cup (2 sticks) plus 1 tablespoon unsalted butter, softened

1 cup granulated sugar

1 large egg

glaze

1 large egg

Pinch of salt

3 tablespoons coarse or granulated sugar

special equipment

3-inch star-shaped cookie cutter (measured from one point to an opposite point)

make the dough

1. Place the almonds, cake flour, cinnamon, and salt in the bowl of a food processor and process until the nuts are finely ground, about 30 seconds. Set aside.

2. In an electric mixer, using the paddle attachment, beat the butter and sugar at medium speed until well blended, about 2 minutes. Scrape down the sides of the bowl and beat in the egg. At low speed, add the dry ingredients one-third at a time and mix just until blended. Scrape the dough out onto a work surface and shape into two disks. Wrap each one in plastic wrap, and refrigerate for at least 2 hours, until chilled (or up to 3 days).

roll and cut the cookies

3. Position two racks near the center of the oven and preheat the oven to 300°F. Lightly grease two baking sheets.

4. Lightly flour a work surface. Remove one of the disks of dough from the refrigerator. It will be very firm. Pound it a few times with a rolling pin to soften it, then roll it out to a thickness of ⅛ inch. Using a 3-inch star-shaped cookie cutter, cut out as many cookies as possible from the dough. Carefully transfer the cookies to one of the prepared baking sheets, spacing them 1 inch apart. Gather the scraps of the dough together, flatten them into a disk, wrap in plastic wrap, and refrigerate until firm enough to roll out. Reroll the scraps one time only to make more cookies. Repeat the rolling and cutting process with the remaining dough.

glaze and bake the cookies

5. In a small bowl, whisk together the egg and salt until blended. Using a pastry brush, brush the cookies with the glaze. Sprinkle with the sugar.

6. Bake the cookies, two sheets at a time, for 17 to 22 minutes, or until they are set and their bottoms are evenly golden brown; switch the positions of the baking sheets halfway through for even baking. Cool the cookies on the baking sheets on wire racks for 5 minutes, then transfer the cookies to the racks and cool completely.

STORE IN AN AIRTIGHT CONTAINER AT ROOM TEMPERATURE FOR UP TO 2 WEEKS.

glazed lemon–poppy seed hearts

MAKES **ABOUT 36 COOKIES**

These pretty cookies are made from a lemony shortbread dough that is sown with crunchy poppy seeds and topped with a sweet glaze and candied lemon peel. Meltingly tender, they make a welcome addition to any holiday cookie tray. You could also wrap them individually in plastic and tie them with a festive ribbon to hand out to all your sweethearts on Valentine's Day.

lemon cookies

1 cup (2 sticks) unsalted butter, softened

½ cup granulated sugar

1 large egg yolk

1 tablespoon finely grated lemon zest

¾ teaspoon lemon extract

½ teaspoon vanilla extract

⅛ teaspoon ground cardamom

Pinch of salt

2 cups all-purpose flour

⅓ cup poppy seeds

candied lemon garnish

1 lemon

1 cup granulated sugar, divided

⅓ cup water

glaze

Basic Sugar Glaze (page 360)

special equipment

2½-inch heart-shaped cookie cutter

make the dough

1. In the bowl of an electric mixer, using the paddle attachment, beat the butter and sugar at medium speed until combined, about 1 minute. Add the egg yolk, lemon zest, vanilla and lemon extracts, cardamom, and salt and mix until combined, scraping down the sides of the bowl as necessary. At low speed, add the flour and poppy seeds and mix until combined. Turn the dough out onto a piece of plastic wrap, pat it into a rectangle, and wrap it. Refrigerate the dough for at least 1 hour, until firm (or up to 3 days).

meanwhile, make the lemon garnish

2. Using a vegetable peeler, peel the lemon lengthwise. Stacking 3 strips of peel on top of one another, thinly slice them crosswise; repeat with the remaining strips. Set aside. Place ⅓ cup of the sugar in a small bowl.

3. In a small heavy saucepan, combine the water and the remaining ⅔ cup sugar and bring to a boil, stirring to dissolve the sugar. Add the lemon peel and boil for 3 minutes. Remove the lemon peel with a slotted spoon and toss with the reserved sugar until coated. Transfer the peel to a plate and let dry for about 30 minutes.

4. Transfer the lemon peel to a sieve and shake to remove the excess sugar.

make the glaze

5. Prepare the sugar glaze as directed on page 360. Set aside.

cut and bake the cookies

6. Position two racks near the center of the oven and preheat the oven to 350°F. Grease two baking sheets.

7. Divide the dough in half. On a lightly floured work surface, roll out one piece of dough about 3⁄16 inch thick. Using a 2½-inch heart-shaped cookie cutter, cut out as many cookies as possible from the dough and transfer to the prepared baking sheets, spacing them 1 inch apart. Gather up the scraps of dough, reroll them, and cut out more hearts. Repeat the process with the remaining piece of dough. Bake the cookies, two sheets at a time, for 14 to 16 minutes, until they are pale brown around the edges; switch the position of the baking sheets halfway through baking. Place the baking sheets on wire racks and glaze the cookies while hot.

glaze and garnish the cookies

8. Using a small offset metal spatula, spread about a teaspoon of the glaze evenly over each cookie. Garnish each cookie with a piece of candied lemon peel. Transfer the cookies to a wire rack and cool completely.

STORE IN AN AIRTIGHT CONTAINER AT ROOM TEMPERATURE FOR UP TO 5 DAYS.

peanut butter shortbread rounds

MAKES **ABOUT 40 COOKIES**

These are very tender, intensely peanutty cookies—shortbread is a great vehicle for peanut flavor. The secret to their success is in using natural peanut butter, which has no added oil, sugar, or salt. The sugar in regular peanut butter would throw the balance of this recipe off. Natural peanut butter is now available in many supermarkets, and you'll also find it in any healthy food store.

1 cup (2 sticks) unsalted butter, cut into tablespoons

½ cup granulated sugar

¼ cup firmly packed light brown sugar

⅔ cup natural peanut butter

¾ teaspoon salt

1 teaspoon vanilla extract

2 cups all-purpose flour

special equipment

2-inch round cookie cutter

make the dough

1. In the bowl of an electric mixer, using the paddle attachment, beat the butter at medium speed for 1 minute to soften it. Gradually add the sugars and beat until well blended, about 1½ minutes. Add the peanut butter, salt, and vanilla extract and mix at medium-low speed until blended, scraping down the sides of the bowl as necessary. At low speed, add the flour and mix just until blended. Turn the dough out onto a work surface, divide in half, and shape it into two disks. Wrap each disk in plastic wrap and refrigerate until chilled, at least 2 hours (or up to 3 days).

cut and bake the cookies

2. Position a rack in the center of the oven and preheat the oven to 300°F. Line two baking sheets with parchment paper.

3. Place one of the chilled dough disks on a lightly floured work surface. Using a rolling pin, roll the dough out to a thickness of ¼ inch. Using a 2-inch round cookie cutter, cut out as many cookies as possible from the dough. Arrange on one of the prepared baking sheets, spacing them ¾ inch apart. Gather up the scraps, rewrap them, and chill for about 15 minutes before rerolling and cutting out more cookies.

4. Bake the cookies, one sheet at a time, for 24 to 28 minutes, until they are just firm but not browned. Cool the cookies on the baking sheet for 10 minutes, then transfer them carefully to a wire rack and cool completely. Repeat the rolling, cutting, and baking procedure with the remaining dough.

Peanut Butter Jamwiches: Prepare the dough as above, but roll it out slightly thinner, to 3⁄16 inch, and use a 1¾-inch round cookie cutter to cut out the cookies. Reduce the baking time to 18 to 20 minutes, and cool as directed. Spread the bottoms of half of the cookies with 1 teaspoon raspberry jam each (total amount of jam is about ¾ cup). Top with the remaining cookies, forming sandwiches. Makes about 35 sandwich cookies.

Chocolate Peanut Butter Shortbread Rounds: Prepare the dough as above, but reduce the flour to 1⅔ cups and add ⅓ cup Dutch-processed cocoa powder, sifted, with the flour. Makes about 40 cookies.

STORE IN AN AIRTIGHT CONTAINER AT ROOM TEMPERATURE FOR UP TO A WEEK.

Cookie Bite **Because it is made without salt, sugar, or stabilizers, natural peanut butter should be stored in the refrigerator; it will keep for up to 6 months.**

almond java rounds

MAKES **ABOUT 38 COOKIES**

These almond butter cookies are infused with rich, fresh-roasted coffee flavor. The ground coffee adds a little crunch as well. Not surprisingly, the cookies are great with a cup of coffee or espresso. The addition of hard-boiled egg yolks, a European technique, gives the cookies a buttery, melt-in-your mouth texture.

½ cup whole blanched almonds

1 cup confectioners' sugar, divided

¼ teaspoon ground cinnamon

2 hard-boiled large egg yolks, chilled

2 cups all-purpose flour

1½ teaspoons baking powder

¼ teaspoon salt

1¼ cups (2½ sticks) unsalted butter

1½ tablespoons freshly and finely ground Swiss almond mocha coffee or espresso beans

1 teaspoon vanilla extract

½ teaspoon almond extract

1 large egg, lightly beaten, for egg wash

special equipment

2¼-inch fluted round cookie cutter

make the dough

1. Place the almonds and ⅓ cup of the confectioners' sugar in the bowl of a food processor and process until the nuts are finely ground, about 30 seconds. Transfer to a medium bowl and stir in the remaining ⅔ cup confectioners' sugar and the cinnamon.

2. Place a fine sieve over a small bowl and force the egg yolks through it using a spoon; set aside.

3. In a medium bowl, whisk together the flour, baking powder, and salt; set aside.

4. In the bowl of an electric mixer, using the paddle attachment, beat the butter and coffee at medium speed until creamy, about 1 minute. Add the almond mixture and egg yolks and beat until well blended. Beat in the vanilla and almond extracts. At low speed, add the flour mixture and mix just until combined.

5. Turn the dough out onto a work surface and gather it into a ball. Divide the dough in half and shape each piece into a disk. Wrap each disk in plastic wrap and refrigerate for at least 2 hours. (The dough can be frozen, for up to 1 month.)

cut out and bake the cookies

6. Position a rack in the center of the oven and preheat the oven to 350°F. Lightly grease two baking sheets.

7. Remove one of the dough disks from the refrigerator. Lightly dust a work surface with flour, place the dough on it, and sprinkle it with a little more flour. Pound the dough a few times with a rolling pin to soften it. Roll the dough out to a thickness of ⅛ inch. Using a 2¼-inch fluted round cookie

cutter, cut out as many cookies as possible and transfer them to one of the baking sheets, spacing them 1 inch apart. Gather the dough scraps, pat them into a disk, wrap them in plastic wrap, and chill before rerolling and cutting out more cookies (reroll the scraps only once). Repeat the rolling and cutting process with the remaining dough.

8. Brush the cookies lightly with the beaten egg. Bake the cookies, one sheet at a time, for 12 to 15 minutes, until golden brown. Cool the cookies on the baking sheets on a wire rack for 5 minutes, then transfer them to the wire rack and cool completely.

STORE IN AN AIRTIGHT CONTAINER AT ROOM TEMPERATURE FOR UP TO 2 WEEKS.

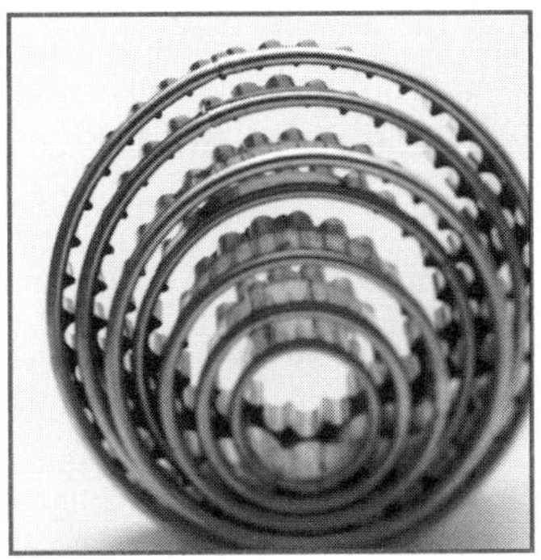

maple walnut leaves

MAKES **ABOUT 52 COOKIES**

These "leaves" are made from basic sugar cookie dough flavored with maple and walnut. Perfect flavor-wise and shape-wise for fall, the cookies go well with a cup of coffee (grown-ups) or a glass of milk (kids). You'll find turbinado sugar, which is light brown, as "Sugar in the Raw" in the supermarket or health food store.

½ cup walnuts, toasted and cooled

¾ cup granulated sugar, divided

2¼ cups all-purpose flour

½ cup cake flour (not self-rising)

½ teaspoon salt

1 cup (2 sticks) unsalted butter, softened

1 large egg yolk

¼ cup pure maple syrup

¼ teaspoon maple flavoring

1 large egg, lightly beaten with 1 teaspoon water for egg wash

Turbinado sugar for sprinkling

special equipment

2¾-inch (measured crosswise) maple leaf–shaped cookie cutter

make the dough

1. Place the walnuts and ¼ cup of the granulated sugar in the bowl of a food processor and process until the nuts are finely ground, about 30 seconds.
2. Sift together the flours and salt into a medium bowl. Stir in the ground walnuts until well blended. Set aside.
3. In the bowl of an electric mixer, using the paddle attachment, beat the butter and the remaining ½ cup sugar at medium-high speed until light in texture, about 2 minutes. Beat in the egg yolk, maple syrup, and maple flavoring until well blended. At low speed, gradually add the flour mixture, mixing until just blended. Divided the dough in half and shape into 2 disks. Wrap each in plastic wrap and refrigerate for at least 2 hours, until firm enough to roll.

cut and bake the cookies

4. Position a rack in the center of the oven and preheat the oven to 350°F.
5. On a lightly floured surface, roll out half of the dough (leave the remaining dough refrigerated) to a thickness of ⅛ inch. Using a 2¾-inch maple leaf cookie cutter, cut out as many cookies as possible from the dough and arrange them on ungreased baking sheets, spacing them 1 inch apart. Gather up the scraps and reroll them (refrigerate them for 10 minutes if they get too soft to roll). Brush the cookies with the egg wash and sprinkle with turbinado sugar.
6. Bake the cookies, one sheet at a time, for 10 to 12 minutes, until golden brown around the edges. Transfer the cookies to a wire rack and cool completely. Repeat with the remaining dough.

STORE **IN AN AIRTIGHT CONTAINER AT ROOM TEMPERATURE FOR UP TO A WEEK.**

pistachio shortbread cookies

MAKES **ABOUT 46 COOKIES**

This recipe is from Chris Broberg, one of the most innovative, tasteful, and kind pastry chefs I know. Chris has a knack for creating sweets that are sophisticated but not fussy, and that never lose the fun of dessert. Pistachio is a subtle flavor, but once people give these buttery cookies a try, maybe two, they generally go for the whole plate.

½ cup shelled unsalted pistachio nuts*

¾ cup granulated sugar, divided

1⅔ cups all-purpose flour

¼ cup cornstarch

¼ teaspoon salt

¾ cup (1½ sticks) unsalted butter

1 large egg yolk

special equipment

2-inch fluted or scalloped round cookie cutter

*__Note:__ If you can only find salted nuts, place them in a sieve and rinse under cold running water. Dry them thoroughly with paper towels.

make the dough

1. Position a rack in the center of the oven and preheat the oven to 325°F. Line two baking sheets with parchment paper or foil.
2. Place the pistachios and ¼ cup of the sugar in the bowl of a food processor and process until the nuts are finely ground, about 30 seconds. Add the flour, cornstarch, and salt and pulse until blended. Set aside.
3. In the bowl of an electric mixer, using the paddle attachment, beat the butter and the remaining ½ cup sugar at medium-high speed until light, about 2 minutes. Add the egg yolk and mix at low speed until blended, scraping down the sides of the bowl as necessary. Add the dry ingredients, mixing until combined.

cut and bake the cookies

4. Scrape the dough out onto a work surface and knead it a few times, until smooth. Divide it in half and shape each half into a disk.
5. Place one of the disks on a large piece of waxed paper, place another piece of waxed paper over it, and, using a rolling pin, roll it out to a thickness of ⅛ inch. Carefully peel off the top piece of waxed paper, then replace it loosely and flip over the dough. Peel off the second piece of waxed paper. Using a 2-inch fluted or scalloped round cookie cutter, cut out as many cookies as possible from the dough. Arrange the cookies ½ inch apart on the prepared baking sheets. Gather up the scraps and reroll them between sheets of waxed paper. Bake the cookies, one sheet at a time, for 13 to 16 minutes, until just lightly colored around the edges. Watch the cookies carefully, as their color will change very quickly. Transfer the cookies to a wire rack and cool completely. Repeat with the remaining dough.

STORE **IN AN AIRTIGHT CONTAINER AT ROOM TEMPERATURE FOR UP TO 5 DAYS.**

chocolate-drizzled toasted coconut cookies

MAKES **ABOUT 42 COOKIES**

Generous drizzles of chocolate and sprinkles of toasted coconut add depth of flavor to these tender, buttery coconut sablé cookies. The hint of rum in the dough brings out the coconut flavor, and the chocolate lends a touch of sophistication.

coconut cookies

⅓ cup slivered almonds

⅔ cup confectioners' sugar, divided

⅓ cup sweetened shredded coconut

⅛ teaspoon salt

¾ cup (1½ sticks) unsalted butter, softened

1 large egg yolk

1 tablespoon dark rum

1 teaspoon vanilla extract

1⅓ cups all-purpose flour

garnish

3 ounces bittersweet chocolate, chopped

⅓ cup sweetened shredded coconut, toasted and finely chopped

special equipment

2-inch fluted round cookie cutter

make the dough

1. Place the almonds and ⅓ cup of the confectioners' sugar in the bowl of a food processor and process until the almonds are finely ground, 20 to 30 seconds. Add the coconut and process until the coconut is finely chopped, about 20 seconds. Transfer the mixture to a medium bowl and stir in the remaining ⅓ cup confectioners' sugar until combined.

2. In the bowl of an electric mixer, using the paddle attachment, beat the butter at medium speed until creamy, about 1 minute. Add the almond-coconut mixture and beat at low speed until combined. Scrape down the sides of the bowl and beat at medium speed until well blended.

3. In a small bowl, combine the egg yolk with the rum and vanilla. Beat the egg mixture into the dough, mixing at medium speed until well blended. At low speed, add the flour and mix just until blended. Scrape the dough out onto a work surface and pat it into a ball. Divide the dough in half and pat each piece into a disk. Wrap each disk in plastic wrap and refrigerate for at least 2 hours, until firm (or up to 2 days).

cut out and bake the cookies

4. Position a rack in the center of the oven and preheat the oven to 350°F. Lightly butter two baking sheets. Remove one of the disks of dough from the refrigerator and place it on a lightly floured work surface. Sprinkle it with a little flour. Pound the dough a few times with a rolling pin to soften it, then roll the dough out to a thickness of ⅛ inch. Using a 2-inch fluted round cookie cutter, cut out as many cookies as possible and transfer them to the prepared baking sheets, spacing them about 1 inch apart. Gather the dough scraps into a ball, wrap in plastic wrap, and refrigerate for about 15 minutes before rerolling. Repeat with the remaining disk of dough.

5. Bake the cookies, one sheet at a time, for 11 to 13 minutes, just until light golden brown around the edges. Transfer the cookies to a wire rack and cool completely.

garnish the cookies

6. Melt the chocolate in the top of a double boiler over simmering water, stirring until smooth. Set aside.

7. Place a sheet of foil or waxed paper under the rack with the cookies on it. Transfer the melted chocolate to a small sealable plastic bag, seal the bag, and snip a tiny hole in one of the bottom corners of the bag. Drizzle the chocolate over the cookies in parallel lines. Sprinkle the toasted coconut over the cookies. Refrigerate the cookies for 10 minutes to set the chocolate.

STORE IN AN AIRTIGHT CONTAINER AT ROOM TEMPERATURE FOR UP TO 5 DAYS.

Cookie Bite **To toast coconut, spread it on a baking sheet in an even layer and bake in a 350°F oven, stirring three or four times during baking, for 6 to 10 minutes, or until golden. Cool completely before using.**

seafood cat cookies

MAKES **ABOUT 220 TINY COOKIES**

I'd always been a dog person, considering cats to be supercilious, mostly decorative creatures, until I married a cat lover and became the owner of two enchanting felines—though it's true they behave more like dogs than cats (big greeters, love ice cream, come running when they're called). When they're not napping or racing around the apartment like miniature thoroughbreds, Emily and Jemal are looking for handouts. Here's one of their favorite snacks—tuna-and-sardine-infused treats that are the perfect rewards for good behavior.

1 cup all-purpose flour

½ cup cornmeal

¼ cup wheat germ

¼ teaspoon salt

One 6-ounce can chunk light tuna packed in vegetable oil

1 large canned sardine (about ¾ ounce)

1 large egg

special equipment

1¾-inch-long by ¾-inch-wide (at its widest point) fish-shaped cookie cutter (I use a cutter that is actually intended to be a flower petal)

1. Position two racks near the center of the oven and preheat the oven to 350°F. Line two baking sheets with parchment paper.

2. In a medium bowl, combine the flour, cornmeal, wheat germ, and salt. Set aside.

3. Place the tuna, with its oil, in the bowl of a food processor and process until finely chopped, about 15 seconds. Add the sardine and process until it is finely chopped, about 15 seconds. Add the egg and process until blended. Scrape down the sides of the bowl and process for a few more seconds. Sprinkle the flour mixture over the tuna mixture and pulse until blended, then process just until the dough forms a clump when pinched, about 15 seconds.

4. Turn the dough out onto a work surface and shape it into a disk. Using a rolling pin, roll the dough out to a thickness of ⅛ inch; sprinkle the dough and work surface lightly with flour, if necessary, to prevent sticking. Using a 1¾-inch-long by ¾-inch wide fish-shaped cookie cutter, cut out as many cookies as possible from the dough and arrange them on the prepared baking sheets, spacing them ¼ inch apart. Gather up and reroll the scraps, continuing to cut out more cookies until all the dough is used.

5. Bake the cookies, two sheets at a time, for 14 to 16 minutes, switching the position of the sheets halfway through baking, until they are just beginning to turn a very light golden brown. Let the cookies cool completely on the baking sheets.

STORE **IN AN AIRTIGHT CONTAINER IN THE REFRIGERATOR FOR UP TO 1 MONTH.**

miss kitty dog biscuits

MAKES **ABOUT 25 BISCUITS**

This recipe was given to me by Carey Campbell, a pastry chef and former editorial assistant at *Chocolatier* magazine. Her yellow lab, Duffy, enjoys these biscuits (when he's not chewing on his owner's pantyhose). What do they taste like? According to my husband, who taste-tested every recipe in this book, these are "texturally perfect but rather pale, flavor-wise, when compared with the sardine complexity of the cat cookies [see page 94]."

1½ cups whole wheat flour

½ cup all-purpose flour

½ cup cornmeal

½ cup quick-cooking rolled oats

3 tablespoons creamy peanut butter

½ cup canola oil

2 large eggs

½ cup water

1 tablespoon vanilla extract

2 tablespoons wheat germ

special equipment

2½-inch cat-shaped cookie cutter

1. Position a rack in the center of the oven and preheat the oven to 350°F. Line two baking sheets with parchment paper.
2. In a medium bowl, combine the flours, cornmeal, and oats. Set aside.
3. In the bowl of an electric mixer, using the paddle attachment, beat the peanut butter and canola oil until blended. Add the eggs one at a time, beating well after each addition, then add the water and vanilla extract. At low speed, add the dry ingredients, mixing just until blended.
4. Turn the dough out onto a work surface and knead it once or twice, just until smooth (it will be a little greasy). Sprinkle the work surface and the dough with flour and, using a rolling pin, roll the dough out to a thickness of 3/16 inch. Using a 2½-inch cat-shaped cookie cutter, cut out as many biscuits from the dough as possible and arrange them on the prepared baking sheets, spacing them 1 inch apart. Sprinkle the biscuits lightly with wheat germ, then pat it gently into the dough with your fingers. Gather up the dough scraps (you may have to knead the scraps a few times to make them stick together) and reroll, cutting out more biscuits.
5. Bake the biscuits, one sheet at a time, for 18 to 20 minutes, until lightly browned and hard. Transfer the biscuits to a wire rack and cool completely.

STORE **IN AN AIRTIGHT CONTAINER AT ROOM TEMPERATURE FOR UP TO 3 MONTHS.**

sacristains

MAKES **ABOUT 90 COOKIES**

I learned to make these delicious cookies during my salad days at cooking school in Paris. They were always a hit during coffee hour, for two reasons: their dryish texture and faintly nutty flavor make them perfect with espresso, and it was easy to sneak them into the café. A sacristain is a buttery twist of puff pastry sprinkled with chopped almonds and sugar. It's been a classic in France for so long that the origin of its name is lost. Since the sacristan is the person responsible for the sacristy, the rooms where the sacred vestments and equipment are kept in a Catholic church, a popular theory is that the "twist" presentation is modeled after the ornate candlesticks in a church. Watch these cookies carefully as they bake—don't let them get too brown.

½ recipe Really Rapid Puff Pastry (page 358; freeze the remaining half for another use)

1 large egg, beaten with 1 teaspoon water for egg wash

½ cup coarse sugar, divided

½ cup slivered almonds, finely chopped, divided

1. Dust a work surface with flour and roll out the dough to a 12 by 16-inch rectangle (about 1⁄16 inch thick), dusting it with flour as necessary. Using a chef's knife, trim the edges of the rectangle so that they are even.
2. Using a pastry brush, brush the dough all over with the egg wash. Sprinkle half of the sugar and half of the chopped almonds evenly over the dough. Roll the rolling pin lightly over the dough so the almonds and sugar adhere. Carefully turn the rectangle upside down. Brush it with the egg wash and sprinkle it with the remaining nuts and sugar. Roll the pin lightly over the dough once again. Using the chef's knife, cut the dough lengthwise into three equal rectangles (each approximately 3¾ by 15½ inches). Cut each rectangle crosswise into ½ by 3¾-inch strips. Holding a strip at both ends, give it three twists and place it on an ungreased baking sheet. Repeat with the remaining twists, leaving about an inch between the cookies. Refrigerate the cookies on the baking sheets for at least 15 minutes (or up to 1 day).
3. Position a rack in the center of the oven and preheat the oven to 375°F.
4. Bake the cookies, one sheet at a time, for 10 minutes, until they are starting to brown on the bottom. Remove the baking sheet from the oven and turn each twist upside down. Bake the twists for another 8 to 12 minutes, until evenly golden brown. Transfer the cookies to a wire rack and cool completely.

STORE **IN AN AIRTIGHT CONTAINER AT ROOM TEMPERATURE, IN A DRY ENVIRONMENT, FOR UP TO 3 DAYS.**

little crullers

MAKES **ABOUT 16 MINIATURE CRULLERS**

The word "cruller" comes from a Danish word for twist, or curly, and a cruller has always been a "twisted cake." Freshly made, these miniature crullers are exceptional—as they melt in your mouth they tease you with an indescribable blend of familiar, cozy flavors. This recipe can be doubled—and it probably should be, considering how fast they'll disappear. These are best the day they are made.

1⅓ cups all-purpose flour

1 teaspoon baking powder

¼ teaspoon salt

1 large egg

⅔ cup granulated sugar, divided

1 tablespoon unsalted butter, softened

1 teaspoon finely grated lemon zest

¼ teaspoon ground cinnamon

1 teaspoon vanilla extract

¼ cup whole milk

Vegetable oil for deep-frying

make the dough

1. Sift together the flour, baking powder, and salt into a medium bowl, then whisk until well-blended; set aside.

2. In a medium bowl, whisk together the egg, ⅓ cup of the sugar, the butter, lemon zest, and cinnamon. Stir in half of the flour mixture until blended. Stir in the milk, then stir in the remaining flour mixture until a soft dough forms. Cover the bowl with plastic wrap and refrigerate for 1 hour.

shape and fry the crullers

3. Scrape the chilled dough out onto a lightly floured work surface. Using a rolling pin, roll out the dough into an 8-inch square. Using a pizza cutter or large knife, cut the square into quarters. Cut each quarter into four 1 by 4-inch strips. Fold each strip over lengthwise, so that it is doubled in thickness, and pinch the ends together so they do not open while frying. Twist each strip once, and transfer to a floured baking sheet. Let the strips stand at room temperature while you heat the oil.

4. Pour at least 2 inches of oil into a deep pan, filling it no more than halfway, and heat over medium heat to 375°F. Line a baking sheet with paper towels. Place the remaining ⅓ cup sugar in a shallow bowl or pie pan.

5. When the oil is ready, use a pancake turner to slide two or three crullers into it. When the crullers are lightly browned on the underside, about 1½ minutes, turn them over with a slotted spoon. When they are golden brown all over, transfer them to the paper towel–lined baking sheet to drain briefly. Repeat with the remaining strips. Roll the crullers in the sugar while still warm.

tangerine kumquat rounds

MAKES **ABOUT 60 COOKIES**

Kumquats resemble tiny, oval oranges (the word is from two Cantonese words, *kam*, meaning "gold," and *kwat*, meaning "orange"). The entire fruit, including the skin, is eaten; the rind is very tart and refreshing. Here, the fruit is sliced and candied in a sugar syrup, then used to top rounds of cookie dough that have been pepped up with a shot of tangerine zest. Because the candied kumquats are slightly chewy, I recommend just popping a whole cookie in your mouth, for a burst of citrus flavor.

kumquat slices

15 kumquats, rinsed and dried

1 cup water

1 cup granulated sugar

2 tablespoons light corn syrup

tangerine cookies

2 cups all-purpose flour

½ teaspoon baking powder

¼ teaspoon salt

1 cup (2 sticks) unsalted butter, softened

½ cup confectioners' sugar

1 tablespoon finely grated tangerine zest

1 teaspoon vanilla extract

Coarse sugar for sprinkling

special equipment

Candy thermometer

1¾-inch fluted round cookie cutter

make the kumquat slices

1. Line a baking sheet with aluminum foil.
2. Using a small sharp knife, cut ¼ inch off the ends of each kumquat. Cut the kumquats crosswise into ⅛-inch slices (about 5 slices per kumquat). Remove the seeds as you slice the kumquats.
3. In a small heavy saucepan, combine the water, sugar, and corn syrup. Bring to a boil over medium-high heat, stirring just until the sugar is dissolved. Add the kumquat slices, reduce to a simmer, and simmer until the kumquats are translucent and tender, about 20 minutes.
4. Increase the heat to high and cook the syrup until it registers 220°F on a candy thermometer. Immediately remove the pan from the heat. Drain the kumquats, discarding the syrup. Using a spoon, carefully transfer the slices to the lined baking sheet, making sure they do not touch. Let cool while you make the cookies.

make the dough

5. Sift together the flour, baking powder, and salt into a medium bowl. Whisk to blend, and set aside.
6. In the bowl of an electric mixer, using the paddle attachment, beat the butter and confectioners' sugar at medium-high speed until smooth, about 1 minute. Beat in the tangerine zest and vanilla. At low speed, gradually add the flour mixture, mixing until the dough starts to come together in large clumps. Scrape the dough out onto a work surface and shape it into a disk. Wrap in plastic wrap and refrigerate for 30 minutes, or until firm enough to roll.

cut out and bake the cookies

7. Position a rack in the center of the oven and preheat the oven to 350°F. Line two baking sheets with parchment paper or foil.

8. Place the dough on a lightly floured work surface. Sprinkle it lightly with flour and, using a rolling pin, roll it out to a thickness of 1/8 inch. Using a 1 3/4-inch fluted cookie cutter, cut out as many rounds as possible and arrange them an inch apart on the prepared baking sheets. Gather up the scraps, reroll them, and cut out more rounds.

9. Place a candied kumquat slice on top of each cookie and sprinkle with coarse sugar. Bake the cookies, one sheet at a time, for 9 to 11 minutes, until they are set and golden brown on the bottom. Transfer the cookies to a wire rack and cool completely.

STORE IN AN AIRTIGHT CONTAINER AT ROOM TEMPERATURE FOR UP TO 3 DAYS.

welsh skillet cakes

MAKES **ABOUT 40 COOKIES**

These little cakes look like puffy, silver dollar pancakes. My Welsh grandmother frequently made these tender sweets for family tea, cooking them in a heavy cast-iron pan over an open hearth.

3/4 cup currants or chopped raisins

2 cups all-purpose flour

3/4 cup granulated sugar

2 teaspoons baking powder

1/4 teaspoon ground cinnamon

1 teaspoon finely grated lemon zest

1/2 cup (1 stick) cold unsalted butter, cut into 1/2-inch cubes

2 large eggs

1 teaspoon vanilla extract

Confectioners' sugar for sprinkling

special equipment

2-inch round cookie cutter

make the dough

1. Put the currants or raisins in a sieve set over a saucepan of boiling water (the water should not touch the fruit). Cover the pan and steam until the currants or raisins are softened, about 2 minutes. Remove the sieve from the pan and let the fruit cool completely.

2. In the bowl of a food processor, combine the flour, sugar, baking powder, cinnamon, and lemon zest and pulse until blended. Scatter the butter pieces over the flour mixture and pulse until the mixture resembles coarse meal.

3. Crack the eggs into a small bowl. Add the vanilla extract and whisk until the eggs are lightly beaten. Sprinkle the cooled currants or raisins over the flour mixture. With the motor running, add the egg mixture through the feed tube, and process until the dough just comes together, a few seconds. Scrape the dough out onto a lightly floured work surface and shape it into a disk. Wrap in plastic wrap and refrigerate for at least 2 hours, until chilled.

cut out and cook the cakes

4. Flour a work surface and roll the chilled dough out to a thickness of 3/16 inch, sprinkling it lightly with flour as necessary to prevent sticking. Using a 2-inch round cookie cutter, cut out as many rounds from the dough as possible. Reroll the scraps and cut out more rounds, until all the dough is used.

5. Preheat an ungreased griddle or large skillet over medium heat for 3 minutes. Place as many dough rounds as possible in the pan, without crowding, and cook for 3 to 4 minutes, until the cakes are puffed. Using a pancake turner, flip the cakes over and cook for another 2 to 3 minutes, until lightly browned on the second side. Transfer the cakes to a wire rack to cool slightly. Repeat with the remaining dough.

6. Sprinkle the cakes with confectioners' sugar just before serving.

STORE **IN AN AIRTIGHT CONTAINER AT ROOM TEMPERATURE FOR UP TO 3 DAYS, BUT THESE ARE BEST SHORTLY AFTER THEY ARE MADE.**

bar cookies

• dark victory brownies • midnight brownies • double chocolate brownies • brooklyn heights brownies • deluxe bittersweet chocolate pecan brownies • caramel coconut pecan brownies • chocolate peanut butter surprise bars • peanut butter brownies • chocolate cheesecake bars • chocolate espresso cheesecake bars • turtle bars • chocolate chip pecan blondies • crunchy peanut bars • chocolate hazelnut truffle squares • chocolate-peanut magic bars • flosso bars • chocolate-dipped earl grey shortbread wedges • fruit and nut bars • white chocolate key lime bars • lebkuchen bars • blueberry crumble bars • lusty lemon bars • orange cream bars • caramel almond squares • party dates • lattice-topped linzer bars • raspberry almond shortbread squares • tropical shortbread bars • chocolate walnut bars • white chocolate–macadamia nut cookie bark • white chocolate eggnog bars • almond cherry bars • sour cream apple crumble bars • coconut custard squares •

If cookies are one of the easiest mediums in baking, bar cookies are one of the easiest cookies—all that business of portioning individual cookies is completely eliminated. And they are among the most versatile: cakey or chewy, crunchy, or even brittle or hard. They accommodate many additions, and in abundance—nuts and chips, fillings, and icings.

Decadence is king here. This is where you'll find many over-the-top recipes in terms of chocolate—Dark Victory Brownies, Chocolate Cheesecake Bars, Chocolate Hazelnut Truffle Squares, Midnight Brownies—and nuts—Turtle Bars, Chocolate-Peanut Magic Bars, Crunchy Peanut Bars. Bar cookies can also be turned into an excellent dessert; simply dollop ice cream over the cookie and serve.

Like drop cookies, these cookies are formed from a soft dough, or, to be precise, a rich batter which is thinner than a dough and can be poured. It is placed in a cake pan or other baking pan. It's important that the batter be spread or pressed evenly all the way to the sides of the pan. After baking, the "cake" is cut into squares. Use straight-sided pans for the recipes in this chapter. Lining the pans with aluminum foil will help you remove the "cakes" more easily, and ease cleanup as well. When lining, allow enough foil to extend over the sides of the pan so that you can use the overhang as handles to lift the cooled bars from the pan.

There is much debate about the proper texture of brownies. There are three basic brownie camps: those who like them chewy, those who prefer them fudgy and dense, and a third group who insist on the cakey frosted variety. I've included a recipe in this chapter to please every brownie aficionado. Whichever recipe you use, remember that the most important factor in the outcome of your brownie is the quality of the chocolate you use. The better the chocolate, the better the brownie. When testing for doneness, insert a toothpick into the center of the brownies. It should emerge with a few moist crumbs clinging to it—this is the endpoint you are looking for to achieve a moist brownie.

dark victory brownies

MAKES **16 BROWNIES**

I love sour cream in chocolate cake so much, I decided to see how it would work in brownies. I got exactly what I hoped for: extremely moist, slightly cakey, deep dark brownies with serious, in-your-face chocolate flavor. My own dark victory. Leave the pecans out, if you prefer, or use walnuts or skinned hazelnuts instead.

3 ounces bittersweet chocolate, coarsely chopped

14 tablespoons (1¾ sticks) unsalted butter, cut into tablespoons

½ cup Dutch-processed cocoa powder

1¼ cups granulated sugar

3 large eggs

⅓ cup sour cream

2 teaspoons vanilla extract

½ cup all-purpose flour

⅛ teaspoon salt

1 cup pecans, coarsely chopped

1. Position a rack in the center of the oven and preheat the oven to 325°F. Line a 9-inch square pan with aluminum foil so that the foil extends 2 inches beyond two opposite sides of the pan. Grease the foil.

2. In the top of a double boiler over barely simmering water, heat the bittersweet chocolate and butter, stirring occasionally, until melted and smooth. Transfer to a medium bowl.

3. Using a wooden spoon, beat in the cocoa powder and sugar until well blended. Beat in the eggs one at a time, mixing well after each addition. Beat in the sour cream and vanilla extract. Add the flour and salt and mix just until blended. Stir in the pecans.

4. Scrape the batter into the prepared pan and bake for 40 to 45 minutes, until a toothpick inserted into the center of the brownies comes out with a few moist crumbs clinging to it. Place the pan on a wire rack and cool completely.

5. Using the foil as handles, lift the brownies out of the pan. Cut the brownies into 16 squares.

STORE **IN AN AIRTIGHT CONTAINER AT ROOM TEMPERATURE FOR UP TO 5 DAYS, OR REFRIGERATE FOR UP TO 2 WEEKS OR FREEZE FOR UP TO A MONTH.**

midnight brownies

MAKES 16 BROWNIES

This recipe is from Lisa Yockelson, one of two brownie recipes she contributed to this book. As contributing editor of *Chocolatier* and *Pastry Art & Design* magazines, Lisa has written many articles and created dozens of recipes. She's also the author of several baking books; her most recent is *Baking by Flavor* (John Wiley & Sons, 2002). She's a baking fanatic, it's fair to say, and at *Chocolatier*, we refer to her as "The Brownie Lady." A classic chocolate brownie with a chewy, nougaty center, this rendition is named for the Milky Way Midnight bar that goes into it. The brownies themselves are deep and dark, like midnight—and they make a great midnight snack.

1 cup all-purpose flour

⅓ cup cake flour

⅓ cup Dutch-processed cocoa powder

¼ teaspoon baking powder

¼ teaspoon salt

Five 1.76-ounce Milky Way Midnight bars, chilled and cut into large dice

1 cup (2 sticks) unsalted butter, cut into tablespoons

5 ounces unsweetened chocolate

5 large eggs

2 cups superfine sugar

2 teaspoons vanilla extract

1. Position a rack in the center of the oven and preheat the oven to 325°F. Line a 9-inch square baking pan with aluminum foil so that the foil extends 2 inches beyond two opposite sides of the pan. Lightly grease the foil.
2. Sift together the flours, cocoa powder, baking powder, and salt into a medium bowl. Stir until combined. In a small bowl, toss the candy bar chunks with 1½ teaspoons of the sifted mixture.
3. In the top of a double boiler over barely simmering water, heat the butter and unsweetened chocolate, stirring occasionally until melted. Remove the pan from the heat and let the mixture cool until tepid.
4. In a large bowl, whisk the eggs for 1 minute to blend, then add the sugar and whisk for 45 seconds, or until just incorporated. Whisk in the chocolate mixture, then the vanilla extract. Sift the flour mixture over the top and slowly whisk it in, mixing until just blended. Stir in the candy.
5. Scrape the batter into the prepared pan, spreading it evenly, and smooth the top, using a rubber spatula. Bake the brownies for 45 to 50 minutes, or until puffed and set. A toothpick inserted into the center of the brownies should come out with a few moist crumbs clinging to it.
6. Cool the brownies completely in the pan on a rack. Using the ends of the foil as handles, lift the brownies out of the pan. Refrigerate for 2 hours, or until firm enough to cut.
7. Cut the brownies into 16 squares.

STORE IN AN AIRTIGHT CONTAINER AT ROOM TEMPERATURE FOR UP TO 5 DAYS.

double chocolate brownies

MAKES 16 BROWNIES

Pastry chef at New York's high-profile Ilo restaurant, Pat Coston regularly satisfies the food-savvy with sophisticated and sleek plated desserts, but he also knows how to make a great brownie. This recipe produces a cakey, incredibly light, moist brownie with a real chocolate kick. Pat uses Valrhona Manjari chocolate (see Sources, page 376), but any high-quality bittersweet chocolate will do. For a fudgier texture, refrigerate the brownies for at least 2 hours before serving.

11 ounces bittersweet chocolate, 5 ounces coarsely chopped, 6 ounces cut into ¼- to ½-inch chunks

¾ cup (1½ sticks) unsalted butter, cut into tablespoons

1 cup cake flour (not self-rising)

¼ teaspoon salt

3 large eggs, at room temperature

1 cup granulated sugar

⅓ cup firmly packed light brown sugar

2 teaspoons vanilla extract

1. Position a rack in the center of the oven and preheat the oven to 325°F. Line a 9-inch square pan with aluminum foil so that the foil extends 2 inches beyond two opposite sides of the pan. Grease the bottom and sides of the pan.
2. In the top of a double boiler over barely simmering water, heat the coarsely chopped chocolate and the butter, stirring occasionally, until melted and smooth. Remove the top of the double boiler from the bottom and set the chocolate mixture aside to cool.
3. Sift together the flour and salt into a medium bowl. Gently whisk to blend. Set aside.
4. In the bowl of an electric mixer, using the whisk attachment beat the eggs, granulated sugar, brown sugar, and vanilla extract at high speed until very light and thick, about 5 minutes (the mixture should leave a ribbon trail when the whisk is lifted). Switch to the paddle attachment. At low speed, add the chocolate mixture (it's okay if it's still warm), mixing until blended. Add the flour mixture, mixing just until blended. Using a wooden spoon, stir in the chocolate chunks.
5. Scrape the batter into the prepared pan and smooth the top. Bake the brownies for 45 to 50 minutes, until a toothpick inserted into the center comes out with a few moist crumbs clinging to it. Place the pan on a wire rack and cool completely.
6. Using the foil as handles, lift the brownies out of the pan. Cut into 16 squares.

STORE IN AN AIRTIGHT CONTAINER AT ROOM TEMPERATURE FOR UP TO 5 DAYS, OR REFRIGERATE FOR UP TO 2 WEEKS OR FREEZE FOR UP TO A MONTH.

brooklyn heights brownies

MAKES 9 BROWNIES

There is nothing faint-hearted about these glazed brownies—they are unapologetically dense and rich, just like the high-brow area for which they're named. Whatever you do, don't overbake them. If you want a chewier texture, chill them for a few hours: they will become more fudge-like, and more like a confection. You could then cut them into 1½-inch squares and put them in petit four paper cases to serve after dinner with coffee. Really, though, these are the companion milk has sought for years.

fudge brownies

½ cup (1 stick) unsalted butter, cut into tablespoons

9 ounces bittersweet chocolate, coarsely chopped

1 ounce unsweetened chocolate, coarsely chopped

¾ cup granulated sugar

3 large eggs

1½ teaspoons vanilla extract

½ cup all-purpose flour

⅛ teaspoon salt

¾ cup walnuts, coarsely chopped

chocolate glaze

1½ ounces bittersweet chocolate, coarsely chopped

1 tablespoon unsalted butter

1 tablespoon light corn syrup

2 tablespoons heavy cream

garnish

9 perfect walnut halves, toasted

make the brownies

1. Position a rack in the center of the oven and preheat the oven to 325°F. Line an 8-inch square baking pan with aluminum foil so that the foil extends 2 inches beyond two opposite sides of the pan. Lightly grease the foil.

2. In the top of a double boiler over barely simmering water, heat the butter with the bittersweet and unsweetened chocolates, stirring occasionally, until melted and smooth. Transfer to a large bowl.

3. Using a wooden spoon, stir in the sugar. Stir in the eggs one at a time, mixing well after each addition. Mix in the vanilla extract. Add the flour and salt and mix vigorously until the batter pulls away from the sides of the bowl. Stir in the walnuts.

4. Scrape the batter into the prepared pan and smooth the top with a rubber spatula. Bake for 35 to 40 minutes, or until a cake tester inserted in the center of the brownies comes out with a few moist crumbs clinging to it; do not overbake.

5. Cool the brownies in the pan on a wire rack for 45 minutes. Using the ends of the foil as handles, lift the brownies out of the pan. Cool the brownies completely.

make the glaze

6. In a small saucepan, combine the chocolate, butter, and corn syrup and heat over low heat, stirring constantly, until the chocolate and butter are melted. Remove from the heat.

7. In a small saucepan, or in a small container in a microwave oven, bring the cream to a simmer. Whisk the hot cream into the chocolate mixture. Transfer the glaze to a small bowl and let cool for 10 minutes.

glaze and garnish the brownies

8. Invert the cooled brownies onto a wire rack. Remove the foil and place the rack over a baking sheet, leaving the brownies smooth side up. Pour the slightly cooled glaze over the brownies and, using a small metal offset spatula, spread it evenly over the top. Place the brownies in the refrigerator for 30 minutes, or until the glaze is set.

9. Using a chef's knife, cut the brownies into 9 squares. Place a toasted walnut half on each brownie.

STORE IN AN AIRTIGHT CONTAINER AT ROOM TEMPERATURE FOR UP TO 5 DAYS, OR REFRIGERATE FOR UP TO 2 WEEKS OR FREEZE FOR UP TO A MONTH.

Cookie Bite **The best knife to use for chopping chocolate is an offset serrated knife, which breaks the chocolate into fine pieces and allows you to chop a large amount of chocolate without tiring your hand.**

deluxe bittersweet chocolate pecan brownies

MAKES 16 BROWNIES

Here's another exceptional brownie recipe from Lisa Yockelson, my friend, colleague, and baking expert nonpareil. The brownies are tall, dense, fudgy, and intensely chocolaty. Nut lovers will especially appreciate them: they are studded with pecans and topped with a sweet, crunchy nut topping.

pecan crunch

1 cup coarsely chopped pecans

1 tablespoon light brown sugar

¼ teaspoon vanilla extract

1 tablespoon unsalted butter, melted and cooled

chocolate pecan brownies

1 cup all-purpose flour

¼ cup cake flour (not self-rising)

3 tablespoons Dutch-processed cocoa powder

¼ teaspoon baking powder

¼ teaspoon salt

1 cup (6 ounces) miniature semisweet chocolate morsels

1 cup (2 sticks) unsalted butter, cut into tablespoons

4 ounces unsweetened chocolate, coarsely chopped

1 ounce bittersweet chocolate, coarsely chopped

4 large eggs

2 cups granulated sugar

1. Position a rack in the center of the oven and preheat the oven to 325°F. Butter the bottom and sides of a 9-inch square baking pan.

make the pecan crunch

2. In a small bowl, thoroughly toss together the pecans and brown sugar. Stir the vanilla extract into the melted butter, and toss the walnuts with the butter mixture until well coated. Set aside.

make the brownies

3. Sift together the flours, cocoa, baking powder, and salt into a medium bowl. In a small bowl, toss the chocolate morsels with 1¼ teaspoons of the sifted mixture to coat. Set both mixtures aside.

4. In the top of a double boiler, over barely simmering water, heat the butter, unsweetened chocolate, and bittersweet chocolate, stirring occasionally until melted. Remove the pan from the heat and let the mixture cool until tepid.

5. In a large bowl, whisk the eggs until blended. Add the sugar and whisk until well blended, 1 to 2 minutes. Whisk in the chocolate mixture and vanilla extract. Sift the flour mixture over the top and slowly whisk it in, mixing just until blended. Stir in the chocolate morsels and chopped pecans (not the pecan crunch mixture).

6. Scrape the batter into the prepared pan, spreading it evenly, and smooth the top, using a rubber spatula. Sprinkle the pecan crunch evenly over the top of the batter. Bake the brownies for 40 to 45 minutes, or until puffed and set. A toothpick inserted into the center of the brownies should come out with a few moist crumbs clinging to it.

1½ teaspoons vanilla extract

½ cup chopped pecans

Confectioners' sugar for dusting (optional)

7. Cool the brownies completely in the pan on a rack, then refrigerate for 2 hours, or until firm enough to cut.

8. Cut the brownies into 16 squares. Just before serving, sprinkle a light dusting of sifted confectioners' sugar over the top of the brownies, if you like.

STORE IN AN AIRTIGHT CONTAINER AT ROOM TEMPERATURE FOR UP TO 5 DAYS.

caramel coconut pecan brownies

MAKES 24 BROWNIES

These are as rich and sinful as brownies get. A layer of chewy caramel permeates a rich coconut brownie, which is strewn with nutty pecans. Prebaking the first layer of brownies prevents the caramel from sinking to the bottom. For an extra-fudgy, really chewy texture, serve the brownies chilled.

caramel layer

½ cup granulated sugar

¼ cup light corn syrup

3 tablespoons water

⅓ cup heavy cream

1 tablespoon unsalted butter

coconut brownies

8 ounces semisweet or bittersweet chocolate, coarsely chopped

4 ounces unsweetened chocolate, coarsely chopped

1 cup (2 sticks) unsalted butter, cut into tablespoons

½ teaspoon salt

1 teaspoon vanilla extract

2 cups granulated sugar

4 large eggs

½ cup all-purpose flour

1 cup sweetened flaked coconut

1½ cups pecan pieces

1. Position a rack in the center of the oven and preheat the oven to 325°F. Grease the bottom and sides of a 9 by 13-inch baking pan.

make the caramel layer

2. In a small heavy saucepan, combine the sugar, corn syrup, and water and cook over medium heat, stirring constantly and occasionally washing down the sides of the pan with a wet pastry brush, until the sugar dissolves. Stop stirring, increase the heat to medium-high, and cook until the sugar caramelizes and turn a deep amber color, 7 to 9 minutes (watch the mixture carefully, as it burns easily). Remove the pan from the heat and add the cream and butter (the mixture will bubble up furiously), stirring until the butter is melted. Let the caramel cool while you make the brownies.

make the brownies

3. Place both chocolates and the butter in the top of a double boiler over simmering water and heat, stirring occasionally, until melted and smooth. Transfer the chocolate mixture to a large bowl.

4. Stir in the salt, vanilla extract, and sugar. Stir in the eggs one at a time, blending well after each addition. Stir in the flour until blended. Stir in the coconut and pecans.

5. Scrape half of the batter into the prepared pan and spread it evenly. Bake for 10 minutes.

6. Remove the pan from the oven, scrape the cooled caramel over the brownie layer (it may be necessary to heat it for a few seconds to make it easier to pour and spread), and spread it evenly. Scrape the remaining

brownie batter over the caramel, spreading it evenly. Bake the brownies for 35 to 40 minutes, until a toothpick inserted into the center comes out with a few moist crumbs clinging to it. Cool completely in the pan on a wire rack.

7. Run a small knife around the sides of the pan to loosen the cooled brownies. Cover the pan and refrigerate for at least 2 hours, or until well chilled.

8. Cut the brownies into 24 bars, using a sharp knife. Serve chilled or at room temperature.

STORE IN AN AIRTIGHT CONTAINER AT ROOM TEMPERATURE FOR UP TO A WEEK, OR REFRIGERATE FOR UP TO 2 WEEKS.

chocolate peanut butter surprise bars

MAKES **16 BROWNIES**

The surprise in these chocolate-peanut wonder bars is the miniature peanut butter cups hidden in the center. The result is high-impact chocolate flavor combined with peanut butter—a hallowed combination.

1 cup (2 sticks unsalted butter)

5 ounces unsweetened chocolate

1 cup all-purpose flour

3 tablespoons Dutch-processed cocoa powder

¼ teaspoon baking powder

¼ teaspoon salt

4 large eggs

1½ cups granulated sugar

½ cup firmly packed light brown sugar

2 teaspoons vanilla extract

16 miniature peanut butter cups

1. Position a rack in the center of the oven and preheat the oven to 325°F. Line a 9-inch square baking pan with aluminum foil so that the foil extends 2 inches beyond two opposite sides of the pan. Lightly grease the bottom and sides of the pan.
2. Place the butter and chocolate in the top of a double boiler over simmering water and heat, stirring occasionally, until melted and smooth. Remove the pan from the heat and cool the chocolate mixture until tepid.
3. Sift together the flour, cocoa powder, baking powder, and salt into a medium bowl. Stir until blended.
4. In the bowl of an electric mixer, using the whisk attachment, beat the eggs at medium speed until blended. Gradually beat in both sugars, mixing just until blended. Using a wooden spoon, stir in the chocolate mixture and vanilla extract. Stir in the flour mixture, mixing until blended.
5. Scrape half of the brownie batter into the prepared pan and smooth the top. Arrange the peanut butter cups evenly over the batter, in four rows of four cups each. Press down lightly on each cup. Scrape the remaining batter over the cups and carefully spread it into an even layer, without moving the cups. Bake for 45 to 50 minutes, until a toothpick inserted into the center of the brownies comes out with a few moist crumbs clinging to it. Cool the brownies completely in the pan on a wire rack.
6. Using the ends of the foil as handles, lift the brownies out of the pan. Cover with plastic wrap and refrigerate for at least 2 hours.
7. Remove the plastic wrap from the brownies and invert them onto a cutting board. Peel off the foil. Reinvert the brownies and cut into 16 squares.

Chocolate Peppermint Surprise Bars: Replace the peanut butter cups with Peppermint Patties.

STORE **IN AN AIRTIGHT CONTAINER AT ROOM TEMPERATURE FOR UP TO A WEEK, OR FREEZE UP TO A MONTH.**

peanut butter brownies

MAKES 9 BROWNIES

On the theory that peanut butter–chocolate lovers never get enough, I offer this loose variation of Chocolate Peanut Butter Surprise Bars (page 112). No surprises here: instead of a brownie with a peanut butter center, the whole bottom layer is peanut butter. These are best when chilled.

peanut butter layer

1 cup creamy peanut butter

⅓ cup granulated sugar

1 large egg

brownie layer

1 cup granulated sugar

⅓ cup firmly packed light brown sugar

½ cup (1 stick) unsalted butter, cut into tablespoons

2 ounces unsweetened chocolate, coarsely chopped

1 tablespoon light corn syrup

½ cup all-purpose flour

½ teaspoon baking powder

⅛ teaspoon salt

2 large eggs, at room temperature

1½ teaspoons vanilla extract

¼ cup unsalted peanuts, chopped

1. Position a rack in the center of the oven and preheat the oven to 325°F. Line an 8-inch square baking pan with aluminum foil so that the foil extends 2 inches beyond two opposite sides of the pan. Lightly butter the bottom and sides of the pan.

make the peanut butter layer

2. In the bowl of an electric mixer, using the paddle attachment, beat the peanut butter, sugar, and egg at medium speed until blended, about 1 minute. Scrape the mixture into the prepared pan and smooth or pat it into an even layer. Set aside.

make the brownie layer

3. In a medium saucepan, combine the sugars, butter, chocolate, and corn syrup. Heat over low heat, stirring constantly, until melted and smooth. Remove the pan from the heat and let cool for 20 minutes, or until tepid.

4. In a small bowl, whisk together the flour, baking powder, and salt; set aside.

5. Whisk the eggs one at a time, into the cooled chocolate mixture, mixing well after each addition. Whisk in the vanilla extract. Using a wooden spoon, stir in the flour mixture until blended. Scrape the brownie batter over the peanut butter layer and smooth the top with a rubber spatula. Sprinkle the peanuts evenly over the batter.

bake the brownies

6. Bake the brownies for 45 to 52 minutes, or until a toothpick inserted in the center of the brownies comes out with a few moist crumbs clinging to it.

7. Cool the brownies in the pan on a wire rack for 1 hour, then cover the pan with plastic wrap and refrigerate for at least 2 hours until chilled.

8. Using the ends of the foil as handles, lift the brownies out of the pan. Using a sharp knife, cut into 9 squares. Serve chilled.

STORE IN AN AIRTIGHT CONTAINER IN THE REFRIGERATOR FOR UP TO A WEEK.

chocolate cheesecake bars

MAKES **12 BARS**

Purists may beg to differ, but in my opinion, chocolate and cream cheese blend beautifully. Their textures are similar and their flavors marry well; the understated tang of the creamy cheese mixture cuts the sweetness of the chocolate in the chewy brownie layer, and the pecans add crunch and a nutty sweetness that ties it all together.

chocolate layer

6 ounces semisweet chocolate, coarsely chopped

3 ounces unsweetened chocolate, coarsely chopped

1 cup all-purpose flour

¼ teaspoon salt

1 cup (2 sticks) unsalted butter, softened

1½ cups granulated sugar

3 large eggs

1 teaspoon vanilla extract

cheesecake layer

1 pound cream cheese, softened

⅓ cup granulated sugar

1 large egg

1 tablespoon heavy cream

1 teaspoon vanilla extract

garnish

½ cup pecans, coarsely chopped

1. Line a 9 by 13-inch baking pan with aluminum foil so that the foil extends 2 inches beyond the two short ends of the pan. Lightly grease the bottom and sides of the pan.

make the chocolate layer

2. In the top of a double boiler over barely simmering water, melt the semisweet and unsweetened chocolates, stirring occasionally until smooth. Cool the chocolate until tepid.

3. In a small bowl, gently whisk together the flour and salt.

4. In the bowl of an electric mixer, using the paddle attachment, beat the butter and sugar at medium speed until combined, about 1 minute. Beat in the eggs one at a time, beating well after each addition and scraping down the side of the bowl as necessary. Beat in the melted chocolate and vanilla extract. At low speed, blend in the flour mixture.

5. Scrape the chocolate mixture into the prepared pan and spread it into an even layer. Place the pan on a flat surface in the freezer for 15 minutes.

6. Position a rack in the center of the oven and preheat the oven to 300°F.

make the cheesecake layer

7. In the clean mixer bowl, using the paddle attachment or beaters, beat the cream cheese and sugar at medium speed until smooth, about 1 minute. Beat in the egg, cream, and vanilla extract until smooth. Scrape down the sides of the bowl and beat for another 30 seconds.

8. Scrape the cheese mixture over the chilled chocolate layer and spread it into an even layer. Sprinkle the chopped pecans over the cheese layer. Bake the bars for 70 to 75 minutes, or until a toothpick inserted into the center comes out with a few moist crumbs clinging to it. Cool the bars completely in the pan on a wire rack.

9. Using the foil as handles, lift the bars from the pan. Cut into 12 bars. Store the bars in an airtight container in the refrigerator; let them stand at room temperature for at least 1 hour before serving.

STORE IN AN AIRTIGHT CONTAINER IN THE REFRIGERATOR FOR UP TO 4 DAYS.

Cookie Bite When cream cheese is called for in a recipe, always use full-fat "block-style" cream cheese, such as Philadelphia brand. Don't substitute light, nonfat, whipped, or natural cream cheese.

chocolate espresso cheesecake bars

MAKES **24 BARS**

Here, chocolate is drizzled on the brandy-kissed sour cream topping that caps an espresso-infused cheesecake layer, which sits on a dense brownie base. These bars are rich, so I recommend coffee or milk as an accompaniment. They are a favorite in my husband's office (and I think they may well be responsible for his alpha male–top dog status there).

brownie layer

4 ounces bittersweet chocolate, coarsely chopped

½ cup (1 stick) unsalted butter, cut into tablespoons

2 large eggs

1 cup granulated sugar

1 tablespoon instant espresso powder, such as Medaglia d'Oro

¼ teaspoon salt

1 teaspoon vanilla extract

½ cup all-purpose flour

chocolate espresso cheesecake layer

⅓ cup brewed coffee

1 tablespoon unsalted butter

4 ounces bittersweet chocolate, coarsely chopped

2 teaspoons vanilla extract

One 8-ounce package cream cheese, softened

½ cup granulated sugar

⅔ cup sour cream

2 large eggs

1 large egg yolk

1. Position a rack in the center of the oven and preheat the oven to 325°F. Line a 9 by 13-inch baking pan with aluminum foil so that the foil extends 2 inches beyond the short ends of the pan. Grease the foil.

make the brownie layer

2. In the top of a double boiler over barely simmering water, melt the chocolate and butter, stirring occasionally until smooth. Remove from the heat.

3. In a medium bowl, whisk the eggs until smooth. Whisk in the sugar, espresso powder, salt, and vanilla extract. Stir in the chocolate and butter mixture until blended. Stir in the flour just until combined. Scrape the batter into the prepared pan and spread it evenly. Set aside.

make the cheesecake layer

4. In the top of a double boiler, combine the coffee, butter, and chocolate. Set over barely simmering water and stir occasionally until the chocolate and butter are completely melted and the mixture is smooth. Whisk in the vanilla extract. Remove the top of the double boiler from the bottom and set the mixture aside to cool.

5. In the bowl of an electric mixer, using the paddle attachment, beat the cream cheese at medium speed until smooth and creamy, about 1 minute. Gradually beat in the sugar, scraping down the sides of the bowl as necessary. Add the cooled chocolate mixture and mix until blended. Mix in the sour cream. Reduce the speed to low and add the eggs and egg yolk one at a time, mixing until well blended.

6. Scrape the mixture over the brownie batter in the pan and spread it evenly. Bake the bars for 30 to 35 minutes, until the cheesecake layer is set but still a little shiny in the center. Place the pan on a wire rack while you make the sour cream topping. Leave the oven on.

sour cream topping

1½ cups sour cream

¼ cup granulated sugar

1 tablespoon brandy

chocolate drizzle

1½ ounces bittersweet chocolate, coarsely chopped

make the topping

7. In a medium bowl, whisk together the sour cream, sugar, and brandy. Scrape the topping over the warm bars and, using a small offset metal spatula, spread it evenly. Bake the bars for an additional 10 minutes, or just until the topping is set (don't worry if the cheesecake layer rises and cracks in a spot or two; it will settle while cooling). Set the pan on a wire rack and cool completely.

8. Chill the bars for at least 2 hours (or up to 2 days, covered well).

garnish the bars

9. In the top of a double boiler over barely simmering water, melt the chocolate, stirring occasionally until smooth. Scrape the chocolate into a small sealable plastic bag and seal the bag. Cut a tiny hole in one of the bottom corners and drizzle the chocolate diagonally across the bars in a zigzag pattern.

10. Dip a sharp chef's knife into hot water and dry it thoroughly. Cut into 24 bars, wiping the knife clean after each cut.

STORE IN AN AIRTIGHT CONTAINER IN THE REFRIGERATOR FOR UP TO 5 DAYS.

turtle bars

MAKES **16 BARS**

Although these are very chewy, gooey, and crunchy, they are a relatively tidy re-creation of that candy classic, the chocolate-covered concoction of nuts and caramel with a humped shape and blobby chocolate frame that resembles a turtle. This version is composed of a pastry crust topped with clusters of pecans and buttery caramel, all drizzled with dark chocolate.

crust

Sweet Pastry Crust #2 (page 354)

caramel pecan topping

1 cup heavy cream

1 cup firmly packed light brown sugar

¼ teaspoon salt

¾ cup light corn syrup

½ cup (1 stick) unsalted butter, cut into tablespoons

2 teaspoons vanilla extract

1½ cups coarsely chopped toasted pecans, divided

chocolate drizzle glaze

1½ ounces bittersweet chocolate, coarsely chopped

make the crust

1. Prepare and bake the pastry crust according to the directions on page 354.

make the topping

2. In a medium-sized heavy saucepan, combine the cream, brown sugar, salt, corn syrup, and butter and cook over medium heat, stirring occasionally, until the butter is melted and the sugar is dissolved. Increase the heat to high and boil the mixture, without stirring, until it registers 238°F on a candy thermometer. Remove the pan from the heat and allow the caramel to cool for 10 minutes.

3. Stir the vanilla extract into the caramel. Sprinkle 1 cup of the pecans over the cooled crust. Pour the caramel over the pecans. Sprinkle the remaining ½ cup pecans evenly over the caramel. Set the pan on a wire rack and let cool at room temperature until set, about 2 hours.

glaze the bars

4. In the top of a double boiler over barely simmering water, melt the chocolate, stirring occasionally until smooth. Remove the pan from the heat and scrape the chocolate into a small sealable plastic bag. Seal the bag and snip a small hole in one of its bottom corners. Drizzle the melted chocolate in diagonal lines over the caramel and pecan bars. Refrigerate for 10 minutes to set the chocolate.

5. Run a sharp thin knife around the edges of the pan to release the bars, then cut into 16 squares.

STORE **IN AN AIRTIGHT CONTAINER AT ROOM TEMPERATURE FOR UP TO 5 DAYS.**

PREVIOUS PAGE cookie shop chocolate chip cookies 166, white chocolate chunk fudge cookies 64

CLOCKWISE FROM TOP LEFT crunchy peanut bars 120, coconut tea cakes 214, chocolate toffee brownie bites 218

FACING PAGE bittersweet chocolate madeleines 222, orange almond madeleines 220

TOP *glazed lemon ginger shortbread wedges* 204

BOTTOM lemon-fennel pretzel cookies 172, fig pillows 258

ABOVE triple-ginger pecan biscotti 183, mandelbrot 178

TOP RIGHT chocolate meringue swirls 200

BOTTOM RIGHT amaretti 192

CLOCKWISE FROM TOP LEFT orange cream bars 132, sour cream apple crumble bars 146, lemon curd bites 270

FACING PAGE brandied eggnog cookies 290, caramel almond squares 134

FOLLOWING PAGE savory cheese palmiers 348, black olive and feta cheese rusks 344, rosemary cheese crisps 336

chocolate chip pecan blondies

MAKES 24 BARS

Blondies are brownies without the chocolate, usually flavored with brown sugar. Here I've reintroduced chocolate to the formula in a big way: not only are there chocolate chips inside, but there's a white chocolate drizzle on top. I like the hint of dark rum in the batter—it really boosts the flavor of the pecans—but you can omit it if you prefer.

chocolate chip pecan blondies

1½ cups all-purpose flour

½ teaspoon baking powder

¼ teaspoon salt

1 cup (2 sticks) unsalted butter, softened

2 cups firmly packed light brown sugar

3 large eggs, at room temperature

2 teaspoons vanilla extract

2 tablespoons dark rum or brandy (optional)

1½ cups coarsely chopped pecans, divided

¾ cup semisweet chocolate morsels

white chocolate drizzle

1½ ounces good-quality white chocolate, chopped

make the blondies

1. Position a rack in the center of the oven and preheat the oven to 350°F. Line a 9 by 13-inch square baking pan with aluminum foil so that the foil extends 2 inches beyond the two short ends of the pan. Lightly grease the foil.

2. In a medium bowl, whisk together the flour, baking powder, and salt; set aside.

3. In the bowl of an electric mixer, using the paddle attachment, beat the butter and brown sugar at medium speed until light in color and texture, about 2 minutes. Scrape down the sides of the bowl. Beat in the eggs one at a time, beating well after each addition. Beat in the vanilla extract and the rum, if using. At low speed, mix in the dry ingredients just until combined. Using a wooden spoon, stir in ¾ cup of the pecans and the semisweet morsels.

4. Scrape the batter into the prepared pan and smooth the top. Sprinkle the remaining ¾ cup pecans over the batter. Bake the bars for 35 to 40 minutes, until they are golden brown and a toothpick inserted in the center of the pan comes out clean but not dry; don't overbake. Cool completely in the pan on a wire rack.

garnish the bars

5. Melt the white chocolate in the top of a double boiler over barely simmering water, stirring until smooth. Scrape the chocolate into a small sealable plastic bag and seal the bag. Cut a small hole in one of the bottom corners of the bag and drizzle the chocolate randomly over the cooled bars. Refrigerate the bars for 10 minutes, or until the chocolate is set.

6. Lift up the foil to remove the bars from the pan. Place them on a cutting board and remove the foil. Use a long sharp knife to cut into 24 squares.

STORE IN AN AIRTIGHT CONTAINER AT ROOM TEMPERATURE FOR UP TO 5 DAYS.

crunchy peanut bars

MAKES 36 BARS

Have you ever had a PayDay, the candy bar that is a dense cluster of nuts held together with caramel. It capitalizes on the combination of salty and sweet (plus crunchy and slightly greasy) that many people crave. These bars are like a PayDay only better, because they are homemade and because I added some peanut butter flavor to the caramel. These are my husband's desert island food choice: he could live on them.

brown sugar crust

1¼ cups all-purpose flour

½ teaspoon salt

½ cup (1 stick) unsalted butter, softened

½ cup firmly packed light brown sugar

peanut topping

4 tablespoons (½ stick) unsalted butter

⅔ cup light corn syrup

1⅔ cups (10 ounces) peanut butter chips

2 teaspoons vanilla extract

2¼ cups (12 ounces) salted peanuts

make the crust

1. Position a rack in the center of the oven and preheat the oven to 350°F. Grease the bottom and sides of a 9 by 13-inch baking pan.

2. In a medium bowl, stir together the flour and salt; set aside.

3. In the bowl of an electric mixer, using the paddle attachment or beaters, beat the butter with the brown sugar at medium speed until combined, about 1 minute. At low speed, add the flour mixture and mix just until crumbly, 10 to 15 seconds.

4. Pat the dough into the bottom of the prepared pan. Prick the dough well with a fork. Bake the crust for 15 to 18 minutes, until golden brown around the edges. Transfer the pan to a wire rack to cool while you prepare the topping. Leave the oven on.

make the topping

5. In a large saucepan, combine the butter, corn syrup, and peanut butter chips and heat over medium heat, stirring constantly, until the chips are melted and the mixture is smooth, about 5 minutes. Remove the pan from the heat and stir in the vanilla extract.

6. Pour the topping over the crust, using a spatula to spread it to the edges of the pan. Sprinkle the peanuts evenly over the topping, and press them lightly into the topping. Bake the bars for 12 to 15 minutes, until the topping is bubbly. Cool the bars completely in the pan on a wire rack.

7. Run a small sharp knife around the edges of the pan to release the bars. Carefully invert the bars onto a baking sheet then reinvert it onto a cutting board. Using a sharp knife, cut into 36 bars.

STORE IN AN AIRTIGHT CONTAINER AT ROOM TEMPERATURE FOR UP TO 5 DAYS, OR FREEZE FOR UP TO A MONTH.

chocolate hazelnut truffle squares

MAKES 16 BARS

Nothing complements the flavor of chocolate like hazelnuts, and hazelnuts are a real presence in this delicious bar. A thin, nut-studded brownie base is topped with a silky chocolate hazelnut truffle layer. For an elegant touch, serve these truffle bars in gold foil petit four cases.

chocolate hazelnut brownie layer

1½ ounces bittersweet chocolate, coarsely chopped

4 tablespoons (½ stick) unsalted butter, cut into tablespoons

1 large egg

½ cup granulated sugar

1 tablespoon hazelnut liqueur, such as Frangelico

¼ cup all-purpose flour

½ cup hazelnuts, toasted, skinned, and coarsely chopped

hazelnut truffle layer

6 ounces bittersweet chocolate, coarsely chopped

6 tablespoons (¾ stick) unsalted butter, cut into tablespoons

¼ cup praline paste (page 364, or see Sources, page 376)

¼ cup granulated sugar

Pinch of salt

½ cup heavy cream

1 teaspoon vanilla extract

1 large egg

2 large egg yolks

garnish

Confectioners' sugar for dusting

16 hazelnuts, toasted and skinned

1. Position a rack in the center of the oven and preheat the oven to 325°F. Grease the bottom and sides of a 9-inch square baking pan.

make the brownie layer

2. In the top of a double boiler over barely simmering water, combine the chocolate and butter and heat, stirring occasionally, until completely melted and smooth. Remove the top part of the double boiler from the bottom and allow the mixture to cool for 10 minutes, or until just warm.

3. In a medium bowl, whisk together the egg and sugar until blended. Whisk in the cooled chocolate-butter mixture and the hazelnut liqueur. Using a rubber spatula, stir in the flour just until blended. Stir in the hazelnuts. Scrape the batter into the prepared pan and spread it evenly.

make the truffle layer

4. In the top of a double boiler over barely simmering water, combine the chocolate and butter and heat, stirring occasionally, until completely melted and smooth. Remove the pan from the heat and whisk in the praline paste. Whisk in the sugar, salt, heavy cream, and vanilla extract. Whisk in the egg and yolks one at a time, blending well after each addition.

5. Scrape the truffle mixture over the brownie layer and spread it evenly. Bake the bars for 25 to 30 minutes, until the top is puffed and set and no longer shiny. Cool the bars in the pan on a wire rack.

6. Refrigerate the cooled bars for at least 2 hours, until chilled.

garnish the brownies

7. Dip a sharp chef's knife into hot water and dry it thoroughly. Cut into 16 squares.

8. Dust the tops of the squares with sifted confectioners' sugar and top each square with a toasted hazelnut.

STORE IN AN AIRTIGHT CONTAINER IN THE REFRIGERATOR FOR UP TO A WEEK.

chocolate-peanut magic bars

MAKES 16 BARS

In the 1960s, Borden's printed a recipe for Magic Cookie Bars on the can of milk, which consisted of a graham cracker crust topped with a rich combination of sweetened condensed milk, semisweet chocolate morsels, coconut, and chopped nuts. Many variations have emerged since that time. Here's mine, with peanut butter cookies rather than graham crackers in the crust, and peanut butter morsels added to the mix. It's a mega-nutty, chocolate-charged bar that, like its precursor, has a magical way of vanishing.

crust

12 chocolate–peanut butter sandwich cookies

4 tablespoons (½ stick) unsalted butter, melted

topping

⅓ cup creamy peanut butter

One 14-ounce can sweetened condensed milk

1 cup sweetened shredded coconut

¾ cup peanut butter morsels

¾ cup semisweet chocolate chunks or morsels

¾ cup unsalted peanuts

1. Position a rack in the center of the oven and preheat the oven to 350°F. Line a 9-inch square baking pan with aluminum foil so that the foil extends 2 inches beyond two opposite sides of the pan. Lightly grease the foil.

make the crust

2. Place the cookies in the bowl of a food processor and process until fine crumbs form. Transfer the crumbs to a medium bowl and stir in the melted butter until combined. Transfer the crumb mixture to the prepared pan and pat it into an even layer.

make the topping

3. Place the peanut butter in a medium bowl and whisk in the condensed milk ¼ cup at a time until blended. Scatter the coconut, peanut butter morsels, semisweet chunks, and peanuts evenly over the crust. Drizzle the condensed milk mixture evenly over the topping, leaving a ¼-inch border around the edges of the pan. Bake the bars for 25 to 30 minutes, until they are lightly golden brown and bubbling. Cool the bars completely in the pan set on a wire rack.

4. Using the foil ends as handles, remove the bars from the pan. Carefully invert them onto a baking sheet or cutting board. Peel off the foil and reinvert the bars. Using a sharp knife, cut into 16 squares.

STORE IN AN AIRTIGHT CONTAINER AT ROOM TEMPERATURE FOR UP TO 5 DAYS.

flosso bars

MAKES **16 BARS**

Jack Flosso is the owner of the Flosso-Hornmann Magic Shop, the oldest magic store in New York, which also happens to be a few doors away from *Chocolatier*'s headquarters. Over the years, I've shared many laughs with Jack and his friends—and learned a trick or two. A talented magician and comedian, Jack is very sweet, somewhat complex, and a little nutty—just like these delicious bars, another variation of the classic Magic Bar. I've done a little chocolate revision of the crust, altered the proportions somewhat, and . . . presto: Flosso!

chocolate crust

6 tablespoons (3/4 stick) unsalted butter, melted

1½ cups chocolate wafer cookie crumbs

topping

1¼ cups sweetened shredded coconut

¾ cup slivered almonds, toasted and coarsely chopped

4½ ounces bittersweet bar chocolate, cut into ¼-inch pieces

One 14-ounce can sweetened condensed milk

1. Position a rack in the center of the oven and preheat the oven to 350°F. Line a 9-inch square baking pan with aluminum foil so that the foil extends 2 inches beyond two opposite sides of the pan. Grease the foil.

make the crust

2. In a medium bowl, combine the melted butter and chocolate wafer crumbs. Transfer the crumbs to the prepared pan and pat them into an even layer.

making the topping

3. Scatter the coconut, almonds, and chocolate evenly over the crust. Drizzle the condensed milk evenly over the topping, leaving a ¼-inch border all around the edges of the pan. Bake the bars for 25 to 30 minutes, until they are bubbling and light golden brown. Cool the bars completely in the pan set on wire rack.

4. Using the foil ends as handles, remove the bars from the pan. Carefully invert them onto a baking sheet or cutting board. Peel off the foil and reinvert the bars. Using a sharp knife, cut into 16 squares.

STORE **IN AN AIRTIGHT CONTAINER AT ROOM TEMPERATURE FOR UP TO A WEEK.**

chocolate-dipped earl grey shortbread wedges

MAKES 16 WEDGES

Earl Grey tea is named for Charles Grey, a nineteenth-century earl. The tea, an amalgamation of Indian and Sri Lankan teas, has a distinct bergamot fragrance. The buttery flavor of shortbread is a perfect foil for the perfumy tea. A quick dip in chocolate gives the wedges a beautiful finish, for both the eye and the palate. Serve with Earl Grey tea or another black tea; it may sound like overkill, but the pairing works wonderfully.

earl grey shortbread

2 tablespoons Earl Grey tea leaves

¾ cup (1½ sticks) unsalted butter, cut into tablespoons

½ cup granulated sugar

1 teaspoon vanilla extract

¼ teaspoon salt

½ cup cake flour (not self-rising)

1 cup all-purpose flour

chocolate garnish

2 ounces bittersweet chocolate, coarsely chopped

½ teaspoon vegetable oil

make the shortbread

1. Grease the bottom and sides of a 9-inch round cake pan.
2. In a medium saucepan, combine the tea leaves and butter and heat over low heat, stirring occasionally, until the butter is completely melted. Remove the pan from the heat and set aside to cool and infuse for 10 minutes.
3. Strain the butter through a fine sieve into a large bowl. Discard the tea leaves. Stir in the sugar, vanilla, and salt. Add the flours and stir until just blended. Scrape the dough into the prepared pan and pat it into an even layer. Cover the surface of the dough with plastic wrap and refrigerate for at least 2 hours, until firm (or up to 2 days).
4. Position a rack in the center of the oven and preheat the oven to 325°F.
5. Bake the chilled shortbread for 35 to 40 minutes, until golden brown. While the shortbread is still hot, cut it into 16 wedges with a thin sharp knife. Transfer the wedges to a wire rack and cool completely.

garnish the wedges

6. In the top of a double boiler over barely simmering water, melt the chocolate, stirring occasionally until smooth. Remove the pan from the heat and stir in the vegetable oil.
7. Line a baking sheet with parchment or waxed paper. Pick up one of the shortbread wedges and brush off any crumbs. Holding it over the pan of chocolate, spoon some of the chocolate over the tip of the wedge, up to about an inch from the point. Set the wedge on the prepared baking sheet and repeat with the remaining wedges. Let the wedges stand until the chocolate is set, about 1 hour at room temperature (or 15 minutes in the refrigerator).

STORE IN AN AIRTIGHT CONTAINER AT ROOM TEMPERATURE FOR UP TO 5 DAYS.

fruit and nut bars

MAKES 16 BARS

If you've ever wanted to whip up your own health bar or granola-style bar, here is the blueprint. This is a very chewy bar, filling but not heavy, flavorful but not too sweet—and so much better than commercial fruit and nut bars. I like dried apricots because their subtle tang goes well with the honey and almond flavors and the faint ginger undernote. But you can experiment with any dried fruit you like.

fruit and nut bars

1 cup quick-cooking rolled oats

2/3 cup all-purpose flour

1/4 teaspoon ground cinnamon

1/4 teaspoon ground ginger

1/4 teaspoon salt

1/8 teaspoon baking powder

1/2 cup firmly packed light brown sugar

3/4 cup (about 5 ounces) dried apricots, chopped into 1/4-inch pieces

1/2 cup slivered almonds

1/4 cup toasted honey wheat germ

1 large egg, lightly beaten

1/4 cup vegetable oil

1/4 cup honey or Lyle's Golden Syrup

1 teaspoon vanilla extract

drizzle glaze

1/2 cup confectioners' sugar

2 teaspoons whole milk

1/8 teaspoon almond extract

make the bars

1. Position a rack in the center of the oven and preheat to 350°F. Line a 9-inch square baking pan with aluminum foil so that the foil extends 2 inches beyond two opposite sides of the pan. Grease the foil.

2. In a medium bowl, stir together the oats, flour, cinnamon, ginger, salt, and baking powder until well blended. Stir in the brown sugar (breaking up any lumps), chopped apricots, almonds, and wheat germ.

3. In another medium bowl, whisk together the egg, vegetable oil, honey or syrup, and vanilla. Stir the wet ingredients into the oat mixture just until blended; the mixture will not be very moist. Scrape the batter into the prepared pan and smooth the top. Bake the bars for 25 to 30 minutes, until golden brown. Place the pan on a wire rack and cool completely.

4. Invert the bars onto a baking sheet or plate and peel off the foil. Reinvert the bars onto a cutting surface.

glaze the bars

5. In a small bowl, whisk together all the ingredients until smooth. Scrape the glaze into a small sealable plastic bag and seal the bag. Using scissors, snip a tiny hole in one of the bottom corners of the bag. Drizzle the glaze diagonally over the bars in a zigzag pattern. Let the glaze set for 10 minutes.

6. Cut the bars into 16 squares.

STORE IN AN AIRTIGHT CONTAINER AT ROOM TEMPERATURE FOR UP TO 5 DAYS.

white chocolate key lime bars

MAKES **16 BARS**

Ginger and lime are both strong flavors, but they marry perfectly, particularly in this variation of the Florida treasure, Key lime pie. Key lime is a shade tangier than the variety you find in the grocery store, Persian limes. Fresh Key limes are virtually impossible to find, so I recommend bottled Key lime juice, available in many supermarkets and gourmet food shops. If you can't find it, then use fresh-squeezed regular lime juice—avoid bottled reconstituted lime juice. These bars can be made ahead and frozen; freeze them uncut and they will cut cleanly. Use a good-quality white chocolate, like Lindt, for the topping.

gingersnap crust

2 cups gingersnap crumbs

2 tablespoons granulated sugar

7 tablespoons unsalted butter, melted

key lime filling

1 large egg

4 large egg yolks

Two 14-ounce cans sweetened condensed milk

1 teaspoon freshly grated lime zest

1 cup bottled Key lime juice or freshly squeezed regular lime juice

¼ teaspoon salt

white chocolate topping

¼ cup whole milk

¼ cup heavy cream

8 ounces good-quality white chocolate, chopped

make the crust

1. Position a rack in the center of the oven and preheat the oven to 350°F. Line a 9 by 13-inch baking pan with aluminum foil so that the foil extends 2 inches beyond the short ends of the pan.

2. In a medium bowl, combine the gingersnap crumbs and sugar. Add the melted butter and mix until well blended. Press the mixture into the bottom of the pan in an even layer.

3. Bake the crust until set, 7 to 9 minutes. Place the pan on a wire rack to cool while you make the filling. Reduce the oven temperature to 325°F.

make the filling

4. In a large bowl, whisk together the egg and yolks until well blended. Whisk in the condensed milk until blended. Whisk in the lime zest, lime juice, and salt. Pour the filling over the prepared crust. Bake until the filling is set, 20 to 22 minutes. Set the pan on a wire rack and let cool for 20 minutes.

5. Refrigerate the bars for at least 2 hours, until chilled.

make the topping

6. In a medium saucepan, bring the milk and cream to a gentle boil. Remove from the heat, add the chopped chocolate, and let stand for 30 seconds to melt the chocolate. Stir until the chocolate is completely melted and the mixture is smooth. Set the topping aside to cool, stirring occasionally, for 15 minutes, or until thickened.

7. Pour the cooled white chocolate topping over the chilled bars and, using a small offset metal spatula, spread it evenly. Freeze the bars in the pan for at least 1 hour before cutting.

8. Lift the bars out of the pan by the aluminum foil ends. Remove the foil and cut into 16 bars. Serve chilled.

STORE IN AN AIRTIGHT CONTAINER IN THE REFRIGERATOR FOR UP TO 3 DAYS, OR FREEZE FOR UP TO 3 WEEKS.

Cookie Bite **Sweetened condensed milk is a mixture of 60 percent whole milk and 40 percent sugar. The milk mixture is heated to remove about 60 percent of its water. The resulting milk is high in fat (about 8 percent) and has an ivory color and sticky, syrupy consistency.**

lebkuchen bars

MAKES 24 BARS

Lebkuchen is a classic German ginger cookie; it's softer and chewier than crisp gingersnaps or gingerbread. This bar cookie version is like a really moist and cakey gingerbread. The Germans bake their lebkuchen in a variety of shapes—rings, bars, and hearts—and have been doing so since about 800 A.D. The dough, with its many spices, needs to "ripen" overnight before baking. Lebkuchen keeps for up to two months, so these are a good choice to make ahead for your Christmas cookie tin.

lebkuchen

½ cup honey

½ cup firmly packed light brown sugar

⅓ cup granulated sugar

3 tablespoons unsalted butter, cut into tablespoons

1½ cups all-purpose flour, sifted

¾ teaspoon baking soda

1½ teaspoons ground cinnamon

1 teaspoon ground cardamom

½ teaspoon ground cloves

½ teaspoon freshly grated nutmeg

½ teaspoon ground ginger

½ cup sliced unblanched almonds

⅓ cup candied orange peel, finely chopped

1 large egg, lightly beaten

2 tablespoons freshly squeezed orange juice

1 teaspoon finely grated orange zest

1 teaspoon vanilla extract

¼ teaspoon almond extract

make the dough

1. In a large nonreactive saucepan, combine the honey, brown sugar, granulated sugar, and butter and cook over medium-high heat, stirring occasionally, until the sugar is dissolved, the butter is melted, and the mixture just begins to boil. Remove the pan from the heat and let cool for 15 minutes.

2. Sift together the flour, baking soda, cinnamon, cardamom, cloves, nutmeg, and ginger into a medium bowl. Set aside.

3. Stir the almonds, candied orange peel, egg, orange juice, orange zest, and vanilla and almond extracts into the cooled honey mixture. Add the dry ingredients and stir until blended. Place a piece of plastic wrap directly on the surface of the dough. Cover the top of the pan with another piece of plastic wrap and let the dough stand at room temperature for 8 hours, or overnight (do not refrigerate).

bake the lebkuchen

4. Position a rack in the center of the oven and preheat the oven to 350°F. Butter and flour a 9-inch square baking pan.

5. Place the dough in the prepared pan and, with a spatula, spread it into an even layer. Bake the lebkuchen for 25 to 30 minutes, or until a toothpick inserted into the center comes out clean.

while the bars are baking, make the glaze

6. In a medium bowl, whisk together the confectioners' sugar, orange juice, ginger, and vanilla extract until smooth.

orange-ginger glaze

1 cup confectioners' sugar

2 tablespoons freshly squeezed orange juice

¼ teaspoon finely grated peeled ginger

¼ teaspoon vanilla extract

glaze the bars

7. When the bars are done, place the pan on a wire rack. Using a small offset metal spatula, spread the glaze evenly over the warm bars. Let the bars cool completely.

8. Using a sharp knife, cut the glazed square into 24 bars.

STORE IN AN AIRTIGHT CONTAINER AT ROOM TEMPERATURE FOR UP TO 2 MONTHS.

Cookie Bite The aromatic spice cardamom, a member of the ginger family, is the dried fruit of a plant native to India. Cardamom is sold in small pods (each pod contains about 20 tiny seeds) or as whole or ground seeds.

blueberry crumble bars

MAKES 24 BARS

These are like mini blueberry crumbles, but they're much firmer and neater, which makes them portable and therefore ideal for picnics and outdoor concerts. They are the perfect summer treat at any time, with tart fresh blueberries under the sweet crumble topping. Blueberries are in season in late spring and throughout the summer; use frozen berries only as a last resort.

crust

Brown Sugar Crust #2 (page 356), unbaked

blueberry filling

¾ cup granulated sugar

1 tablespoon cornstarch

½ teaspoon ground cinnamon

¼ teaspoon ground ginger

2 cups blueberries

crumb topping

1 cup all-purpose flour

⅓ cup firmly packed dark brown sugar

¼ cup granulated sugar

1 teaspoon ground cinnamon

¼ teaspoon salt

6 tablespoons (¾ stick) unsalted butter, melted

make the crust

1. Position a rack in the center of the oven and preheat the oven to 350°F.
2. Make the crust as directed on page 356, but do not bake it.

make the filling

3. In a medium bowl, combine the sugar, cornstarch, cinnamon, and ginger. Add the blueberries and toss to coat well. Spread the blueberry mixture evenly over the crust.

make the topping

4. In a medium bowl, stir together the flour, sugars, cinnamon, and salt until blended. Stir in the melted butter until the mixture comes together. Sprinkle the topping evenly over the blueberry filling.
5. Bake the bars for 48 to 50 minutes, until the topping is lightly browned and the filling is bubbling. Cool the bars completely in the pan on a wire rack.
6. Cut into 24 bars.

STORE IN AN AIRTIGHT CONTAINER AT ROOM TEMPERATURE FOR UP TO 1 WEEK.

Cookie Bite If you plan to use frozen blueberries in this recipe, seek out IQF (individually quick-frozen) fruit, which is available in many supermarkets. It's not necessary to thaw the berries before using.

lusty lemon bars

MAKES 18 BARS

Not for the faint of heart, these bars are mouth-puckeringly lemony. They are the perfect balance between sweet and tart, with a creamy rich filling and slightly spicy ginger crust. I like to serve them chilled, with a dollop of vanilla bean–speckled whipped cream.

crust

Brown Sugar Ginger Crust (page 355)

lemon topping

½ cup all-purpose flour

⅛ teaspoon salt

5 large eggs

2¾ cups granulated sugar

1 cup freshly squeezed lemon juice

2 teaspoons finely grated lemon zest

Confectioners' sugar for dusting

make the crust

1. Make and bake the ginger crust as directed on page 355.

make the topping

2. In a small bowl, combine the flour and salt; set aside.
3. In a large bowl, whisk the eggs and sugar together until smooth. Add the lemon juice and zest and whisk until blended. Whisk in the flour mixture until combined.
4. Pour the topping over the crust. Bake the bars for 30 to 35 minutes, until the filling is set and lightly browned in spots. Let the bars cool completely in the pan on a wire rack.
5. Cut the bars into 18 rectangles. Just before serving, dust the tops of the bars with confectioners' sugar.

STORE IN AN AIRTIGHT CONTAINER IN THE REFRIGERATOR FOR UP TO 5 DAYS.

Cookie Bite Lemons that yield a generous amount of juice are soft and feel heavy in the hand. One large lemon yields about ¼ cup of juice.

orange cream bars

MAKES 16 BARS

Remember when you were a kid how all-consuming, how crucial, the choice of what to buy when the ice cream truck stopped on your block? My pick was always the Creamsicle. There's something soothing about the way vanilla-infused cream softens the sweet acidity of oranges, creating a new flavor in the process. Here a thin shortbread crust topped with an orange curd filling, a creamy sour cream mixture prettily piped in a filigree pattern on top, recaptures that pleasure in bar cookie form. So refreshing, they are perfect for summertime, but a great choice in winter too, when oranges are especially plentiful.

shortbread crust

1¼ cups all-purpose flour

⅔ cup confectioners' sugar

Pinch of salt

10 tablespoons (1¼ sticks) cold unsalted butter, cut into ½-inch cubes

orange curd filling

2 large eggs

4 large egg yolks

¾ cup granulated sugar

1 tablespoon freshly squeezed lemon juice

½ cup freshly squeezed orange juice

2 tablespoons finely grated orange zest

Pinch of salt

½ cup (1 stick) unsalted butter, softened

make the crust

1. Position a rack in the center of the oven and preheat the oven to 325°F. Line a 9-inch square baking pan with aluminum foil so that the foil extends 2 inches beyond two opposite sides of the pan. Grease the foil.

2. Place the flour, sugar, and salt in the bowl of a food processor and process until blended. Scatter the butter pieces over the mixture and pulse the machine six to eight times, until the mixture resembles coarse meal. Process until the mixture forms large clumps and holds together when pinched between two fingers, 15 to 20 seconds.

3. Scrape the dough into the prepared pan and pat it into an even layer. Using a fork, prick the dough at 1-inch intervals. Bake the crust for 30 to 35 minutes, until golden brown around the edges. Set the pan on a wire rack and cool completely.

make the filling

4. Set a fine-mesh sieve over a medium bowl and set aside. In a medium-sized heavy nonreactive saucepan, whisk together the eggs, yolks, and sugar until blended. Stir in the citrus juices, orange zest, salt, and butter and cook over medium heat, whisking constantly, until the mixture thickens, 7 to 8 minutes (do not let the mixture boil, or it will curdle). Immediately strain the mixture through the sieve, pressing it through with a rubber spatula.

5. Transfer ¼ cup of the curd to a medium bowl, cover, and refrigerate. Scrape the remaining warm curd onto the cooled shortbread crust and spread it into an even layer. Place the pan in the refrigerator for 30 minutes, or until the curd is cool.

topping

¾ cup sour cream

¼ cup heavy cream

2 tablespoons granulated sugar

1 teaspoon vanilla extract

Orange food coloring

make the topping

6. Preheat the oven to 350°F.

7. Whisk the sour cream, heavy cream, sugar, and vanilla extract into the reserved orange curd. Transfer ¼ cup of the topping to a small bowl and set aside. Scrape the remaining topping over the cooled orange curd layer and spread it evenly.

8. Add a small amount of orange food coloring to the reserved ¼ cup topping, just enough to turn it a pale orange. Scrape this mixture into a small sealable plastic bag and seal the bag. Snip a tiny hole in one of the bottom corners of the bag. Pipe the colored topping in a free-form filigree pattern over the bars.

9. Bake the bars for 10 minutes, just until the topping is set. Place the pan on a wire rack and cool completely, then chill the bars for at least 2 hours (or up to a day).

10. Using a thin sharp knife, cut the bars into 16 squares, wiping the blade clean after each cut. Serve chilled.

STORE IN AN AIRTIGHT CONTAINER IN THE REFRIGERATOR FOR UP TO 5 DAYS, OR FREEZE FOR UP TO A MONTH.

caramel almond squares

MAKES **30 BARS**

I have to admit: I am caramel-obsessed. These are my kind of bars: a sweet, gooey caramel topping, enhanced with orange and honey and studded with sliced almonds, tops a buttery pastry crust, for a crunchy, but kind of chewy, very addictive cookie.

crust

Sweet Pastry Crust #1 (page 353)

caramel almond topping

⅓ cup water

1 cup granulated sugar

⅓ cup heavy cream

7 tablespoons unsalted butter, cut into tablespoons

3 tablespoons honey

2 cups sliced blanched almonds

1 teaspoon finely grated orange zest

make the crust

1. Make and bake the crust as directed on page 353. Leave the oven on at 350°F.

make the topping

2. In a medium-sized heavy saucepan, combine the water and sugar and cook over medium heat, stirring constantly and occasionally washing down the sides of the pan with a wet pastry brush, until the sugar is dissolved. Increase the heat to high and cook, without stirring, until the caramel turns a dark amber color. Immediately remove the pan from the heat and stir in the heavy cream (be careful—the mixture will bubble up). Add the butter and honey and stir until the butter is melted. Stir in the almonds and orange zest, tossing the almonds until they are completely coated.

3. Pour the hot caramel mixture over the pastry base and, using a small offset metal spatula, spread it into an even layer, making sure that the nuts are evenly distributed. Bake for 12 minutes, or until the almonds are lightly toasted and the caramel is bubbling. Cool the bars in the pan on a wire rack for at least 1 hour.

4. Run a sharp knife around the edges of the pan to release the bars. Carefully invert the bars onto a cutting board. Turn them right side up. Using a serrated knife, cut into 30 squares.

STORE **IN AN AIRTIGHT CONTAINER AT ROOM TEMPERATURE FOR UP TO 5 DAYS.**

party dates

MAKES **16 BARS**

The origin of the cornball, retro name for these bars is a dessert we were regularly served during college. It didn't do a thing to spark romance, but it did inspire these, which I think are the best date bars ever. These offer a taste of the Middle East: the fruity, musky flavor of dates pairs perfectly with pecan, orange brings out the fruitiness, and cinnamon adds depth.

crust

Sweet Pastry Crust #2 (page 354)

date filling

2 cups pitted dates, but in half

⅓ cup granulated sugar

1½ cups water

1 teaspoon finely grated orange zest

¼ teaspoon salt

1 cinnamon stick

topping

⅔ cup all-purpose flour

¼ cup firmly packed dark brown sugar

2 tablespoons granulated sugar

½ teaspoon ground cinnamon

⅛ teaspoon salt

½ cup pecans, coarsely chopped

4 tablespoons (½ stick) unsalted butter, melted

Confectioners' sugar for dusting

make the crust

1. Make and bake the pastry crust as directed on page 354. Leave the oven on at 350°F.

make the filling

2. In a medium saucepan, combine the dates, sugar, water, orange zest, salt, and cinnamon stick. Bring to a boil, then reduce to a simmer and simmer until the dates are tender when pierced with a fork, 15 to 20 minutes. Let the mixture cool for 10 minutes.

3. Remove the cinnamon stick from the cooled date mixture and transfer it to the bowl of a food processor. Process until smooth, about 30 seconds. Scrape the filling onto the cooled crust and spread it evenly, covering the crust completely.

make the topping

4. In a medium bowl, stir together the flour, sugars, cinnamon, and salt until blended. Stir in the pecans. Stir in the melted butter until the mixture comes together.

5. Sprinkle the topping evenly over the date filling, covering it. Bake the bars for 25 to 30 minutes, until the pecans are lightly browned. Cool the bars completely in the pan on a wire rack.

6. Using a sharp thin knife, cut into 16 bars. Sift a light dusting of confectioners' sugar over the bars before serving.

STORE **IN AN AIRTIGHT CONTAINER AT ROOM TEMPERATURE FOR UP TO 5 DAYS.**

lattice-topped linzer bars

MAKES **16 BARS**

For a sophisticated alternative to traditional Valentine's Day sweets, try these delicious and pretty bars that uphold the raspberry linzer tart tradition. I've added a combination of ground hazelnuts and almonds to the classic linzer dough to make it especially tender and flavorful. Use the best-quality raspberry preserves you can find.

hazelnut-almond dough

1½ cups all-purpose flour

1 teaspoon baking powder

½ teaspoon ground cinnamon

¼ teaspoon ground cloves

¼ teaspoon salt

½ cup slivered almonds

½ cup hazelnuts, toasted and skinned

½ cup granulated sugar

9 tablespoons unsalted butter, softened

⅓ cup firmly packed light brown sugar

1 large egg

½ teaspoon vanilla extract

¼ teaspoon almond extract

filling

½ cup raspberry preserves

Confectioners' sugar for dusting

make the dough

1. In a medium bowl, whisk together the flour, baking powder, cinnamon, cloves, and salt. Set aside.
2. In a food processor, combine the almonds, hazelnuts, and granulated sugar and process until the nuts are finely ground. Set aside.
3. In the bowl of an electric mixer, using the paddle attachment, beat the butter and brown sugar at medium-high speed until light and creamy, about 2 minutes. Beat in the egg until blended, scraping down the sides of the bowl as necessary. Beat in the ground nuts, vanilla extract, and almond extract. At low speed, add the flour mixture one-third at a time, mixing just until blended.

assemble the bars

4. Remove one-third of the dough and set aside. Press the remaining two-thirds of the dough into the bottom of an ungreased 8-inch square baking pan. Spread the raspberry preserves evenly over the dough. Cover the pan with plastic wrap and place the pan in the refrigerator. Shape the remaining dough into a 4-inch square and place it between two 12-inch squares of waxed paper. Roll the dough out to an 8-inch square. Place the dough square, still between the waxed paper, on a baking sheet and refrigerate for 45 minutes.

bake the bars

5. Position a rack in the center of the oven and preheat the oven to 350°F.
6. Remove the baking pan and the dough square from the refrigerator. Peel off the top piece of waxed paper from the dough. Replace the paper loosely and flip over the dough. Peel off the other piece of waxed paper. Using a

pizza or pastry wheel, cut the square into twelve ½-inch-wide strips. Arrange 6 of the strips across the raspberry filling, about 1 inch apart. Repeat with the remaining strips, arranging them perpendicular to the first 6 strips, to make a lattice pattern.

7. Bake the bars for 30 to 35 minutes, until the pastry is golden brown. Place the pan on a wire rack and cool completely.

8. Sift confectioners' sugar lightly over the cooled bars. Using a sharp knife, cut into 16 squares.

STORE IN AN AIRTIGHT CONTAINER AT ROOM TEMPERATURE FOR UP TO 3 DAYS, OR REFRIGERATE FOR UP TO A WEEK.

raspberry almond shortbread squares

MAKES **16 BARS**

These bars are much like a linzer torte, but with a generous crumb topping rather than the lattice pastry crust. Between the buttery shortcrust base and the almond-flavored topping is a raspberry filling reinforced by black raspberry liqueur, with lemon zest to punch up the flavor. These are the perfect choice for brunch, tea, or a picnic; and they are sure to be a best seller at a bake sale.

crust

Sweet Pastry Crust #2 (page 354)

raspberry filling

¾ cup seedless raspberry preserves

½ teaspoon finely grated lemon zest

2 teaspoons Chambord or kirsch

almond crumb topping

4 tablespoons (½ stick) unsalted butter, softened

¼ cup firmly packed light brown sugar

2 tablespoons canned almond paste

½ cup plus 2 tablespoons all-purpose flour

Pinch of salt

⅓ cup coarsely chopped blanched almonds

glaze

½ cup confectioners' sugar

1 tablespoon whole milk

¼ teaspoon almond extract

make the crust

1. Prepare and bake the pastry crust as directed on page 354. Leave the oven on at 350°F.

make the filling

2. In a small bowl, mix together the raspberry preserves, lemon zest, and liqueur; set aside.

make the topping

3. In the bowl of an electric mixer, using the paddle attachment or beaters, beat the butter, sugar, and almond paste at medium speed until smooth, about 45 seconds. Add the flour and salt and mix at low speed just until crumbly. Using a wooden spoon, stir in the almonds.

assemble and bake the bars

4. Scrape the raspberry filling onto the cooled crust and spread it evenly. Sprinkle the almond topping evenly over the filling.

5. Bake the bars for 30 to 32 minutes, or until lightly browned. Transfer the pan to a wire rack. Run a small sharp knife around the edges of the pan to loosen the bars (otherwise, the raspberry filling will stick to the sides of the pan). Let them cool completely in the pan.

6. Using a sharp thin knife, cut the bars into 16 squares and place on a sheet of aluminum foil or waxed paper.

glaze the bars

7. In a small bowl, whisk together the confectioners' sugar, milk, and almond extract until smooth. Scrape the glaze into a small sealable plastic bag. Seal the bag and snip a tiny hole in one of the bottom corners of the bag. Drizzle the glaze over the top of the bars. Let the glaze set for 10 minutes before serving.

STORE **IN AN AIRTIGHT CONTAINER AT ROOM TEMPERATURE FOR 2 DAYS, OR REFRIGERATE FOR UP TO A WEEK.**

tropical shortbread bars

MAKES 16 BARS

The basic shortbread recipe of sugar, flour, and butter has inspired many different variations. Its high proportion of fat to flour yields a pure, buttery taste, making it perfect as a base for many bar cookies, but its real beauty is that it welcomes additions to the dough. Here, macadamia nuts, sweet coconut, and tangy lime combine to create a flirty tropical spin on dignified traditional Scottish shortbread.

¾ cup salted macadamia nuts, divided

1 cup all-purpose flour, divided

½ cup cornstarch

½ cup granulated sugar

¼ cup plus ⅓ cup sweetened flaked coconut, divided

1½ teaspoons finely grated lime zest

¾ cup (1½ sticks) cold unsalted butter, cut into ½-inch cubes

1. Position a rack in the center of the oven and preheat the oven to 300°F. Lightly grease a 9-inch square baking pan.
2. Chop ½ cup of the macadamia nuts and reserve them for topping the shortbread.
3. Place the remaining ¼ cup macadamia nuts and ½ cup of the flour in the bowl of a food processor and process until the nuts are finely chopped, about 10 seconds. Add the remaining ½ cup flour, the cornstarch, sugar, ¼ cup of the coconut, and the lime zest and process until blended, about 30 seconds. Scatter the butter cubes over the flour mixture and pulse 6 to 7 times, then process for another 6 seconds, or until the crumbs are fine and powdery. Process for another 8 to 10 seconds, until the crumbs form clumps and the dough holds together easily when pressed.
4. Press the dough evenly into the bottom of the prepared pan. Sprinkle the reserved chopped macadamia nuts and the remaining ⅓ cup coconut on top of the shortbread. Press down lightly so they adhere to the shortbread.
5. Bake the shortbread for 48 to 52 minutes, until the coconut is lightly golden and the shortbread is just beginning to turn golden brown around the edges. Place the pan on a wire rack and let cool for 15 minutes.
6. While the shortbread is still warm, use a sharp knife to cut it into 16 squares. Transfer the shortbread squares to the wire rack and cool completely.

STORE IN AN AIRTIGHT CONTAINER AT ROOM TEMPERATURE FOR UP TO 2 WEEKS.

chocolate walnut bars

MAKES 16 BARS

Picture a pecan pie. Now replace the pecans with walnuts and chocolate chunks. That will give you an idea of what awaits you when you whip up these chewy, delicious bar cookies. Be sure to use a good-quality bittersweet chocolate.

crust

Sweet Pastry Crust #2 (page 354)

walnut topping

1/3 cup heavy cream

6 tablespoons (3/4 stick) unsalted butter, cut into tablespoons

1/2 cup light corn syrup

1/2 cup granulated sugar

1 1/2 cups coarsely chopped walnuts

3 ounces bittersweet chocolate, cut into 1/4-inch chunks, divided

2 large eggs

2 tablespoons dark rum

1 teaspoon vanilla extract

make the crust

1. Make and bake the crust as directed on page 354. Reduce the oven temperature to 300°F.

make the topping

2. In a small heavy saucepan, combine the cream, butter, corn syrup, and sugar and cook over medium heat, stirring constantly, until the butter melts and the sugar dissolves. Increase the heat and bring the syrup to a boil. Attach a candy thermometer to the pan and cook, without stirring, until the thermometer registers 230°F, 3 to 4 minutes. Remove the pan from the heat and stir in the walnuts. Transfer the mixture to a medium bowl and let cool for 15 minutes.

3. Add one-third of the chocolate chunks into the walnut mixture, stirring until the chocolate is completely melted. Let cool for another 10 minutes.

4. In a small bowl, whisk together the eggs, rum, and vanilla extract until blended. Stir the egg mixture into the walnut mixture, then stir in the remaining chocolate chunks.

assemble and bake the bars

5. Pour the topping over the cooled shortbread crust, spreading it evenly. Bake for 30 to 35 minutes, until the center is set. Place the pan on a wire rack and let cool for 3 hours, or until firm enough to cut.

6. Run a thin knife around the sides of the pan to loosen the bars. Cut into 16 bars. (To give the bars a firmer texture for cleaner cutting, refrigerate them for 30 minutes before cutting.)

STORE IN AN AIRTIGHT CONTAINER AT ROOM TEMPERATURE FOR UP TO 2 DAYS.

white chocolate–macadamia nut cookie bark

MAKES **ABOUT FORTY 2 BY 2½-INCH PIECES**

This is a quick way to make a batch of cookies: you bake one large rectangular cookie, from which you break off irregular pieces. (The name comes from the candy, said to resemble tree bark.) This is a good beginner recipe for children (they might prefer the peanut butter variation), as well as a good one for grown-ups and kids to make together. Whoever's in charge, though, remember: don't overbake, or the delicious chocolaty, nutty cookies will become dry as tree bark.

2 cups plus 2 tablespoons all-purpose flour

½ teaspoon baking soda

½ teaspoon salt

1 cup (2 sticks) unsalted butter, melted and slightly cooled

¾ cup granulated sugar

½ cup firmly packed light brown sugar

2 teaspoons vanilla extract

4 ounces good-quality white chocolate, cut into ¼-inch squares

¾ cup semisweet chocolate morsels

¾ cup coarsely chopped unsalted macadamia nuts*

special equipment

11½ by 17½-inch jellyroll pan

***Note:** If you can only find salted nuts, place them in a sieve and rinse them under cold running water. Dry them thoroughly with paper towels.

1. Position a rack in the center of the oven and preheat the oven to 350°F. Grease the bottom and sides of an 11½ by 17½-inch jellyroll pan.
2. Sift together the flour, baking soda, and salt into a medium bowl. Set aside.
3. In the bowl of an electric mixer, using the paddle attachment, beat the melted butter with sugars at medium speed until combined, about 2 minutes. Beat in the vanilla extract. At low speed, add the flour mixture, mixing just until blended. Using a wooden spoon, stir in the white chocolate, semisweet morsels, and macadamia nuts.
4. Scrape the dough into the prepared pan and, using a small offset metal spatula, spread it into an even layer, covering the bottom of the pan completely (the dough will be spread thin). Bake for 15 to 18 minutes, just until lightly golden brown around the edges. The bark should still be quite soft; it will firm up as it cools. (Overbaking the cookie bark will make it too dry and crisp.) Place the pan on a wire rack and cool completely.
5. Using your hands, break the bark into irregularly shaped 2 by 2½-inch pieces.

Chocolate Peanut Butter Cookie Bark: Substitute ¾ cup peanut butter morsels for the white chocolate and coarsely chopped unsalted roasted peanuts for the macadamia nuts.

STORE **IN AN AIRTIGHT CONTAINER AT ROOM TEMPERATURE FOR UP TO A WEEK.**

white chocolate eggnog bars

MAKES 24 BARS

These holiday-flavored bars are rich, but not overwhelmingly so. The flavor of eggnog can be somewhat elusive; what defines it are nutmeg and brandy, or rum. These are included here, and the cinnamon note in the graham cracker crust pairs well with the nutmeg. White chocolate, just a hint of its sweetness as a thin topping, serves to mellow the faint spiciness and adds a nice finish to the festive bars.

cinnamon graham cracker crust

2 cups cinnamon graham cracker crumbs

9 tablespoons unsalted butter, melted

eggnog filling

12 ounces cream cheese, softened

2/3 cup granulated sugar

2 teaspoons cornstarch

1 large egg

2 large egg yolks

1/3 cup heavy cream

3 tablespoons brandy or dark rum

1 1/2 teaspoons vanilla extract

1/4 teaspoon freshly grated nutmeg

white chocolate topping

1/2 cup heavy cream

5 ounces good-quality white chocolate, chopped

garnish

Freshly grated nutmeg

make the crust

1. Position a rack in the center of the oven and preheat the oven to 350°F. Line a 9 by 13-inch baking pan with aluminum foil so that the foil extends 2 inches beyond the two short ends of the pan. Lightly grease the foil.

2. In a medium bowl, combine the graham cracker crumbs and melted butter. Transfer the crumbs to the prepared pan and pat them into an even layer. Bake the crust for 8 minutes, or until it is slightly puffed and set. Place the pan on a wire rack and let cool while you make the filling. Reduce the oven temperature to 325°F.

make the filling

3. In the bowl of an electric mixer, using the paddle attachment, beat the cream cheese and sugar at medium speed until smooth and light, about 1 minute. Beat in the cornstarch. Add the egg and egg yolks, one at a time, beating until blended and scraping down the sides of the bowl as necessary. Beat in the heavy cream, brandy or rum, vanilla extract, and nutmeg.

4. Scrape the filling into the slightly cooled crust. Bake for 15 to 20 minutes, until the filling is set. Place the pan on a wire rack and cool for 30 minutes.

5. Refrigerate the bars for at least 1 hour, until chilled.

make the topping

6. In a small saucepan, bring the cream to a gentle boil. Remove the pan from the heat and immediately add the white chocolate. Let the mixture stand for 30 seconds to melt the chocolate, then stir until the chocolate is completely melted and the mixture is smooth. Set the topping aside to cool, stirring occasionally, for 15 minutes or until thickened.

7. Pour the topping over the chilled bars and, using a small offset metal spatula, spread evenly. Refrigerate the bars for at least 2 hours before cutting (or freeze for 1 hour).

8. Lift the bars out of the pan using the aluminum foil as handles. Remove the foil and cut into 24 bars. Serve chilled, dusted very lightly with freshly grated nutmeg.

STORE IN AN AIRTIGHT CONTAINER IN THE REFRIGERATOR FOR UP TO A WEEK.

almond cherry bars

MAKES **16 BARS**

Frangipane, or almond cream, is a classic ingredient in many French-style tarts and cakes. It's a creamy filling that becomes somewhat cake-like once it's baked. It goes well with chocolate, fruits, and other nuts. Here I pair its mellow flavor with cherry—chopped dried cherries in the filling, and a cherry preserve layer—and top the whole thing off with a drizzle of almond-flavored glaze.

crust

Sweet Pastry Crust #2 (page 354)

almond cherry filling

⅓ cup dried sour cherries, chopped

⅓ cup freshly squeezed orange juice

⅔ cup plus 2 tablespoons granulated sugar, divided

1 cup sliced blanched almonds

2 large eggs

½ cup (1 stick) unsalted butter, cut into tablespoons, softened

½ teaspoon vanilla extract

¼ teaspoon almond extract

1 tablespoon all-purpose flour

cherry layer

⅔ cup cherry preserves

drizzle glaze

½ cup confectioners' sugar

2 tablespoons heavy cream

¼ teaspoon almond extract

make the crust

1. Prepare and bake the pastry crust according to the directions on page 354, and cool completely. Leave the oven on at 350°F.

make the filling

2. Place the cherries, orange juice, and 2 tablespoons of the sugar in a small saucepan and bring to a boil over medium-high heat. Boil until the liquid is almost completely absorbed by the cherries, 2 to 2½ minutes; watch carefully so that the mixture does not burn. Remove the pan from the heat and cool completely.

3. Place the almonds and the remaining ⅔ cup sugar in the bowl of a food processor and process until the almonds are finely ground, about 45 seconds. Add the eggs and process until blended. Scatter the softened butter pieces over the almond mixture and process until blended and creamy, about 30 seconds. Add the vanilla extract, almond extract, and flour and pulse until blended. Add the cooled cherries and process until blended, about 5 seconds.

assemble and bake the bars

4. Using a small offset metal spatula, spread the cherry preserves in a thin layer over the cooled crust. Scrape the almond cherry filling over the layer of preserves and spread it evenly. Bake the bars for 35 to 38 minutes, until they are golden brown and a toothpick inserted in the center comes out clean. Set the pan on a wire rack and cool completely.

glaze the bars

5. In a small bowl, combine the confectioners' sugar, heavy cream, and almond extract, stirring until smooth. Transfer the glaze to a small sealable plastic bag and seal the bag. Using scissors, snip a tiny hole in one of the bottom corners of the bag. Drizzle the glaze over the bars diagonally in a zigzag pattern. Allow the glaze to set for 10 minutes, then cut the bars into 16 squares.

STORE IN AN AIRTIGHT CONTAINER AT ROOM TEMPERATURE FOR UP TO 3 DAYS, OR REFRIGERATE FOR UP TO A WEEK.

Cookie Bite **Cherry pits (which should not be eaten, of course) have the flavor of almonds—perhaps this is why the fruit and nuts combine so well in recipes.**

sour cream apple crumble bars

MAKES 16 BARS

Apple pie is America, it's Mom, it's those golden afternoons when the world was young and so were we. But just as every American has one vote, each of us is entitled to our own apple pie recipe. This is mine, in cookie form: a beautiful buttery crust, a juicy apple filling flavored with warm cinnamon, apple brandy, and tangy sour cream, and a sweet crumbly topping. Like the pie, these bars are great served warm, with a scoop of vanilla ice cream or a healthy dollop of sweet whipped cream.

crust

Sweet Pastry Crust #2 (page 354)

apple filling

1 pound Granny Smith apples (about 3 medium)

2 teaspoons freshly squeezed lemon juice

2 tablespoons frozen apple juice concentrate

2 teaspoons cornstarch

2 tablespoons Calvados or brandy

3 tablespoons unsalted butter

½ cup firmly packed light brown sugar

topping

1 cup all-purpose flour

¼ cup granulated sugar

⅓ cup firmly packed dark brown sugar

1 teaspoon ground cinnamon

¼ teaspoon salt

7 tablespoons unsalted butter, melted

make the crust

1. Prepare and bake the crust as directed on page 354, and cool completely. Leave the oven on at 350°F.

make the filling

2. Peel and core the apples, cut into ½-inch cubes, and place in a medium bowl. Add the lemon juice, apple concentrate, cornstarch, and Calvados or brandy and toss to combine.

3. In a large skillet, melt the butter over medium-high heat. Add the sugar and cook, stirring constantly until any lumps of sugar are broken up. Add the apple mixture and bring to a boil. Cook for 5 minutes, or until the apples are softened on the outside but still slightly crunchy on the inside. Transfer to a medium bowl and cool while you make the topping.

make the topping

4. In a medium bowl, stir together the flour, sugars, cinnamon, and salt until well blended. Add the melted butter and mix with a fork, stirring until the dry ingredients are uniformly moistened. Set aside.

make the sour cream mixture

5. In a small bowl, whisk the egg until blended. Whisk in the sour cream, cinnamon, salt, and currants or raisins.

assemble and bake the bars

6. Fold the sour cream mixture into the cooled apple mixture and spread it evenly over the crust. Sprinkle the topping evenly over the filling and press

sour cream mixture

1 large egg

½ cup sour cream

½ teaspoon ground cinnamon

¼ teaspoon salt

⅓ cup currants or chopped raisins

Confectioners' sugar for dusting

down lightly on it with your fingers. Bake the bars for 35 to 40 minutes, until golden brown around the edges and set. Cool the bars completely in the pan set on a wire rack. (The bars can be served warm, but they will not cut as cleanly.)

7. Using a sharp knife, cut the bars into 16 squares. Sprinkle with sifted confectioners' sugar before serving.

STORE IN AN AIRTIGHT CONTAINER IN THE REFRIGERATOR FOR UP TO 5 DAYS.

Cookie Bite I love the tartness of Granny Smith apples in this bar cookie, but some other varieties are also wonderful: try Rome Beauty, Winesap, York Imperial, Cortland, or Northern Spy.

coconut custard squares

MAKES **16 BARS**

When I was a kid, one of my favorite desserts was coconut custard pie. The combination of the creamy, slippery-smooth coconut custard and the buttery crust transported me. These squares are a variation of the American classic. The coconut flavor is punched up by the addition of dark rum, and the silky custard is topped off with cashew chunks—a little crunch that gives you more time to savor the tropical goodness.

crust

Sweet Pastry Crust #2 (page 354)

coconut filling

2 large eggs

1 large egg yolk

¾ cup granulated sugar

1 cup coconut milk (available in the Asian section of most supermarkets)

1 teaspoon vanilla extract

2 tablespoons dark rum

1 tablespoon all-purpose flour

Pinch of salt

1 cup sweetened shredded coconut

topping

¾ cup coarsely chopped unsalted roasted cashews

Confectioners' sugar for dusting

make the crust

1. Prepare and bake the pastry crust as directed on page 354, and cool completely. Leave the oven on at 350°F.

make the filling and topping

2. In a medium bowl, whisk the eggs, egg yolk, and granulated sugar until blended. Slowly whisk in the coconut milk. Whisk in the vanilla extract, rum, flour, and salt.

3. Sprinkle the coconut evenly over the cooled crust. Pour the filling through a fine sieve over the coconut, covering the crust completely. Sprinkle the chopped cashews over the top. Bake for 25 to 30 minutes, until the filling is set and the edges are golden brown. Cool completely in the pan on a wire rack.

4. Sprinkle the bars lightly with sifted confectioners' sugar. Using a sharp knife, cut into 16 squares.

STORE **IN AN AIRTIGHT CONTAINER IN THE REFRIGERATOR FOR UP TO 3 DAYS.**

hand-formed cookies

• classic vanilla sugar cookies • melting moments • gingersnaps • cinnamon sugar crinkles • ginger quakes • benne wafers • chinese almond cookies • ANZAC tiles • russian tea cakes • cinnamon doughnut holes • kourabiedes • lemon cornmeal cookies • butter pecan cookies • pfeffernüsse • cocomacs • cookie shop chocolate chip cookies • brandy snaps • chocolate-dipped almond crescents • chocolate crackles • classic pine nut macaroons • lemon-fennel pretzel cookies • chocolate pretzel cookies • ginger fortune cookies • mandelbrot • almond anise biscotti • pistachio biscotti • hazelnut biscotti • triple-ginger pecan biscotti • caramelized pecan–orange biscotti • chocolate almond biscotti • double-chocolate pecan biscotti • molasses spice cookies •

Requiring a light touch and some practice, hand-formed cookies are shaped by hand into simple shapes such as flattened rounds, crescents, or rusk-shaped biscotti or into more complex shapes such as pretzels and even fortune cookies. They are not to be confused with what I call Decorator Cookies, for specific holidays and other special occasions, which have simpler flavors but more ornate decorations (see page 303). Hand-formed cookies have a rustic, or homespun, look and lots of character.

In this chapter, you will find Gingersnaps, Brandy Snaps, Lemon-Fennel Pretzel Cookies, sesame-flavored Benne Wafers, and the fashionable Italian biscotti. The word "biscotti" means "twice cooked" (just as the French word "biscuit" does). In Italy, *biscotti* actually refers to a wide array of crisp cookies, not all of which are twice baked, but Americans have seized on the ultra-crispy full-flavored style, which has become hugely popular in the last few years, riding the wave of the coffee boom—for these sturdy, flavorful biscuits are perfect for dunking in coffee, or tea.

Generally the dough for hand-formed cookies is stiff, and it is sometimes chilled before being shaped. It is important that your hands be cool and that you handle the dough as little as possible. If the dough becomes warm, the cookies are more likely to spread and to lose their shape. Shaping cookies by hand is a source of personal satisfaction. The results are real crowd pleasers, all over the world.

classic vanilla sugar cookies

MAKES ABOUT 38 COOKIES

These timeless cookies have been an American favorite for as long as Americans have baked. They're wonderfully tender, with a crunchy exterior from the coarse sugar sprinkled on top. Using the seeds from a fresh vanilla bean imparts truer vanilla flavor than extract. These cookies go perfectly with tea; coffee might overwhelm the delicate vanilla fragrance. You'll make them over and over again, because they never fail to satisfy.

½ cup granulated sugar

½ plump vanilla bean

2½ cups all-purpose flour

¾ teaspoon baking powder

½ teaspoon salt

1 cup (2 sticks) unsalted butter, softened

½ cup confectioners' sugar

1 large egg

Coarse sugar for sprinkling

1. Position a rack in the center of the oven and preheat the oven to 375°F. Lightly grease two baking sheets.
2. Put the granulated sugar in a small bowl. Using a small sharp knife, split the vanilla bean lengthwise in half. Scrape the small seeds from the interior of the pod into the bowl containing the sugar; discard the pod. Using your fingers, rub the sugar and vanilla seeds together until well blended. Set aside.
3. In a medium bowl, whisk together the flour, baking powder, and salt; set aside.
4. In the bowl of an electric mixer, using the paddle attachment, beat the butter, confectioners' sugar, and vanilla-sugar mixture at medium-high speed until light in texture and color, about 2 minutes. Add the egg and beat until well blended, scraping down the sides of the bowl as necessary. Reduce the speed to low, add the flour mixture, and mix just until blended.
5. Roll the dough into 1-inch balls and arrange 2 inches apart on the prepared baking sheets. Moisten your palm to prevent sticking, and flatten each cookie into a 1¾-inch disk. Sprinkle the cookies generously with coarse sugar. Bake, one sheet at a time, for 9 to 11 minutes, until golden brown around the edges. Transfer the cookies to wire racks and cool completely.

STORE IN AN AIRTIGHT CONTAINER AT ROOM TEMPERATURE FOR UP TO A WEEK.

melting moments

MAKES ABOUT 36 COOKIES

This is a classic Scottish cookie that will literally melt in your mouth. The cornstarch makes the cookies very tender; the oats give them some texture, and also their ephemeral flavor—just a subtle drumbeat of oat on your palate before it all melts away. These cookies don't travel well, so invite your friends to your place.

1¼ cups all-purpose flour

¾ cup cornstarch

¼ teaspoon salt

1 cup (2 sticks) unsalted butter, softened

1⅓ cups confectioners' sugar, divided

1 large egg yolk

1½ teaspoons vanilla extract

⅔ cup quick-cooking rolled oats

1. Position a rack in the center of the oven and preheat the oven to 350°F.
2. In a medium bowl, whisk together the flour, cornstarch, and salt; set aside.
3. In the bowl of an electric mixer, using the paddle attachment, beat the butter and ⅔ cup of the confectioners' sugar at medium-high speed until creamy and light, about 2 minutes. Beat in the egg yolk and vanilla until blended, scraping down the sides of the bowl as necessary. At low speed, add the flour mixture and mix just until blended, then stir the dough with a wooden spoon, scraping up any ingredients from the bottom of the bowl and blending them into the dough.
4. Place the oats and remaining ⅔ cup confectioners' sugar in two separate shallow dishes or pie pans.
5. Pull off pieces of the dough and shape them into 1-inch balls. Roll the balls in the oats and arrange 2 inches apart on ungreased baking sheets. Using the heel of your hand, gently flatten each ball to a 1½-inch disk. Bake the cookies, one sheet at a time, for 14 to 16 minutes, until very lightly browned around the edges. Let cool on the baking sheets for 10 minutes.
6. Dredge the tops of the cookies in the confectioners' sugar (handle the cookies with care; they are extremely fragile). Place on wire racks and cool completely.

STORE IN AN AIRTIGHT CONTAINER IN A COOL, DRY PLACE FOR UP TO A WEEK.

gingersnaps

MAKES ABOUT 60 COOKIES

This is the classic: a ginger and molasses cookie with a crisp texture, a sugar glaze patina, and a flavor with a multitude of spicy and zesty notes. The word "snap" in the name of a cookie probably derives from a German or Middle Dutch word, *snappen*, "to seize quickly." People will be snapping up these delicious cookies as soon as they're put on a plate.

2⅔ cups all-purpose flour

2 teaspoons ground ginger

1 teaspoon baking soda

½ teaspoon ground cinnamon

¼ teaspoon ground cloves

¼ teaspoon salt

¾ cup (1½ sticks) unsalted butter, softened

1⅓ cups granulated sugar

1 tablespoon finely chopped crystallized ginger

2 large eggs, at room temperature

¼ cup unsulphured (mild) molasses

¼ teaspoon finely grated lemon zest

2 tablespoons turbinado or coarse sugar, for sprinkling

make the dough

1. In a large bowl, whisk together the flour, ground ginger, baking soda, cinnamon, cloves, and salt. Set aside.
2. In the bowl of an electric mixer, using the paddle attachment, beat the butter, sugar, and crystallized ginger at medium speed until light, about 2 minutes. Beat in the eggs one at a time, beating well after each addition and scraping down the sides of the bowl as necessary. Add the molasses and lemon zest and beat until combined. At low speed, add the dry ingredients and mix just until blended. Cover the bowl with plastic wrap and chill the dough for 30 minutes (or up to a day).
3. Position a rack in the upper third of the oven and preheat the oven to 350°F. Grease two baking sheets.

shape and bake the cookies

4. Roll the dough into 1-inch balls and arrange the balls on the prepared baking sheets, spacing them about 1½ inches apart. Moisten your palm to prevent sticking, and flatten each cookie into a perfect 1½-inch round. Sprinkle the tops of the cookies with the turbinado or coarse sugar and bake, one sheet at a time, for 9 to 11 minutes, or until they are puffed and lightly golden around the edges. Cool the cookies on the baking sheets on a wire rack for 5 minutes, then transfer the cookies to the rack and cool completely.

STORE IN AN AIRTIGHT CONTAINER FOR UP TO 1 WEEK, OR FREEZE FOR UP TO 1 MONTH.

cinnamon sugar crinkles

MAKES **ABOUT 34 COOKIES**

Also known as Snickerdoodles, these have been popular, especially in New England, since the 1800s. They're so old-fashioned they've become fashionable again. Snickerdoodles are probably German in origin, and their name may be a corruption of the German word "schneckennudeln," which translates as "crinkly noodles." The signature crinkle emerges when the cinnamon-sugar coating bakes up just right. The cookies are crisp on the outside, chewy on the inside, and full of cinnamon flavor, with a subtle backnote of nutmeg.

cookies

2½ cups all-purpose flour

1 tablespoon baking powder

¼ teaspoon freshly grated nutmeg

¼ teaspoon salt

¾ cup (1½ sticks) unsalted butter, softened

1⅓ cups granulated sugar

1 tablespoon unsulphured (mild) molasses

2 large eggs

1 teaspoon vanilla extract

topping

1 tablespoon ground cinnamon

¼ cup granulated sugar

1. Position a rack in the center of the oven and preheat the oven to 350°F. Grease two baking sheets.

make the dough

2. Sift together the flour, baking powder, nutmeg, and salt into a medium bowl. Stir until well blended; set aside.

3. In the bowl of an electric mixer, using the paddle attachment, beat the butter, sugar, and molasses at medium-high speed until light, about 1½ minutes. Add the eggs one at a time, beating well after each addition. Beat in the vanilla extract. Scrape down the sides of the bowl and beat for 30 seconds more. At low speed, add the flour mixture and mix just until blended.

make the topping

4. In a small bowl, gently whisk together the cinnamon and sugar.

shape and bake the cookies

5. Shape the dough into 1¼-inch balls (using about 1½ tablespoons of dough for each cookie). Roll each ball in the cinnamon-sugar mixture to coat completely, and arrange the balls on the baking sheets, spacing them 2½ inches apart. Flatten each cookie into a 2-inch disk. Bake the cookies, one sheet at a time, for 16 to 18 minutes, until the tops are crinkly and they are puffed and lightly browned around the edges. Transfer the cookies to a wire rack and cool completely.

STORE **IN AN AIRTIGHT CONTAINER AT ROOM TEMPERATURE FOR UP TO A WEEK.**

ginger quakes

MAKES **ABOUT 58 COOKIES**

These are similar to gingersnaps in flavor, but softer and chewier. The recipe was adapted from one of my mother's favorites; Ginger Quakes were a fixture around our house during the holidays. I punched up the ginger flavor by adding fresh ginger. The unusual (and optional) addition of rendered bacon fat gives the cookies a very subtle smoky-salty endnote. They are truly addictive. As my husband says, "Everything tastes better with bacon."

2½ cups all-purpose flour

2 teaspoons baking soda

1 tablespoon ground ginger

1 teaspoon ground cinnamon

½ teaspoon salt

¾ cup (1½ sticks) unsalted butter, softened

1 cup firmly packed light brown sugar

2 teaspoons rendered bacon fat (optional)

1 large egg

⅓ cup unsulphured (mild) molasses

2 tablespoons finely minced fresh ginger

1 teaspoon finely grated orange zest

½ cup turbinado or coarse sugar, for coating

1. Position a rack in the center of the oven and preheat the oven to 350°F. Line two baking sheets with parchment paper or foil.
2. In a medium bowl, whisk together the flour, baking soda, ground ginger, cinnamon, and salt. Set aside.
3. In the bowl of an electric mixer, using the paddle attachment, beat the butter and brown sugar at medium-high speed until light and creamy, about 2 minutes. Beat in the bacon fat, if using. Add the egg and mix until blended, scraping down the sides of the bowl as necessary. Add the molasses, ginger, and orange zest and mix until blended. At low speed, add the flour mixture, mixing just until blended.
4. Place the turbinado or coarse sugar in a shallow dish or pie plate. Roll the dough into 1-inch balls. Roll each ball in the sugar, coating it completely. Arrange the balls on the prepared baking sheets, spacing them 2 inches apart. Bake the cookies, one sheet at a time, for 8 to 10 minutes, until the edges are set and the tops are cracked but the centers are still soft. Transfer the cookies to a wire rack and cool completely.

STORE **IN AN AIRTIGHT CONTAINER AT ROOM TEMPERATURE FOR UP TO A WEEK.**

Cookie Bite **Here's a quick way to mince ginger: Peel, then slice the ginger into thin rounds. Arrange the rounds close together between two sheets of waxed paper and pound lightly with a meat pounder until finely minced. If any large pieces remain, finely chop them with a large knife.**

benne wafers

MAKES ABOUT 40 COOKIES

Crunchy, flavorful sesame seeds coat this buttery cookie, which is flavored with brown sugar and orange. "Benne" is the word for sesame in a certain African language. These cookies have been popular in the South, particularly South Carolina, since slaves first brought the seeds from Africa. According to legend, the seeds bring good luck to those who eat them. Buy your sesame seeds in a health food store where they are sold in bulk. They will be less expensive than those in the small jars in the supermarket.

1¼ cups sesame seeds, divided

1½ cups all-purpose flour

1½ teaspoons baking powder

⅛ teaspoon salt

6 tablespoons (¾ stick) unsalted butter, melted and cooled

¾ cup firmly packed light brown sugar

¼ cup granulated sugar

2 large eggs

1 teaspoon finely grated orange zest

1 teaspoon toasted sesame oil

1½ teaspoons vanilla extract

1. Position a rack in the center of the oven and preheat the oven to 350°F. Grease two baking sheets.

2. Put the sesame seeds in a large skillet, place over medium heat, and toast the seeds, shaking the pan often, until they are light golden brown. Immediately transfer the seeds to a medium bowl and cool completely.

3. In a medium bowl, whisk together the flour, baking powder, and salt; set aside.

4. In the bowl of an electric mixer, using the paddle attachment, mix together the melted butter, brown sugar, and granulated sugar at medium speed until combined, about 30 seconds. Add the eggs one at a time, beating well after each addition and scraping down the sides of the bowl as necessary. Add the orange zest, sesame oil, and vanilla extract and beat just until blended. At low speed, add the dry ingredients, and then 1 cup of the sesame seeds, mixing until just combined. Cover the bowl with plastic wrap and chill the dough for 15 minutes.

5. Place the remaining ¼ cup sesame seeds in a pie plate. Shape the dough into 1-inch balls. Dip each ball into the sesame seeds, covering just one half of the ball. Place the balls, with the sesame seeds on top, on the prepared baking sheets, spacing them 2 inches apart. Using your palm, gently press down on the balls to flatten them into 1½-inch disks.

6. Bake the cookies, one sheet at a time, until golden, 11 to 13 minutes. Transfer the cookies to a wire rack to cool completely.

STORE IN AN AIRTIGHT CONTAINER AT ROOM TEMPERATURE FOR UP TO 2 WEEKS.

chinese almond cookies

MAKES ABOUT 42 COOKIES

Years ago, before mass-produced fortune cookies, these were the cookies that were typically served in Chinese restaurants at the end of the meal. My American addition to the recipe is cornmeal, which works well with the nutty almond flavor. Yes, the recipe calls for lard. Let me just say that bona fide, meltingly tender Chinese almond cookies cannot be made without this unfairly-maligned fat. If you can't find it at your supermarket, substitute an equal amount of softened butter.

2½ cups all-purpose flour

½ cup yellow cornmeal

1¼ teaspoons baking powder

⅛ teaspoon salt

¾ cup lard

¾ cup (1½ sticks) unsalted butter, softened

¾ cup granulated sugar

1 large egg

2 teaspoons almond extract

½ teaspoon vanilla extract

About 42 blanched whole almonds

1. Position a rack in the center of the oven and preheat the oven to 350°F.
2. In a medium bowl, whisk together the flour, cornmeal, baking powder, and salt. Set aside.
3. In the bowl of an electric mixer, using the paddle attachment, beat the lard and butter at medium speed until smooth, about 30 seconds. Add the sugar and beat until well blended, about 1 minute. Add the egg and almond and vanilla extracts and beat until blended, about 1 minute. At low speed, add the dry ingredients, mixing just until blended.
4. Shape the dough into 1¼-inch balls and arrange them about 2 inches apart on ungreased baking sheets. Moisten your palm to prevent sticking, and flatten each ball into a 2-inch round. Press an almond into the center of each cookie. Bake, one sheet at a time, for 12 to 15 minutes, until golden brown just around the edges. Transfer the cookies to a wire rack and cool completely.

STORE IN AN AIRTIGHT CONTAINER AT ROOM TEMPERATURE FOR UP TO A WEEK.

ANZAC tiles

MAKES ABOUT 36 COOKIES

Talk about an unlikely source for a cookie name: ANZAC is the acronym for Australian and New Zealand Army Corps. The original cookies were baked for soldiers, who used to joke that their ANZAC ration was bulletproof. Here is a modern, more flavorful and tender version of the classic, though it retains the secret ingredient: sweet, caramely (almost like butterscotch) Lyle's Golden Syrup, a pure sugarcane syrup. You can substitute dark corn syrup, but they won't be quite as good.

1 cup all-purpose flour, sifted

1¼ cups old-fashioned rolled oats

1 cup sweetened flaked coconut

1 teaspoon finely grated lemon zest

1 teaspoon baking soda

⅛ teaspoon salt

10 tablespoons (1¼ sticks) unsalted butter, cut into tablespoons

3 tablespoons Lyle's Golden Syrup or dark corn syrup

¾ cup granulated sugar

2 teaspoons vanilla extract

1. Position a rack in the upper third of the oven and preheat the oven to 325°F. Lightly grease two baking sheets.
2. In a medium bowl, stir together the flour, oats, coconut, lemon zest, baking soda, and salt; set aside.
3. In a small saucepan, combine the butter, syrup, and sugar and cook over medium-high heat, stirring constantly, until the butter is melted and the sugar is dissolved. Remove the pan from the heat and let the mixture cool for 10 minutes.
4. Stir the vanilla extract into the butter mixture, then stir the mixture into the dry ingredients just until combined.
5. Form the dough into 1-inch balls and arrange them 3 inches apart on the prepared baking sheets. Moisten your palm to prevent sticking, and flatten each ball into a 1½-inch round. Bake the cookies, one sheet at a time, for 12 to 14 minutes, just until they are lightly browned all over. Transfer the cookies to a wire rack and cool completely.

STORE IN AN AIRTIGHT CONTAINER AT ROOM TEMPERATURE FOR UP TO A WEEK.

Cookie Bite Before measuring the Golden Syrup or corn syrup, spray the tablespoon lightly with nonstick cooking spray. It will prevent the sticky syrup from sticking to the spoon.

russian tea cakes

MAKES ABOUT 44 COOKIES

These are also known as Mexican Wedding Cakes, or Bride's Cakes. If those names have you puzzled, consider: a small cake like this might be closer to the original wedding cake than one of those large multitiered extravaganzas. Our ritual of showering the bridal couple with rice is an offshoot of the medieval-era custom of throwing grain. Grain evolved into baked goods (made with flour), and for centuries biscuits were crumbled over the heads of the happy couple. These cakes would crumble very well, but I'd rather eat them. They're very tender with a delicate, faintly nutty flavor. Rolling them in confectioners' sugar while they're still warm is a classic touch.

cookies

½ cup walnuts, toasted

½ cup pecans, toasted

2 cups all-purpose flour, divided

½ teaspoon salt

1 cup (2 sticks) unsalted butter, softened

⅓ cup granulated sugar

1 teaspoon finely grated orange zest

1 teaspoon vanilla extract

garnish

⅔ cup confectioners' sugar

make the cookies

1. Position a rack in the center of the oven and preheat the oven to 325°F. Grease two baking sheets.
2. In the bowl of a food processor, combine the walnuts, pecans, and 2 tablespoons of the flour. Process until the nuts are finely ground, about 30 seconds. Transfer the mixture to a medium bowl. Add the remaining flour and the salt and stir well to combine.
3. In the bowl of an electric mixer, using the paddle attachment, beat the butter and sugar at medium-high speed until light, about 2 to 3 minutes. Beat in the orange zest and vanilla extract. At low speed, add the flour-nut mixture and mix just until combined.
4. Form the dough into ¾-inch balls and arrange them 2 inches apart on the prepared baking sheets. Bake the cookies, one sheet at a time, for 17 to 20 minutes, until lightly browned. Let the cookies cool on the baking sheet for 5 minutes.

garnish the cookies

5. Place the confectioners' sugar in a pie plate or shallow bowl. While the cookies are still warm, dredge their tops in the confectioners' sugar until well coated (it will melt a little). Transfer the dusted cookies to a wire rack and cool completely. Sift the remaining sugar over the tops of the cookies before serving.

STORE IN AN AIRTIGHT CONTAINER AT ROOM TEMPERATURE FOR UP TO 5 DAYS.

cinnamon doughnut holes

MAKES ABOUT 30 DOUGHNUT HOLES

A doughnut hole is not technically a cookie. It is, as they say, sui generis: a thing unto itself. But these will be right at home on any cookie tray, and, trust me, no one will complain. These are very light, with a cinnamon flavor and a sandy-textured sugar coating. They're actually very easy to make; you just need to be very careful working with the hot oil.

doughnut holes

2 cups plus 2 tablespoons all-purpose flour

1 teaspoon baking powder

½ teaspoon baking soda

½ teaspoon ground cinnamon

¼ teaspoon salt

2 large eggs

⅔ cup granulated sugar

⅔ cup sour cream

1 teaspoon vanilla extract

cinnamon sugar

⅔ cup granulated sugar

1 teaspoon ground cinnamon

Vegetable oil for deep-frying

All-purpose flour for shaping

make the dough

1. Sift together the flour, baking powder, baking soda, cinnamon, and salt into a medium bowl. Set aside.

2. In a medium bowl, whisk together the eggs and sugar until blended. Whisk in the sour cream and vanilla extract. Using a wooden spoon, gradually stir in the flour mixture just until combined; the dough will be sticky. Cover the bowl with plastic wrap and let the dough rest at room temperature for 1½ hours.

make the cinnamon sugar

3. In a small bowl, combine the sugar and cinnamon. Set aside.

shape and fry the doughnut holes

4. Pour at least 2 inches of oil into a deep pan, filling it no more than halfway, and heat over medium heat to 375°F. Line a baking sheet with paper towels.

5. Sprinkle about 2 tablespoons of flour onto a plate. Pinch off a rounded tablespoon of the dough and dip one side of it into the flour, using just enough flour to let you form the dough into a ball (you don't want to dredge the dough in flour; use as little flour as possible). Be gentle when rolling the dough; don't compress the dough, or the doughnut holes will be heavy. Gently place the dough into the hot oil (fry only as many pieces at a time as fit without crowding) and repeat with the remaining dough. Fry the holes for about 3 minutes, occasionally turning with a slotted spoon, until they are evenly browned all over. With the spoon, remove each hole as soon as it is done and place on the lined baking sheet to drain for a few minutes.

6. While they are still warm, roll the holes in the cinnamon sugar until completely coated.

STORE IN AN AIRTIGHT CONTAINER AT ROOM TEMPERATURE FOR UP TO A DAY, BUT THESE ARE BEST THE DAY THEY ARE MADE.

kourabiedes

MAKES ABOUT 34 COOKIES

Pronounced "koo-rah-bee-YAY-dehs," these are classic melt-in-the-mouth Greek cookies. They're tender and buttery, flavored with spicy cloves and a subtle hint of brandy. Similar in some ways to the cookies known as *bizcochos de boda* (Mexican wedding cakes) in Oaxaca and *kipfel* in Austria, kourabiedes are traditional at Greek christenings, weddings, and holiday celebrations. (The clove is a symbol of the Magis' gift of rare spices to the infant Jesus.) Confectioners' sugar dusting is the classic finish, but I've tinkered with the recipe a bit: I added ground pistachios to the dough and garnished each finished cookie with a pistachio half (another popular Greek ingredient), instead of the traditional whole clove, which isn't so pleasant to eat.

¼ cup unsalted pistachio nuts, plus 34 halves (cut lengthwise) for garnish*

½ cup confectioners' sugar

1 cup (2 sticks) unsalted butter, softened

1 tablespoon honey

⅛ teaspoon salt

⅛ teaspoon ground cloves

1 large egg yolk

1 tablespoon brandy

1 teaspoon vanilla extract

2 cups all-purpose flour, sifted

Confectioners' sugar for dusting

***Note:** If you can only find salted pistachio nuts, place the nuts in a sieve and run cold water over them for a few seconds. Dry them thoroughly with paper towels.

1. Place the pistachio nuts and confectioners' sugar in the bowl of a food processor and process until the nuts are finely ground, about 30 seconds. Set aside.
2. In the bowl of an electric mixer, using the paddle attachment, beat the butter, honey, and salt at medium-high speed until creamy, about 1 minute. Add the pistachio-sugar mixture, cloves, egg yolk, brandy, and vanilla extract and beat until light, about 2 minutes. At low speed, add the flour and mix until just combined. Cover the bowl and refrigerate the dough until firm enough to shape, about 30 minutes.
3. Position a rack in the center of the oven and preheat the oven to 350°F. Grease two baking sheets.
4. Shape the chilled dough into 1-inch balls and arrange them 1 inch apart on the prepared baking sheets. Insert a pistachio half into each cookie. Bake the cookies, one sheet at a time, for 15 to 18 minutes, until barely beginning to color. Transfer the cookies to wire racks and cool completely.
5. Just before serving, sift confectioners' sugar over the cookies until coated.

STORE IN AN AIRTIGHT CONTAINER AT ROOM TEMPERATURE FOR UP TO 5 DAYS.

lemon cornmeal cookies

MAKES ABOUT 40 COOKIES

Known as *crumiri* in Italy, these are a traditional cookie from the Piedmont region, where cornmeal is extremely popular, although it is used most often in polenta. The cornmeal creates a pleasingly coarse texture and offers a subtle flavor that is the perfect platform for the lemony endnote.

1¼ cups all-purpose flour

¾ cup yellow cornmeal

¼ teaspoon salt

¾ cup (1½ sticks) unsalted butter, softened

⅔ cup granulated sugar

1 teaspoon finely grated lemon zest

½ teaspoon vanilla extract

1 large egg

1 large egg yolk

Coarse sugar for sprinkling

1. Position a rack in the center of the oven and preheat the oven to 350°F. Grease two baking sheets.
2. In a medium bowl, whisk together the flour, cornmeal, and salt. Set aside.
3. In the bowl of an electric mixer, using the paddle attachment, beat the butter, sugar, lemon zest, and vanilla extract at medium-high speed until light, about 2 minutes. Beat in the egg, then the yolk, beating well after each addition and scraping down the sides of the bowl as necessary. At low speed, add the flour mixture and mix just until blended.
4. Shape the dough into 1-inch balls and arrange them 2 inches apart on the prepared baking sheets. Moisten your palm to prevent sticking, and flatten each ball into a 1½-inch disk. Sprinkle the cookies with coarse sugar and bake, one sheet at a time, for 12 to 14 minutes, until lightly golden around the edges. Transfer to a wire rack and cool completely.

STORE IN AN AIRTIGHT CONTAINER AT ROOM TEMPERATURE FOR UP TO A WEEK.

butter pecan cookies

MAKES ABOUT 28 COOKIES

This cookie is my rendition of the Pecan Sandy, that store-bought favorite. With a crumbly texture, lots of both finely and coarsely chopped pecans, and a buttery flavor, these cookies will have the kids and the grown-ups in a donnybrook over who controls the cookie tin.

1½ cups all-purpose flour

½ cup pecans, finely ground in food processor, plus 1 cup coarsely chopped pecans

¾ teaspoon salt

1 cup (2 sticks) unsalted butter, softened

¾ cup firmly packed light brown sugar

1 large egg

1 tablespoon vanilla extract

1. In a medium bowl, whisk together the flour, ground pecans, and salt. Set aside.

2. In the bowl of an electric mixer, using the paddle attachment, beat the butter at medium speed until creamy, about 1 minute. Gradually add the light brown sugar. Scrape down the sides of the bowl, and beat at medium-high speed for 2 minutes, until light and fluffy. Beat in the egg and vanilla extract, scraping down the sides of the bowl as necessary. Reduce the speed to low and add the flour mixture, in two additions, mixing until blended. Stir in the chopped nuts. Cover the bowl with plastic wrap and chill the dough for 1 hour.

3. Position two racks near the center of the oven and preheat the oven to 350°F.

4. Shape the dough into 1¼-inch balls and arrange on the baking sheets (the cookies will not spread, so you don't need to leave much space between them). Moisten your palm to prevent sticking, and flatten each cookie into a 2-inch disk. Bake the cookies, two sheets at a time, for 8 to 10 minutes, switching the position of the sheets halfway through baking, until they are lightly browned around the edges. Let the cookies cool for 10 minutes on the baking sheets, then transfer them to a wire rack to cool completely.

STORE IN AN AIRTIGHT CONTAINER AT ROOM TEMPERATURE FOR UP TO A WEEK, OR FREEZE FOR UP TO A MONTH.

pfeffernüsse

MAKES ABOUT 80 SMALL COOKIES

The name translates as "peppernuts," and it's right on target: these German classic are very assertive, with not only pepper, but also a brash blend of other spices and citrus, and a coating of confectioners' sugar to temper it. The dough needs to ripen for at least 8 hours before baking, so allow extra time. Warning: after a few days, these cookies will get rock hard. Storing them with an apple slice (placed in an open plastic bag) will keep them soft. Replace the apple with a fresh slice after a few days.

⅓ cup slivered almonds

2¼ cups all-purpose flour

½ teaspoon baking powder

⅛ teaspoon baking soda

¼ teaspoon salt

¼ teaspoon ground white pepper

1 teaspoon ground cinnamon

¼ teaspoon ground cloves

¼ teaspoon ground cardamom

½ cup (1 stick) unsalted butter, softened

¾ cup granulated sugar

2 large eggs

1 large egg yolk

⅓ cup finely chopped candied orange peel

1½ teaspoons finely grated lemon zest

3 tablespoons Lyle's Golden Syrup or dark corn syrup

2 tablespoons brandy

1 teaspoon vanilla extract

1 cup confectioners' sugar, sifted

make the dough

1. Place the almonds in the bowl of a food processor and process until finely ground, about 15 seconds. Transfer the nuts to a medium bowl and stir in the flour, baking powder, baking soda, salt, white pepper, cinnamon, cloves, and cardamom until blended.

2. In the bowl of an electric mixer, using the paddle attachment, beat the butter and sugar at medium speed until well blended, about 1 minute. Add the eggs and egg yolk and beat at medium-high speed until well blended and light, about 2 minutes. Add the candied orange peel, lemon zest, syrup, brandy, and vanilla extract and mix until blended. At low speed, gradually beat in the flour mixture just until blended. Cover the bowl and refrigerate the dough for at least 8 hours (or up to 3 days).

shape and bake the cookies

3. Position a rack in the upper third of the oven and preheat the oven to 350°F. Grease two baking sheets.

4. Pull off small pieces of dough and shape them into ¾-inch balls. Arrange the balls on the prepared baking sheets, spacing them 1 inch apart. Bake the cookies, one sheet at a time, for 12 to 14 minutes, until golden brown on the bottom. Transfer the cookies to a wire rack and cool completely.

5. Place the confectioners' sugar in a large sealable plastic bag. Add 4 cookies at a time to the bag and shake to coat well with the sugar.

STORE IN AN AIRTIGHT CONTAINER WITH AN APPLE SLICE (SEE HEADNOTE ABOVE) AT ROOM TEMPERATURE FOR UP TO 1 MONTH.

cocomacs

MAKES ABOUT 48 COOKIES

These little cookies carry the appealing flavor of a tropical island. Coconut and macadamia nuts combine in a crispy-on-the-outside, chewy-on-the-inside treat. The nutmeg endnote lingers as you reach for another of these unassuming cookies.

2¼ cups all-purpose flour

1 teaspoon baking soda

¼ teaspoon salt

⅓ cup solid vegetable shortening

½ cup (1 stick) unsalted butter, melted and cooled

½ cup granulated sugar

½ cup firmly packed light brown sugar

1 large egg

1 large egg yolk

⅛ teaspoon freshly grated nutmeg

¾ teaspoon vanilla extract

1½ cups sweetened flaked coconut, divided

1½ cups unsalted macadamia nuts, chopped*

***Note:** If you can only find salted nuts, place them in a sieve and rinse them under cold water. Dry them thoroughly with paper towels.

1. Position a rack in the center of the oven and preheat the oven to 350°F. Line 2 baking sheets with parchment paper or foil.
2. In a medium bowl, whisk together the flour, baking soda, and salt. Set aside.
3. In the bowl of an electric mixer, using the paddle attachment, beat the vegetable shortening, melted butter, and sugars at medium speed until well blended, about 1 minute. Beat in the egg and egg yolk, one at a time, mixing until blended and scraping down the sides of the bowl as necessary. Beat in the nutmeg, vanilla extract, and coconut. At low speed, add the flour mixture, mixing just until combined. Using a wooden spoon, stir in the macadamia nuts.
4. Pinch off pieces of the dough and shape into 1-inch balls. Arrange the balls on the prepared baking sheets, spacing them 1½ inches apart. Moisten your palm to prevent sticking, and flatten each ball slightly into a 1½-inch disk. Bake the cookies, one sheet at a time, for 10 to 12 minutes, until golden brown on the bottom. Transfer the cookies to a wire rack and cool completely.

STORE IN AN AIRTIGHT CONTAINER AT ROOM TEMPERATURE FOR UP TO A WEEK.

cookie shop chocolate chip cookies

MAKES ABOUT 60 COOKIES

Adding ground rolled oats to chocolate chip cookies became popular in the 1980s, when chocolate chip cookie stores were all the rage. The oats result in a slightly coarser texture and nuttier flavor than the standard chocolate chip cookie. This version is buttery, crisp on the outside, and soft on the inside—and loaded with chocolate chips.

2 cups all-purpose flour

1 teaspoon baking soda

1 teaspoon baking powder

1 teaspoon salt

¾ cup old-fashioned rolled oats

2½ cups (15 ounces) semisweet chocolate morsels, divided

1 cup (2 sticks) plus 2 tablespoons unsalted butter, softened

¾ cup granulated sugar

¾ cup firmly packed light brown sugar

2 teaspoons vanilla extract

2 large eggs

1. Position two racks near the center of the oven and preheat the oven to 375°F. Line two baking sheets with parchment paper.
2. Sift together the flour, baking soda, baking powder, and salt into a medium bowl. In the bowl of a food processor, combine the oats and ½ cup of the chocolate morsels and process until finely ground, about 45 seconds. Stir the oat mixture into the flour mixture and set aside.
3. In the bowl of an electric mixer, using the paddle attachment, beat the butter, sugars, and vanilla extract at medium speed until creamy, about 2 minutes. Beat in the eggs one at a time, beating well after each addition and scraping down the sides of the bowl as necessary. At low speed, add the dry ingredients, mixing just until combined. Using a wooden spoon, stir in the remaining 2 cups chocolate morsels.
4. Measure out rounded tablespoonfuls of the dough and, using wet hands, roll each portion into a ball. Arrange the balls 2 inches apart on the prepared baking sheets. Moisten your palm to prevent sticking, and flatten the balls into 1¾-inch disks.
5. Bake the cookies, two sheets at a time, for 11 to 13 minutes, just until golden brown; switch the positions of the baking sheets halfway through baking for even browning. Transfer the cookies to wire racks and cool completely.

STORE IN AN AIRTIGHT CONTAINER AT ROOM TEMPERATURE FOR UP TO A WEEK.

brandy snaps

MAKES ABOUT 32 COOKIES

This is an adaptation of a classic cookie from England. Treacle was an essential ingredient in that original formula, as was the step of rolling each wafer into a cylinder while still warm, then, when cooled, piping decorative swirls of whipped cream into the ends. I left in the treacle (Lyle's Golden Syrup is also known as light treacle) but omitted the whipped cream because it reduces the cookie's snap-like quality.

¾ cup all-purpose flour

¼ teaspoon ground ginger

¼ teaspoon ground cinnamon

Pinch of salt

½ cup (1 stick) unsalted butter, cut into tablespoons

⅓ cup Lyle's Golden Syrup or unsulphured molasses

½ cup granulated sugar

1 tablespoon brandy

1. Position two racks near the center of the oven and preheat the oven to 325°F. Lightly grease two baking sheets.
2. In a medium bowl, whisk together the flour, ginger, cinnamon, and salt; set aside.
3. In a medium-sized heavy saucepan, combine the butter, syrup or molasses, and sugar. Bring to a simmer over medium heat, stirring occasionally, until the butter is melted and the mixture is smooth. Let the mixture boil for 30 seconds. Remove the pan from the heat and stir in the flour mixture until blended. Stir in the brandy.
4. Using 2 level teaspoonfuls per cookie, drop the batter onto the prepared baking sheets, spacing the cookies at least 4 inches apart (you will be able to fit 6 cookies on a large baking sheet). Bake the cookies, two sheets at a time, for 7 to 9 minutes, until they are bubbling and lightly browned. Let the cookies cool on the baking sheets for 2 minutes.
5. Using a metal spatula, carefully transfer one cookie at a time to a work surface, laying it face down. Quickly roll the cookie around the handle of a wooden spoon. Slide the cookie off the handle and place it seam side down on a wire rack to cool completely. (If the cookies become too firm to roll, return them to the oven briefly to soften them.)

STORE IN AN AIRTIGHT CONTAINER AT ROOM TEMPERATURE, IN A DRY ENVIRONMENT, FOR UP TO 3 DAYS.

chocolate-dipped almond crescents

MAKES ABOUT 64 COOKIES

Almond crescents are sandy-textured, rich in almond flavor, and exceptionally tender. Since the classic recipe appears in many American cookbooks, I decided to refashion them a bit. These chic uptown crescents are dipped in chocolate and sprinkled with lightly toasted sliced almonds. For a simpler cookie, omit the chocolate and almonds, and dredge the cookies in superfine sugar while they're still warm.

cookies

2½ cups all-purpose flour

¼ teaspoon salt

1 cup slivered almonds

½ cup granulated sugar

1½ cups (3 sticks) unsalted butter, softened

⅛ teaspoon almond extract

garnish

6 ounces bittersweet chocolate, coarsely chopped

½ teaspoon vegetable oil

⅔ cup sliced blanched almonds, lightly toasted

make the dough

1. In a medium bowl, whisk together the flour and salt. Set aside.
2. Place the almonds and sugar in the bowl of a food processor and process until the almonds are finely ground, about 45 seconds.
3. In the bowl of an electric mixer, using the paddle attachment, beat the butter, ground almond mixture, and almond extract at medium-high speed until light in texture and color, about 2 minutes. Reduce the speed to low and mix in the flour mixture just until combined. Cover the bowl with plastic wrap and refrigerate for at least 2 hours, until firm (or up to 3 days).

shape and bake the cookies

4. Position two racks near the center of the oven and preheat the oven to 325°F.
5. Pinch off small pieces of the chilled dough and shape into ¾-inch balls. Roll each ball into a 2½-inch log (about ½ inch thick). Form each log into a crescent shape (make the ends thinner than the centers) and arrange 1 inch apart on ungreased baking sheets. Bake the cookies, two sheets at a time, for 13 to 15 minutes, switching the position of the sheets halfway through baking, until lightly golden on the bottom (but not on top). Transfer the cookies to wire racks and cool completely.

garnish the cookies

6. Line a baking sheet with parchment or waxed paper. In the top of a double boiler over barely simmering water, melt the bittersweet chocolate, stirring occasionally until smooth. Remove the pan from the heat and whisk in the vegetable oil. Place the sliced almonds in a bowl.

7. Dip about ½ inch of one end of a crescent into the chocolate, letting the excess drip off. Hold the cookie over the bowl of almonds, and sprinkle a few almonds onto the top of the chocolate-dipped end. Set the cookie on the prepared baking sheet. Repeat with the remaining cookies. Let the cookies stand at room temperature for about an hour, until set. (You can refrigerate or freeze the cookies to speed up the process.)

STORE IN AN AIRTIGHT CONTAINER AT ROOM TEMPERATURE FOR UP TO A WEEK.

Cookie Bite To soften butter quickly, place the unwrapped cold stick on a microwave-safe plate and microwave at the defrost setting (30 percent) for 30 to 40 seconds.

chocolate crackles

MAKES ABOUT 36 COOKIES

These are known in some circles as Black and Whites; I prefer the "Crackle" designation to set these apart from New York yin-yang–style Black and White Cookies (page 72). The balls of dough are coated with snowy white confectioners' sugar so that during baking, the sugar coating forms cracks that reveal the dramatically dark chocolate cookie underneath. These are very chocolaty and moist, with a subtle coffee note from the Kahlúa.

5 ounces bittersweet chocolate, coarsely chopped

1 ounce unsweetened chocolate, coarsely chopped

4 tablespoons (½ stick) unsalted butter

1½ cups all-purpose flour

¾ teaspoon baking powder

¼ teaspoon salt

2 large eggs, at room temperature

⅔ cup granulated sugar

2 tablespoons Kahlúa

1 teaspoon vanilla extract

½ cup confectioners' sugar, sifted

1. In the top of a double boiler, combine the bittersweet chocolate, unsweetened chocolate, and butter and heat over barely simmering water, stirring occasionally, until melted and smooth. Remove the pan from the heat and let the mixture cool slightly.

2. In a medium bowl, whisk together the flour, baking powder, and salt until blended; set aside.

3. In the bowl of an electric mixer, using the whisk attachment, beat the eggs with the sugar at medium-high speed until pale, about 2 minutes. Reduce the speed to low and mix in the cooled chocolate mixture. Add the Kahlúa and vanilla extract and mix until combined. Add the flour mixture and mix just until blended. Cover the bowl with plastic wrap and refrigerate for at least 1½ hours, until firm enough to shape (or up to 2 days).

4. Position a rack in the center of the oven and preheat the oven to 325°F.

5. Place the confectioners' sugar in a pie plate or shallow bowl. Shape the dough into 1¼-inch balls. Coat each ball well in the confectioners' sugar and arrange on ungreased baking sheets, spacing them at least 1½ inches apart. Bake the cookies, one sheet at a time, for 12 to 15 minutes, until their tops are cracked and their edges are set but they are still soft in the center. Let the cookies cool on the baking sheets for 5 minutes, then transfer them to a cooling rack and cool completely.

STORE IN AN AIRTIGHT CONTAINER AT ROOM TEMPERATURE FOR UP TO A WEEK.

Cookie Bite **If you have any doubt about the freshness of your baking powder, drop a pinch in some warm water. If it is fresh, it will fizz up. If not, it will sink to the bottom of the container.**

classic pine nut macaroons

MAKES **ABOUT 26 COOKIES**

These Italian cookies appear on cookie trays across the country around the holidays. Fragrant pine nuts coat a sweet, soft, and chewy almond macaroon cookie for a symphony of textures and flavors. Taste one of your pine nuts before using to make sure they are still good; they can turn rancid quickly.

One 8-ounce can almond paste

¾ cup granulated sugar

2 large egg whites, at room temperature

2 cups pine nuts

Coarse sugar for sprinkling

1. Position a rack in the center of the oven and preheat the oven to 325°F. Line two baking sheets with parchment paper or foil.
2. Break up the almond paste into large chunks and place in the bowl of a food processor, along with the sugar. Process until no large chunks remain, about 15 seconds. Add the egg whites and process until blended. Scrape down the sides of the bowl and pulse until the mixture is smooth.
3. Line a third baking sheet or a tray with foil and spread the pine nuts on it. Using wet hands, roll a piece of the dough (it will be sticky) into a 1-inch ball, roll it in the pine nuts, covering it completely, and place it on a prepared baking sheet. Repeat with the remaining dough and nuts, wetting your hands before rolling each ball of dough and arranging the cookies 1½ inches apart on the baking sheets. Sprinkle the cookies with coarse sugar.
4. Bake, one sheet at a time, for 20 to 25 minutes, until the cookies are puffed and pale golden brown. Cool the cookies completely on the baking sheets on a wire rack. Using a pancake turner, gently scrape the cookies off the paper or foil.

STORE **IN AN AIRTIGHT CONTAINER AT ROOM TEMPERATURE FOR UP TO 2 DAYS.**

Cookie Bite **Pine nuts are the seeds of certain varieties of pine tree, found hidden in the scales of pine cones. They are used frequently in Middle Eastern and Italian cooking.**

lemon-fennel pretzel cookies

MAKES 24 COOKIES

The playful pretzel shape belies a very grown-up flavor pairing here. The tantalizing flavor of anise from the fennel seeds harmonizes beautifully with lemon in the rich dough. A sprinkle of coarse sugar, applied late in the game, brings it all into balance. Not a ballpark pretzel by any means . . . if they sold pretzels at the opera, these would be a sensation.

pretzel dough

¾ teaspoon fennel seeds

½ cup (1 stick) unsalted butter, softened

⅓ cup granulated sugar

Pinch of salt

1 tablespoon finely grated lemon zest

½ teaspoon vanilla extract

1 large egg

2 large egg yolks

2 cups all-purpose flour

sugar coating

1 large egg, lightly beaten with 1 teaspoon water for egg wash

Coarse sugar for sprinkling

make the dough

1. Using a mortar and pestle, finely crush the fennel seeds. Alternatively, you can place the seeds in a small sealable plastic bag, seal the bag, and run a rolling pin over the bag, crushing the seeds as fine as possible. Set aside.

2. In the bowl of an electric mixer, using the paddle attachment, beat the butter and sugar at medium speed until well blended, about 1 minute. Beat in the salt, lemon zest, crushed fennel, and vanilla extract. Add the egg and egg yolks one at a time, beating well after each addition and scraping down the sides of the bowl as necessary. At low speed, gradually add the flour, mixing until combined.

3. Scrape the dough out onto a work surface and knead it a few times, until it is smooth. Shape the dough into a 10-inch log about 1¾ inches in diameter. Wrap the log in plastic wrap and let stand at room temperature for 1 hour (or refrigerate the dough for up to 3 days; bring to room temperature before shaping).

shape and bake the cookies

4. Position two racks near the center of the oven and preheat the oven to 350°F. Line two baking sheets with parchment paper or foil.

5. Using a large knife, cut the log into 12 equal slices. Using your hands, divide each slice in half. Roll one of the dough pieces into a ball (keep the other pieces covered loosely with plastic wrap so they don't dry out), then, on a lightly floured surface, roll the ball into a 9-inch-long rope, slightly tapering the ends. Cross the ends of the rope, about 1½ inches from each end, then

flop the resulting O-shape over the ends to form a pretzel shape (see below), and place on a prepared baking sheet. Repeat with the remaining dough, spacing the pretzels 1 inch apart.

6. Using a pastry brush, brush each pretzel with the egg wash. Brush the pretzels a second time, then sprinkle them generously with coarse sugar. Bake the cookies, two sheets at a time, for 18 to 20 minutes, switching the position of the sheets halfway through baking, until the pretzels are a light golden brown (the bottom of the pretzels should be golden brown). Transfer the cookies to a wire rack and cool completely.

STORE IN AN AIRTIGHT CONTAINER AT ROOM TEMPERATURE FOR UP TO A WEEK.

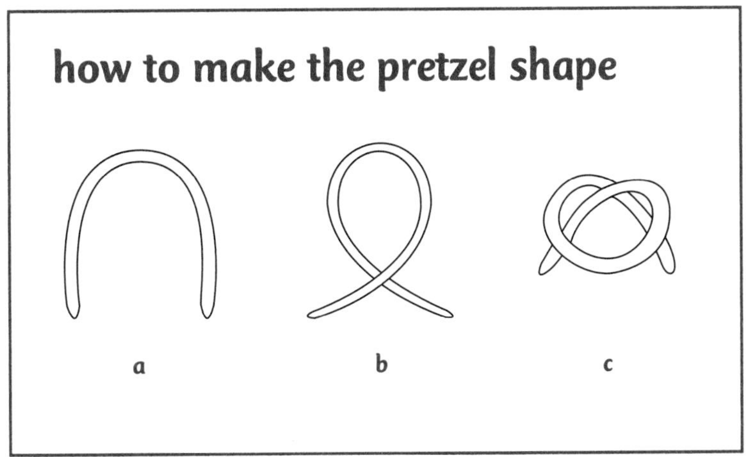

chocolate pretzel cookies

MAKES 32 COOKIES

Pretzel cookies always remind me of the buttery ones that came in the assorted Danish cookie selection we'd get as a gift around the holidays. I've added chocolate, as is my wont. According to Maida Heatter, whom I would never argue with, the classic pretzel shape was created by a German monk, and it represents arms crossed across a chest; that stern, impatient adult gesture was appropriate, as pretzels were traditionally given to children after they'd learned their prayers. This chocolaty dough is fairly easy to work with once it's been chilled. The shaped pretzels are sprinkled with coarse sugar and decadently drizzled with bittersweet chocolate. The answer to a chocoholic's prayer.

chocolate pretzel cookies

3 ounces semisweet or bittersweet chocolate, coarsely chopped

2¼ cups all-purpose flour

1 tablespoon Dutch-processed cocoa powder, sifted

¼ teaspoon salt

¾ cup (1½ sticks) unsalted butter, softened

⅔ cup granulated sugar

1 tablespoon light corn syrup

2 large eggs

glaze

3 tablespoons heavy cream

Coarse sugar for sprinkling

chocolate drizzle garnish

2½ ounces semisweet or bittersweet chocolate, coarsely chopped

make the dough

1. In a double boiler over barely simmering water, melt the chocolate, stirring occasionally until smooth. Remove the pan from the heat and let the chocolate cool.

2. In a medium bowl, whisk together the flour, cocoa powder, and salt; set aside.

3. In the bowl of an electric mixer, using the paddle attachment, beat the butter and sugar at medium speed until well blended, about 2 minutes. Add the corn syrup and beat for another minute. Add the eggs one at a time, beating well after each addition and scraping down the sides of the bowl as necessary. Add the cooled chocolate and beat until blended. At low speed, add the flour mixture, mixing just until the dough is blended and comes together. Cover the bowl and refrigerate the dough until firm enough to handle, about 1 hour (or up to 3 days).

shape and bake the cookies

4. Position a rack in the center of the oven and preheat the oven to 350°F. Lightly grease two baking sheets.

5. Turn the dough out onto a work surface and shape it into a 14-inch log. Using a large knife, cut the log into 16 equal slices. Using your hands, divide each slice in half. Roll one of the dough pieces into a ball, then on a lightly floured surface, roll the ball into a 9-inch-long rope, slightly tapering the

ends. Cross the ends of the rope about 1½ inches up from each end, then flop the resulting O-shape over the ends to form a pretzel shape (see page 173), and place on a prepared baking sheet. Repeat with the remaining dough, spacing the pretzels 1 inch apart.

6. Brush the pretzels lightly with the heavy cream and sprinkle with coarse sugar. Bake for 10 to 12 minutes, until almost firm to the touch. Transfer the pretzels to a wire rack and cool completely.

garnish the pretzels

7. Line two baking sheets with aluminum foil and arrange the cooled cookies on them.

8. In the top of a double boiler over barely simmering water, melt the chocolate, stirring occasionally until smooth. Scrape the melted chocolate into a small sealable plastic bag and seal the bag. Using scissors, snip a small hole in one of the bottom corners of the bag. Drizzle the chocolate over the cookies in diagonal lines. Refrigerate the cookies for 15 minutes, until the chocolate is set.

STORE IN AN AIRTIGHT CONTAINER AT ROOM TEMPERATURE FOR UP TO A WEEK.

ginger fortune cookies

MAKES ABOUT 42 COOKIES

This recipe was inspired by a chocolate fortune cookie recipe from Carole Harlam, a regular *Chocolatier* contributor. These cookies require a little time and patience, but they are perfect for a special gift (you might pack them in a tissue paper–lined Chinese take-out container) or Asian-themed dinner (you can customize the fortunes for each guest). The batter must be refrigerated for at least 8 hours before baking, so plan ahead. Shaping the cookies takes some practice, but once you've mastered the technique, it's pretty easy. Avoid making these cookies on a rainy or humid day—they will absorb moisture from the air and, when broken apart, will not have the snap that a fortune cookie should have. I've also included Carole's original chocolate version.

4 large egg whites

2 teaspoons water

1 teaspoon vanilla extract

½ cup (1 stick) unsalted butter, at room temperature

¼ cup honey

1 teaspoon minced peeled fresh ginger

½ teaspoon finely grated lemon zest

¼ teaspoon salt

1⅓ cups confectioners' sugar

1 cup all-purpose flour

About forty-two 5 by ½-inch strips of paper

make the batter

1. In a small bowl, whisk together the egg whites, water, and vanilla; set aside.
2. In the bowl of an electric mixer using the paddle attachment, beat the butter, honey, ginger, lemon zest, and salt at medium speed until blended. At low speed, gradually add the confectioners' sugar and beat until blended. Add the egg white mixture, beating until blended (the batter will not be smooth at this point) and scraping down the sides of the bowl with a rubber spatula as necessary. Using the rubber spatula, stir in the flour, mixing until the batter is thoroughly blended and forms a smooth paste.
3. Scrape the batter into a small container. Cover the surface of the batter with plastic wrap and refrigerate for at least 8 hours (or up to 3 days).

bake and shape the cookies

4. To make the fortunes, write a message on each strip of paper. (To customize them, write the initials of the designated person on one end of the strip, and make sure that the initials are exposed when forming the cookie.)
5. Position a rack in the center of the oven and preheat the oven to 325°F. Have a baking sheet and a muffin tin at hand.
6. Using the rim of a bowl as a guide, draw two 4-inch circles, spaced well apart, on a sheet of parchment paper the same size as the baking sheet. Place the parchment sheet upside down on the baking sheet (so that the pencil lines

are against the baking sheet). Using a small offset metal spatula, spread 1 tablespoon of the batter into a thin layer inside one of the outlines. Repeat to make another round. Bake for 7 to 8 minutes, until the cookies are browned around the edges and set. Let rest for about 30 seconds.

7. Using a metal spatula, transfer one of the cookies to a work surface. Place a fortune along the center. Quickly fold the bottom edge of the cookie over to meet the top edge, without flattening the interior of the circle. Quickly shape the cookie by pinching the bottom flat side in the center and folding it in half so that the ends meet. Place the formed cookie into one of the muffin tins for 5 minutes to hold its shape while cooling. Immediately shape the second cookie (if it has cooled too much and does not bend easily, return the baking sheet to the oven for 30 seconds to soften the cookie). Repeat with the remaining batter to form more cookies. Transfer the fortune cookies to a wire rack to cool completely.

Chocolate Fortune Cookies: Omit the ginger and lemon zest, and replace ½ cup of the flour with ½ cup Dutch-processed cocoa powder, sifted. Bake the cookies for 8 to 9 minutes, until set. Shape as directed above.

STORE IN AN AIRTIGHT CONTAINER AT ROOM TEMPERATURE, IN A DRY ENVIRONMENT, FOR UP TO 3 DAYS.

mandelbrot

MAKES ABOUT 44 COOKIES

Sometimes referred to as "Jewish biscotti," this almond cookie gets its name from two German words: *mandel* ("almond") and *brot* ("bread"). Mandelbrot are twice-baked like biscotti, and therefore very crisp—the perfect dunking cookie for coffee or tea. This version is fragrant with almonds and citrus zest and has a wonderful eggy-yellow color.

3 cups all-purpose flour

2 teaspoons baking powder

½ teaspoon salt

4 large eggs

1 cup granulated sugar

¾ cup vegetable oil

1 teaspoon vanilla extract

1 teaspoon almond extract

1 teaspoon finely grated lemon zest

1 teaspoon finely grated orange zest

1 cup slivered almonds, toasted and coarsely chopped

Coarse sugar for sprinkling

1. Position two racks near the center of the oven and preheat the oven to 325°F. Line two baking sheets with parchment paper.

2. Sift together the flour, baking powder, and salt into a medium bowl. Set aside.

3. In the bowl of an electric mixer, using the paddle attachment, beat the eggs at medium speed just until blended. Increase the speed to medium-high and gradually beat in the sugar. Continue to beat until the mixture is light in texture and color, about 2 minutes. Reduce the speed to medium and beat in the oil, extracts, and lemon and orange zest. At low speed, add the flour mixture, mixing just until combined. Using a wooden spoon, stir in the almonds. Let the dough stand at room temperature for 10 minutes to firm up slightly.

4. Turn the dough out onto a work surface (it will be soft and sticky) and divide it into quarters. Use a spoon to form a strip of batter down one of the baking sheets with one portion of the dough: the strip should be about 9 inches long and 2½ inches wide and positioned about 2 inches from a long side of the baking sheet. Spoon another strip of batter onto the baking sheet, and two more strips on the other sheet. Sprinkle the loaves generously with coarse sugar.

5. Bake the loaves for 30 to 35 minutes, switching the position of the baking sheets halfway through baking, until light golden brown. Remove from the oven and reduce the oven temperature to 300°F.

6. Transfer the warm loaves to a cutting board and, using a serrated knife, cut crosswise into ½-inch slices. Line the baking sheets with clean parchment

paper. Arrange the slices cut side down on the baking sheets and bake for another 18 to 22 minutes, switching the position of the sheets again halfway through baking, until they are crisp and just beginning to turn a very light golden color. Transfer to a wire rack and cool completely.

Pecan Date Mandelbrot: Omit the almond extract. Substitute 1½ cups pecans, toasted and coarsely chopped, for the almonds. Add 1½ cups (about 8 ounces) chopped (¼-inch pieces) pitted Medjool dates with the pecans.

STORE IN AN AIRTIGHT CONTAINER AT ROOM TEMPERATURE FOR UP TO A WEEK.

Cookie Bite Use a neutral-tasting vegetable oil, such as canola oil or a blended vegetable oil, in this recipe. Strongly flavored oils, such as olive oil or peanut oil, will mask the delicate almond and citrus flavors in this cookie.

almond anise biscotti

MAKES ABOUT 34 COOKIES

A combination of almond paste and toasted almonds gives these cookies a real almond intensity, while the anise seeds provide a fragrant backnote. Anise, with its distinctive, perfumy licorice-like flavor, is frequently paired with nuts in Italy, particularly in biscotti. Canned almond paste is a little more expensive than the type sold in tubes, but the flavor is much better.

2 cups all-purpose flour

1½ teaspoons baking powder

½ teaspoon salt

½ cup canned almond paste

4 tablespoons (½ stick) unsalted butter, softened

⅔ cup granulated sugar

2 large eggs, at room temperature

2 teaspoons vanilla extract

1 tablespoon anise seeds

1½ cups slivered almonds, toasted

1. Position two racks near the center of the oven and preheat the oven to 325°F. Line two baking sheets with parchment paper.

2. Sift together the flour, baking powder, and salt into a medium bowl. Gently whisk to combine. Set aside.

3. In the bowl of an electric mixer, using the paddle attachment, beat the almond paste and butter at medium speed until blended, about 1 minute. Gradually beat in the sugar and continue to beat until well blended, about 1 minute. Beat in the eggs one at a time, mixing well after each addition and scraping down the sides of the bowl as necessary. Beat in the vanilla extract. At low speed, add the dry ingredients, mixing just until combined. Add the anise seeds and almonds and mix for a few seconds, until blended. Using a wooden spoon, stir the dough a few times until the nuts are evenly incorporated.

4. Turn the dough out onto a lightly floured work surface and divide it in half. With lightly floured hands, gently form each piece into a 12-inch log about 1¾ inches wide. Place the two logs on one of the prepared baking sheets. Using the heel of your hand, flatten the logs to a width of 2 inches. Place the baking sheet on the upper oven rack and bake for 35 minutes, or until the logs just start to brown lightly. Set the baking sheet on a wire rack and cool for 10 minutes. Reduce the oven temperature to 300°F.

5. Carefully transfer the logs to a cutting surface. Using a serrated knife, cut the logs on the diagonal into ½-inch slices. Line the baking sheet on which you baked the logs with clean parchment paper. Arrange the slices cut side down on the two baking sheets, ½ inch apart. Bake for an additional 18 to 22 minutes, switching the position of the baking sheets halfway through baking, until the biscotti are dry and barely beginning to color around the edges. Transfer the cookies to wire racks and cool completely.

STORE IN AN AIRTIGHT CONTAINER AT ROOM TEMPERATURE FOR UP TO 2 WEEKS.

pistachio biscotti

MAKES ABOUT 40 BISCOTTI

This recipe was given to me by Carole Harlam, a good friend and colleague who has created dozens of great recipes for *Chocolatier* magazine over the years. These beautiful biscotti are studded with bright green pistachio nuts and enlivened with the addition of olive oil and the subtle flavors of cinnamon, honey, and orange. As a leavener, Carole uses bicarbonate of ammonia, or baker's ammonia; it's a professional's secret ingredient that gives cookies a wonderfully crisp texture. It must be stored in an airtight container, or it will quickly lose its potency.

2 cups bleached all-purpose flour

3/4 cup granulated sugar

3/4 teaspoon bicarbonate of ammonia (available from The Baker's Catalogue; see Sources, page 376) or 1 1/2 teaspoons baking powder

1/4 teaspoon salt

1 teaspoon ground cinnamon

1 1/2 cups shelled unsalted pistachio nuts (about 6 1/2 ounces)*

2 large eggs

1/4 cup honey

1/4 cup high-quality olive oil

Grated zest of 1 large navel orange

***Note:** If you can only find salted nuts, place them in a sieve and rinse them under cold running water. Dry them thoroughly with paper towels.*

1. Position a rack in the center of the oven and preheat the oven to 350°F. Line a large baking sheet with parchment paper.
2. In a large bowl, whisk together the flour, sugar, bicarbonate of ammonia or baking powder, salt, and cinnamon. Stir in the pistachio nuts. Set aside.
3. In a small bowl, whisk together the eggs, honey, olive oil, and orange zest. Use a fork to stir the egg mixture into the dry ingredients, stirring until the dough clumps together.
4. Turn the dough out onto a lightly floured work surface and press the dough together. Divide the dough in half. With lightly floured hands, gently shape each half into a log 13 to 14 inches long. Carefully transfer the logs to the prepared baking sheet, placing them at least 3 inches apart. Bake for 25 to 30 minutes, until the logs are well risen and firm. Set the baking sheet on a wire rack and cool the logs completely. Reduce the oven temperature to 325°F.
5. Peel away the parchment paper and transfer the logs to a cutting surface. Using a serrated knife, cut the logs on the diagonal into 1/2-inch slices. Line the baking sheet with clean parchment paper and place the biscotti, standing up, on the baking sheet.
6. Bake the biscotti for 10 to 15 minutes, until dry. Set the baking sheet on a wire rack and allow the biscotti to cool completely.

STORE IN AN AIRTIGHT CONTAINER AT ROOM TEMPERATURE FOR UP TO 2 WEEKS.

hazelnut biscotti

MAKES ABOUT 40 BISCOTTI

The hazelnut is the national nut of Italy, so it's only natural to add it to the Italian national cookie, biscotti. The result is a sweet, intensely nutty cookie that begs to be enjoyed with coffee or espresso. To ensure this recipe's success, make sure your hazelnuts are fresh; because of their high oil content, they can easily turn rancid.

1¾ cups all-purpose flour

1 teaspoon baking powder

¼ teaspoon salt

5 tablespoons unsalted butter, softened

½ cup granulated sugar

½ cup firmly packed light brown sugar

2 large eggs

1 teaspoon vanilla extract

½ teaspoon almond extract

1⅓ cups hazelnuts, toasted, skinned, and coarsely chopped

Coarse sugar for sprinkling

1. Position two racks near the center of the oven and preheat the oven to 325°F. Line two baking sheets with parchment paper.
2. In a medium bowl, whisk together the flour, baking powder, and salt. Set aside.
3. In the bowl of an electric mixer, using the paddle attachment, beat the butter, granulated sugar, and brown sugar at medium speed until well blended, about 1 minute. Beat in the eggs one at a time, beating well after each addition and scraping down the sides of the bowl as necessary. Beat in the vanilla and almond extracts. At low speed, add the flour mixture, mixing just until blended. Add the hazelnuts and mix until combined.
4. Scrape the dough out onto a floured work surface and gather it into a disk (the dough will be quite sticky). Divide the dough in half. Sprinkle the surface with more flour and shape each piece into a 12-inch log. Transfer the logs to one of the prepared baking sheets, spacing them about 3 inches apart (the logs will spread). With the heel of your hand, flatten the logs slightly, until they are 2 inches wide. Brush each log lightly with water and sprinkle generously with coarse sugar. Place the baking sheet on the upper oven rack and bake for 30 to 35 minutes, until the logs just start to brown lightly. Set the baking sheet on a wire rack and cool for 10 minutes. Reduce the oven temperature to 300°F.
5. Slide a pancake turner under each log to loosen it from the parchment paper. Carefully transfer the logs to a cutting surface. Line the baking sheet with clean parchment paper. Using a serrated knife, cut the logs on the diagonal into ½-inch slices. Arrange the slices cut side down and ½ inch apart on the two baking sheets. Bake for an additional 18 to 22 minutes, switching the position of the baking sheets halfway through baking, until the biscotti are dry and beginning to color around the edges. Transfer the cookies to wire racks and cool completely.

STORE IN AN AIRTIGHT CONTAINER AT ROOM TEMPERATURE FOR UP TO A WEEK.

triple-ginger pecan biscotti

MAKES **ABOUT 40 BISCOTTI**

These are the gingery-est ginger biscotti you'll ever find, and one of my favorite recipes in the book. I combined ground ginger, fresh ginger, and crystallized ginger in a buttery biscotti dough studded with lots of pecans; a pinch of freshly ground black pepper really brings the ginger flavor to life.

1¾ cups all-purpose flour

1 teaspoon baking powder

¾ teaspoon ground ginger

¼ teaspoon salt

Pinch of freshly ground black pepper

5 tablespoons unsalted butter, softened

1 cup granulated sugar

2 large eggs

1 tablespoon peeled and finely grated fresh ginger

1 teaspoon vanilla extract

⅓ cup chopped crystallized ginger

1 cup pecans

1. Position two racks near the center of the oven and preheat the oven to 325°F. Line two baking sheets with parchment paper.
2. In a medium bowl, whisk together the flour, baking powder, ground ginger, salt, and pepper. Set aside.
3. In the bowl of an electric mixer, using the paddle attachment, beat the butter and sugar at medium speed until well blended, about 1 minute. Beat in the eggs one at a time, beating well after each addition and scraping down the sides of the bowl as necessary. Beat in the fresh ginger and vanilla extract. At low speed, add the flour mixture, mixing just until blended. Stir in the crystallized ginger and pecans and mix until combined.
4. Scrape the dough out onto a floured work surface and gather it into a disk (the dough will be quite sticky). Divide the dough in half. Sprinkle the surface with more flour and shape each piece into a 12-inch log. Transfer the logs to one of the prepared baking sheets, spacing them about 3 inches apart (the logs will spread). With the heel of your hand, flatten the logs slightly, until they are 2 inches wide. Place the baking sheet on the upper oven racks and bake for 35 minutes, or until the logs just start to brown lightly. Set the baking sheet on a wire rack and cool for 10 minutes. Reduce the oven temperature to 300°F.
5. Slide a pancake turner under each log to loosen it from the parchment paper. Carefully transfer the logs to a cutting surface. Line the baking sheet with clean parchment paper. Using a serrated knife, cut the logs on the diagonal into ½-inch slices. Arrange the slices cut side down and ½ inch apart on the two baking sheets. Bake for an additional 18 to 22 minutes, switching the position of the baking sheets halfway through baking, until the biscotti are dry and barely beginning to color around the edges. Transfer the cookies to wire racks and cool completely.

STORE **IN AN AIRTIGHT CONTAINER AT ROOM TEMPERATURE FOR UP TO A WEEK.**

caramelized pecan–orange biscotti

MAKES ABOUT 54 BISCOTTI

This recipe is from Gerhard Weitzel, a talented Vancouver pastry chef who owned a well-known patisserie there for many years. As soon as I tasted these unusual biscotti, I asked Gerhard for the recipe, and he graciously complied. Caramelized pecans are a favorite among pastry chefs because they deliver so much flavor and crunch. Gerhard adds lots of orange zest and hints of anise and cinnamon for a flavor combination that will delight biscotti lovers.

pecan praline

1 cup granulated sugar

¼ cup water

1 cup (about 4 ounces) pecan halves

biscotti

3 cups all-purpose flour

1 cup granulated sugar

2½ teaspoons baking powder

1 teaspoon ground anise

1 teaspoon ground cinnamon

6 tablespoons olive oil

4 large eggs

1 large egg yolk

Finely grated zest of 4 oranges (about 2½ tablespoons)

make the pecan praline

1. Lightly brush a baking sheet with vegetable oil. In a medium-sized heavy saucepan, combine the sugar and water and cook over medium heat, stirring constantly, until the sugar dissolves. Increase the heat to high and bring the syrup to a boil. Cook without stirring, occasionally brushing down the sides of the pan with a wet pastry brush, until the syrup turns a dark caramel. Immediately add the pecans and stir to coat with the caramel. Quickly turn the mixture out onto the oiled baking sheet. Cool for 20 minutes, or until hardened.

2. Transfer the praline to a cutting board and, using a large knife, finely chop it. Set aside.

make and bake the biscotti

3. Position two racks near the center of the oven and preheat the oven to 350°F. Line two baking sheets with parchment paper.

4. In the bowl of an electric mixer, using the paddle attachment, beat the flour, sugar, baking powder, anise, and cinnamon on low speed until combined. In a large glass measuring cup, gently whisk together the olive oil, eggs, yolk, and orange zest. Add this mixture all at once to the dry ingredients and mix, still on low speed, just until combined; do not overmix. Add the chopped pecan praline and mix for a few seconds, until blended.

5. Scrape the dough out onto a floured work surface and divide it into thirds. Shape each portion into a 12-inch-long log. Transfer the logs to one of the prepared baking sheets, spacing them about 3 inches apart (the logs will

spread). With the heel of your hand, flatten the logs slightly, until they are about 2 inches wide. Place the baking sheet on the upper oven rack and bake for about 25 minutes, or until the dough is set. Set the baking sheet on a wire rack and cool for 10 minutes. Reduce the oven temperature to 325°F.

6. Slide a pancake turner under each log to loosen it from the parchment paper. Carefully transfer the logs to a cutting surface. Line the baking sheet with clean parchment paper. Using a serrated knife, cut the logs on the diagonal into ½-inch slices. Arrange the slices cut side down and ½ inch apart on the two baking sheets and bake for about 15 minutes, or until dry and crisp. Transfer the biscotti to a wire rack and cool completely.

Cranberry Orange Biscotti: Substitute ⅔ cup dried cranberries, coarsely chopped, for the pecan praline.

STORE IN AN AIRTIGHT CONTAINER AT ROOM TEMPERATURE FOR UP TO 2 WEEKS.

chocolate almond biscotti

MAKES ABOUT 40 BISCOTTI

This cookie has the crisp, crunchy, rustic texture of biscotti, but the addition of chocolate makes it richer than most. It is also more handsome than most biscotti, with lots of toasted almonds creating a nice color contrast to the dark dough. These are irresistible crumbled over ice cream.

One 3.5-ounce bar bittersweet chocolate, coarsely chopped

1¾ cups all-purpose flour

1 teaspoon baking powder

¼ teaspoon salt

¾ cup Dutch-processed cocoa powder

9 tablespoons unsalted butter, softened

1¼ cups granulated sugar

2 large eggs

1 teaspoon vanilla extract

1 cup miniature semisweet chocolate morsels

1 cup blanched whole almonds, toasted and coarsely chopped

Coarse sugar for sprinkling

1. Position two racks near the center of the oven and preheat the oven to 325°F. Line two baking sheets with parchment paper.
2. In the top of a double boiler over barely simmering water, melt the chocolate, stirring occasionally until smooth. Set the chocolate aside to cool.
3. In a medium bowl, whisk together the flour, baking powder, and salt. Sift the cocoa powder over the dry ingredients and whisk to combine. Set aside.
4. In the bowl of an electric mixer, using the paddle attachment, beat the butter and sugar at medium speed until well blended, about 1 minute. Beat in the eggs one at a time, beating well after each addition and scraping down the sides of the bowl as necessary. Beat in the cooled melted chocolate and the vanilla extract. At low speed, add the flour mixture, mixing just until blended. Stir in the chocolate morsels and almonds and mix until combined.
5. Scrape the dough out onto a work surface and gather it into a disk. Divide the dough in half. Sprinkle the surface lightly with flour and shape each piece into a 12-inch log. Transfer the logs to one of the prepared baking sheets, spacing them about 3 inches apart (the logs will spread slightly). With the heel of your hand, flatten the logs slightly, until they are 2 inches wide. Sprinkle the logs with coarse sugar. Place the baking sheet on the upper oven rack and bake for 40 minutes, or until the logs spring back when lightly touched. Set the baking sheet on a wire rack and cool for 20 minutes. Reduce the oven temperature to 300°F.
6. Carefully transfer the logs to a cutting surface. Line the baking sheet with clean parchment paper. Using a serrated knife, cut the logs on the diagonal into ½-inch slices. Arrange the slices cut side down and ½ inch apart on the two baking sheets. Bake for an additional 15 to 20 minutes, switching the position of the baking sheets halfway through baking, until the biscotti are dry. Transfer the biscotti to wire racks and cool completely.

STORE IN AN AIRTIGHT CONTAINER AT ROOM TEMPERATURE FOR UP TO A WEEK.

double-chocolate pecan biscotti

MAKES ABOUT 40 BISCOTTI

This recipe is from Irina Brandler, who assisted in researching this book. Irina is a talented caterer and baker who has a bakery on City Island in New York. Her biscotti are very chocolaty and not too sweet, with great interplay between the pecan and the slight note of anise. These are great with coffee.

1½ cups all-purpose flour

½ cup Dutch-processed cocoa powder, preferably Valrhona

1½ teaspoons baking powder

¼ teaspoon salt

½ cup (1 stick) unsalted butter, softened

1 cup granulated sugar

2 large eggs

1½ teaspoons vanilla extract

1 tablespoon Pernod (anise liqueur) (optional)

¾ cup pecans

3 ounces milk chocolate, finely chopped

1 large egg, beaten with 1 teaspoon water for egg wash

Coarse sugar for sprinkling

1. Position two racks near the center of the oven and preheat the oven to 350°F. Line two baking sheets with parchment paper or foil.
2. Sift together the flour, cocoa powder, baking powder, and salt into a medium bowl; whisk to combine. Set aside.
3. In the bowl of an electric mixer, using the paddle attachment, beat the butter and sugar at medium speed until well blended, about 1 minute. Beat in the eggs one at a time, beating well after each addition and scraping down the sides of the bowl as necessary. Beat in the vanilla extract and Pernod, if using. Reduce the speed to low and add the flour mixture one-third at a time, mixing just until blended. Stir in the pecans and milk chocolate.
4. Scrape the dough out onto a lightly floured work surface and gather it into a disk (it will be sticky). Divide the dough in half. Sprinkle the work surface lightly with more flour and shape each piece into a 12-inch log. Transfer the logs to one of the prepared baking sheets, spacing them about 3 inches apart (the logs will spread slightly). With the heel of your hand, flatten the logs slightly, until they are 1¾ inches wide. Brush the top of each log with the egg wash and sprinkle with coarse sugar. Place the baking sheet on the upper oven rack and bake for 25 to 30 minutes, until the logs spring back when lightly touched. Set the baking sheet on a wire rack and cool for 20 minutes. Reduce the oven temperature to 250°F.
5. Slide a pancake turner under each log to loosen it from the parchment paper. Carefully transfer the logs to a cutting surface. Line the baking sheet with clean parchment paper or foil. Using a serrated knife, cut the logs on the diagonal into ½-inch slices. Arrange the slices cut side down and ½ inch apart on the two baking sheets. Bake for an additional 20 to 25 minutes, switching the position of the baking sheets halfway through baking, until the biscotti are dry. Transfer the biscotti to wire racks and cool completely.

STORE IN AN AIRTIGHT CONTAINER AT ROOM TEMPERATURE FOR UP TO A WEEK.

molasses spice cookies

MAKES ABOUT 46 COOKIES

These thin, crisp cookies dipped in sugar are classic: simple, but with deep flavor, very much like gingerbread. They're great for baking at holiday time, when you want the house to fill with the scent of warm spices.

2 cups all-purpose flour

1 teaspoon baking soda

1½ teaspoons ground cinnamon

¼ teaspoon ground cloves

¼ teaspoon ground cardamom

¾ cup (1½ sticks) unsalted butter, softened

½ cup granulated sugar

½ cup firmly packed dark brown sugar

¼ cup unsulphured (mild) molasses

1 tablespoon finely minced peeled ginger

1 large egg

1½ teaspoons vanilla extract

⅓ cup coarse or granulated sugar, for coating

1. Sift together the flour, baking soda, cinnamon, cloves, and cardamom into a medium bowl. Whisk to combine, and set aside.
2. In the bowl of an electric mixer, using the paddle attachment, beat the butter and both sugars at medium-high speed until light and creamy, about 2 minutes. Beat in the molasses and ginger, mixing until blended. Add the egg and vanilla, mixing until well blended and scraping down the sides of the bowl as necessary. At low speed, mix in the dry ingredients one-third at a time. Cover the bowl with plastic wrap and refrigerate the dough for 30 minutes, until it is firm enough to shape.
3. Position a rack in the center of the oven and preheat the oven to 350°F. Line two baking sheets with parchment paper or foil.
4. Place the coarse or granulated sugar in a small bowl. Shape the dough into 1-inch balls. Dip the top of each ball in the sugar, coating one half of it, and arrange the balls sugared side up on the prepared baking sheets, spacing them 2 inches apart. Bake the cookies, one sheet at a time, for 12 to 15 minutes, until they are puffed and barely darker around the edges; don't overbake, or the cookies will be too hard when cool. Transfer the cookies to wire racks and cool completely.

STORE IN AN AIRTIGHT CONTAINER AT ROOM TEMPERATURE FOR UP TO 3 WEEKS.

piped and molded cookies

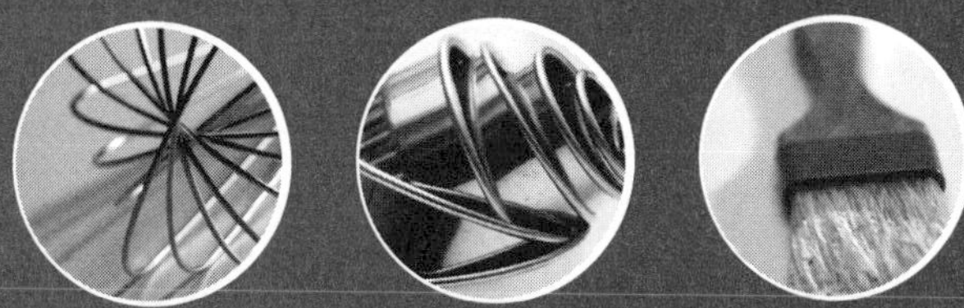

• cats' tongues • amaretti • classic spritz cookies • chocolate-dipped peanut butter swirls • macadamia kisses • chocolate-dipped meringue kisses • wellingtons • chocolate meringue swirls • vanilla-scented shortbread • brown sugar pecan shortbread • lime cornmeal shortbread • glazed lemon ginger shortbread wedges • chocolate espresso shortbread • vanilla honey tuiles • pirouettes • two-tone tuile corkscrews • financiers • almond raspberry tea cakes • coconut tea cakes • chocolate almond gems • chocolate toffee brownie bites • madeleines • orange almond madeleines • bittersweet chocolate madeleines •

The cookies in this chapter are formed by piping the dough out through a pastry bag or by placing the dough into molds before baking. These delicate, pretty cookies are always eagerly anticipated and they are expected at certain times of the year. There are classics that any baker should have in her or his repertoire, such as popular and easy cookies like the meringues and spritz cookies as well as traditional French cookies like the madeleines, financiers, and langues de chat (cats' tongues). You'll also find some tantalizing cookies that may be unfamiliar to you—Wellingtons and Amaretti, for example. This chapter includes a number of mini-cakes too—Coconut Tea Cakes, Chocolate Almond Gems—which always add variety and surprise to cookie trays. In addition, there are cookies that you will want to have if you're assembling fancy desserts—several types of tuiles, and simple, graceful Pirouettes. Shortbread, which is generally molded in a cake or tart pan before baking, makes a starring appearance in this chapter.

Follow the directions in each recipe for information on refrigerating the dough (or not). If you are piping out spritz cookies, for example, you don't want the dough to be too stiff, or it'll resist being pushed through your pastry bag.

cats' tongues

MAKES **ABOUT 60 COOKIES**

These classic cookies are popular in Spain and in France, where they are called langues de chat, because of their resemblance to a cat's tongue. They're light and delicate, with vanilla as the strongest flavor note. The batter is simple, with few ingredients, but the cookies can be temperamental. Overmixing the batter after adding the flour will make them tough, piping the thin batter into perfect little tongues takes a little practice, and overbaking by even a minute will make them too crisp and brown. Don't let their cat-like stubbornness discourage you, though: these simple, elegant cookies are perfect with a cup of Darjeeling tea, and despite their fragility, they really stand up to a bowl of ice cream.

½ cup (1 stick) unsalted butter, softened

¾ cup granulated sugar

¼ teaspoon salt

4 large egg whites, at room temperature, lightly beaten

1 teaspoon vanilla extract

¾ cup all-purpose flour, sifted

special equipment

Large pastry bag fitted with a 5/16-inch plain tip (such as Ateco #3)

1. Position a rack in the center of the oven and preheat the oven to 375°F. Line two baking sheets with parchment paper.

2. In the bowl of an electric mixer, using the paddle attachment, beat the butter, sugar, and salt at medium speed until well blended and light, about 1 minute. Reduce the speed to low and add the egg whites, beating until well blended and scraping down the sides of the bowl as needed. Beat in the vanilla extract. Sift the flour over the batter, and gently fold it in until well blended.

3. Scrape the batter into a large pastry bag fitted with a 5/16-inch plain tip. Pipe the batter onto the prepared sheets in 2½-inch-long fingers, spacing the cookies at least 2 inches apart (they will spread). Bake the cookies, one sheet at a time, for 7 to 10 minutes, until golden brown around the edges. Cool the cookies on the baking sheets for 10 minutes, then carefully transfer them to a wire rack and cool completely (the cookies will stick a bit to the paper).

STORE **IN AN AIRTIGHT CONTAINER AT ROOM TEMPERATURE FOR UP TO 5 DAYS.**

amaretti

MAKES ABOUT 40 COOKIES

These are Italian-style macaroons. You might think that the name refers to *amore*, "love," but in fact, translated literally, *amaretti* means "little bitter things," a reference to the bitter almonds classically used to make them. Almond paste can be purchased in tubes or in cans; use the canned, which has more flavor and a better texture. The result is sublime almond flavor with a memorable crunchy-chewy texture.

One 8-ounce can almond paste

2/3 cup granulated sugar

2 large egg whites, at room temperature

Coarse sugar for sprinkling

special equipment

Large pastry bag fitted with a 3/8-inch plain tip (such as Ateco #4)

1. Position a rack in the center of the oven and preheat the oven to 325°F. Line two baking sheets with parchment paper.
2. Crumble the almond paste into the bowl of an electric mixer and, using the paddle attachment, beat at low speed for about 30 seconds. Gradually add the sugar and mix until blended (the mixture will be very crumbly). Add the egg whites in four additions, mixing well after each addition. Increase the speed to medium and beat until smooth, 2 to 3 minutes.
3. Scrape the batter into a large pastry bag fitted with a 3/8-inch plain tip. Pipe the batter onto the prepared baking sheets in 1-inch mounds, spacing them about 1 inch apart. Pour some water into a small bowl. Dip a finger into the water and smooth the top of each cookie, eliminating the peak; redip your finger in the water as necessary. Sprinkle the cookies with coarse sugar and bake, one sheet at a time, for 18 to 22 minutes, until they are golden brown and their surfaces are cracked.
4. Carefully turn each sheet of parchment paper, with the cookies sticking to it, upside down on a work surface and brush it lightly with cold water, without splashing the cookies. Turn the sheets right side up and let stand until you are able to pull the cookies easily off the paper, about 1 minute. If they stick, brush the paper again. Cool the cookies completely on a wire rack.

STORE IN AN AIRTIGHT CONTAINER AT ROOM TEMPERATURE FOR UP TO 2 DAYS, BUT THESE ARE BEST THE DAY THEY ARE MADE.

classic spritz cookies

MAKES 36 TO 48 COOKIES, DEPENDING ON SHAPE

During the holidays, spritz cookies are found on every cookie tray in Scandinavia. They have a subtle vanilla-almond flavor and ultrabuttery texture. They can be piped into different shapes and dressed up with drizzled chocolate, chopped nuts, raspberry jam, or even sprinkles. The dough keeps very well in the freezer up to 2 months, making these a good treat to whip up for unexpected guests.

cookies

2⅓ cups all-purpose flour

¼ teaspoon salt

1 cup (2 sticks) unsalted butter, softened

1 cup confectioners' sugar

1 large egg

2 teaspoons vanilla extract

¼ teaspoon almond extract

optional garnish

⅓ cup finely chopped slivered almonds

special equipment

Large pastry bag fitted with a medium closed star tip (such as Ateco #5)

1. Position a rack in the center of the oven and preheat the oven to 400°F. Grease two baking sheets.
2. In a medium bowl, whisk together the flour and salt; set aside.
3. In the bowl of an electric mixer, using the paddle attachment, beat the butter at medium speed until creamy, about 30 seconds. Gradually beat in the confectioners' sugar. Beat in the egg, vanilla, and almond extract. Scrape down the sides of the bowl and beat for another 30 seconds. At low speed, add the flour mixture in three additions, mixing just until blended.
4. Scrape the dough into a large pastry bag fitted with a medium closed star tip, and follow the directions below for piping various shapes. Sprinkle the cookies with the almonds, if desired. Bake the cookies, one sheet at a time, for 7 to 10 minutes, until they are just golden brown around the edges. Transfer the cookies to a wire rack and cool completely.

STORE IN AN AIRTIGHT CONTAINER AT ROOM TEMPERATURE FOR UP TO A WEEK.

spritz cookie shapes

fingers Pipe 2½-inch-long fingers about 2 inches apart onto the baking sheets.

crescents Pipe 2-inch crescent shapes about 2 inches apart onto the baking sheets.

swirls Pipe 1¼-inch swirled rosettes about 2 inches apart onto the baking sheets.

christmas wreaths Pipe 1¾-inch wreaths about 2 inches apart onto the baking sheets.

s shapes Pipe 1¾-inch-long S shapes about 2 inches apart onto the baking sheets.

chocolate-dipped peanut butter swirls

MAKES ABOUT 46 COOKIES

These cookies require some piping ability. If you're strictly a simple-rosette-and-even-that's-pushing-it pastry bag piper, pipe out 2¼-inch-long fingers of dough instead of the trickier S shapes. Whatever the shape, these are buttery, tender cookies with great peanut butter flavor. I added some chocolate for the classic flavor marriage and some peanuts for more texture.

peanut butter cookies

⅓ cup unsalted dry-roasted peanuts

2¼ cups all-purpose flour, divided

1 cup (2 sticks) unsalted butter, softened

¼ cup creamy peanut butter

¾ cup firmly packed light brown sugar

½ cup confectioners' sugar

1 large egg

½ teaspoon salt

1 tablespoon vanilla extract

garnish

4 ounces bittersweet chocolate, coarsely chopped

1 teaspoon vegetable oil

¼ cup unsalted dry-roasted peanuts, finely chopped

special equipment

Large pastry bag fitted with a medium closed star tip (such as Ateco #5)

make the cookies

1. Position a rack in the center of the oven and preheat the oven to 375°F. Grease two baking sheets.

2. Place the peanuts and 1 cup of the flour in the bowl of a food processor and process until the nuts are finely ground, about 30 seconds. Transfer the mixture to a medium bowl. Add the remaining 1¼ cups flour and stir to combine; set aside.

3. In the bowl of an electric mixer, using the paddle attachment, beat the butter and peanut butter at medium speed until creamy, about 30 seconds. Gradually beat in the light brown and confectioners' sugar. Beat in the egg, salt, and vanilla extract. Scrape down the sides of the bowl and beat for another 30 seconds. At low speed, add the flour mixture in three additions, mixing just until blended.

4. Scrape one-third of the dough at a time (it's easier to work with a small amount of dough) into a large pastry bag fitted with a medium closed star tip. Pipe 2¼-inch-long tight S shapes of dough onto the prepared baking sheets, spacing them about 1½ inches apart. The dough will be somewhat difficult to pipe at first, but it will soften up as your hands warm it. (If a piece of peanut clogs the tip during piping, use a knife to gently open up the prongs of the tip slightly.) Bake the cookies, one sheet at a time, for 8 to 10 minutes, until golden brown around the edges. Transfer the cookies to a wire rack and cool completely.

garnish the cookies

5. In the top of a double boiler over barely simmering water, melt the chocolate, stirring occasionally until smooth. Remove the pan from the heat and whisk in the vegetable oil. Line a baking sheet with parchment or waxed paper.

6. Dip ½ inch of the top side of one end of each cookie into the chocolate, and place them on the paper-lined sheet. Sprinkle the peanuts over the chocolate. Refrigerate the cookies for about 10 minutes, until the chocolate is set.

STORE IN AN AIRTIGHT CONTAINER AT ROOM TEMPERATURE FOR UP TO 5 DAYS.

macadamia kisses

MAKES **ABOUT 60 COOKIES**

Macadamia nuts are perhaps the most indulgent of nuts, in terms of richness, opulence, and voluptuousness of flavor. They are certainly the priciest. But these cookies are worth it. Infused with the flavor and fragrance of macadamia, they are crunchy on the outside and soft and chewy on the inside.

¾ cup unsalted macadamia nuts*

2 tablespoons confectioners' sugar

1¼ cups granulated sugar, divided

¼ cup water

4 large egg whites, at room temperature

½ teaspoon cream of tartar

Pinch of salt

Confectioners' sugar for dusting

special equipment

Candy thermometer

Large pastry bag fitted with a large plain tip (such as Ateco #6)

***Note:** If you can only find salted nuts, place them in a sieve and rinse them under cold running water. Dry the nuts thoroughly with paper towels.

1. Position two racks near the center of the oven and preheat to 250°F. Line two baking sheets with parchment paper.

2. Place the macadamia nuts and confectioners' sugar in the bowl of a food processor and process until the nuts are finely chopped, about 20 seconds (do not overprocess the nuts, or they will become oily and turn to a paste). Set aside.

3. In a small heavy saucepan, combine 1 cup of the granulated sugar and the water and cook over medium heat, stirring constantly, until the sugar dissolves. Stop stirring, and reduce the heat to low.

4. In the bowl of an electric mixer, using the whisk attachment, beat the egg whites at medium speed until foamy. Add the cream of tartar and salt and beat at high speed until soft peaks form. Gradually add the remaining ¼ cup sugar and beat until stiff peaks form.

5. Attach a candy thermometer to the side of the pan. Increase the heat under the saucepan to high and boil the sugar syrup until it registers 248°F (firm ball stage). With the mixer off, add about ¼ cup of the hot syrup to the egg whites, then beat at medium speed until blended, about 5 seconds. Continue adding the hot syrup ¼ cup at a time, mixing well after each addition. Remove the bowl from the mixer stand and fold in ½ cup of the ground macadamia nuts (the meringue will still be hot).

6. Scrape the meringue into a large pastry bag fitted with a large plain tip. Pipe the meringue onto the prepared baking sheets, forming kisses about 1½ inches wide at the base and spacing them ¾ inch apart. (The remaining meringue will hold up enough to be piped after the first batch of meringues has baked.) Sprinkle the kisses with some of the remaining macadamia nuts.

Bake the meringues, two sheets at a time, for about 40 to 50 minutes, or until dry on the outside but still soft inside. Transfer the cookies to a wire rack and cool completely. Dust the meringues lightly with sifted confectioners' sugar before serving.

STORE IN AN AIRTIGHT CONTAINER IN A COOL, DRY PLACE FOR UP TO A WEEK.

Cookie Bite **Buttery-rich and slightly sweet, macadamia nuts grow on a tree native to Australia. Today Hawaii is the biggest producer; macadamias are also grown in California. Their shells are extremely hard, which is why they are always sold shelled.**

chocolate-dipped meringue kisses

MAKES **ABOUT 44 COOKIES**

Light and crisp, these creamy-white meringue cookies deliver a wonderful sweetness that marries very nicely, flavor- and texture-wise, with their chocolate base. Make them on a low-humidity day, or they will be sticky.

meringue kisses

3 large egg whites, at room temperature

¼ teaspoon cream of tartar

Pinch of salt

¾ cup superfine sugar

½ teaspoon vanilla extract

chocolate garnish

4 ounces bittersweet chocolate, coarsely chopped

1 teaspoon vegetable oil

special equipment

Large pastry bag fitted with a medium star tip (such as Ateco #5)

make the meringue kisses

1. Position two racks near the center of the oven and preheat the oven to 200°F. Line two baking sheets with parchment paper or foil.

2. In the bowl of an electric mixer, using the whisk attachment, beat the egg whites at medium-low speed until frothy. Add the cream of tartar and salt and, gradually increasing the speed to medium-high, beat until soft peaks form. Add the sugar 1 tablespoon at a time, and continue beating until the whites form stiff, shiny peaks. Beat in the vanilla extract.

3. Scrape about half of the meringue into a large pastry bag fitted with a medium star tip. Pipe the meringue into 1½-inch-diameter rosettes on the prepared baking sheets, spacing them about ½ inch apart. Repeat with the remaining meringue. Bake the meringues for 1½ to 2 hours, or until they are firm to the touch. Set the baking sheets on wire racks and cool completely.

garnish the cookies

4. Line a baking sheet with parchment paper or foil. In the top of a double boiler over barely simmering water, melt the chocolate, stirring occasionally until smooth. Remove from the heat and stir in the vegetable oil. Dip the bottom of each meringue kiss into the melted chocolate, letting the excess drip off, and set on the lined sheet. Refrigerate for 15 to 20 minutes (but no longer), or freeze for 10 minutes, until the chocolate is set.

STORE **IN AN AIRTIGHT CONTAINER IN A COOL, DRY PLACE FOR UP TO 3 DAYS.**

> **Cookie Bite** **Cream of tartar, or potassium tartrate, is commonly used to stabilize egg whites so that they whip up well and do not separate or become clumpy.**

wellingtons

MAKES ABOUT 32 COOKIES

This recipe was given to me by Ann Amernick, owner of Amernick, a patisserie in Washington, D.C., that sells elegant, European-style cakes and pastries, and co-owner and pastry chef of Palena, a chic restaurant that caters to the Washington elite. Ann got the recipe from a Dutch baker, Antoon Van Tol, whose shop she bought. It's an old Northern European recipe, and it's very unusual. These cookies start off looking like disks of white chocolate topped with nuts, but when baked, they puff up beautifully and turn into fragrant macaroons with cracked tops. The cookies need to dry at room temperature for 8 hours before baking, so plan accordingly.

¾ cup canned almond paste

1¼ cups granulated sugar

2 teaspoons finely grated lemon zest

3 large egg whites

½ cup sliced blanched almonds

special equipment

Large pastry bag fitted with a ½-inch plain tip (such as Ateco #6)

1. Line two baking sheets with parchment paper or foil.
2. In the bowl of an electric mixer, using the paddle attachment combine the almond paste, sugar, and lemon zest at low speed. Increase the speed to medium and beat until the almond paste is in small, lentil-sized particles and no large lumps remain. Reduce the speed to low and add the egg whites in 3 additions, mixing well and scraping down the sides of the bowl as necessary. Increase the speed to medium and beat until the batter is smooth, about 2 minutes.
3. Scrape the batter into a large pastry bag fitted with a ½-inch plain tip. Pipe the batter onto the prepared baking sheets in 1½-inch mounds, spacing them about 1 inch apart. Sprinkle the sliced almonds over the cookies, pressing them down lightly so that they stick. Set the cookies aside to dry at room temperature, uncovered, for 8 hours (or up to 24 hours).
4. Position two racks near the center of the oven and preheat the oven to 325°F.
5. Bake the cookies for 18 to 20 minutes, switching the position of the sheets halfway through baking, until they are puffed and lightly browned. Let the cookies cool on the baking sheets for 2 minutes. Using a pancake turner, scrape the cookies off the baking sheets (they tend to stick), cleaning the spatula occasionally, and cool completely on a wire rack.

STORE IN AN AIRTIGHT CONTAINER IN A COOL, DRY PLACE FOR UP TO 3 DAYS.

chocolate meringue swirls

MAKES ABOUT 62 COOKIES

Sold in pastry shops throughout Europe, these sweet nothings are crisp on the outside and soft and chewy on the inside—just the very lightest kiss of chocolate on your tongue. Seek out bittersweet chocolate with 70 percent cocoa solids—its intensity is strong enough to stand up to all that egg white.

One 3½-ounce bar Lindt Excellence 70% Cocoa dark chocolate, coarsely chopped

1¼ cups granulated sugar, divided

¼ cup water

4 large egg whites, at room temperature

½ teaspoon cream of tartar

Pinch of salt

Confectioners' sugar for dusting (optional)

special equipment

Candy thermometer

Large pastry bag fitted with a large star tip (such as Ateco #6)

1. Position two racks near the center of the oven and preheat the oven to 250°F. Line two large baking sheets with parchment paper.
2. In the top of a double boiler over barely simmering water, melt the chocolate, stirring occasionally until smooth. Remove the pan from the heat and let the chocolate cool slightly.
3. In a small heavy saucepan, combine 1 cup of the sugar and the water. Cook over medium heat, stirring constantly, until the sugar dissolves. Reduce the heat to low.
4. In the bowl of an electric mixer, using the whisk attachment, beat the egg whites at medium speed until foamy. Add the cream of tartar and salt and beat at high speed until soft peaks form. Gradually add the remaining ¼ cup sugar and beat until stiff peaks form (if the meringue is not stiff enough at this point, it will not hold its shape later).
5. Attach a candy thermometer to the side of the saucepan. Increase the heat to high and boil the sugar syrup until it registers 248°F (firm ball stage). With the mixer off, add about ¼ cup of the hot syrup to the egg whites, then beat at medium speed until blended, about 5 seconds. Continue adding the hot syrup ¼ cup at a time, mixing well after each addition. Remove the bowl from the mixer stand and whisk in the melted chocolate just until blended.
6. Scrape some of the hot meringue into a large pastry bag fitted with a large star tip. Pipe the meringue onto the prepared baking sheets, forming rosettes about 1½ inches wide at the base and spacing them ¾ inch apart. (The remaining meringue will hold up to be piped after the first batch of meringues has baked.) Bake the meringues for 25 to 30 minutes, or until dry on the outside but still soft inside. Transfer the cookies to a wire rack and cool completely. Dust the meringues lightly with sifted confectioners' sugar, if you like, before serving.

STORE IN AN AIRTIGHT CONTAINER IN A COOL, DRY PLACE FOR UP TO A WEEK.

vanilla-scented shortbread

MAKES 24 COOKIES

This recipe makes shortbread with a deep, buttery texture and flavor and a vivid vanilla endnote. It is also slightly chewier than classic shortbread. Because vanilla is the star, I urge you to use a fresh vanilla bean. If you can't get one, substitute 2 teaspoons good-quality Tahitian vanilla extract, added right before the final spin in the food processor.

1 plump vanilla bean

1 cup all-purpose flour

½ cup cornstarch

¼ teaspoon salt

½ cup granulated sugar

½ teaspoon finely grated orange zest

¾ cup (1½ sticks) cold unsalted butter, cut into ½-inch cubes

2 teaspoons coarse sugar, for sprinkling

special equipment

Two 7½-inch fluted tart pans with removable bottoms or two 9-inch glass pie pans

1. Position a rack in the lower third of the oven and preheat the oven to 300°F. Have two 7½-inch fluted tart pans with removable bottoms or two 9-inch glass pie pans at hand.
2. Using a paring knife, split the vanilla bean lengthwise. Scrape the tiny seeds of the vanilla bean into a small bowl; discard the bean and set the seeds aside.
3. Place the flour, cornstarch, and salt in the bowl of a food processor and pulse until blended. Add the sugar, vanilla bean seeds, and orange zest and process for a few seconds, until blended. Scatter the butter cubes over the flour mixture and pulse 6 or 7 times, then process for 6 seconds, or until the crumbs are fine and powdery. Process for another 5 to 7 seconds, until the crumbs are clumpier and the dough holds together easily when pressed.
4. Press the dough evenly and firmly into the tart pans (if using pie pans, press the dough only into the bottom of the pans, not up the sides). Press the back of the tines of a fork all around the edges of each pan, and sprinkle the shortbread with the coarse sugar. Bake the shortbread for 40 to 45 minutes, until it is just barely colored a creamy beige; don't let it brown. Place the pans on a wire rack and let cool for 15 minutes.
5. Remove the rims of the pans if you are using the tart pans, and cut each round into 12 wedges while it is still very warm. Transfer the triangles to the wire rack and cool completely.

STORE IN AN AIRTIGHT CONTAINER AT ROOM TEMPERATURE FOR UP TO A WEEK.

brown sugar pecan shortbread

MAKES 32 COOKIES

Shortbread is an ideal medium to convey a variety of flavors. In this simply delicious version, bourbon gives it a subtly sweet flavor that goes well with the pecans, and brown sugar gives it a deep caramel flavor. These rich, tender cookies taste great with coffee, tea, or milk.

shortbread

1¼ cups all-purpose flour

½ cup pecans

¼ teaspoon salt

10 tablespoons (1¼ sticks) unsalted butter, softened

¼ cup granulated sugar

¼ cup firmly packed light brown sugar

1 tablespoon bourbon

1½ teaspoons vanilla extract

garnish

Coarse sugar for sprinkling

⅓ cup coarsely chopped pecans

make the shortbread

1. Position a rack in the lower third of the oven and preheat the oven to 325°F. Line a 9-inch square baking pan with aluminum foil so that the foil extends over two opposite sides of the pan. Lightly butter the foil.

2. Place the flour, pecans, and salt in the bowl of a food processor and process until the nuts are finely ground, about 15 seconds; set aside.

3. In the bowl of an electric mixer, using the paddle attachment, beat the butter at medium speed until creamy, about 30 seconds. Add the granulated and brown sugars and continue beating until the mixture is light in texture, 2 to 3 minutes. Scrape down the sides of the bowl and beat in the vanilla extract and bourbon. At low speed, beat in the flour mixture one-third at a time, scraping down the sides of the bowl after each addition. Scrape the dough into the prepared pan and, using a small offset metal spatula, spread it evenly.

garnish and bake the shortbread

4. Sprinkle the dough evenly with coarse sugar and the chopped pecans. Bake the shortbread for 35 to 40 minutes, until lightly browned around the edges. Place the pan on a wire rack and let cool for 15 minutes.

5. Lift up the foil ends and remove the shortbread from the pan. Using a large knife, cut the square into quarters. Cut each quarter into quarters again, and cut each square diagonally in half, to make 32 triangles. Transfer the triangles to the wire rack and cool completely.

STORE IN AN AIRTIGHT CONTAINER AT ROOM TEMPERATURE FOR UP TO A WEEK.

lime cornmeal shortbread

MAKES **16 COOKIES**

Here's a nice twist on conventional shortbread: tender cornmeal shortbread with the zesty flavor of lime. The cornmeal gives the cookies a slightly crunchy texture and lovely yellow color. Great with iced tea in the summer, or with hot tea in the winter.

¾ cup all-purpose flour

½ cup stone-ground yellow cornmeal

¼ cup cornstarch

⅛ teaspoon salt

½ cup granulated sugar

1 teaspoon finely grated lime zest

¾ cup (1½ sticks) cold unsalted butter, cut into ½-inch cubes

½ teaspoon vanilla extract

2 teaspoons coarse sugar, for sprinkling

special equipment

9-inch fluted tart pan with a removable bottom

1. Position a rack in the center of the oven and preheat the oven to 300°F. Have a 9-inch fluted tart pan with a removable bottom at hand.
2. Place the flour, cornmeal, cornstarch, and salt in the bowl of a food processor and pulse until blended. Add the sugar and lime zest and process for a few seconds, until blended. Scatter the butter cubes over the flour mixture and pulse 6 or 7 times. Add the vanilla extract, then process for another 6 seconds, or until the crumbs are fine and powdery. Process for another 5 to 7 seconds, until the crumbs are clumpier and the dough holds together easily when pressed.
3. Press the crumbs evenly and firmly into the tart pan. Press the back of the tines of a fork all around the edges of the pan, and sprinkle the shortbread with the coarse sugar. Bake the shortbread for 45 to 50 minutes, until it is just barely colored around the edges; don't let it brown. Place the pan on a wire rack and let cool for 15 minutes.
4. Remove the rim of the pan, and cut the round into 16 wedges while it is still very warm. Transfer the triangles to the wire rack and cool completely.

STORE **IN AN AIRTIGHT CONTAINER AT ROOM TEMPERATURE FOR UP TO A WEEK.**

glazed lemon ginger shortbread wedges

MAKES 12 COOKIES

If you put two powerhouse personalities in a room together, it is usually a social disaster, but with these cookies, that rule does not apply. Two compelling flavors add up to a refreshing, memorable shortbread. There is nothing subtle about its sweet-tart-with-a-real-ginger-kick flavor.

glaze

Lemon Glaze (page 360)

shortbread

¾ cup all-purpose flour

½ cup cake flour (not self-rising)

9 tablespoons unsalted butter, softened

½ cup granulated sugar

½ teaspoon ground ginger

¼ teaspoon salt

2 teaspoons finely grated lemon zest

¼ cup finely chopped crystallized ginger

make the glaze

1. Prepare the glaze according to the directions on page 360.

make the shortbread

2. Position a rack in the lower third of the oven and preheat the oven to 300°F. Have a 9-inch round cake pan at hand.

3. Sift the flours together into a medium bowl. Gently whisk to combine, and set aside.

4. In the bowl of an electric mixer, using the paddle attachment, beat the butter, sugar, ground ginger, salt, and lemon zest at medium-low speed until well blended (don't overbeat; you don't want to incorporate a lot of air). Add the crystallized ginger and mix until blended. At low speed, add the flour in three additions, mixing just until the dough starts to come together and is no longer crumbly.

5. Press the dough evenly and firmly into the cake pan. Press the back of the tines of a fork all around the edges. Bake the shortbread for 35 to 40 minutes, until it is just barely colored a creamy beige; don't let it brown. Place the pan on a wire rack and let cool for 10 minutes.

glaze the shortbread

6. Remove the shortbread round from the pan and, using a sharp knife, cut it into 12 wedges. Spread a generous amount of the glaze onto each wedge, letting it drip over the sides. Transfer the triangles to the wire rack and cool completely.

STORE IN AN AIRTIGHT CONTAINER AT ROOM TEMPERATURE FOR UP TO 3 DAYS.

chocolate espresso shortbread

MAKES 12 COOKIES

These dark wedges of buttery chocolate shortbread are pepped up with an intense shot of ground espresso beans. Chocolate-covered espresso beans add a final flourish. This is the perfect cookie to bring out with coffee after dinner, as an after-dessert.

shortbread

⅔ cup all-purpose flour

⅓ cup cake flour (not self-rising)

⅓ cup Dutch-processed cocoa powder

9 tablespoons unsalted butter, softened

½ cup granulated sugar

1 tablespoon finely ground espresso beans

¼ teaspoon salt

Coarse sugar for sprinkling

garnish

½ ounce bittersweet chocolate, coarsely chopped

12 chocolate-covered espresso beans

make the shortbread

1. Position a rack in the lower third of the oven and preheat the oven to 300°F. Have a 9-inch round cake pan at hand.
2. Sift the flours and cocoa powder together into a medium bowl. Gently whisk to combine, and set aside.
3. In the bowl of an electric mixer, using the paddle attachment, beat the butter, sugar, espresso, and salt at medium-low speed until well blended (don't overbeat; you don't want to incorporate a lot of air). At low speed, add the flour mixture in three additions, mixing just until the dough starts to come together and is no longer crumbly.
4. Press the dough evenly and firmly into the cake pan. Press the back of the tines of a fork all around the edges to make a decorative border. Sprinkle with coarse sugar. Bake the shortbread for 35 to 40 minutes, until it is no longer shiny and is set. Place the pan on a wire rack and let cool for 15 minutes.
5. Using a sharp knife, cut the warm round into 12 wedges.

garnish the cookies

6. In the top of a double boiler over barely simmering water, melt the chocolate, stirring occasionally until smooth. Spoon a small dot of chocolate into the center of a shortbread wedge, and place a chocolate-covered espresso bean on the chocolate. Repeat with the remaining wedges. Let the chocolate set completely before serving.

STORE IN AN AIRTIGHT CONTAINER AT ROOM TEMPERATURE FOR UP TO A WEEK.

vanilla honey tuiles

MAKES ABOUT 40 COOKIES

A tuile (pronounced "tweel") is a delicate, crisp cookie popular in Europe, often used to garnish desserts. In this recipe, the sweetness of honey rounds out the vanilla flavor of the simple, no-frills cookies nicely. If, like me, you're tempted to add chocolate to just about anything though, you'll be glad to know that tuiles accept chocolate quite happily, as the two variations demonstrate. This recipe has a built-in-time-saver: you don't need to refrigerate the batter before baking, as you do with most tuile recipes.

½ cup confectioners' sugar, plus extra for dusting

½ cup all-purpose flour

Pinch of salt

4 tablespoons (½ stick) unsalted butter, softened

1 tablespoon plus 1 teaspoon honey

¾ teaspoon vanilla extract

1 large egg white

special equipment

Large plastic top (such as one from a coffee can or cottage cheese container)

1. Position a rack in the center of the oven and preheat the oven to 300°F. Line two baking sheets with parchment paper.

make a round template

2. Cut a 3-inch circle out of the center of a large plastic top, such as one from a coffee can or cottage cheese container, leaving the rim intact. (An X-acto knife is handy for this task.)

make the batter

3. Sift the confectioners' sugar, flour, and salt into a medium bowl. Gently stir until blended. Set aside.

4. In the bowl of an electric mixer, using the paddle attachment, beat the butter and honey at medium speed until creamy, about 1 minute. Beat in the vanilla extract. Add the dry ingredients in two additions, alternating with the egg white, and beat until combined. Scrape down the sides of the bowl. Increase the speed to medium-high and beat the batter until very smooth and lighter in color, about 1 minute.

shape and bake the tuiles

5. Place the template flat side down on one of the baking sheets. Drop about 1 teaspoon of the batter into the center of the template and, using a small metal offset spatula, spread the batter evenly across the template. When the interior of the circle is covered, remove the template. (Scrape any excess batter from the template back into the bowl of batter.) Repeat to form as many tuiles as possible. Bake the tuiles, one sheet at a time, for 9 to 11 minutes, just until they are golden brown and set.

6. Have a rolling pin ready. Using an offset metal spatula or pancake turner, immediately and carefully remove the tuiles one at a time from the sheet and press each one over the rolling pin to give it a curved shape (they will cool very quickly). Transfer the tuiles to a plate. Repeat with the remaining batter.

7. Dust the tuiles with sifted confectioners' sugar before serving.

   Chocolate-Flecked Honey Tuiles: Place ½ ounce bittersweet chocolate, coarsely chopped, in the bowl of a food processor and pulse until ground, making sure not to overprocess and melt the chocolate. Transfer the chocolate to a small bowl and refrigerate until cold, about 30 minutes. Stir the chocolate into the batter before forming the tuiles.

   Chocolate Honey Tuiles: Reduce the amount of flour to 6 tablespoons, and add 2 tablespoons Dutch-processed cocoa powder to the dry ingredients. Bake the tuiles for 9 to 11 minutes, until set.

STORE IN AN AIRTIGHT CONTAINER AT ROOM TEMPERATURE FOR UP TO A WEEK.

pirouettes

MAKES ABOUT 50 COOKIES

These are extremely light, delicate rolled wafers, also known as cigarettes. They take some practice, but once you get the rolling procedure down, it's very easy. These cookies are far more delicate than any packaged variety. Fairly plain, with a subtle buttery flavor, they are perfect for dipping in chocolate or filling with ganache, or served as a foil to richer cookies or brownies on a dessert buffet. They're also ideal to dip in tea.

7 tablespoons unsalted butter, softened

1¼ cups confectioners' sugar

4 large egg whites, at room temperature

1 teaspoon vanilla extract

½ teaspoon finely grated lemon zest

¾ cup all-purpose flour

Confectioners' sugar for dusting

special equipment

Large plastic top (such as one from a coffee can or cottage cheese container)

1. Position a rack in the lower third of the oven and preheat the oven to 350°F. Lightly grease two baking sheets.

make a round template

2. Cut a 2½-inch circle out of the center of a large plastic top, such as one from a coffee can or cottage cheese container, leaving the rim intact. (An X-acto knife is handy for this task.)

make the batter

3. In the bowl of an electric mixer, using the paddle attachment, beat the butter at medium speed until very creamy, about 2 minutes. Beat in the confectioners' sugar 1 tablespoon at a time, and continue to beat until the mixture is light and fluffy, about 2 minutes. Beat in the egg whites one-quarter at a time, beating well after each addition. Beat in the vanilla extract and lemon zest. Reduce the speed to low and add the flour, mixing just until combined.

form and bake the cookies

4. Have a wooden spoon or ⅜-inch-thick dowel at hand. Place the template flat side down on one of the baking sheets. Drop 1 heaping teaspoon of the batter into the center of the template and, using a small metal offset spatula, spread the batter evenly across the template. When the interior of the circle is covered, remove the template. (Scrape any excess batter from the template back into the bowl containing the batter.) Repeat to form as many rounds as possible. Bake the cookies, one sheet at a time, for 6 to 8 minutes, or until pale golden brown. Remove the baking sheet from the oven and place it on a wire rack.

5. Remove a cookie from the sheet and invert it onto a work surface. Quickly roll the cookie snugly up around the wooden spoon or dowel. Slip the cookie off the form and transfer it to a wire rack to cool. Repeat with the other cookies. If the cookies become too brittle to roll, return them to the oven just until they soften, about 15 seconds.

6. Lightly dust the pirouettes with sifted confectioners' sugar when cool.

STORE IN AN AIRTIGHT CONTAINER AT ROOM TEMPERATURE FOR UP TO A WEEK.

Cookie Bite **It is easier to separate eggs when they are cold because they are not as fluid as when they are at room temperature. Place the cold, separated egg whites in a bowl, covered with plastic wrap, and bring to room temperature before using.**

two-tone tuile corkscrews

MAKES ABOUT 60 COOKIES

Though time-consuming and a little tricky to master, these crispy, spiral-shaped cookies make a show-stopping garnish for slices of cake, mousses, ice cream, and other desserts.

½ cup (1 stick) unsalted butter, softened

1¼ cups confectioners' sugar

¼ cup honey

1 teaspoon vanilla extract

1 cup all-purpose flour

2 large egg whites

2 teaspoons unsweetened cocoa powder

special equipment

Thin piece of plastic or cardboard for making a template

1. Position a rack in the center of the oven and preheat the oven to 300°F. Have one or two nonstick baking sheets at hand.

make a template

2. Cut a 2 by 9-inch rectangle from a thin piece of plastic or cardboard. Then cut a rectangle that measures 1 by 7 inches from the center of the rectangle, leaving a 1-inch border. (An X-acto knife is handy for this task.)

make the batter

3. In the bowl of an electric mixer, using the paddle attachment, beat the butter and sugar on medium speed until well blended, about 2 minutes. Add the honey and vanilla extract and mix until blended, about 1 minute. Add the flour and egg whites and mix until batter becomes a smooth paste, about 1 minute.

shape and bake the tuiles

4. In a small bowl, combine 3 tablespoons of the tuile batter with the cocoa powder, stirring until smooth. Spoon the chocolate tuile batter into a small sealable plastic bag and seal the bag, pressing out as much of the air as possible.

5. Have a wooden spoon with a ½-inch-diameter handle or a ½-inch wooden dowel at hand. Place the template on one of the baking sheets. Drop about 1 teaspoon of the batter into the center of the template and, using a small metal offset spatula, spread the batter evenly across the template. When the interior of the rectangle is covered, remove the template. (Scrape any excess batter from the template back into the bowl containing the batter.) Using scissors, snip a tiny hole in a bottom corner of the sealed bag containing the chocolate batter. Squeezing the bag gently, pipe a thin line of batter down the center of the rectangle (the line can be straight, zigzag, or any design you like). Repeat to form as many tuiles as possible. Bake the tuiles for 4 to 6 minutes, until they are a very light golden brown.

6. Very gently (the tuiles are extremely delicate at this point), slide an offset metal spatula or pancake turner about 1 inch under a short side of one of the tuiles. Using your fingers, gently peel the tuile off the baking sheet and carefully wrap it around the handle of the wooden spoon or the dowel to form a spiral shape. Slide the tuile off the form and transfer it to a plate. Repeat with the remaining tuiles.

STORE IN AN AIRTIGHT CONTAINER AT ROOM TEMPERATURE FOR UP TO A WEEK.

financiers

MAKES ABOUT 29 COOKIES

This is a classic French cookie, an essential part of any petits fours presentation. It's crisp on the outside, tender on the inside, and springy, sweet, and nutty overall. Traditionally, these are baked in the shape of a gold bar. The Financier was created by a baker whose shop was located near the financial center of Paris, and it was intended to flatter and entice the financiers who frequented the shop. Because the small shallow rectangular molds used to make the classic form are expensive and not especially versatile, I call for mini muffin pans, which work just as well.

glaze

Almond Glaze (page 360)

financier batter

10 tablespoons (1¼ sticks) unsalted butter, cut into tablespoons

1 cup slivered almonds

1 cup confectioners' sugar

½ cup granulated sugar

6 large egg whites, at room temperature

1 tablespoon dark rum

1 teaspoon vanilla extract

½ teaspoon almond extract

½ cup all-purpose flour, sifted

⅛ teaspoon salt

special equipment

Two 12-cup miniature muffin pans (1-ounce cups)

1. Position a rack in the center of the oven and preheat the oven to 375°F. Spray two miniature muffin pans with nonstick cooking spray.

make the glaze

2. Prepare the glaze as directed on page 360, and set aside.

make the financiers

3. Melt the butter in a medium saucepan over medium heat. Continue to cook until the solids at the bottom of the pan turn light brown and the butter is fragrant, about 4 minutes. Remove the pan from the heat and let the butter cool until tepid.

4. Place the almonds and confectioners' sugar in the bowl of a food processor and process until the nuts are finely ground, about 45 seconds. Transfer the mixture to a medium bowl and stir in the granulated sugar, egg whites, rum, vanilla extract, and almond extract until well blended. Using a rubber spatula, gently fold in the sifted flour and salt. Fold in the browned butter.

5. Pour the batter into a liquid measuring cup. Pour the batter into the prepared muffin pans, filling the cups three-quarters full. Bake the financiers for 15 to 18 minutes, until they are a deep golden brown around the edges. Unmold the financiers and place them on a wire rack set on a baking sheet.

glaze the financiers

6. While the financiers are still warm, using a small offset metal spatula, spread a scant teaspoon of the glaze over the top of each one, letting it melt and drip a little over the sides. Let the glazed cookies cool completely.

STORE IN AN AIRTIGHT CONTAINER AT ROOM TEMPERATURE FOR UP TO 3 DAYS, BUT THESE ARE BEST THE DAY THEY ARE MADE.

almond raspberry tea cakes

MAKES ABOUT 22 MINIATURE CAKES

These are similar to Financiers (page 212), but lighter. They have a slight crispiness on the outside, accented by the sweet glaze, and are chewy inside. The cakes are flecked with tiny bits of almond skin and each is garnished with a whole raspberry, which just peeks out of the top after they are baked. If you want, you can skip the glaze and leave them unadorned, or simply dust the cooled cakes with sifted confectioners' sugar.

tea cakes

1 cup sliced unblanched almonds

¾ cup confectioners' sugar

1 large egg

1 large egg yolk

¼ teaspoon almond extract

5 tablespoons unsalted butter, melted and cooled

3 tablespoons all-purpose flour, sifted

2 large egg whites, at room temperature

Pinch of salt

About 22 raspberries

glaze

¾ cup confectioners' sugar, sifted

4 to 5 teaspoons hot water

special equipment

Two 12-cup miniature muffin pans (1-ounce cups)

Optional large pastry bag fitted with a medium plain tip (such as Ateco #5)

make the tea cakes

1. Position a rack in the center of the oven and preheat the oven to 375°F. Spray two 12-cup miniature muffin pans with nonstick cooking spray.

2. Place the almonds and confectioners' sugar in the bowl of a food processor and process until the nuts are finely ground, about 30 seconds. Transfer the mixture to the bowl of an electric mixer fitted with the paddle attachment or beaters. Add the egg, egg yolk, and almond extract and beat at high speed until light, about 2 minutes. Using a rubber spatula, gently fold in the melted butter and flour.

3. In a clean mixer bowl, using the whisk attachment, beat the egg whites and salt at high speed until the whites are stiff but not dry. Using the rubber spatula, gently fold the whites into the batter.

4. Spoon the batter into the prepared muffin pans (or pipe it through a large pastry bag fitted with a medium plain tip), filling the cups two-thirds full. Place a raspberry on top of each tea cake and push it halfway down into the batter. Bake for 12 to 15 minutes, until the cakes are a deep golden brown around the edges. Immediately unmold the cakes and place them on a wire rack set on a baking sheet.

glaze the cakes

5. In a medium bowl, whisk together the confectioners' sugar and just enough water to make an icing thin enough to drizzle. Scrape the icing into a small sealable plastic bag and seal the bag. Cut a small hole in one of the bottom corners of the bag and drizzle the icing in parallel lines over the cakes, letting it drip down a little over the sides. Let the icing set completely.

STORE IN AN AIRTIGHT CONTAINER IN THE REFRIGERATOR FOR UP TO 3 DAYS, BUT THESE ARE BEST THE DAY THEY ARE MADE.

coconut tea cakes

MAKES ABOUT 24 MINIATURE CAKES

These cakes are to the dessert world what the little black dress is to the fashion world—always appropriate, always a winner. The tender miniature cakes are topped with a fluffy frosting and flaky coconut, like an old-fashioned coconut layer cake. The tea cakes can be made ahead, but the frosting should be made the day of serving.

coconut tea cakes

¾ cup all-purpose flour

⅓ cup cake flour (not self-rising)

1 teaspoon baking powder

¼ teaspoon salt

6 tablespoons (¾ stick) unsalted butter, softened

¾ cup granulated sugar

1 large egg, at room temperature

1 large egg yolk, at room temperature

1 teaspoon vanilla extract

¼ teaspoon almond extract

⅓ cup light coconut milk (available in the Asian section of most supermarkets)

⅓ cup sweetened shredded coconut

white silk frosting

1 large egg white

¾ cup granulated sugar

2½ tablespoons water

1 teaspoon light corn syrup

⅛ teaspoon cream of tartar

make the tea cakes

1. Position a rack in the center of the oven and preheat the oven to 350°F. Thoroughly butter two miniature muffin pans, dust the pans with flour, and tap out the excess. Alternatively, line the cups with miniature paper cupcake liners.

2. Sift together the all-purpose flour, cake flour, baking powder, and salt into a medium bowl. Whisk to combine, and set aside.

3. In the bowl of an electric mixer, using the paddle attachment, beat the butter and sugar at medium-high speed until light, about 3 minutes. Add the egg and yolk one at a time, beating well after each addition and scraping down the sides of the bowl as necessary. Beat in the vanilla and almond extracts. At low speed, add half of the flour mixture, mixing just until blended. Add the coconut milk and mix until blended. Add the remaining flour mixture and mix until combined. Add the coconut and mix until blended.

4. Spoon the batter into the prepared molds, filling them three-quarters full. Bake for 15 to 18 minutes, until the cakes are golden brown and a toothpick inserted into the center of one comes out clean. Cool the cakes in the pans on a wire rack for 5 minutes, then invert the pans and unmold the cakes. Let them cool on the wire rack for 10 minutes before you make the frosting.

make the frosting

5. In the top of double boiler over simmering water, whisk together the egg white, sugar, water, corn syrup, cream of tartar, and salt until foamy. Beat with a hand-held electric mixer at high speed until the mixture forms soft,

Pinch of salt

½ teaspoon vanilla extract

¼ teaspoon almond extract

garnish

1 cup sweetened shredded coconut

24 candied violets or candied rose petals

special equipment

Two 12-cup miniature muffin pans (1-ounce cups)

Hand-held electric mixer (for frosting)

shiny peaks, 5 to 7 minutes. Remove the pan from the heat and add the vanilla and almond extracts. Beat the frosting for another 2 minutes, or until it thickens slightly. The frosting should be used immediately.

garnish the tea cakes

6. Using a small offset metal spatula, spread the frosting generously over the tea cakes.

7. Sprinkle the tops of the cakes with the coconut, dividing it evenly and covering the frosting completely. Top each tea cake with a candied violet or rose petal.

STORE THE UNFROSTED CAKES IN AN AIRTIGHT CONTAINER AT ROOM TEMPERATURE FOR UP TO A WEEK; THE FROSTED CAKES CAN BE STORED IN AN AIRTIGHT CONTAINER AT ROOM TEMPERATURE FOR NO MORE THAN A DAY.

Cookie Bite To bring eggs to room temperature quickly, submerge the eggs (still in their shells) in a bowl of warm water for about 10 minutes. Dry the eggs thoroughly before cracking.

chocolate almond gems

MAKES ABOUT 24 MINIATURE CAKES

The flavors of chocolate and toasted almond are showcased beautifully in these moist little cakes. They have a slightly coarse, nutty texture and are topped off with a rich glaze and crunchy toasted almonds. These are pretty, elegant cakes that make a sophisticated and unexpected addition to a cookie plate. They're perfect with cappuccino or coffee.

chocolate almond cupcakes

½ cup (1 stick) unsalted butter, divided

2 ounces unsweetened chocolate, coarsely chopped

½ cup slivered almonds, toasted

¾ cup granulated sugar, divided

2 large eggs

¼ teaspoon salt

½ cup all-purpose flour

¼ cup amaretto liqueur

¼ teaspoon almond extract

glaze

3½ ounces semisweet chocolate, coarsely chopped

¼ cup heavy cream

garnish

¼ cup slivered almonds, toasted and finely chopped

special equipment

Two 12-cup miniature muffin pans (1-ounce cups)

make the cupcakes

1. Position a rack in the center of the oven and preheat the oven to 350°F. Spray two 12-cup miniature muffin pans generously with nonstick cooking spray, or butter them well.

2. In the top of a double boiler over barely simmering water, combine 4 tablespoons (½ stick) of the butter and the unsweetened chocolate and heat, stirring occasionally, until melted and smooth. Remove the top of the double boiler from the bottom and set the chocolate mixture aside to cool.

3. Place the almonds and ¼ cup of the sugar in the bowl of a food processor and process until the almonds are finely ground, about 1 minute. Set aside.

4. In the bowl of an electric mixer, using the paddle attachment, beat the remaining 4 tablespoons butter with the remaining ½ cup sugar at medium-high speed until well blended, about 2 minutes. Add the eggs one at a time, beating well after each addition and scraping down the sides of the bowl as necessary. Beat in the salt, the ground almond mixture, and then the melted chocolate mixture. At low speed, add the flour, mixing just until combined. Beat in the amaretto and almond extract until blended.

5. Spoon the batter into the prepared muffin cups, filling them almost to the rim. Place the muffin pans on a baking sheet and bake for 15 to 18 minutes, until the cakes are puffed and a toothpick inserted into the center of one comes out clean. Cool the cupcakes in the pans set on a wire rack for 10 minutes, then remove the cupcakes from the pans and cool on the wire rack while you make the glaze.

glaze and garnish the cupcakes

6. Place the semisweet chocolate in the bowl of a food processor and process just until finely ground, about 30 seconds.

7. In a small saucepan, bring the cream to a gentle boil. With the food processor running, pour the hot cream through the feed tube onto the chocolate. Process until smooth, about 20 seconds. Scrape the glaze into a small bowl.

8. Using a small offset metal spatula, spread glaze over the top of each cake until it is covered. Place the cupcakes on a plate. Sprinkle the tops with the almonds. Refrigerate until the glaze is set, about 10 minutes.

STORE IN AN AIRTIGHT CONTAINER AT ROOM TEMPERATURE FOR UP TO 3 DAYS, OR REFRIGERATE FOR UP TO A WEEK.

chocolate toffee brownie bites

MAKES ABOUT 24 MINIATURE CAKES

Whether you're looking to become the star of your bake sale or just seeking a bit more respect at home, these cookie-brownie-cupcake hybrids are the ticket. This is a rich and chewy chocolate brownie topped with a lustrous glaze and studded with buttery, chewy toffee bits. Resistance is futile.

brownies

½ cup (1 stick) unsalted butter, cut into tablespoons

2 ounces unsweetened chocolate, coarsely chopped

½ cup all-purpose flour

⅛ teaspoon baking powder

Pinch of salt

1 cup granulated sugar

2 large eggs

1½ teaspoons vanilla extract

¼ teaspoon almond extract

chocolate glaze

5 ounces bittersweet chocolate, coarsely chopped

½ cup plus 1 tablespoon heavy cream

1 tablespoon light corn syrup

⅓ cup almond brickle chips, such as Heath Bits O' Brickle

special equipment

Two 12-cup miniature muffin pans (1-ounce cups)

make the brownies

1. Position a rack near the center of the oven and preheat the oven to 325°F. Grease two 12-cup miniature muffin pans well and dust them with flour.
2. In the top of a double boiler over barely simmering water, combine the butter and chocolate and heat, stirring occasionally, until melted and smooth. Transfer the mixture to a medium bowl and cool until tepid.
3. Sift the flour, baking powder, and salt together into a medium bowl. Stir until combined.
4. Stir the sugar, eggs, vanilla, and almond extract into the chocolate mixture until well combined. Add the flour mixture and stir until blended.
5. Spoon the batter into the prepared muffin cups, filling them two-thirds full. Bake the brownie bites for 14 to 16 minutes, until set but still soft in the center; a toothpick inserted into a brownie should come out with a few moist crumbs clinging to it. Let the cookies cool in the pan on a wire rack for 10 minutes, then invert the cookies onto the rack and cool completely.

make the glaze

6. In the top of a double boiler over simmering water, combine the chocolate, cream, and corn syrup and heat, stirring occasionally, until the chocolate is completely melted and the mixture is smooth. Remove the bowl from the heat and stir in the brickle bits.

glaze and garnish the brownie bites

7. Place the rack with the cookies on it on a baking sheet. Arrange the brownie bites, still inverted, so that they are no more than ¼ inch apart. Pour the glaze over the bites, covering the tops and sides. Use a small offset metal spatula to smooth glaze over any exposed spots. Refrigerate until the glaze is set, about 10 minutes. Serve at room temperature or chilled.

STORE IN AN AIRTIGHT CONTAINER AT ROOM TEMPERATURE FOR UP TO 3 DAYS, OR REFRIGERATE FOR UP TO A WEEK.

madeleines

MAKES ABOUT 28 COOKIES

This shell-shaped cookie is said to have been created by a young woman named Madeleine, chef of King Stanislas, to honor the occasion when the French writer Voltaire dined with the king. Afterward, the king's daughter suggested they be named after the chef herself. I learned this recipe from a well-known Parisian pastry chef, Denis Rufel, as a student at cooking school in Paris. These little cakes are perfect for dunking in tea and need no adornment. They are best served shortly after they are made.

¾ cup (1½ sticks) unsalted butter, cut into tablespoons

2 tablespoons honey

1½ cups all-purpose flour

2 teaspoons baking powder

Pinch of salt

4 large eggs, at room temperature

⅔ cup granulated sugar

2 tablespoons dark brown sugar

1 teaspoon vanilla extract

special equipment

Two regular madeleine pans (don't use nonstick pans; they will result in overly brown madeleines)

make the batter

1. In a small saucepan, melt the butter over medium heat. Remove the pan from the heat and stir in the honey. Let the mixture cool until tepid.
2. Sift together the flour, baking powder, and salt into a medium bowl. Set aside.
3. Place the eggs in a medium bowl and gently whisk them just until blended and smooth (you don't want to whip them at all or incorporate much air). Using a rubber spatula, stir in the granulated and brown sugars until well blended, breaking up any lumps of brown sugar. Very gently fold in the flour mixture all at once until just blended (do not overwork the batter).
4. Stir the vanilla extract into the honey-butter mixture and add this to the batter, stirring just until combined. Cover the bowl with plastic wrap and let the batter stand at room temperature for 30 minutes, until it has thickened slightly.

bake the madeleines

5. Position a rack in the center of the oven and preheat the oven to 425°F. Spray two madeleine pans thoroughly with nonstick cooking spray, or brush them with melted butter.
6. Place a dollop of batter in each mold, filling them two-thirds full and mounding the batter slightly in the center. Bake, one pan at a time, for 9 to 10 minutes, or until the madeleines are golden brown and domed in the center. Invert the madeleines onto a wire rack and remove the mold. Serve the madeleines warm or at room temperature.

   Lavender Madeleines: Add 1 teaspoon dried lavender to the butter before melting it. Strain the melted butter through a fine sieve into a small bowl, then stir in the honey.

STORE IN AN AIRTIGHT CONTAINER AT ROOM TEMPERATURE FOR UP TO A DAY.

orange almond madeleines

MAKES **ABOUT 24 COOKIES**

This cookie is adapted from a recipe given to me by Denise Mondot, the talented pastry chef at the Westin St. Francis Hotel in San Francisco. The classic French madeleine is meant to be a little dry, all the better to absorb liquid when dunked into hot tea, but these madeleines are very moist, more to most Americans' taste. They are flavored with almonds and Fiori di Sicilia, an exotic citrus-vanilla flavoring available by mail-order; you can substitute orange extract if necessary. I find that dark, nonstick madeleine pans produce overly browned madeleines, so I recommend baking them in the shiny stainless steel variety.

madeleines

½ cup slivered almonds

¾ cup granulated sugar, divided

½ cup all-purpose flour

¼ teaspoon salt

5 large egg whites, at room temperature

¾ cup (1½ sticks) unsalted butter, cut into tablespoons

½ teaspoon vanilla extract

¼ teaspoon Fiori di Sicilia (available from The Baker's Catalogue; see Sources, page 376) or orange extract

sugar glaze

1 cup confectioners' sugar

2 tablespoons unsalted butter, melted

3 tablespoons whole milk

¼ teaspoon vanilla extract

special equipment

Two regular madeleine pans (don't use nonstick pans)

make the batter

1. Place the almonds and 1 tablespoon of the sugar in the bowl of a food processor and blend until finely ground, about 1 minute. Transfer the almonds to a medium bowl. Add the remaining sugar, the flour, and salt and stir until well blended. Slowly whisk in the egg whites until blended.

2. In a small saucepan, melt the butter over medium heat. Continue to cook until the solids at the bottom of the pan turn light brown and the butter is fragrant, about 5 minutes. Remove from the heat and whisk butter into the almond mixture until combined. Whisk in the vanilla extract and Fiori di Sicilia. Cover the bowl and refrigerate the batter for at least 2 hours, until cold (or up to 24 hours).

bake the madeleines

3. Place two racks near the center of the oven and preheat the oven to 375°F. Spray two madeleine pans thoroughly with nonstick cooking spray. Place the pans in the freezer for 10 minutes to set the spray.

4. Place a dollop of batter in each mold, filling them two-thirds full. Bake for 15 to 17 minutes, or until the madeleines are golden brown and the centers spring back when lightly touched. Immediately remove the madeleines from the molds and place them on a wire rack to cool while you make the glaze.

glaze the madeleines

5. Put the confectioners' sugar in a medium bowl. Gradually whisk in the butter, milk, and vanilla extract until smooth.

6. Place the rack with the madeleines on it over a baking sheet. Dip a madeleine scalloped side down in the glaze, letting the excess drip off, then place the madeleine on the cooling rack (glazed side up). Glaze the remaining madeleines. Serve the madeleines immediately, or store in an airtight container until ready to serve.

STORE IN AN AIRTIGHT CONTAINER AT ROOM TEMPERATURE FOR UP TO A DAY.

Cookie Bite **Using whole milk rather than low-fat or nonfat produces a whiter, less translucent glaze.**

bittersweet chocolate madeleines

MAKES ABOUT 34 COOKIES

People get very passionate about madeleines. Add some bittersweet chocolate to the recipe, and you may see a full-blown love affair. These are cakey, like all good madeleines, and a little dry, all the better for dunking in tea or coffee. They're particularly good with a strong, fragrant tea like Earl Grey.

¾ cup (1½ sticks) unsalted butter, cut into tablespoons

5 ounces bittersweet chocolate, coarsely chopped

1⅓ cups all-purpose flour

2 tablespoons plus 2 teaspoons nonalkalized cocoa powder

2 teaspoons baking powder

Pinch of salt

4 large eggs, at room temperature

¾ cup granulated sugar

2 tablespoons light brown sugar

1 teaspoon vanilla extract

Confectioners' sugar for dusting

special equipment

Two regular madeleine pans (don't use nonstick pans; they will result in overly brown madeleines)

make the batter

1. In a small saucepan, melt the butter over medium heat. Continue to cook until the solids at the bottom of the pan turn light brown and the butter is fragrant, about 4 minutes. Remove the pan from the heat and let the butter cool until tepid.

2. In the top of double boiler over barely simmering water, melt the chocolate, stirring occasionally, until smooth. Remove the pan from the heat and allow the chocolate to cool until tepid.

3. Sift together the flour, cocoa powder, baking powder, and salt into a medium bowl. Set aside.

4. Place the eggs in a medium bowl and, using a rubber spatula, stir them just until they are blended and smooth (you don't want to whip them or incorporate much air). Stir in the granulated and light brown sugars until well blended. Very gently, fold in the flour mixture all at once until just blended (do not overwork the batter). Stir the vanilla extract into the cooled butter, then add this to the batter, stirring just until combined. Stir in the melted chocolate. Cover the bowl with plastic wrap and let stand at room temperature for 30 minutes or until the batter has thickened slightly.

bake the madeleines

5. Position a rack in the center of the oven and preheat the oven to 425°F. Spray two madeleine pans thoroughly with nonstick cooking spray.

6. Place a dollop of batter in each mold, filling them two-thirds full and mounding the batter slightly in the center. Bake, one pan at a time, for 8 to 10 minutes, or until the madeleines are set and domed in the center; do not overbake, or the madeleines will be crusty. Invert the madeleines onto a wire rack. Dust the madeleines lightly with sifted confectioners' sugar.

STORE IN AN AIRTIGHT CONTAINER AT ROOM TEMPERATURE FOR UP TO A DAY, BUT THESE ARE BEST EATEN WHILE STILL WARM.

refrigerator cookies

• golden raisin cookies • key lime cookies • ginger bites • chocolate mint wafers • white chocolate lemon cookies • chocolate cherry almond crisps • glazed rosemary-lemon butter cookies • tweed crisps • mocha chip cookies • deep chocolate sablés • chocolate blackouts • orange poppy seed spirals • cinnamon almond streusel cookies • chocolate pistachio checkerboard cookies • palmiers • chocolate peanut butter spirals • honey-roasted peanut butter cookies •

Think of refrigerator cookies, at least in part, as your "emergency cookies." You form the dough into logs, wrap in plastic, and refrigerate (or freeze). When it's time to make cookies, you simply slice and bake. That makes it easy to dazzle your guests with warm-from-the-oven batches of Chocolate Pistachio Checkerboard Cookies, Palmiers, or Cinnamon Almond Streusel Cookies. These are simple cookies in the sense that they don't contain a lot of mix-ins (since those can make neat slicing problematic), but not simple at all when it comes to flavor: White Chocolate Lemon, Glazed Rosemary-Lemon Butter, Key Lime, Orange Poppy Seed, Chocolate Cherry Almond. Prepare your palate for very sophisticated and deep, dramatic flavors.

You can freeze most of these doughs; they will generally keep for a month. Wrap the plastic-wrapped dough logs in aluminum foil or freezer paper. To thaw, transfer the dough to the refrigerator for at least two hours before unwrapping, slicing, and baking. You can also slice and bake frozen dough; just add a few minutes to the baking time.

golden raisin cookies

MAKES **ABOUT 34 COOKIES**

This recipe is from Pat Coston, pastry chef at Ilo in New York City. Pat is a sly one, a bit mischievous, but he was born and raised in America's Heartland, and this cookie is evidence of both sides of his nature: a very simple, crisp cookie, chock-full of sweet golden raisins. The raisins are soaked in rum, which gives the cookie a subtle warm, spicy flavor. This dough can be frozen for up to a month; even better, you can just slice and bake as is—there's no need to defrost it.

1 cup golden raisins

¼ cup dark rum

½ cup (1 stick) unsalted butter, softened

½ cup confectioners' sugar

1 large egg

Pinch of salt

1 teaspoon vanilla extract

1⅔ cups all-purpose flour

Coarse sugar for sprinkling

make the dough

1. In a small bowl, combine the raisins and rum. Set aside to soak for at least 1 hour.
2. In the bowl of an electric mixer, using the paddle attachment, beat the butter and confectioners' sugar at medium-high speed until well blended and light, about 1 minute. Add the egg, salt, and vanilla extract and beat until blended but not smooth (the dough will look curdled at this point). Scrape down the sides of the bowl. At low speed, add the flour, mixing until just until blended. Drain the raisins, discarding (or drinking) the rum, add them to the dough, and mix until combined.
3. Scrape the dough out onto a work surface and shape it into a 12-inch log about 1¾ inches in diameter. Wrap the log in plastic wrap and refrigerate for at least 2 hours, until firm (or up to 3 days).

slice and bake the cookies

4. Position a rack in the center of the oven and preheat the oven to 350°F. Line two baking sheets with parchment paper.
5. Remove the dough log from the refrigerator. Using a large sharp knife, cut it into ¼-inch slices and arrange the slices ½ inch apart on the prepared baking sheets (the cookies will not spread). Sprinkle the cookies with coarse sugar. Bake, one sheet at a time, for 9 to 11 minutes, until very lightly golden on the underside. Transfer the cookies to wire racks and cool completely.

STORE **IN AN AIRTIGHT CONTAINER AT ROOM TEMPERATURE FOR UP TO A WEEK.**

key lime cookies

MAKES ABOUT 54 COOKIES

Ginger provides a subtle backnote to the lime in this refreshing, slightly chewy cookie. It's difficult to find Key limes at markets (and even if you do, they will yield very little juice), but bottled Key lime juice is readily available in gourmet shops and better supermarkets. Watch these cookies carefully as they bake. They are done when they just begin to lightly brown around the edges but are still pale. Overbaked by even a minute, they become browned and crisp and the delicate flavor is lost.

2 cups all-purpose flour

¾ cup confectioners' sugar

¼ teaspoon baking powder

¼ teaspoon salt

1 tablespoon grated lime zest

½ teaspoon ground ginger

¾ cup (1½ sticks) cold unsalted butter, cut into tablespoons

2 tablespoons bottled Key lime or freshly squeezed regular lime juice

1 teaspoon vanilla extract

Coarse sugar for sprinkling

make the dough

1. In the bowl of a food processor, combine the flour, confectioners' sugar, baking powder, salt, lime zest, and ginger and pulse a few times until combined. Scatter the butter pieces over the flour mixture and process for 25 to 30 seconds, until the butter is in small pieces.

2. In a small cup, combine the lime juice and vanilla extract. With the machine running, add the lime juice mixture through the feed tube and process for a few seconds, until the dough starts to come together.

3. Turn the dough out onto a work surface. Knead it a few times, until it comes together. Divide the dough in half and roll each piece into an 8-inch log. Wrap each log in plastic wrap and refrigerate for at least 2 hours, until firm (or up to 3 days).

slice and bake the cookies

4. Position a rack in the center of the oven and preheat the oven to 325°F.

5. Unwrap the dough. Slice each log into rounds about ¼ inch thick and place the cookies 1 inch apart on ungreased baking sheets. Sprinkle the cookies lightly with coarse sugar. Bake the cookies, one sheet at a time, for 14 to 18 minutes, until very lightly golden around the edges; do not overbake. Transfer the cookies to wire racks and cool completely.

STORE IN AN AIRTIGHT CONTAINER AT ROOM TEMPERATURE FOR UP TO 2 WEEKS.

ginger bites

MAKES ABOUT 32 COOKIES

Chewy but tender, these shortbread cookies are little bursts of sweet-hot ginger in your mouth. They're great with lemon-flavored iced tea in summer, or a hot cup of plain Orange Pekoe tea in winter.

2 cups all-purpose flour

1 tablespoon ground ginger

¼ teaspoon ground cinnamon

½ teaspoon baking powder

½ teaspoon salt

1 cup (2 sticks) unsalted butter, softened

¼ cup granulated sugar

¼ cup firmly packed light brown sugar

⅓ cup finely chopped crystallized ginger

½ teaspoon finely grated lemon zest

make the dough

1. Sift together the flour, ginger, cinnamon, baking powder, and salt into a medium bowl; set aside.

2. In the bowl of an electric mixer, using the paddle attachment, beat the butter and sugars at medium-high speed until light in texture and color, about 2 minutes. Beat in the crystallized ginger and lemon zest until combined. Reduce the speed to low and add the flour mixture, mixing just until blended.

3. Scrape the dough out onto a work surface and shape it into an 18-inch log 1½ to 1¾ inches in diameter. Cut the log into two 9-inch logs. Wrap each dough log in plastic wrap and refrigerate for at least 2 hours, until firm (or up to 3 days).

slice and bake the cookies

4. Position two racks near the center of the oven and preheat the oven to 325°F.

5. Unwrap the dough. Cut the logs into ⅜-inch-thick slices and arrange the cookies on ungreased baking sheets, spacing them 2 inches apart. Bake, two sheets at a time, for 23 to 25 minutes, switching the position of the sheets halfway through baking, until the edges are lightly golden. Transfer the cookies to a wire rack and cool completely.

STORE IN AN AIRTIGHT CONTAINER AT ROOM TEMPERATURE FOR UP TO A WEEK.

chocolate mint wafers

MAKES ABOUT 76 COOKIES

These mint-chocolate wafers coated in chocolate will remind you of Thin Mints, the Girl Scout classics. Made with fresh ingredients, home baking, and a coating of real chocolate, though, they are ever so much better; Scout's honor.

chocolate mint wafers

2 cups all-purpose flour

½ cup Dutch-processed cocoa powder, sifted

¼ teaspoon salt

1 cup (2 sticks) unsalted butter, softened

1 cup granulated sugar

2 teaspoons vanilla extract

½ teaspoon mint extract

chocolate coating

7 ounces bittersweet chocolate, coarsely chopped

1 teaspoon vegetable oil

make the dough

1. In a medium bowl, whisk together the flour, cocoa powder, and salt. Set aside.

2. In the bowl of an electric mixer, using the paddle attachment, beat the butter at medium-high speed until creamy, about 30 seconds. Gradually add the sugar and beat until well blended, about 1 minute. Beat in the vanilla and mint extracts. At low speed, add the flour mixture, mixing just until combined.

3. Scrape the dough out onto a work surface and knead it a few times to incorporate any crumbs and smooth out the dough. Divide the dough in half. Shape each piece into an 11-inch log about 1¼ inches in diameter. Wrap each log in plastic wrap and refrigerate for at least 2 hours, until firm (or up to 2 days).

slice and bake the wafers

4. Position a rack in the center of the oven and preheat the oven to 350°F. Line two baking sheets with parchment paper.

5. Unwrap one of the dough logs. Using a sharp knife, slice it into 3/16-inch rounds and arrange the rounds 2 inches apart on the prepared baking sheets. Bake the wafers, one sheet at a time, for 8 to 11 minutes, until they are slightly firm around the edges; the cookies should still be soft—they will firm up as they cool. Let the cookies cool on the baking sheet for 2 minutes, then carefully transfer them to a wire rack and cool completely. Repeat with the remaining dough.

coat the wafers with chocolate

6. In the top of a double boiler over barely simmering water, melt the chocolate, stirring occasionally until smooth. Remove the pan from the heat and stir in the vegetable oil.

7. Line two baking sheets with aluminum foil, waxed paper, or parchment paper. Dip one side of the top of a cookie in the melted chocolate, covering about 1 inch of it, and place the cookie on one of the prepared sheets. Repeat with the remaining cookies. Place the baking sheets in the refrigerator for about 15 minutes, or until the chocolate is set.

STORE IN AN AIRTIGHT CONTAINER AT ROOM TEMPERATURE FOR UP TO A WEEK.

white chocolate lemon cookies

MAKES ABOUT 72 COOKIES

In this easy slice-and-bake cookie, the sweetness of white chocolate meets the tang of lemon, with crunchy almonds as a backnote. High-quality white chocolate is not white in color—it's pale gold. That indicates that it contains real cocoa butter.

7 ounces good-quality white chocolate, coarsely chopped

½ cup sliced unblanched almonds

2 cups all-purpose flour

¼ teaspoon baking soda

½ teaspoon salt

1 cup (2 sticks) unsalted butter, softened

½ cup granulated sugar

½ cup firmly packed light brown sugar

2 large eggs

1 tablespoon finely grated lemon zest

½ teaspoon vanilla extract

make the dough

1. Place the white chocolate in the bowl of a food processor and pulse until it is in small pieces. Add the almonds and process for a few seconds more, until the chocolate is finely chopped and the almonds are broken up. Set aside.

2. In a medium bowl, gently whisk together the flour, baking soda, and salt. Set aside.

3. In the bowl of an electric mixer, using the paddle attachment, beat the butter at medium speed until creamy. Gradually add the sugars and beat until light and fluffy, about 2 minutes. Add the eggs one at a time, beating well after each addition and scraping down the sides of the bowl as necessary. Beat in the lemon zest and vanilla extract. At low speed, add the white chocolate-almond mixture and mix just for a few seconds. Add the flour mixture in three batches, mixing just until combined. Scrape the dough out onto a large piece of plastic wrap and shape it into a rough disk (the dough will be quite sticky). Wrap the dough in the plastic wrap and refrigerate for 1½ hours, or until firm enough to shape.

4. Divide the dough in half. On a floured work surface, shape each piece into a 12-inch log about 1¼ inches in diameter. Wrap each log in plastic wrap and refrigerate for at least 2 hours, until firm (or up to 3 days).

slice and bake the cookies

5. Position a rack in the center of the oven and preheat the oven to 350°F. Line two baking sheets with parchment paper.

6. Unwrap one of the logs (leave the other log refrigerated until ready to use). Slice the log into 3/16-inch-thick rounds, slicing only enough cookies to fit on one of the prepared baking sheets, and arrange them about 1 inch apart on

the baking sheet. Bake the cookies for 11 to 13 minutes, until the edges just start to turn lightly golden. Transfer the cookies to wire cooling racks and cool completely. Repeat with the remaining dough.

White Chocolate Pistachio Nut Cookies: Replace the almonds with ⅔ cup shelled unsalted pistachio nuts. Reduce the amount of lemon zest to 1 teaspoon, and add ¼ teaspoon almond extract to the dough with the vanilla extract.

STORE IN AN AIRTIGHT CONTAINER AT ROOM TEMPERATURE FOR UP TO A WEEK, OR FREEZE FOR UP TO 3 MONTHS.

chocolate cherry almond crisps

MAKES ABOUT 80 COOKIES

Cherry-almond is a classic flavor pairing in European baking. Here it takes the form of a tender yet crispy chocolate-speckled cookie, fragrant with almonds and a delicate cherry backnote. These cookies are also great drizzled with white chocolate.

1⅔ cups all-purpose flour

⅓ cup nonalkalized cocoa powder

1 teaspoon baking powder

¾ teaspoon baking soda

¼ teaspoon salt

3 ounces bittersweet chocolate, coarsely chopped

½ cup slivered almonds, toasted

½ cup granulated sugar

10 tablespoons (1¼ sticks) unsalted butter, softened

½ cup firmly packed light brown sugar

⅓ cup cherry preserves

1 large egg

1 teaspoon vanilla extract

make the dough

1. Sift together the flour, cocoa powder, baking powder, baking soda, and salt into a medium bowl. Stir to combine well, and set aside.
2. Place the chocolate, almonds, and granulated sugar in the bowl of a food processor and process until the nuts are finely ground, about 30 seconds. Stir the nut mixture into the sifted dry ingredients.
3. In the bowl of an electric mixer, using the paddle attachment, beat the butter and brown sugar at medium-high speed until well blended, about 2 minutes. Reduce the speed to medium and beat in the cherry preserves. Beat in the egg and vanilla extract, scraping down the sides of the bowl as necessary. At low speed, add the dry ingredients, mixing just until combined.
4. Scrape the dough out onto a work surface and shape it into a ball, kneading it a few times if necessary to smooth it out. Divide the dough into quarters, and shape each piece into a 9-inch log about 1 inch in diameter (sprinkle the surface with a little flour if necessary to prevent the dough from sticking). Wrap each log in plastic wrap and refrigerate for at least 2 hours, until firm (or up to 2 days).

slice and bake the cookies

5. Position a rack in the center of the oven and preheat the oven to 350°F. Line two baking sheets with parchment paper or aluminum foil.
6. Unwrap one log of dough. Using a large sharp knife, slice the log into ¼-inch-thick rounds, and arrange the rounds on the prepared baking sheets, spacing them 1½ inches apart. Bake the cookies, one sheet at a time, for 10 to 12 minutes, until the surface is cracked but the cookies are still soft; they will firm up as they cool. Let the cookies cool on the sheets for 5 minutes, then transfer them to a wire rack and cool completely. Repeat with the remaining logs.

STORE IN AN AIRTIGHT CONTAINER AT ROOM TEMPERATURE FOR UP TO A WEEK.

glazed rosemary-lemon butter cookies

MAKES **ABOUT 70 COOKIES**

Fragrant, woodsy rosemary mingles with tart lemon in this unusual but delectable butter cookie. Don't use dried rosemary for this—it'll be like eating pine needle cookies.

cookies

2 cups all-purpose flour

½ teaspoon baking powder

¼ teaspoon salt

1 cup (2 sticks) unsalted butter, softened

1 cup granulated sugar

2 large egg yolks

2 teaspoons vanilla extract

2 tablespoons finely grated lemon zest

1¼ teaspoons finely chopped fresh rosemary

glaze

Lemon Glaze (page 360)

make the dough

1. Sift the flour, baking powder, and salt into a medium bowl, and set aside.
2. In the bowl of an electric mixer, using the paddle attachment, beat the butter at medium speed until creamy, about 30 seconds. Add the sugar and beat until blended, about 1 minute. Add the egg yolks, vanilla extract, lemon zest, and rosemary and beat until blended. Scrape down the sides of the bowl and beat for another 30 seconds. Reduce the speed to low and add the dry ingredients, mixing just until a smooth dough forms.
3. Scrape the dough out onto a work surface and divide it in half. Shape each piece into an 11-inch log about 1¼ inches in diameter. Wrap each log in plastic wrap and refrigerate for at least 1 hour, until firm (or up to 3 days).
4. Position a rack in the center of the oven and preheat the oven to 350°F.

make and glaze the cookies

5. Prepare the glaze as directed on page 360. Set aside.
6. Unwrap one of the logs (leave the other log refrigerated until ready to use). Slice the log into ¼-inch-thick rounds, cutting only enough cookies to fit on one baking sheet, and arranging them about 1 inch apart on an ungreased baking sheet. Refrigerate the remaining dough until the cookies have baked. Bake until the edges of the cookies just start to turn golden, 9 to 11 minutes. Transfer the cookies to a wire rack and let them cool for just 2 to 3 minutes (the cookies should be glazed while they are still warm).
7. Using a small offset metal spatula, spread a thin layer of the glaze (about a scant ½ teaspoon) onto each warm cookie. Transfer the cookies to a wire rack and cool completely. Repeat the cutting, baking, and glazing process with the remaining dough.

Glazed Blueberry-Lemon Butter Cookies: Substitute ½ cup (about 3 ounces) dried blueberries for the rosemary.

STORE **IN AN AIRTIGHT CONTAINER AT ROOM TEMPERATURE FOR UP TO A WEEK.**

tweed crisps

MAKES ABOUT 60 COOKIES

Tiny bits of chocolate speckled through the dough give these cookies a tweedy look. They bake up nice and crisp on the outside. The real star of the cookies, though, is coconut, which imparts a slightly chewy texture and a sweet rich taste.

2 cups sweetened flaked coconut

2 ounces bittersweet or semisweet chocolate, coarsely chopped

1¾ cups all-purpose flour

1 teaspoon baking powder

Pinch of salt

1 cup (2 sticks) unsalted butter, softened

⅔ cup granulated sugar

⅓ cup firmly packed light brown sugar

1 large egg

1 teaspoon vanilla extract

make the dough

1. In the bowl of a food processor, combine the coconut and chocolate and process until the chocolate is finely ground, about 45 seconds. Set aside.

2. In a medium bowl, whisk together the flour, baking powder, and salt. Set aside.

3. In the bowl of an electric mixer, using the paddle attachment, beat the butter and sugars at medium-high speed until light, about 2 minutes. Beat in the egg until blended. Scrape down the sides of the bowl and beat in the vanilla extract. Beat in the coconut mixture until blended. At low speed, gradually add the flour mixture, mixing until blended. Divide the dough in half and shape each half into a disk. Wrap each disk in plastic wrap and refrigerate for 1 hour, or until firm enough to shape.

4. Remove the dough from the refrigerator and shape each disk into an 11-inch log. Wrap each log in plastic wrap and refrigerate for at least 2 hours, until firm (or up to 3 days).

slice and bake the cookies

5. Position two racks near the center of the oven and preheat the oven to 325°F. Line two baking sheets with parchment paper.

6. Unwrap one of the logs of dough. Using a large sharp knife, cut the log into 3/16-inch slices and arrange the slices 2 inches apart on the prepared baking sheets. Rewrap and refrigerate the remaining dough in between batches. Bake the cookies, two sheets at a time, for 15 to 18 minutes, switching the position of the baking sheets halfway through baking, until they are just lightly browned on the bottom; they will still be soft to the touch, but they will firm up after cooling. Transfer the cookies to a wire rack and cool completely. Repeat with the remaining dough.

STORE IN AN AIRTIGHT CONTAINER AT ROOM TEMPERATURE FOR UP TO A WEEK.

mocha chip cookies

MAKES ABOUT 48 COOKIES

These delicious, buttery cookies combine chocolate and a robust coffee flavor. Try using flavored coffee beans, such as hazelnut or vanilla, for a different taste.

2 ounces semisweet chocolate, coarsely chopped

1 cup all-purpose flour

2 tablespoons nonalkalized cocoa powder

½ teaspoon baking powder

⅛ teaspoon salt

9 tablespoons unsalted butter, softened

⅓ cup firmly packed light brown sugar

¼ cup granulated sugar

2 teaspoons finely ground coffee beans

1 large egg yolk

1 teaspoon vanilla extract

6 ounces (1 cup) miniature semisweet chocolate morsels

make the dough

1. In the top of a double boiler over barely simmering water, melt the chocolate, stirring occasionally until smooth. Set aside until ready to use.

2. Sift together the flour, cocoa powder, baking powder, and salt into a medium bowl. Gently whisk until combined. Set aside.

3. In the bowl of an electric mixer, using the paddle attachment, beat the butter, sugars, and ground coffee at medium-high speed until light and fluffy, about 3 minutes. Beat in the egg yolk until blended, scraping down the sides of the bowl as necessary. Beat in the vanilla extract. At low speed, add the flour mixture in three batches, mixing just until combined. Using a wooden spoon, stir in the miniature semisweet morsels. Scrape the dough out onto a piece of plastic wrap and press it into a disk. Wrap the disk in the plastic wrap and refrigerate until firm enough to shape, about 1 hour.

4. Remove the dough from the refrigerator and place it on a floured work surface. Shape the dough into a 12-inch log about 1½ inches in diameter. Wrap the log in plastic wrap and refrigerate for at least 2 hours, until firm (or up to 3 days).

slice and bake the cookies

5. Position a rack in the center of the oven and preheat the oven to 350°F. Line two baking sheets with aluminum foil.

6. Using a large sharp knife, cut the dough log into ¼-inch slices and arrange them 1½ inches apart on the prepared baking sheets. Bake, one sheet at a time, for 11 to 13 minutes, until they are no longer shiny; the cookies will still be quite soft, but they will firm up as they cool. Transfer the cookies to a wire rack and cool completely.

STORE IN AN AIRTIGHT CONTAINER AT ROOM TEMPERATURE FOR UP TO 1 WEEK, OR FREEZE FOR UP TO 3 MONTHS.

deep chocolate sablés

MAKES **ABOUT 48 COOKIES**

These are simple, not too sweet, very chocolaty cookies. Make sure you chop the bittersweet chocolate fine (an offset serrated knife is best for this task), or the dough will be difficult to slice, and the cookies won't be perfectly round.

¾ cup (1½ sticks) unsalted butter, softened

1 cup confectioners' sugar

½ cup Dutch-processed cocoa powder, sifted

2 large eggs

1 teaspoon vanilla extract

¼ teaspoon salt

1¾ cups all-purpose flour

3 ounces semisweet or bittersweet chocolate, finely chopped

¼ cup coarse or granulated sugar

make the dough

1. In the bowl of an electric mixer, using the paddle attachment, beat the butter and confectioners' sugar at medium speed until well blended, about 1 minute. Add the cocoa powder and mix until well blended, scraping down the sides of the bowl as necessary. Add the eggs one at a time, beating well after each addition and scraping down the sides of the bowl as necessary (the mixture won't be completely smooth at this point; it should look a little curdled). Beat in the vanilla extract and salt. Reduce the speed to low and add the flour one-third at a time, mixing just until blended. Add the chocolate and beat for a couple of seconds, just until combined.

2. Scrape the dough out onto a lightly floured work surface. Divide it in half and shape it into two 8-inch logs about 1¼ inches in diameter (the dough will be soft). Sprinkle the sugar over the work surface and roll the dough logs in it, coating each well. Wrap each log in plastic wrap and refrigerate for at least 2 hours, until firm (or up to 3 days).

slice and bake the cookies

3. Position a rack in the center of the oven and preheat the oven to 350°F. Line 2 baking sheets with parchment paper or foil.

4. Using a large sharp knife, cut the dough logs into ¼-inch slices and arrange them 1 inch apart on the prepared baking sheets. Bake, one sheet at a time, for 8 to 10 minutes, until the cookies are no longer shiny; they will still be soft, but they will firm up as they cool. Transfer the cookies to a wire rack and cool completely.

STORE **IN AN AIRTIGHT CONTAINER AT ROOM TEMPERATURE FOR UP TO A WEEK.**

chocolate blackouts

MAKES **ABOUT 42 COOKIES**

Inspired by the Brooklyn Blackout Cake, these are very dark chocolate cookies made with chocolate cookie crumbs, chocolate morsels, and cocoa powder. Accented with walnuts and a coating of more cookie crumbs, they are a moist and chewy riverboat ride down the heart of chocolate darkness.

¾ cup chocolate wafer cookie crumbs, divided

1 cup (6 ounces) semisweet chocolate morsels

1 cup all-purpose flour

½ cup Dutch-processed cocoa powder

1¼ teaspoons baking powder

¼ teaspoon baking soda

⅛ teaspoon salt

9 tablespoons unsalted butter, softened

¾ cup granulated sugar

½ cup firmly packed light brown sugar

1 large egg

1½ teaspoons vanilla extract

¾ cup coarsely chopped walnuts

make the dough

1. Place ½ cup of the cookie crumbs in a medium bowl and set aside.
2. Place the chocolate morsels in the bowl of a food processor and process for 20 to 30 seconds, until finely chopped. Stir the chopped morsels into the cookie crumbs in the bowl and set aside.
3. In another medium bowl, gently whisk together the flour, cocoa powder, baking powder, baking soda, and salt. Set aside.
4. In the bowl of an electric mixer, using the paddle attachment, beat the butter, granulated sugar, and light brown sugar at medium-high speed until light, about 2 minutes. Beat in the egg and vanilla extract, scraping down the sides of the bowl as necessary. At low speed, add the flour mixture, mixing just until combined. Add the chocolate and cookie crumb mixture and the walnuts and mix until blended.
5. Scrape the dough out onto a lightly floured work surface and shape it into a 13-inch log about 1¾ inches in diameter. Sprinkle the remaining ¼ cup cookie crumbs into a rough 2 by 13-inch rectangle alongside the dough log. Roll the log in the crumbs, coating it completely. Wrap the dough log in plastic wrap and refrigerate for at least 2 hours, until firm (or up to 3 days).

slice and bake the cookies

6. Position a rack in the center of the oven and preheat the oven to 350°F. Line two baking sheets with parchment paper or foil.
7. Using a large sharp knife, cut the dough log into ¼-inch slices and arrange them 1½ inches apart on the prepared baking sheets. Bake, one sheet at a time, for 11 to 13 minutes, until the cookies are no longer shiny, they will still be soft, but they will firm up as they cool. Transfer the cookies to a wire rack and cool completely.

STORE **IN AN AIRTIGHT CONTAINER AT ROOM TEMPERATURE FOR UP TO A WEEK.**

orange poppy seed spirals

MAKES ABOUT 50 COOKIES

The centerpiece of these lightly orange-flavored cookies is the dramatic spiral of crunchy, sweet, delicious poppy seed filling that kicks them into high gear. Buy the poppy seeds from a health food store or a market that sells them in bulk; they will be cheaper and fresher than the small containers in the spice section at the supermarket.

orange cookie dough

2¼ cups all-purpose flour

1½ teaspoons baking powder

½ teaspoon salt

1 cup (2 sticks) unsalted butter, softened

¾ cup plus 2 tablespoons granulated sugar

2 teaspoons finely grated orange zest

1 large egg

poppy seed filling

¾ cup poppy seeds

6 tablespoons granulated sugar

1 teaspoon finely grated lemon zest

½ teaspoon ground cloves

2 tablespoons whole milk

1 tablespoon honey

make the dough

1. Sift together the flour, baking powder, and salt into a medium bowl. Set aside.
2. In the bowl of an electric mixer, using the paddle attachment, beat the butter at medium-high speed until creamy, about 30 seconds. Gradually add the granulated sugar, then the orange zest, and beat until light, about 2 minutes. Beat in the egg until well blended, scraping down the sides of the bowl as necessary. At low speed, add the flour mixture, mixing just until blended.
3. Place a large piece of waxed paper on a work surface. Transfer half of the dough to the waxed paper and shape it into a rough rectangle. Cover with another piece of waxed paper. Using a rolling pin, roll the dough out to an 8 by 11-inch rectangle about 3/16 inch thick. Repeat with the other piece of dough. Stack the dough packages on a baking sheet and refrigerate for 45 minutes, or just until firm enough to roll. (If you refrigerate the dough for longer, it will be too firm, and you will need to let it soften at room temperature for 5 to 10 minutes before working with it.)

meanwhile, make the poppy seed filling

4. Place the poppy seeds, sugar, lemon zest, and cloves in the bowl of a food processor and process until blended, about 15 seconds. (Leave the mixture in the processor.)
5. Place the milk and honey in a small microwave-safe container and microwave on high about 1½ minutes (or cook in a small saucepan over high heat), until just beginning to bubble. With the food processor running, pour the milk mixture through the feed tube, mixing just until blended. Scrape the filling into a small bowl, cover with plastic wrap, and refrigerate for 1 hour, until chilled.

assemble and bake the cookies

6. Remove one of the dough packages from the refrigerator and place it on a work surface. Peel off the top sheet of waxed paper. Scrape half of the chilled poppy seed filling onto the dough. Using a small offset metal spatula, spread the filling evenly to within ¼ inch of the edges of the dough. Starting with a long side, roll the dough up tightly jellyroll-style, peeling off the waxed paper as you go. Turn the log seam side down if necessary, and pinch the ends of the log to seal. Rewrap the log and refrigerate for 30 minutes, or until firm enough to cut cleanly. Repeat with the remaining dough and filling.

7. Position a rack in the center of the oven and preheat the oven to 350°F. Butter two baking sheets.

8. Unwrap one of the logs of dough (keep the remaining log refrigerated until you are ready to slice it). Using a large sharp knife, cut the log into ¼-inch slices and arrange the cookies 1 inch apart on the prepared baking sheets. Bake the cookies, one sheet at a time, for 12 to 15 minutes, until very lightly browned around the edges. Transfer to a wire rack and cool completely. Repeat with the remaining dough.

STORE IN AN AIRTIGHT CONTAINER AT ROOM TEMPERATURE FOR UP TO A WEEK.

cinnamon almond streusel cookies

MAKES **ABOUT 45 COOKIES**

These look like little crumb cakes, but they are much more interesting in flavor. There's more going on here than just sweetness. These consist of an almond cookie base, topped with a crumbly almond streusel that has just the right touch of cinnamon and brown sugar.

almond cookie dough

½ cup slivered almonds

2 cups all-purpose flour

⅛ teaspoon salt

¾ cup (1½ sticks) unsalted butter, softened

⅓ cup granulated sugar

⅓ cup firmly packed light brown sugar

¼ teaspoon almond extract

streusel topping

3 tablespoons canned almond paste

2 tablespoons light brown sugar

½ teaspoon ground cinnamon

3 tablespoons unsalted butter, softened

½ cup all-purpose flour

make the dough

1. Place the almonds in the bowl of a food processor and process until finely ground, about 20 seconds. Set aside.

2. In a medium bowl, whisk together flour and salt; set aside.

3. In the bowl of an electric mixer, using the paddle attachment, beat the butter, granulated sugar, and light brown sugar at medium-high speed until light, about 2 minutes. Add the ground almonds and almond extract and beat until well blended. At low speed, gradually add the flour mixture, mixing until combined.

4. Scrape the dough out onto a work surface and knead it a few times, until smooth. Shape the dough into a 13-inch log about 1¾ inches in diameter. Wrap the log in plastic wrap and refrigerate until firm, at least 2 hours (or up to 3 days).

make the streusel topping

5. In a medium bowl, using a wooden spoon, stir together the almond paste, sugar, and cinnamon, breaking up any large lumps. Stir in the butter until blended, using your fingers to break up any remaining lumps. Add the flour and stir until the mixture is crumbly. Set aside.

assemble and bake the cookies

6. Position a rack in the center of the oven and preheat the oven to 325°F. Line two baking sheets with parchment paper. Have a small bowl of cold water and a pastry brush ready.

7. Using a sharp knife, cut the chilled dough log into 3⁄16-inch slices. Holding one of the cookies in your hand, lightly brush the top with water. Sprinkle about a teaspoon of the streusel topping over it, covering the top com-

pletely, and place it on one of the prepared baking sheets. Repeat with the remaining slices, filling both sheets and spacing the cookies ½ inch apart (the cookies will not spread). Refrigerate one of the sheets until ready to bake.

8. Bake the cookies, one sheet at a time, for 13 to 15 minutes, until the topping just begins to turn light golden (the bottom of the cookies should be light golden brown). Gently transfer the cookies to a wire rack and cool completely. Repeat with the remaining dough and topping.

STORE IN AN AIRTIGHT CONTAINER AT ROOM TEMPERATURE FOR UP TO A WEEK.

chocolate pistachio checkerboard cookies

MAKES ABOUT 54 COOKIES

For these pretty and unusual cookies, strips of a chocolate dough are alternated with a fragrant pistachio dough, and the resulting checkerboard pattern is framed in a vanilla dough. The buttery cookies have a sophisticated flavor combination and a little chewiness. They are actually quite easy to make, and the cookie dough log can be frozen for up to a month, nice to have on hand around the holidays.

¼ cup shelled unsalted pistachio nuts*

1 cup plus 1 tablespoon granulated sugar, divided

2 ounces bittersweet chocolate, coarsely chopped

2 cups all-purpose flour

½ teaspoon baking powder

¼ teaspoon salt

1 cup (2 sticks) unsalted butter, softened

1 large egg, separated

1 large egg yolk

1 teaspoon vanilla extract

1 tablespoon sifted Dutch-processed cocoa powder

Green food coloring

***Note:** *If you can only find salted nuts, place them in a sieve and rinse under cold running water. Dry them thoroughly with paper towels.*

make the dough

1. Place the pistachio nuts and 1 tablespoon of the sugar in the bowl of a food processor and process until finely ground, about 30 seconds. Set aside.

2. In the top of double boiler over barely simmering water, melt the chocolate, stirring occasionally, until smooth. Remove the pan from the heat and let the chocolate cool.

3. Sift together the flour, baking powder, and salt into a medium bowl. Set aside.

4. In the bowl of an electric mixer, using the paddle attachment, beat the butter and the remaining 1 cup sugar at medium speed until well blended, about 1 minute. Beat in the egg yolks and vanilla extract (place the egg white in a small container and refrigerate until ready to use). At low speed, add the flour mixture, mixing just until a soft dough is formed.

5. Remove 1 firmly packed cup of the dough and shape it into a 4-inch square; set aside. Transfer 1 loosely packed cup of the dough to a medium bowl and, with your hands, gently knead in the ground pistachio nuts and a small amount of green food coloring to tint it pale green. Form the dough into a 4-inch square; set aside. Add the melted chocolate and cocoa powder to the dough remaining in the bowl of the electric mixer and mix at low speed until blended. Form the dough into a 4-inch square. Wrap each of the doughs in plastic wrap and refrigerate for at least 1 hour, until firm (or up to 3 days).

form the cookies

6. Remove the chocolate and pistachio doughs from the refrigerator. Pat or roll each one into a 5 by 6-inch rectangle. Using a large sharp knife, cut each rectangle crosswise into eight ¾-inch-wide strips. Place a strip of each color

dough side by side. Top the strips with two more strips, alternating the colors to create a checkerboard pattern. Lightly press the dough strips together. Repeat with the remaining strips to form three more checkerboard dough rectangles.

7. Remove the vanilla dough from the refrigerator and divide it into quarters. On a lightly floured surface, roll one of the pieces of dough into a 5 by 6-inch rectangle, sprinkling the dough with flour as necessary to prevent it from sticking. Whisk the reserved egg white until foamy. Using a pastry brush, brush the vanilla dough rectangle with the egg white. Place a checkerboard rectangle lengthwise down the center of the vanilla dough. Wrap the vanilla dough around the checkerboard dough. Trim the ends of the vanilla dough, and use the scraps to patch any exposed areas at the seam. Gently press the seam to seal the dough. Repeat with the remaining dough. Wrap each rectangle in plastic wrap and refrigerate for at least 2 hours, until firm (or up to 2 days).

slice and bake the cookies

8. Position two racks near the center of the oven and preheat the oven to 350°F. Line two baking sheets with parchment paper.

9. Using a large sharp knife, cut the dough rectangles into ¼-inch slices and arrange them 1 inch apart on the prepared baking sheets. Bake, two sheets at a time, for 10 to 12 minutes, switching the position of the sheets halfway through baking, until barely golden around the edges (the cookies will still be soft, but they will firm up as they cool). Transfer the cookies to a wire rack and cool completely.

STORE IN AN AIRTIGHT CONTAINER AT ROOM TEMPERATURE FOR UP TO A WEEK.

palmiers

MAKES ABOUT 36 COOKIES

Named for the palm leaf they resemble, these French cookies are also known as elephant's ears, because that's what they look like too. First made around the turn of the twentieth century, these slices of sugared double rolls of puff pastry are crunchy and buttery and have a wonderful caramel flavor. Okay, strictly speaking, maybe they aren't really cookies. Maybe they're pastries. But they look so at home and beautiful on a cookie tray that I couldn't resist including them. Some people find puff pastry intimidating, but you'll find that my recipe is really easy.

Really Rapid Puff Pastry (page 358)

1 cup plus 3 tablespoons granulated sugar, divided

1 large egg, beaten with 1 teaspoon water for egg wash

roll and fold the dough

1. Cut the puff pastry in half to make two rectangles. Wrap one of the rectangles in plastic wrap and return it to the refrigerator. Sprinkle a work surface with ½ cup of the sugar. Dredge both sides of the dough rectangle in the sugar. Using a floured rolling pin, roll out the dough into a 12 by 13-inch rectangle (see below), turning the dough over frequently so that both sides of the dough absorb as much of the sugar as possible. Fold each longer side two-thirds of the way in towards the center. Fold each side in again so that the folded edges meet at the center. Fold the dough over again from the center, creating six layers of dough. Cut the folded dough crosswise in half, to make two 6½-inch-long strips. Wrap each strip well in plastic wrap. Place the dough on a tray and refrigerate for at least hour, until firm (or up to 2 days). Repeat with the remaining dough.

bake the cookies

2. Position a rack in the center of the oven and preheat the oven to 375°F.

3. Unwrap one strip of dough and trim off the ends, if they are uneven. Using a large sharp knife, cut the dough into ½-inch slices, cutting only as many slices as will fit on one baking sheet, and arrange 2½ inches apart on an ungreased baking sheet. Rewrap the uncut dough and refrigerate until needed. Using a pastry brush, brush the egg wash over the top of each cookie. Sprinkle the cookies generously with sugar.

4. Bake the cookies for 12 minutes, or until the bottoms are just beginning to brown. Remove the sheet from the oven and turn each palmier over. Bake

for another 8 to 12 minutes, until they are golden brown. Transfer the cookies to a wire rack and cool completely. Repeat the slicing and sugaring process with the remaining dough.

STORE IN AN AIRTIGHT CONTAINER AT ROOM TEMPERATURE FOR UP TO 3 DAYS.

how to fold the dough

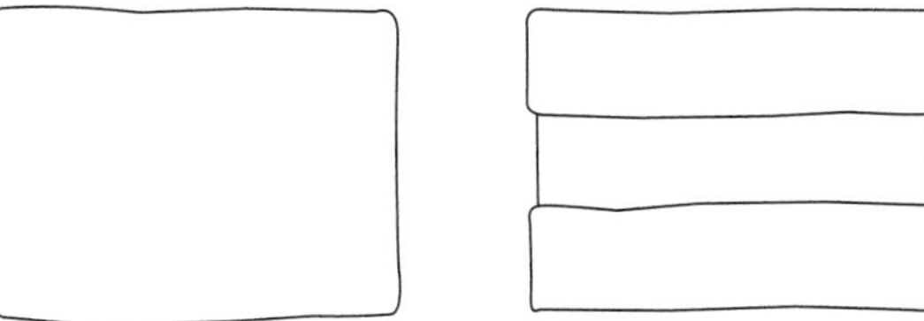

1. Roll the dough into a 12 by 13-inch rectangle
2. Fold each 13-inch side two-thirds of the way in toward the center

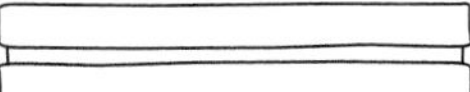

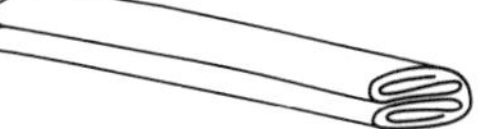

3. Fold each side in again so that the folded edges meet in the center
4. Fold the dough over again from the center forming 6 layers of dough

chocolate peanut butter spirals

MAKES **ABOUT 64 COOKIES**

These somewhat crisp, somewhat chewy, eye-catching cookies are composed of two butter cookie doughs, one chocolate and one peanut butter, swirled together in a spiral pattern. Both flavors are subtle; this cookie is not like a Reese's peanut butter cup. It's a slightly more grown-up approach to this classic flavor pairing, but kids love them too.

chocolate dough

3 ounces semisweet or bittersweet chocolate, coarsely chopped

1 cup all-purpose flour

1½ tablespoons Dutch-processed cocoa powder

¼ teaspoon baking powder

⅛ teaspoon salt

½ cup (1 stick) unsalted butter, softened

½ cup granulated sugar

1 large egg yolk

1 teaspoon vanilla extract

peanut butter dough

1 cup all-purpose flour

¼ teaspoon baking powder

⅛ teaspoon salt

6 tablespoons (¾ stick) unsalted butter, softened

½ cup creamy peanut butter

½ cup granulated sugar

1 large egg yolk

½ teaspoon vanilla extract

make the chocolate dough

1. In the top of a double boiler over barely simmering water, melt the chocolate, stirring occasionally until smooth. Remove the pan from the heat and let the chocolate cool.

2. Sift together the flour, cocoa powder, baking powder, and salt into a medium bowl. Set aside.

3. In the bowl of an electric mixer, using the paddle attachment, beat the butter and sugar at medium-high speed until well blended, about 2 minutes. Beat in the egg yolk and vanilla extract. Beat in the cooled melted chocolate until blended. At low speed, add the flour mixture, mixing just until a soft dough is formed. Scrape the dough out onto a work surface and knead it a few times, just until it is smooth. Shape the dough into a 4-inch square, wrap in plastic wrap, and refrigerate for 1 hour, or until firm enough to roll.

make the peanut butter dough

4. Sift together the flour, baking powder, and salt into a medium bowl. Set aside.

5. In the bowl of an electric mixer, using the paddle attachment or beaters, beat the butter, peanut butter, and sugar at medium-high speed until well blended, about 2 minutes. Beat in the egg yolk and vanilla extract. At low speed, add the flour mixture, mixing just until a soft dough is formed. Scrape the dough out onto a work surface and knead it a few times, just until it is smooth. Shape the dough into a 4-inch square, wrap in plastic wrap, and refrigerate for 1 hour, or until firm enough to roll.

shape the dough

6. Remove the peanut butter dough from the refrigerator and divide it in half. Rewrap one piece and refrigerate until ready to use. Place a large piece of waxed paper on a work surface and dust it lightly with flour. Place the dough on paper and dust it lightly with flour. Using a rolling pin, roll the dough out to a 6 by 10-inch rectangle, dusting the dough with flour as necessary to prevent sticking. Set the dough aside.

7. Repeat the rolling procedure with half of the chocolate dough. Carefully invert the chocolate dough rectangle onto the peanut butter dough rectangle, lining up the edges as closely as possible. Peel the waxed paper off the chocolate dough. Press the chocolate dough into the peanut butter dough. Starting with a long end and using the waxed paper to assist you, roll the doughs up tightly together jellyroll-style. Wrap the log in a piece of plastic wrap. Repeat the process with the remaining doughs. Refrigerate the dough logs for at least 2 hours, until firm (or up to 3 days).

slice and bake the cookies

8. Position two racks near the center of the oven and preheat the oven to 350°F. Line two baking sheets with parchment paper.

9. Unwrap one of the logs of dough (keep the remaining log refrigerated until you are ready to slice it). Using a large sharp knife, cut the dough log into 3/16-inch slices and arrange them 1½ inches apart on the prepared baking sheets. Bake, two sheets at a time, for 10 to 12 minutes, switching the position of the sheets halfway through baking, until barely golden around the edges; the cookies will still be soft, but they will firm up as they cool. Transfer the cookies to a wire rack and cool completely. Repeat with the remaining dough.

STORE **IN AN AIRTIGHT CONTAINER AT ROOM TEMPERATURE FOR UP TO A WEEK.**

honey-roasted peanut butter cookies

MAKES ABOUT 60 COOKIES

Honey-roasted nuts, it seems, were once relegated to the coach section of airplanes. Well, they make a jump to first class as a key ingredient in this killer cookie. Chewy, with 100 percent honey-roasted peanut flavor, the cookies have the added benefit of being a cinch to make.

1¾ cups all-purpose flour

½ teaspoon baking soda

½ teaspoon salt

¾ cup (1½ sticks) unsalted butter, softened

¾ cup granulated sugar

¾ cup firmly packed light brown sugar

¾ cup creamy peanut butter

1 tablespoon honey

2 teaspoons vanilla extract

1 large egg

1 large egg yolk

¾ cup honey-roasted peanuts, chopped

make the dough

1. Sift together the flour, baking soda, and salt into a medium bowl. Set aside.

2. In the bowl of an electric mixer, using the paddle attachment, beat the butter, granulated sugar, and light brown sugar at medium-high speed until creamy and light, about 2 minutes. Beat in the peanut butter, honey, and vanilla extract until blended, scraping down the sides of the bowl as necessary. Beat in the egg and egg yolk one at a time, beating well after each addition. At low speed, gradually add the flour mixture, mixing until blended. Add the peanuts and mix until just blended. Cover the bowl with plastic wrap and refrigerate the dough until firm enough to shape, about 30 minutes.

3. Spread out two lengths of plastic wrap, each about 13 inches long. Spoon half of the dough down the length of each piece of plastic wrap, forming rough logs 9 to 10 inches long. Wrap the logs loosely in the plastic and then gently roll each into a smooth 10½-inch log about 1¾ inches in diameter. Wrap the logs securely and place them in the freezer for at least 1½ hours, until firm (or up to 1 month).

slice and bake the cookies

4. Position a rack in the center of the oven and preheat the oven to 350°F. Line two baking sheets with parchment paper or foil.

5. Unwrap one of the logs of dough. Using a large sharp knife, cut the dough log into ¼-inch-thick slices, cutting only enough slices to fit on one of the prepared baking sheets, and arrange the cookies 1 inch apart on the baking sheets. Return the remaining dough to the freezer until ready to bake more cookies. Bake the cookies for 9 to 11 minutes, until just beginning to turn lightly golden around the edges. Transfer the cookies to a wire rack and cool completely. Repeat with the remaining dough.

STORE IN AN AIRTIGHT CONTAINER AT ROOM TEMPERATURE FOR UP TO A WEEK, OR FREEZE FOR UP TO A MONTH.

filled and sandwich cookies

• oatmeal raspberry thumbprints • chocolate pecan thumbprints • white chocolate pistachio thumbprints • chocolate-filled florentines • chocolate-filled butter cookies • fig pillows • bakery-style hamantaschen • cranberry nut rugelach • sour cherry pockets • raspberry-filled shortbread fingers • pecan tassies • lemon curd bites • ginger pinwheels • pithiviettes • linzer hearts • rum-raisin sandwich cookies • citrus sandwiches • brandied eggnog cookies • glazed hazelnut jam sandwiches • caramel-almond tiger cookies • whoopie pies • chocolate sandwich cookies • amy-oes • chocolate espresso sandwich cookies • french macaroons • chocolate macaroon sandwiches • symphonies • toasted almond crunch cookies • stroopwafels •

Filled and sandwich cookies are all about contrast. The magic of these cookies is in pairing different flavors and textures, whether it's a crisp cookie sandwiched with a creamy filling or a rich dough filled with a tangy curd. These cookies require a little more work—there are a few more steps involved in assembling them—but they are still simple to make and the results are memorable. To streamline the process, the cookies and filling can be prepared one day and assembled the next.

When you make sandwich cookies, it's important that the cookies all be the same size. This isn't a problem with cut-outs, but the dough for drop or hand-formed cookies should be measured accurately. Try to avoid the temptation of using too much filling; not only will you have unfilled cookies left over, but the filling will spill out when you bite into the cookie.

For filled cookies, the dough is easier to work with if it is chilled first. It won't stick to the work surface while being rolled, and is less likely to tear and create a spot for the filling to leak out. If the recipe requires you to cut out squares of dough, use a ruler to measure the squares accurately so that the cookies are consistent.

oatmeal raspberry thumbprints

MAKES ABOUT 36 COOKIES

This recipe is from Marshall Rosenthal, executive pastry chef at the Mystic Lake Casino in Minneapolis, Minnesota. The tender, crumbly cookie has a nutty-oat flavor and is punctuated with a filling of raspberry preserves. Use the finest-quality raspberry preserves possible, or the flavor will be all sweetness, no punch.

1¼ cups walnuts

1¼ cups quick-cooking rolled oats

1 cup all-purpose flour

¼ teaspoon salt

6 tablespoons (¾ stick) unsalted butter, softened

½ cup solid vegetable shortening

½ cup firmly packed light brown sugar

1 large egg yolk

1½ teaspoons vanilla extract

½ cup raspberry preserves

Confectioners' sugar for dusting

1. Position a rack in the center of the oven and preheat the oven to 350°F. Grease two baking sheets.
2. Place the walnuts in the bowl of a food processor and process until finely ground, about 15 seconds. Transfer the nuts to a pie plate or shallow bowl and set aside.
3. In a medium bowl, whisk together the oats, flour, and salt; set aside.
4. In the bowl of an electric mixer, using the paddle attachment, beat the butter, shortening, and brown sugar at medium-high speed until light and creamy, about 2 minutes. Beat in the egg yolk until well blended, scraping down the sides of the bowl as necessary. Beat in the vanilla extract. At low speed, add the oat mixture, mixing just until blended.
5. Pinch off pieces of the dough and shape into 1-inch balls. Roll one of the balls in the ground walnuts, coating it completely. Place the ball on one of the baking sheets and flatten it slightly with your palm, then press your thumb into the center of the cookie to form an indentation. Spoon about ½ teaspoon of the raspberry preserves into the indentation, filling it. Repeat with the remaining dough balls, arranging them 1½ inches apart on the baking sheets.
6. Bake the cookies, one sheet at a time, for 14 to 16 minutes, until golden brown. Transfer the cookies to a wire rack and cool completely.
7. Dust the cookies lightly with sifted confectioners' sugar before serving.

STORE IN AN AIRTIGHT CONTAINER AT ROOM TEMPERATURE FOR UP TO A WEEK.

chocolate pecan thumbprints

MAKES **ABOUT 36 COOKIES**

The recipe for these chewy cookies with the deep flavor of pecan and a generous filling of pure chocolate was given to me by Stephanie Banyas, a good friend who is executive assistant to chef Bobby Flay. Every year at Christmastime, Stephanie and her mother make these cookies, a holiday tradition that delights friends and neighbors who drop by for a visit.

chocolate pecan cookies

2 cups all-purpose flour

½ teaspoon salt

6 tablespoons Dutch-processed cocoa powder

2 tablespoons vegetable oil

1 cup (2 sticks) unsalted butter, softened

1 cup granulated sugar

2 large egg yolks

2 teaspoons vanilla extract

1½ cups pecans, finely ground in a food processor

2 large egg whites

chocolate filling

8 ounces bittersweet chocolate, coarsely chopped

garnish

About 36 pecan halves, lightly toasted

make the cookies

1. Position a rack in the center of the oven and preheat the oven to 350°F. Lightly grease two baking sheets.

2. In a medium bowl, whisk together the flour and salt until thoroughly blended. Set aside.

3. In a small bowl, stir the cocoa powder and oil until thoroughly blended. Set aside.

4. In the bowl of an electric mixer, using the paddle attachment, beat the butter at low speed until creamy, about 1 minute. Gradually add the sugar and beat until blended, 1 to 2 minutes. Add the egg yolks one at a time, beating well after each addition. Beat in the vanilla extract, then the cocoa mixture, scraping down the sides of the bowl as necessary. At low speed, gradually beat in the flour mixture until just mixed.

5. Place the ground pecans in a small bowl. Place the egg whites in a small bowl and beat with a fork until frothy.

6. Pinch off pieces of the dough and roll them into 1-inch balls. Roll each ball first in the egg whites, then in the ground pecans, and place on the prepared baking sheets, spacing the cookies about 1½ inches apart. Using your thumb or the knuckle of your index finger, press a deep indentation into the center of each ball, spreading it into a 1½-inch disk.

7. Bake the cookies, one sheet at a time, for 8 to 10 minutes, just until set. Transfer the cookies to a wire rack and cool completely.

make the filling

8. In the top of a double boiler over barely simmering water, melt the chocolate, stirring occasionally until smooth. Remove the pan from the heat and let the chocolate cool slightly.

fill the cookies

9. Using a small spoon, fill the center of each cookie with melted chocolate. Let stand for 5 minutes, then place a pecan half on the chocolate.

STORE IN AN AIRTIGHT CONTAINER AT ROOM TEMPERATURE FOR UP TO 5 DAYS.

Cookie Bite Dutch-processed cocoa powder is also known as alkalized cocoa powder or European-style cocoa powder.

white chocolate pistachio thumbprints

MAKES **ABOUT 74 COOKIES**

Pistachio and white chocolate is a wonderful, and often neglected, flavor combination. Here crispy-chewy pistachio dough is rolled in ground pistachios and baked, then the thumbprint cookies are filled with melted sweet white chocolate. Use the best brand of white chocolate you can find; it makes all the difference.

pistachio cookies

1¼ cups unsalted shelled pistachio nuts*

2⅓ cups all-purpose flour

½ teaspoon salt

1 cup (2 sticks) unsalted butter, softened

1 cup granulated sugar

2 large eggs, separated

2 teaspoons vanilla extract

white chocolate filling

8 ounces good-quality white chocolate, chopped

1 tablespoon vegetable oil

*__Note:__ If you can only find salted nuts, place them in a sieve and rinse under cold running water. Dry them thoroughly with paper towels.

make the cookies

1. Position a rack in the center of the oven and preheat the oven to 350°F. Line two baking sheets with parchment paper.
2. Place the pistachios in the bowl of a food processor and process until finely ground, about 30 seconds. Transfer to a small bowl and set aside.
3. In a medium bowl, whisk together the flour and salt; set aside.
4. In the bowl of an electric mixer, using the paddle attachment, beat the butter, sugar, and ¼ cup of the ground pistachios at medium-high speed until light, about 2 minutes. Add the egg yolks one at a time, beating well after each addition and scraping down the sides of the bowl as necessary. (Reserve the egg whites in a small bowl for later use.) Beat in the vanilla extract. At low speed, gradually add the flour mixture, mixing just until combined.
5. Beat the egg whites with a fork until frothy. Pinch off pieces of the dough and roll them into ¾-inch balls. Roll each ball first in the egg whites and then in the ground pistachios, and arrange on the prepared baking sheets, spacing the balls 2 inches apart. Using the knuckle of your index finger, press a deep indentation into the center of each ball, spreading it into a 1¼-inch disk.
6. Bake the cookies, one sheet at a time, for 11 to 13 minutes, just until the nuts are lightly browned and the cookies are browned on the bottom. Transfer to a wire rack and cool completely.

fill the cookies

7. In the top of a double boiler over barely simmering water, melt the white chocolate, stirring occasionally until smooth. Stir in the vegetable oil. Remove the top of the double boiler from the bottom.
8. Using a small spoon, fill the indentation in each cookie with melted chocolate. Set the cookies aside for about 45 minutes, or until the chocolate sets.

STORE **IN AN AIRTIGHT CONTAINER AT ROOM TEMPERATURE FOR UP TO 5 DAYS.**

chocolate-filled florentines

MAKES **ABOUT 50 SANDWICH COOKIES**

These are extremely delicate, lacy cookies, very sweet and crisp and lightly flavored with orange. You can just glimpse the coffee-flavored chocolate filling through the fine lattice. Although they are a bit time-consuming, the cookies are very beautiful and rewarding.

florentine cookies

½ cup all-purpose flour

½ teaspoon salt

¾ cup (1½ sticks) unsalted butter, cut into tablespoons

1 cup granulated sugar

¾ cup heavy cream

¼ cup honey

1⅓ cups blanched sliced almonds

¼ cup finely diced candied orange peel

½ teaspoon finely grated orange zest

1 teaspoon vanilla extract

chocolate filling

8 ounces bittersweet chocolate, coarsely chopped

3 tablespoons strong brewed coffee

4 tablespoons (½ stick) unsalted butter

make the florentines

1. Position a rack in the center of the oven and preheat the oven to 325°F. Butter and flour two baking sheets.
2. In a small bowl, whisk together the flour and salt; set aside.
3. In a medium saucepan, combine the butter, sugar, cream, and honey and cook over medium heat, stirring occasionally, until the butter is melted. Stir in the flour mixture, almonds, candied orange peel, and orange zest, and bring to a boil. Remove the pan from the heat and stir in the vanilla extract. Let the mixture cool for 10 minutes.
4. Drop the batter by teaspoonfuls onto one of the prepared baking sheets, leaving at least 2½ inches between the cookies. Bake for 8 to 10 minutes, or until golden brown; the cookies will not be set, and they may still be bubbling. Let cool on the baking sheet on a wire rack for 3 minutes, then carefully transfer the cookies to the rack and cool completely. Repeat with the remaining batter.

make the filling

5. In the top of a double boiler over barely simmering water, and heat, stirring occasionally, until the chocolate is completely melted and the mixture is smooth. Cool the filling for 10 minutes, stirring occasionally.

assemble the cookies

6. Using a small offset metal spatula or the back of a spoon, spread a scant teaspoon of the filling on the bottom of a cookie. Press the bottom of another cookie onto the filling, and press the cookies together to form a sandwich. Repeat with the remaining cookies and filling. Refrigerate the cookies for about 3 minutes, or until the filling is set.

STORE **IN AN AIRTIGHT CONTAINER AT ROOM TEMPERATURE FOR UP TO 2 DAYS, BUT THESE ARE BEST THE DAY THEY ARE MADE.**

chocolate-filled butter cookies

MAKES **ABOUT 45 SANDWICH COOKIES**

These little cookies are filled with a rich chocolate ganache and then drizzled with more chocolate. They are delicate numbers, crispy on the outside and soft on the inside, and extremely addictive, even unfilled. These cookies are especially ideal for sandwiching because they are so thin. Make sure you line the baking sheets with waxed paper (not parchment), or the cookies will stick.

butter cookies

1 cup all-purpose flour

Pinch of salt

1 cup (2 sticks) plus 1 tablespoon unsalted butter, softened

1¼ cups confectioners' sugar

2 large eggs

1 large egg yolk

1 teaspoon vanilla extract

chocolate filling

8 ounces bittersweet chocolate, finely chopped

⅔ cup heavy cream

2 teaspoons kirsch (optional)

chocolate drizzle

1 ounce bittersweet chocolate, coarsely chopped

1 teaspoon vegetable shortening

special equipment

Pastry bag fitted with a 5/16-inch plain tip (such as Ateco #3)

Pastry bag fitted with a medium star tip (such as Ateco #4)

make the cookies

1. Position a rack in the center of the oven and preheat the oven to 325°F. Line two baking sheets with waxed paper.

2. Sift together the flour and salt into a medium bowl. Stir until well blended, and set aside.

3. In the bowl of an electric mixer, using the paddle attachment, beat the butter and confectioners' sugar at medium-high speed until light in texture and color, about 2 minutes. Beat in the eggs and yolk one at a time, mixing well after each addition and scraping down the sides of the bowl as necessary (the mixture will not be smooth at this point). Beat in the vanilla. At low speed, gradually add the flour, mixing just until blended. Remove the bowl from the mixer stand and stir the dough by hand a few times to finish the blending.

4. Scrape the dough into a pastry bag fitted with a 5/16-inch plain tip. Pipe the dough into 1-inch mounds on the prepared baking sheets, spacing them 2 inches apart (the cookies will spread quite a bit). Bake the cookies, one sheet at a time, for 11 to 13 minutes, until they are golden brown around the edges but still pale in the center. Cool the cookies for 1 minute on the baking sheets, then lift them off gently with a pancake turner and transfer them to a wire rack to cool completely.

make the filling

5. Place the chopped chocolate in a medium bowl and set aside. In a small saucepan, bring the cream to a gentle boil. Pour the hot cream over the chocolate and let stand for 30 seconds to melt the chocolate, then gently whisk the mixture until the chocolate is completely melted and the mixture is smooth. Whisk in the kirsch, if using. Let the filling cool to room temperature, about 1½ hours.

6. Cover the bowl of filling with plastic wrap and refrigerate for 1 hour, or until the filling is the consistency of frosting.

assemble the cookies

7. Turn half of the cookies upside down. Scrape the chocolate filling into a pastry bag fitted with a medium star tip. Pipe a rosette of filling onto the flat side of each upside-down cookie. Top with the remaining cookies, pressing them together gently. Arrange the cookies on a wire rack and place the wire rack on a baking sheet lined with foil.

8. In the top of a double boiler over barely simmering water, heat the chocolate and shortening, stirring occasionally, until melted and smooth. Transfer to a small sealable plastic bag and seal the bag. Using scissors, snip a tiny hole in one of the bottom corners of the bag. Drizzle the chocolate in a zigzag pattern over the tops of the cookies. Let the chocolate set at room temperature, about 45 minutes.

STORE IN AN AIRTIGHT CONTAINER AT ROOM TEMPERATURE FOR UP TO 3 DAYS.

fig pillows

MAKES ABOUT 72 COOKIES

A case study in how fresh ingredients, sans preservatives, can make all the difference: these are like Fig Newtons, but much, much better. The dough, cinnamon-scented and soft as a pillow, is stuffed with a fig filling flavored with cinnamon and a touch of brandy.

cinnamon dough

2½ cups all-purpose flour

1½ teaspoons baking powder

½ teaspoon ground cinnamon

¼ teaspoon salt

9 tablespoons unsalted butter, softened

¾ cup firmly packed light brown sugar

2 large eggs

½ teaspoon vanilla extract

fig filling

2 cups halved dried figs

½ cup granulated sugar

1½ cups water

2 teaspoons finely grated lemon zest

¼ teaspoon salt

1 cinnamon stick

1 tablespoon brandy

½ teaspoon vanilla extract

garnish

2 tablespoons heavy cream

Coarse sugar for sprinkling

make the dough

1. In a medium bowl, whisk together the flour, baking powder, cinnamon, and salt. Set aside.

2. In the bowl of an electric mixer, using the paddle attachment, beat the butter and brown sugar at medium speed until combined, about 1 minute. Add the eggs one at a time, and mix until well blended, scraping down the sides of the bowl as necessary. Mix in the vanilla extract. At low speed, add the flour mixture, beating just until the dough starts to come together.

3. Divide the dough into four pieces, and shape each piece into a rough rectangle. Wrap each rectangle in plastic wrap and chill for at lest 30 minutes, until firm (or up to 2 days).

make the filling

4. In a medium saucepan, combine the figs, sugar, water, lemon zest, salt, and cinnamon stick. Bring to a boil, then reduce the heat to a simmer. Simmer for 25 to 30 minutes, until the figs are tender when pierced with a fork. Let the mixture cool for 10 minutes.

5. Remove the cinnamon stick from the fig mixture, and transfer it to the bowl of a food processor. Add the brandy and vanilla extract. Process until smooth, about 30 seconds. Let the filling cool completely.

assemble and bake the cookies

6. Position a rack in the center of the oven and preheat the oven to 350°F. Lightly grease two large baking sheets.

7. Unwrap one of the dough rectangles and place it on a lightly floured work surface. Using a rolling pin, roll the dough into a 9-inch square about 1/16 inch thick. Using a pastry wheel or large sharp knife, cut the square in half,

to make two rectangles. Spoon about ¼ cup of the fig filling lengthwise down the center of each rectangle, mounding it slightly toward the center and leaving about ¼ inch of the dough uncovered at each end. Lightly brush the exposed dough with water. Fold the uncut long edge of each rectangle up over the filling so that it covers about two-thirds of it. Fold the other long edge of each rectangle over, covering the filling completely and overlapping the other edge. Pinch the ends of the dough together to seal the filling. Transfer each loaf to one of the prepared baking sheets, placing it seam side down. Repeat with the remaining dough and filling.

8. Brush the top of each loaf with heavy cream and sprinkle with coarse sugar. Bake the logs, one sheet at a time, for 20 to 25 minutes, until golden brown. Let the logs cool completely on the baking sheets.

9. Using a serrated knife, trim the ends of each log, then slice slightly on the diagonal into ¾-inch strips.

STORE IN AN AIRTIGHT CONTAINER AT ROOM TEMPERATURE FOR UP TO A WEEK.

bakery-style hamantaschen

MAKES **ABOUT 30 COOKIES**

This recipe is from Marcy Goldman, a baker, cookbook author, and all-around expert on the subjects of Jewish baking. She says hamantaschen are her favorite Jewish pastry because they're fruit-filled, unique, and nothing else so smacks of the holidays (they're traditional at Purim) or offers such a "bubbie" (grandmotherly) aura. They were created to celebrate the defeat of Haman, an oppressor in Persia, and they're modeled after the villain's hat. They're small tricorner pastries that welcome just about any filling, but these fruity suggestions are fairly classic. Oil-based hamantaschen are the most common of the home-prepared variety, but Marcy prefers a bakery-style combination of shortening and butter, and so do I.

dough

3 to 3¼ cups all-purpose flour

1¾ teaspoons baking powder

¼ teaspoon salt

½ cup (1 stick) unsalted butter, softened

3 tablespoons solid vegetable shortening

1 cup granulated sugar

2 large eggs

2 tablespoons freshly squeezed orange juice

⅛ teaspoon orange oil (such as Boyajian brand, available from The Baker's Catalogue; see Sources, page 376) or 1 teaspoon vanilla extract

filling

Apricot Orange Filling (page 368), Sour Cherry Filling (made with 1¼ cups dried cherries; page 370), or Prune Filling (page 369)

make the dough

1. In a medium bowl, whisk together 3 cups of the flour, the baking powder, and salt. Set aside.

2. In the bowl of an electric mixer, using the paddle attachment, beat the butter and shortening at medium-high speed until creamy, about 1 minute. Gradually beat in the sugar and beat until light, about 2 minutes. Beat in the eggs one at a time, beating well after each addition and scraping down the sides of the bowl as necessary. Beat in the orange juice and orange oil or vanilla extract until blended (the mixture will look curdled). At low speed, add the flour mixture, mixing until a soft dough forms.

3. Turn the dough out onto a lightly floured work surface and knead gently a few times, adding some or all of the remaining ¼ cup flour if necessary to make smooth dough that is no longer sticky. Divide the dough in half and shape it into two disks. Wrap each disk in plastic wrap and chill for at least 1 hour, until firm.

make the filling

4. Prepare the filling you've chosen as directed on page 368, 369, or 370.

assemble the pastries

5. Position a rack in the center of the oven and preheat the oven to 350°F. Line two baking sheets with parchment paper.

1 large egg, lightly beaten with 1 teaspoon water for egg wash

Coarse sugar for sprinkling

special equipment

3-inch round cookie cutter

6. On a lightly floured work surface, roll one of the dough disks out to a thickness of ⅛ inch. Using a 3-inch round cookie cutter, cut out as many rounds from the dough as possible. Gather up the scraps, reroll the dough, and cut out more rounds until all the dough is used. Repeat with the remaining disk.

7. Brush a round of dough all over with egg wash. Spoon a rounded teaspoon of the filling into the center of the round. Draw three sides of the dough together in the center to form a triangle, leaving a little of the filling (about ½ inch) exposed. Pinch the seams together to seal. Repeat the process with the remaining dough and filling, arranging the pastries 1 inch apart on the prepared baking sheets. Brush the tops of the pastries with the egg wash and sprinkle with coarse sugar.

8. Bake the pastries, one sheet at a time, for 15 to 20 minutes, until lightly golden brown. Transfer the pastries to a wire rack and cool completely.

STORE IN AN AIRTIGHT CONTAINER IN THE REFRIGERATOR FOR UP TO 3 DAYS.

cranberry nut rugelach

MAKES **48 COOKIES**

Rugelach (rūg-uh-luh), which originated in Poland, are very popular throughout Eastern Europe. They have become increasingly popular in the United States as well, especially since they can host so many different fillings. This recipe is from Faith Robyn Fernbach, who worked as an assistant editor at *Chocolatier*. Faith is a food writer, recipe developer, and unofficial Queen of Rugelach. Her cranberry nut rugelach are little drums of crisp cream cheese pastry wrapped around a spiced sugar filling of finely chopped fruit and nuts.

cream cheese dough

1⅓ cups cake flour (not self-rising), sifted

¼ teaspoon salt

⅛ teaspoon baking powder

4 ounces cream cheese, softened

½ cup (1 stick) unsalted butter, slightly softened

1 tablespoon confectioners' sugar

1 large egg yolk

1½ tablespoons sour cream

1½ teaspoons vanilla extract

filling and garnish

¾ cup apricot preserves

½ cup granulated sugar

1 tablespoon ground cinnamon

⅓ cup pecans, chopped

⅓ cup walnuts, chopped

½ cup blanched whole almonds, chopped

1 cup dried cranberries, chopped

make the dough

1. In a medium bowl, whisk together the cake flour, salt, and baking powder; set aside.

2. In the bowl of an electric mixer, using the paddle attachment, beat the cream cheese, butter, and sugar at medium-high speed until very light, about 2 minutes. Add the egg yolk, sour cream, and vanilla extract and mix at medium speed until combined, scraping down the sides of the bowl as necessary. At low speed, add the flour mixture and mix just until combined. Scrape the dough out onto a lightly floured work surface and divide it into three equal pieces. Form each piece into a disk and wrap it in plastic. Refrigerate the dough for at least 6 hours (or overnight).

shape and bake the cookies

3. Position a rack in the center of the oven and preheat the oven to 325°F. Grease two baking sheets.

4. Place the apricot preserves in a bowl. Transfer any large pieces of apricot to a cutting board and finely chop them. Return the fruit to the preserves.

5. In a small bowl, combine the sugar and cinnamon; set aside. In a medium bowl, combine the nuts and cranberries; set aside.

6. On a lightly floured surface, roll out one disk of dough into a 12-inch circle (leave the remaining dough in the refrigerator until needed). Scrape half of the apricot preserves onto the center of the dough and spread it almost to the edges. Sprinkle 2 tablespoons of the cinnamon sugar over the dough.

Sprinkle half of the cranberry-nut mixture (about 2/3 cup) over the dough. Using a sharp knife, cut the circle of dough into 16 wedges. Starting at the outer edge, roll up each triangle.

7. Arrange the rugelach 1 inch apart on the prepared baking sheets, making sure the points are on the bottom. Sprinkle with the remaining cinnamon sugar. Bake for about 20 to 25 minutes, until lightly browned. Transfer the cookies to wire racks and cool completely. Repeat with the remaining dough.

STORE IN AN AIRTIGHT CONTAINER AT ROOM TEMPERATURE FOR UP TO 5 DAYS.

sour cherry pockets

MAKES **32 COOKIES**

These cookies are actually miniature Danish pastry envelopes that enclose a tart homemade cherry filling. To save time, you could use prepared sour cherry preserves; American Spoon Foods makes an excellent one (see Sources, page 376).

filling

Sour Cherry Filling (page 370)

dough

2 cups all-purpose flour

¼ cup granulated sugar

½ teaspoon salt

¼ teaspoon ground cardamom

1 cup (2 sticks) cold unsalted butter, cut into ½-inch cubes

1 teaspoon vanilla extract

1 cup sour cream

1 large egg white, lightly beaten with 1 teaspoon water for egg wash

Confectioners' sugar for dusting

make the filling

1. Prepare the cherry filling as directed on page 370.

make the dough

2. Place the flour, sugar, salt, and cardamom in the bowl of a food processor and process until blended. Sprinkle the butter pieces over the dough and process for about 6 seconds, until the butter pieces are the size of peas. Stir the vanilla extract into the sour cream, then spoon the sour cream mixture over the flour mixture and process just until the dough starts to come together, about 5 seconds.

3. Turn the dough out onto a work surface and divide it in half. Shape each piece into a rough square. Wrap each dough square in plastic wrap and refrigerate for at least 2 hours, until chilled (or up to 24 hours).

shape and bake the cookies

4. Position a rack in the center of the oven and preheat the oven to 375°F.

5. Remove one of the dough squares from the refrigerator, and place it on a floured work surface. Roll it out to an 11-inch square, flouring the dough as needed to prevent sticking. Using a large sharp knife, trim the edges to make them even. Cut the square into quarters. Cut each quarter into quarters again, to make 16 squares.

6. Spoon 1 scant teaspoon of the cherry filling onto the center of one square. Fold one corner over the filling into the center of the square. Brush the opposite corner lightly with the egg wash and fold it into the center, overlapping the first dough flap slightly. Repeat the filling and folding process with the remaining squares, arranging the cookies 1 inch apart on ungreased baking sheets.

7. Bake the cookies, one sheet at a time, for 12 to 15 minutes, until lightly golden. Transfer the cookies to a wire rack and cool completely. Repeat with the remaining square of dough.

8. Dust the cookies lightly with sifted confectioners' sugar before serving.

STORE IN AN AIRTIGHT CONTAINER IN THE REFRIGERATOR FOR UP TO 3 DAYS

raspberry-filled shortbread fingers

MAKES 48 COOKIES

For all its buttery goodness, shortbread is a fairly neutral platform for the succulent sweetness of raspberry. I like to punch up the raspberry flavor with Chambord, though it's not essential. Fresh raspberries combined with raspberry preserves are so refreshing—these are summer cookies, to be enjoyed outdoors, with vanilla ice cream.

shortbread

2 cups all-purpose flour

½ teaspoon baking powder

Pinch of salt

¾ cup (1½ sticks) unsalted butter, softened

⅔ cup granulated sugar

1 large egg

2 teaspoons vanilla extract

1 teaspoon finely grated lemon zest

raspberry filling

¾ cup seedless raspberry preserves

1 tablespoon Chambord liqueur (optional)

48 raspberries (about 1½ pints)

make the shortbread

1. Position a rack in the center of the oven and preheat the oven to 350°F.
2. In a medium bowl, whisk together the flour, baking powder, and salt until well blended; set aside.
3. In the bowl of an electric mixer, using the paddle attachment, beat the butter at medium speed until creamy, about 1 minute. Gradually beat in the sugar and continue to beat until light, about 2 minutes. Add the egg and beat until combined. Scrape down the sides of the bowl and beat for another 30 seconds. Beat in the vanilla extract and lemon zest (the mixture will look curdled). At low speed, add the dry ingredients and mix just until blended.
4. Turn the dough out onto a work surface and divide it into four equal parts. Roll each piece into a 12 by ¾-inch log (sprinkle a little flour on the surface if the dough is sticky). Place the logs 2 inches apart on an ungreased baking sheet. Using your palm, flatten the logs slightly. With your index finger, make a trough about ½ inch wide and ¼ inch deep down the length of each log.

fill and bake the shortbread

5. In a small bowl (or glass measure), stir together the raspberry preserves and Chambord, if using. Spoon about 2 tablespoons of the jam mixture into the depression in each log. Set the remaining jam mixture aside. Bake the logs for 18 to 22 minutes, until golden brown around the edges. Cool the logs on the baking sheet on a wire rack for 10 minutes, then transfer the logs to the rack and cool completely.

6. Transfer the logs to a cutting board. Using a serrated knife, cut each log on the diagonal into twelve ¾-inch cookies. Place a raspberry in the center of each cookie (if the raspberries are large, cut them in half and use just the top half).

7. Heat the remaining jam mixture in the microwave for periods of 7 seconds until it just begins to bubble. Using a pastry brush, lightly coat each raspberry with the jam mixture. Let the jam cool for 10 minutes before serving the cookies.

STORE THE COOKIES, WITHOUT RASPBERRIES, FOR UP TO 5 DAYS IN AN AIRTIGHT CONTAINER AT ROOM TEMPERATURE; ONCE YOU ADD THE RASPBERRIES, THE COOKIES SHOULD BE EATEN THE SAME DAY.

pecan tassies

MAKES 24 TASSIES

These are like miniature pecan pies, and I do mean mini—they can be eaten in one or two bites. The pecan pie dates back to Colonial America, when pecans were stirred into what was called transparent, or sometimes molasses, pie. The sweetening agent varied, but as one culinary authority put it, "The only rule seems to be that it be sweet enough to make the teeth ache." I adhere to the Golden Rule: Lyle's Golden Syrup, a cane syrup available in most supermarkets. It has more dimension than corn syrup and a distinctive flavor, somewhere between buttery and mild brown sugar. To make these tassies, you don't even have to roll the dough out—just shape it into balls and press it into the muffin cups. If you want, you can pipe a little whipped cream and sprinkle some cinnamon on top of these delicious pies.

dough

1¼ cups all-purpose flour

½ cup confectioners' sugar

¼ teaspoon baking powder

⅛ teaspoon salt

½ cup (1 stick) cold unsalted butter, cut into tablespoons

1 large egg

1 teaspoon vanilla extract

pecan filling

1 large egg

½ cup firmly packed light brown sugar

¼ cup Lyle's Golden Syrup or light corn syrup

1 tablespoon unsalted butter, melted

Pinch of salt

1 teaspoon vanilla extract

¾ cup coarsely chopped pecans

make the dough

1. In the bowl of a food processor, combine the flour, confectioners' sugar, baking powder, and salt and process for a few seconds, until blended. Sprinkle the butter pieces over the mixture and pulse about 18 times, until the butter pieces are the size of peas and the mixture resembles coarse meal. In a small bowl, whisk together the egg and vanilla with a fork. Add the mixture to the processor and pulse just until the dough starts to come together (don't let it form a ball around the blade).

2. Turn the dough out onto a work surface and gently press it into a disk. Wrap the dough in plastic wrap and refrigerate for at least 1 hour, until firm (or up to 2 days).

3. Position a rack in the center of the oven and preheat the oven to 325°F. Coat two 12-cup miniature muffin pans with nonstick cooking spray.

make the filling

4. In a medium bowl, whisk together the egg, brown sugar, golden syrup, melted butter, salt, and vanilla extract. Stir in the pecans.

assemble and bake the tassies

5. Remove the dough from the refrigerator and divide it in half. Divide each half into 12 equal portions. Shape each piece of dough into a ball. Place one ball in each muffin cup and press down into the center of the ball with the

special equipment

Two 12-cup miniature muffin pans (1-ounce cups)

knuckle of your index finger to form an indentation, then press the dough up the sides of the cup to its rim. The cups should be completely lined with dough. Spoon the filling into the muffin cups, filling them two-thirds to three-quarters full.

6. Bake the tassies for 25 to 30 minutes, until they are puffed and the crust is light golden brown. Cool them in the pans on a wire rack for 15 minutes. Carefully remove the tassies from the cups and cool them completely on the rack.

STORE IN AN AIRTIGHT CONTAINER AT ROOM TEMPERATURE FOR UP TO 1 WEEK, OR FREEZE FOR UP TO A MONTH.

lemon curd bites

MAKES 24 MINIATURE TARTS

These miniature tarts, or tassies, are made with a tender cream cheese dough and filled with tangy lemon curd. Very posh, very sophisticated. Lemon curd is popular in England, where it's frequently used as a spread. Its silky texture and bright citrus flavor contrast deliciously with the rich pastry shell.

cream cheese dough

1¼ cups all-purpose flour

⅓ cup confectioners' sugar

¼ teaspoon baking powder

⅛ teaspoon salt

½ cup (1 stick) cold unsalted butter, cut into tablespoons

One 3-ounce package cream cheese, cut into ½-inch chunks and frozen for 30 minutes

1 large egg yolk

1 teaspoon vanilla extract

lemon curd filling

1 large egg

4 large egg yolks

1 cup plus 2 tablespoons granulated sugar

½ cup freshly squeezed lemon juice

2 teaspoons finely grated lemon zest

Pinch of salt

6 tablespoons (¾ stick) unsalted butter, cut into tablespoons

garnish

Small fresh spearmint leaves

make the dough

1. In the bowl of a food processor, combine the flour, confectioners' sugar, baking powder, and salt and process for a few seconds, until blended. Sprinkle the butter and cream cheese pieces over the mixture and pulse about 18 times, until the butter pieces are the size of peas and the mixture resembles coarse meal. In a small bowl, whisk together the egg yolk and vanilla with a fork. Add the mixture to the processor and pulse just until the dough starts to come together (don't let it form a ball around the blade).

2. Turn the dough out onto a work surface and gently press it into a disk. Wrap the dough in plastic wrap and refrigerate for at least 1 hour, until firm (or up to 2 days).

make the filling

3. Set a fine-mesh sieve over a medium bowl and set aside. In a medium-sized heavy nonreactive saucepan, whisk together the egg, yolks, and sugar until blended. Stir in the lemon juice and zest, salt, and butter and cook over medium heat, whisking constantly, until the mixture thickens, 7 to 10 minutes (do not let the mixture boil, or it will curdle). Immediately strain the mixture through the sieve, pressing it through with a rubber spatula. Cover the bowl and refrigerate the curd until chilled, about 1 hour.

bake the crusts

4. Position a rack in the center of the oven and preheat the oven to 400°F. Coat two 12-cup miniature muffin pans with nonstick cooking spray. Cut out twenty-four 2-inch squares of aluminum foil.

5. Remove the dough from the refrigerator and divide it in half. Divide each half into 12 equal portions. Shape each piece of dough into a ball. Place one ball in each muffin cup and press down into the center of the ball with the

special equipment

Two 12-cup miniature muffin pans (1-ounce cups)

Pastry bag fitted with a medium star tip (such as Ateco #5)

knuckle of your index finger to form an indentation, then press the dough up the sides of the cup to its rim. The cups should be completely lined with dough. Prick the bottom of each crust with a fork. Line each crust with one of the foil squares and fill with a few pie weights, dried beans, or rice.

6. Bake the crusts for 10 minutes. Transfer the muffin pans to a wire rack and reduce the oven temperature to 350°F. Remove the foil and weights from the crusts and bake the crusts for another 7 to 9 minutes, until golden brown around the edges. Set the muffin pans on a wire rack and cool the crusts completely.

assemble the bites

7. Scrape the chilled lemon curd into a pastry bag fitted with a medium star tip. Pipe a generous rosette of lemon curd into each crust. Garnish each with a mint leaf. Serve the bites immediately, or chill until serving time.

   Grapefruit Curd Bites: For the filling, substitute grapefruit juice and zest for the lemon juice and zest. Reduce the amount of sugar to 1 cup, and proceed with the recipe as directed.

STORE **IN AN AIRTIGHT CONTAINER IN THE REFRIGERATOR FOR UP TO 1 DAY.**

Cookie Bite **Lemons and other citrus fruits will yield much more juice if you microwave them on high power until they are warm to the touch (about 20 to 30 seconds) before juicing them.**

ginger pinwheels

MAKES ABOUT 38 COOKIES

Some special handling is required to create these little pinwheel-shaped pastries, but I find the folding and filling process quite therapeutic. The results are delicious, eye-catching, and memorable. The pastry is fluffy and moist with a hint of ginger flavor, and the filling is spicy ginger with a citrus tang.

ginger dough

2⅓ cups all-purpose flour

¼ cup firmly packed light brown sugar

½ teaspoon salt

½ teaspoon ground ginger

1 cup (2 sticks) cold unsalted butter, cut into ½-inch cubes

1 teaspoon vanilla extract

½ cup sour cream

ginger filling

⅔ cup ginger preserves

1 teaspoon finely grated orange zest

1 large egg white, lightly beaten with 1 teaspoon water for egg wash

make the dough

1. Place the flour, sugar, salt, and ginger in the bowl of a food processor and process until blended. Sprinkle the butter pieces over the dough and process for about 6 seconds, until the butter pieces are the size of peas. Stir the vanilla extract into the sour cream. Spoon the sour cream mixture in dollops over the flour mixture and process just until the dough starts to come together, about 8 seconds.
2. Turn the dough out onto a work surface and knead it a few times to bring it together. Divide it in half and shape each piece into a 4-inch square. Wrap each square in plastic wrap and refrigerate for at least 2 hours, until chilled (or up to 24 hours).

make the filling

3. In a small bowl, stir together the ginger preserves and orange zest. Refrigerate, covered, until ready to use.

assemble and bake the cookies

4. Position a rack in the center of the oven and preheat the oven to 375°F.
5. Remove one of the dough squares from the refrigerator. On a lightly floured work surface, using a rolling pin, roll the dough out into a 11½- to 12-inch square about ⅛ inch thick, dusting the dough with flour as necessary to prevent sticking. Using a pastry wheel or knife, trim the edges so they are even. Cut the dough into sixteen 2¾-inch squares. Arrange the squares 1½ inches apart on ungreased baking sheets. Place the baking sheets in the refrigerator for 15 minutes to chill the squares. (Gather up any scraps, wrap them in plastic wrap, and chill for 30 minutes before rerolling.)

6. Make a diagonal cut from each corner of each square halfway to the center. Spoon a scant teaspoon of ginger filling into the center of each square. Brush alternate tips of the cut portions with the egg wash, pull the brushed tips to the center, and lightly press to seal them together.

7. Bake the pinwheels, one sheet at a time, for 14 to 16 minutes, until golden brown just around the edges. Transfer the cookies to a wire rack and cool completely. Repeat with the remaining dough and filling.

STORE IN AN AIRTIGHT CONTAINER AT ROOM TEMPERATURE FOR UP TO 3 DAYS.

pithiviettes

MAKES ABOUT 44 COOKIES

These cookies are a miniature version of the classic Pithiviers, which takes its name from the French town where it originated. The classic is a large round sandwich of puff pastry filled with almond-scented frangipane. Here, little scalloped rounds of delicate puff pastry enclose an apricot-studded almond filling. A common problem when working with puff pastry is to underbake it, resulting in an unpleasant raw taste. When you think the cookies are done, remove one, cut it in half, and taste it: you'll know immediately whether it's sufficiently baked or needs more time in the oven. If some of the almond filling escapes onto the baking sheet, just trim it off with a sharp paring knife before serving.

pastry

Really Rapid Puff Pastry (page 358)

almond cream filling

½ cup sliced blanched almonds

⅓ cup granulated sugar

1 large egg

4 tablespoons (½ stick) unsalted butter, cut into tablespoons, softened

¼ teaspoon vanilla extract

⅛ teaspoon almond extract

1½ teaspoons all-purpose flour

1 tablespoon finely chopped dried apricots

1 large egg, lightly beaten with 1 teaspoon water for egg wash

garnish

Coarse sugar for sprinkling

Confectioners' sugar for dusting

make the pastry

1. Prepare the puff pastry according to the directions on page 358; refrigerate.

make the filling

2. Place the almonds and sugar in the bowl of a food processor and process until the almonds are finely ground, about 45 seconds. Add the egg and process until blended. Scatter the butter pieces over the almond mixture and process until blended and creamy, about 30 seconds. Add the vanilla extract, almond extract, and flour and pulse until blended. Transfer the filling to a small bowl, and stir in the apricots. Cover the bowl with plastic wrap and refrigerate until ready to use.

assemble the pithiviettes

3. Remove the puff pastry from the refrigerator and divide it in half. Wrap one piece of dough and return it to the refrigerator. On a floured work surface, using a floured rolling pin, roll the dough out to a thickness of ⅛ inch. Using a 2¼-inch scallop-shaped cutter, cut out as many rounds from the dough as possible. Prick each round well with a fork and place them on a baking sheet (no need to leave space between them at this point). Stack and press the dough scraps together and reroll them to cut out more rounds. Prick these and place them on the baking sheet, stacking them between layers of waxed paper. Repeat with the remaining dough. Refrigerate the rounds for at least 30 minutes.

4. Remove 12 of the rounds from the refrigerator and arrange them on an ungreased baking sheet, spacing them 1½ inches apart. Brush each round with egg wash. Spoon ½ teaspoon of the almond filling into the center of each round. Top each round with another round, lining up the scalloped edges. Using a fork, press the edges of each round to seal the dough rounds together (it's important that they be sealed well). Brush the tops of each pithiviette with egg wash. Freeze the cookies for 15 minutes (or, covered, for up to 3 days). Repeat the process with the remaining rounds and filling. Reserve the egg wash.

bake the pithiviettes

5. Position a rack in the center of the oven and preheat the oven to 375°F.

6. Remove the pithiviettes from the freezer. Brush the tops of the rounds again with egg wash and sprinkle with coarse sugar. Bake the rounds for 20 to 25 minutes, until puffed and golden brown. Transfer them to a wire rack and cool completely.

7. Sprinkle the pithiviettes with sifted confectioners' sugar before serving.

STORE IN AN AIRTIGHT CONTAINER AT ROOM TEMPERATURE FOR UP TO 2 DAYS.

linzer hearts

MAKES ABOUT 42 SANDWICH COOKIES

These pretty cookies are a variation of the classic linzertorte, a lattice-topped jam-filled Austrian pastry from the town of Linz (for a different take, see Raspberry Almond Shortbread Squares, page 138). Originally, it had a very cakey texture, but it evolved into a crisp and buttery pastry. I added hazelnuts to deepen the flavor. The hazelnut short dough makes an extremely tender cookie, and consequently, the process of rolling out and cutting the cookies requires some delicacy. Chilling and flouring the dough as directed, however, makes the process relatively stress-free. Be sure to grind the hazelnuts to a fine consistency; if they are too coarse, the dough will be difficult to roll and is more likely to fall apart.

linzer cookies

½ cup blanched hazelnuts, toasted and skinned

½ cup granulated sugar, divided

1 cup (2 sticks) unsalted butter, softened

1 large egg yolk

2 cups all-purpose flour

1 teaspoon finely grated lemon zest

1 teaspoon vanilla extract

⅛ teaspoon salt

raspberry filling

½ cup seedless raspberry preserves

⅓ cup confectioners' sugar for dusting

special equipment

2-inch heart-shaped cookie cutter

¾-inch heart-shaped aspic cutter

make the dough

1. Place the hazelnuts and ¼ cup of the sugar in a food processor and process until finely ground, about 45 seconds. Set aside.

2. In the bowl of an electric mixer, using the paddle attachment, beat the butter with the remaining ¼ cup sugar at medium speed until light, about 1 minute. Add the egg yolk and beat until thoroughly blended. Add the ground hazelnut mixture, flour, lemon zest, vanilla extract, and salt and mix on low speed just until combined. Scrape the dough onto a piece of plastic wrap, flatten it into a disk, and wrap it up. Refrigerate the dough for at least 2 hours, until firm enough to handle.

cut and bake the cookies

3. Arrange two racks near the center of the oven and preheat the oven to 350°F.

4. Place half of the dough on a lightly floured work surface. Sprinkle the dough with flour. Using a floured rolling pin, roll the dough out to a thickness of ⅛ inch, flouring it as necessary to prevent sticking. Use a 2-inch heart-shaped cookie cutter to cut out as many hearts from the dough as possible. Arrange some of the cookies on an ungreased baking sheet, spacing them 1 inch apart. Use a ¾-inch heart-shaped aspic cutter to cut out the center of each cookie. Place the remaining whole cookies on another baking sheet.

5. Bake the cookies for 12 to 14 minutes, until they are lightly golden around the edges. Cool the cookies on the baking sheets on a wire rack for 15 minutes. Using a metal spatula, gently transfer them to the wire rack to cool completely.

6. Continue to reroll the scraps until all the dough is used (no need to rechill the dough). Repeat the cutting and baking process.

assemble the cookies

7. Spoon about ½ teaspoon of the raspberry preserves onto each whole cookie and, with a small offset metal spatula, spread it to within ¼ inch of the edges of the cookie. Place the confectioners' sugar in a fine-mesh sieve and liberally sprinkle the surfaces of the cut-out cookies. Sandwich the tops and bottoms together.

STORE IN AN AIRTIGHT CONTAINER AT ROOM TEMPERATURE FOR UP TO 4 DAYS.

rum-raisin sandwich cookies

MAKES **ABOUT 50 SANDWICH COOKIES**

This is one of my all-time favorites, with a creamy rum raisin filling sandwiched between tender, buttery brown sugar–raisin cookies. Use a high-quality dark rum, such as Myers's, for the best flavor.

rum-raisin cookies

½ cup dark rum

⅔ cup dark raisins

1 cup (2 sticks) unsalted butter, softened

½ cup granulated sugar

½ cup firmly packed light brown sugar

¼ teaspoon salt

1 teaspoon vanilla extract

2 large eggs

2 cups all-purpose flour

½ teaspoon ground cinnamon

1 large egg white, lightly beaten with 1 teaspoon water for egg wash

Turbinado sugar for sprinkling

filling

2 cups confectioners' sugar

4 tablespoons (½ stick) unsalted butter, softened

1 teaspoon vanilla extract

Pinch of salt

special equipment

1¾-inch round cookie cutter

1. Combine the raisins with the rum in a small plastic container with a tight-fitting lid and let macerate at room temperature for at least 6 hours, or overnight.

make the dough

2. Using a slotted spoon, remove ⅓ cup of the raisins from the rum and finely chop them. Place them in a small bowl and add 1 tablespoon of the rum (this will be added to the dough, while the remaining whole raisins will be added to the filling).

3. In the bowl of an electric mixer, using the paddle attachment, beat the butter, sugars, and salt at medium-high speed until light in texture and color, about 3 minutes. Beat in the finely chopped raisins and rum mixture, then the vanilla extract. Add the eggs one at a time, beating well after each addition and scraping down the sides of the bowl as needed. Reduce the speed to low and add the flour and cinnamon, mixing just until blended. Scrape the dough onto a work surface and divide it into quarters. Shape each piece into a disk. Wrap each disk in plastic wrap and refrigerate for at least 2 hours, until firm (or up to 8 hours).

cut and bake the cookies

4. Position a rack in the center of the oven and preheat the oven to 350°F. Lightly butter two baking sheets, or coat them with nonstick cooking spray.

5. Remove one of the disks of dough from the refrigerator. On a floured work surface, roll it out to a thickness of ⅛ inch, sprinkling the dough and work surface with flour as needed to prevent sticking. Dip a 1¾-inch round cookie cutter in flour and cut out as many cookies as possible from the dough. Arrange the cookies on the baking sheets, spacing them 1 inch apart. Rewrap the scraps and refrigerate them until they are firm enough to reroll. Repeat the rolling and cutting process with the scraps and remaining disks of dough.

6. Brush the cookies lightly with the egg wash and sprinkle with turbinado sugar. Bake the cookies, one sheet at a time, until the edges are lightly golden, 9 to 11 minutes. Transfer the cookies to a wire rack and cool completely.

make the filling

7. In the bowl of an electric mixer, using the paddle attachment, beat the sugar and butter at medium speed until the mixture is crumbly, about 1 minute. Add 3 tablespoons of the reserved rum and beat at high speed until smooth. Add the reserved whole raisins, drained, the vanilla extract, and salt and beat until blended.

fill the cookies

8. Using a small offset metal spatula or a knife, spread about 2 teaspoons of the rum raisin filling onto the bottom of a cookie. Place another cookie, right side up, on the filling, to form a sandwich cookie. Repeat with the remaining cookies and filling.

STORE IN AN AIRTIGHT CONTAINER AT ROOM TEMPERATURE FOR UP TO 5 DAYS.

citrus sandwiches

MAKES **ABOUT 50 SANDWICH COOKIES**

These are crispy-chewy cookies, shot through with lemon and orange flavor. For the filling, you need something equally tangy, and I give three choices here: one that reinforces the orange and lemon theme, one with the mellow and delicious flavor of Key lime, and one with orange and green tea.

citrus cookies

2 cups all-purpose flour

¼ teaspoon baking powder

¼ teaspoon salt

14 tablespoons (1¾ sticks) unsalted butter, softened

1 cup granulated sugar

1 large egg yolk

2 teaspoons finely grated lemon zest

2 teaspoons finely grated orange zest

Coarse sugar for sprinkling

citrus filling

¼ cup freshly squeezed orange juice

1 tablespoon freshly squeezed lemon juice

6 tablespoons (¾ stick) unsalted butter, softened

1½ cups confectioners' sugar

1 tablespoon heavy cream

Pinch of salt

make the dough

1. In a medium bowl, whisk together the flour, baking powder, and salt; set aside.

2. In the bowl of an electric mixer, using the paddle attachment, beat the butter and sugar at medium-high speed until well combined, about 1 minute. Beat in the egg yolk and citrus zests. At low speed, add the flour mixture and mix just until blended. Scrape the dough onto a work surface and gather it up into a disk. Wrap the disk in plastic wrap and refrigerate for at least 2 hours, until firm (or up to 3 days).

cut and bake the cookies

3. Position two racks near the center of the oven and preheat the oven to 350°F. Line two baking sheets with parchment paper or foil.

4. Place the chilled dough on a lightly floured work surface and sprinkle it lightly with flour. Using a rolling pin, roll the dough out to a thickness of ⅛ inch. Using a 1½-inch round scalloped cookie cutter, cut out as many cookies as possible from the dough. With a ½-inch round cookie cutter or ½-inch plain pastry tip, cut out the centers of half of the cookies (these will be the tops). Stack and press together the scraps and chill for 15 minutes before rerolling. Carefully transfer the cookies to the prepared baking sheets, spacing them ½ inch apart and placing the tops and bottoms on separate sheets (the tops will take a minute or so less to bake than the bottoms). Sprinkle the cookies with coarse sugar. Bake the cookies, two sheets at a time, for 9 to 11 minutes, or until lightly browned on the bottom (not on top). Transfer the cookies to wire racks and cool completely.

make the filling

5. In a small nonreactive saucepan, bring the orange and lemon juices to a boil over high heat and boil for 3 to 5 minutes, or until reduced to about 1 tablespoon. Let cool completely.

special equipment

1½-inch scalloped round cookie cutter

½-inch round cookie cutter or ½-inch plain pastry tip (such as Ateco #6)

6. In the bowl of an electric mixer, using the paddle attachment, beat the butter, confectioners' sugar, cream, salt, and cooled citrus juices at medium speed until smooth.

assemble the cookies

7. Spread about a teaspoon of the filling onto the bottom of one of the whole cookies. Top with one of the cut-out cookies, right side up, and press the cookies lightly together. Repeat with the remaining cookies and filling. Serve the cookies at room temperature or chilled.

Key Lime Sandwiches: Omit the orange zest in the cookie dough, and add 1 teaspoon finely grated lime zest. Omit the citrus juices and cream in the filling, and add 2 tablespoons bottled Key lime juice or freshly squeezed regular lime juice and 1 teaspoon finely grated lime zest.

Green Tea Orange Sandwiches: Omit the lemon zest in the cookie dough, and increase the orange zest to 1 tablespoon. Omit the citrus juices in the filling, increase the heavy cream to 2½ tablespoons, and add 1½ teaspoons powdered Japanese green tea (available from Katagiri & Company; see Sources, page 378).

STORE IN AN AIRTIGHT CONTAINER AT ROOM TEMPERATURE OR REFRIGERATED FOR UP TO A WEEK.

brandied eggnog cookies

MAKES 30 SANDWICH COOKIES

Just as the scent of a madeleine transported Proust to his memories of childhood, I'd bet that one whiff of these holiday-themed cookies would take you back to your own youth. They're tender, nutmeg-infused squares of shortbread, sandwiched together with a creamy brandy-spiked filling.

eggnog cookies

1 cup (2 sticks) unsalted butter, softened

½ cup granulated sugar

1 large egg yolk

1 teaspoon vanilla extract

¼ teaspoon freshly grated nutmeg

⅛ teaspoon salt

2 cups all-purpose flour

Coarse sugar for sprinkling

brandy cream filling

3 tablespoons unsalted butter, softened

1 cup plus 2 tablespoons confectioners' sugar

1 tablespoon brandy

1 teaspoon vanilla extract

garnish

Freshly grated nutmeg

special equipment

1½-inch fluted square or round cookie cutter

½-inch aspic cutter (of any shape) or ½-inch plain pastry tip (such as Ateco #6)

make the dough

1. In the bowl of an electric mixer, using the paddle attachment, beat the butter and sugar at medium speed until combined, about 1 minute. Add the egg yolk, vanilla extract, nutmeg, and salt and mix until combined, scraping down the sides of the bowl as necessary. At low speed, add the flour and mix until combined. Turn the dough out onto a piece of plastic wrap, pat it into a rectangle, and wrap it up. Refrigerate for at least 1 hour, until firm (or up to 3 days).

cut and bake the cookies

2. Position a rack in the center of the oven and preheat the oven to 350°F. Line two baking sheets with parchment paper or foil.

3. Place the chilled dough on a lightly floured work surface and sprinkle it lightly with flour. Using a rolling pin, roll the dough out to a thickness of ⅛ inch. Using a 1½-inch fluted square or round cookie cutter, cut out as many cookies as possible from the dough. Using a ½-inch aspic cutter (of any shape) or ½-inch plain pastry tip, cut out the centers of half of the cookies (these will be the tops). Stack and press together the scraps and chill for 15 minutes before rerolling. Carefully transfer the cookies to the prepared baking sheets, placing the tops and bottoms on separate sheets (the tops will take a minute or so less to bake than the bottoms). Sprinkle the cookies with coarse sugar. Bake the cookies, one sheet at a time, for 9 to 11 minutes, or until lightly browned on the bottom (not on top). Transfer the cookies to wire racks and cool completely.

make the filling

4. In the bowl of an electric mixer, using the paddle attachment, beat the butter at medium speed until creamy, about 30 seconds. Gradually add the confectioners' sugar, brandy, and vanilla extract and beat until blended. Scrape down the sides of the bowl. Increase the speed to high and beat until the filling is creamy, about 2 minutes.

assemble the cookies

5. Spread about 3/4 teaspoon of the filling onto the bottom of one of the whole cookies. Top with one of the cut-out cookies, right side up, and press the cookies lightly together. Repeat with the remaining cookies and filling. Grate a bit of nutmeg on top of each cookie. Serve the cookies at room temperature or chilled.

STORE IN AN AIRTIGHT CONTAINER AT ROOM TEMPERATURE FOR 3 DAYS OR REFRIGERATED FOR UP TO A WEEK.

Cookie Bite Nutmeg is the seed of a type of fir tree. Freshly grated nutmeg is much more flavorful than the preground nutmeg from the supermarket. The spice mace is actually the dried ground outer membrane of the nutmeg seed; even though we only see it dried, fresh mace is more pungent than nutmeg.

glazed hazelnut jam sandwiches

MAKES **ABOUT 38 SANDWICH COOKIES**

These cookies are a visual as well as a taste delight. The dough, loaded with butter and ground hazelnuts, bakes into very tender, nutty cookies, which are glazed and filled with raspberry jam. The delicate dough is a little tricky to roll out, so roll it between two sheets of waxed paper, as directed. These cookies take some time and effort to make (they are fussy), but they will be noticed.

hazelnut dough

½ cup hazelnuts, toasted and skinned

2½ cups all-purpose flour

⅛ teaspoon salt

1¼ cups (2½ sticks) unsalted butter, softened

¾ cup granulated sugar

glaze and filling

½ cup confectioners' sugar

1 tablespoon plus 1 teaspoon whole milk

¾ cup seedless raspberry jam

special equipment

1¾-inch scalloped round cookie cutter

½-inch round aspic cutter or ½-inch plain pastry tip (such as Ateco #6)

make the dough

1. Place the hazelnuts in the bowl of a food processor and process until finely ground, about 30 seconds. Transfer the nuts to a medium bowl.
2. Add the flour and salt to the bowl and whisk well to combine.
3. In the bowl of an electric mixer, using the paddle attachment, beat the butter at medium speed until creamy, about 30 seconds. Gradually beat in the sugar. Increase the speed to medium-high and beat until well combined and light, about 2 minutes, scraping down the sides of the bowl as necessary. At low speed, gradually add the dry ingredients, mixing just until combined.
4. Scrape the dough out onto a work surface and divide it into three portions. Place one of the pieces on a large piece of waxed paper and flatten it into a disk. Place another piece of waxed paper over it and, using a rolling pin, roll the dough out to 10-inch round about ⅛ inch thick. Repeat with the remaining pieces of dough. Stack the dough rounds, still between layers of waxed paper, and refrigerate for at least 2 hours, until firm (or up to 3 days).

cut and bake the cookies

5. Position a rack in the center of the oven and preheat the oven to 325°F. Line two baking sheets with parchment paper or foil.
6. Remove one of the dough rounds from the refrigerator. Peel off the top piece of waxed paper. Replace it loosely and flip over the dough. Peel off the other piece of waxed paper. Using a 1¾-inch round scalloped cookie cutter, cut out as many cookies as possible from the dough. Using the narrow end of a ½-inch plain pastry tip, cut out a hole from the center of each cookie. Transfer the cookies to one of the baking sheets, spacing them ½

inch apart. Bake for 8 to 12 minutes, until they are just beginning to turn pale golden. Let them cool on the baking sheet for 5 minutes, then transfer to the rack to cool completely.

7. Repeat with the remaining dough rounds, cutting out center holes from only half of the cookies from one of these rounds (to make a total of half cookies with holes and half without). Gather up the dough scraps, shape them into a disk, and reroll between sheets of waxed paper to a thickness of ⅛ inch. Chill for at least 30 minutes before cutting out more cookies (cut out holes from half of these).

glaze and fill the cookies

8. In a small bowl, whisk together the confectioners' sugar and milk until smooth. Using a pastry brush, brush a thin layer of the glaze over the tops of the cookies with holes. Set the cookies aside until the glaze is set, about 10 minutes.

9. Spoon a scant teaspoon of the raspberry jam onto the bottom of each of the whole cookies. Top each with a glazed cookie, right side up, and press down lightly so that the jam seeps through the hole slightly.

STORE IN AN AIRTIGHT CONTAINER AT ROOM TEMPERATURE FOR UP TO 3 DAYS.

caramel-almond tiger cookies

MAKES ABOUT 44 SANDWICH COOKIES

Almond and caramel has become a new classic combination, celebrated in premium ice creams and now in this wonderful cookie. Tender toasted almond shortbread rounds are sandwiched with buttery caramel, then more caramel is drizzled on top in tiger stripes. The drizzle is for visual pizzazz—and because people who love caramel can never get enough.

almond cookies

½ cup slivered almonds, toasted

1½ cups all-purpose flour, divided

½ cup cornstarch

⅛ teaspoon salt

1 cup (2 sticks) unsalted butter, softened

¼ cup granulated sugar

¼ cup confectioners' sugar

¼ teaspoon almond extract

caramel filling

¾ cup granulated sugar

3 tablespoons water

⅓ cup heavy cream

2 tablespoons unsalted butter

Pinch of salt

special equipment

1½-inch fluted round cookie cutter

¾-inch round cutter (or ⅝-inch plain pastry tip, such as Ateco #8)

make the dough

1. Place the almonds and ¼ cup of the flour in the bowl of a food processor and process until the almonds are finely ground, about 45 seconds. Transfer the mixture to a medium bowl and stir in the remaining 1¼ cups flour, the cornstarch, and salt. Set aside.

2. In the bowl of an electric mixer, using the paddle attachment, beat the butter and sugars at medium-high speed until light in texture, about 2 minutes. Beat in the almond extract. At low speed, gradually add the flour mixture, mixing just until combined. Scrape the dough onto a work surface and shape it into a disk. Wrap the dough in plastic wrap and refrigerate for at least 2 hours, until firm enough to handle (or up to 2 days).

cut and bake the cookies

3. Position a rack in the center of the oven and preheat the oven to 350°F.

4. On a lightly floured work surface, using a rolling pin, roll out the dough to a thickness of ⅛ inch, sprinkling it lightly with flour as needed to prevent sticking. Using a 1½-inch fluted round cookie cutter, cut out as many cookies as possible from the dough. Using a ¾-inch round cutter, or the tip of a ¾-inch plain pastry tip, cut out the center of half of the cookies (these cookies will be the tops). Reroll the scraps, chilling the dough for 10 minutes if necessary, and cut out more cookies. Cut out the centers of half of these. Transfer the cookies to ungreased baking sheets, spacing them ½ inch apart. Bake the cookies one sheet at a time, for 10 to 12 minutes, or until just barely beginning to color at the edges. Transfer the cookies to a wire rack and cool completely.

make the filling

5. In a small heavy saucepan, combine the sugar and water and cook over medium heat, stirring constantly, until the sugar dissolves. Increase the heat to high and cook, without stirring and occasionally brushing down the sides of the pan with a wet pastry brush, until the syrup caramelizes and turns a golden amber color, about 4 minutes. Remove the pan from the heat and carefully add the heavy cream (the mixture will bubble up), stirring until smooth. Stir in the butter and salt until the butter is melted. Let the caramel filling cool for 20 minutes, or until it has thickened enough to spread.

assemble the cookies

6. Line a large baking sheet with aluminum foil or waxed paper. Spread a scant teaspoon of the caramel filling over the bottom of each whole cookie. Top each with a cut-out cookie, and place the filled cookies on the lined sheet. Place the saucepan of caramel over low heat and heat, stirring constantly, until it is thin enough to drizzle. Using a spoon, lightly drizzle the tops of the cookies with parallel lines of caramel.

STORE IN AN AIRTIGHT CONTAINER IN A COOL, DRY PLACE FOR UP TO 5 DAYS.

whoopie pies

MAKES ABOUT 28 SANDWICH COOKIES

This recipe is from Pat Howard, mother of Martin Howard, a New York–area pastry chef known for his flashy desserts. Pat Howard would make a batch of these famous treats, and kids from all over the neighborhood would come a-runnin'. They taste like homemade Devil Dogs, only much better—generous rounds of devil's food cake with a lush cream filling. Make them for the kids, but save a bunch for yourself.

chocolate cookies

2 cups all-purpose flour

1 cup nonalkalized cocoa powder

⅜ teaspoon salt

½ cup (1 stick) unsalted butter, softened

1 cup granulated sugar

1 large egg yolk

1 teaspoon vanilla extract

1 teaspoon baking soda

½ cup hot water

½ cup buttermilk

filling

2 cups confectioners' sugar

4 tablespoons (½ stick) unsalted butter, softened

3 tablespoons heavy cream

1 teaspoon vanilla extract

Pinch of salt

make the cookies

1. Position a rack in the center of the oven and preheat the oven to 400°F. Butter two baking sheets.
2. In a medium bowl, whisk together the flour, cocoa powder, and salt until well blended. Set aside.
3. In the bowl of an electric mixer, using the paddle attachment, beat the butter and sugar at medium-high speed until well blended, about 2 minutes. Add the egg yolk and beat until well blended, scraping down the sides of the bowl as necessary. Beat in the vanilla extract. Stir the baking soda into the hot water. Adding one-third of each ingredient at a time, alternately add the hot water mixture, buttermilk, and dry ingredients, ending with the dry ingredients and mixing just until combined.
4. Using wet hands, shape the dough into 1-inch balls and arrange them 2 inches apart on the prepared baking sheets. Moisten your palm and flatten each ball into a 1¼-inch disk. Bake the cookies, one sheet at a time, for 5 to 7 minutes, until their surfaces are cracked; the cookies will still be quite soft, but they will firm up as they cool. Immediately transfer the cookies to a wire rack to cool completely.

make the filling

5. In the bowl of an electric mixer, using the paddle attachment, beat the confectioners' sugar with the butter at medium speed until the mixture is crumbly, about 1 minute. Add the heavy cream and beat at high speed until smooth. Add the vanilla extract and salt and beat until blended.

assemble the cookies

6. Using a small offset metal spatula, spread the bottoms of half of the cookies with 1 heaping teaspoon of filling each. Top with the remaining cookies and press them together gently.

STORE IN AN AIRTIGHT CONTAINER AT ROOM TEMPERATURE FOR UP TO 5 DAYS.

chocolate sandwich cookies

MAKES **ABOUT 64 SANDWICH COOKIES**

Ever wonder how those big cookie companies get their chocolate sandwich cookies so dark? The secret is black cocoa, a super-dark, super-rich cocoa that produces very dark and flavorful cookies. It's available by mail-order from The Baker's Catalogue (see Sources, page 376).

dark chocolate cookies

2 cups all-purpose flour

¼ cup nonalkalized cocoa powder, sifted

¼ cup Dutch-processed black cocoa powder, sifted

1 teaspoon baking soda

¼ teaspoon salt

1 cup (2 sticks) unsalted butter, softened

1 cup granulated sugar

1 cup firmly packed light brown sugar

2 large eggs

2 teaspoons vanilla extract

vanilla cream filling

6 tablespoons (¾ stick) unsalted butter, softened

⅓ cup solid vegetable shortening

2¼ cups confectioners' sugar

2 teaspoons vanilla extract

make the cookies

1. Position a rack in the center of the oven and preheat the oven to 350°F.
2. In a medium bowl, whisk together the flour, cocoa powders, baking soda, and salt until thoroughly blended.
3. In the bowl of an electric mixer, using the paddle attachment, beat the butter at medium speed until creamy, about 30 seconds. Add both sugars and continue beating until the mixture is light in texture and color, 2 to 3 minutes. Scrape down the sides of the bowl. Add the eggs one at a time, beating well after each addition. Beat in the vanilla extract. At low speed, beat in the flour mixture in three additions, scraping down the sides of the bowl after each addition.
4. Drop the dough by slightly rounded teaspoonfuls onto ungreased baking sheets, leaving about 1½ inches between them. Bake, one sheet at a time, for 7 to 9 minutes, until the cookies are puffed (the centers will still be soft). Cool the cookies on the baking sheets on wire racks for 1 to 2 minutes. Using a metal spatula, transfer the cookies to wire racks to cool completely.

make the filling

5. In the bowl of an electric mixer, using the paddle attachment, mix the butter and shortening at low speed until blended. Gradually add the confectioners' sugar and vanilla extract and beat until combined. Increase the speed to high and beat for 3 minutes longer, or until fluffy.

assemble the cookies

6. Using a small offset metal spatula, spread a scant teaspoon of the filling onto the bottom of a cookie. Top with another cookie, right side up, and press the cookies together lightly. Repeat with the remaining cookies and filling.

STORE **IN AN AIRTIGHT CONTAINER AT ROOM TEMPERATURE FOR UP TO A WEEK.**

amy-oes

MAKES ABOUT 33 SANDWICH COOKIES

Amy Berg is the creative and very busy baker behind New York's famed Amy's Cookies. Her cookies are sold at such culinary landmarks as Dean & Deluca, Grace's Marketplace, and Balducci's. This is one of her most popular cookies, a very dark chocolate sandwich cookie, subtly flavored with coffee and filled with a creamy, rich Kahlúa-flavored buttercream. It is crucial that you do not overbake these delicate cookies; if you leave them in the oven for even a minute or two too long, they may have a burnt taste. Amy-oes freeze extremely well.

dark cocoa cookies

1¼ cups all-purpose flour

2 teaspoons instant espresso powder, such as Medaglia d'Oro

¼ teaspoon salt

¾ cup (1½ sticks) unsalted butter, softened

¾ cup granulated sugar

1 large egg

1 teaspoon vanilla extract

¾ cup Dutch-processed cocoa powder, preferably Valrhona, sifted

kahlúa buttercream

3 tablespoons unsalted butter, softened

1 cup plus 2 tablespoons confectioners' sugar

1 tablespoon Kahlúa

1 teaspoon vanilla extract

special equipment

2-inch scalloped round cookie cutter

make the dough

1. In a medium bowl, whisk together the flour, instant espresso powder, and salt. Set aside.

2. In the bowl of an electric mixer, using the paddle attachment, beat the butter at medium speed until creamy, about 30 seconds. Gradually add the sugar and beat until light and fluffy, about 2 minutes. Reduce the speed to low and add the egg, mixing well and scraping down the sides of the bowl as necessary. Mix in the vanilla extract. Gradually add the cocoa powder, mixing until blended. Scrape down the sides of the bowl. Add the flour mixture in three additions, mixing just until blended. Scrape the dough out onto a work surface and divide it in two. Shape each piece into a disk, wrap in plastic wrap, and refrigerate for at least 2 hours, until firm.

cut and bake the cookies

3. Position a rack in the center of the oven and preheat to 325°F. Line two baking sheets with parchment paper.

4. Place one of the dough disks on a very lightly floured work surface, sprinkle it lightly with flour, and, using a rolling pin, roll it out to a thickness of 3/16 inch. Using a 2-inch round scalloped cookie cutter, cut out as many rounds as possible and arrange them ½ inch apart on the prepared baking sheets. Gather up the scraps, reroll them, and cut out more rounds. Bake the cookies, one sheet at a time, for 7 to 9 minutes, until they no longer look wet; the cookies should still be soft to the touch—do not overbake. Transfer the cookies to a wire rack and cool completely. Repeat with the remaining dough.

make the buttercream

5. In the bowl of an electric mixer, using the paddle attachment, beat the butter at medium speed until creamy, about 30 seconds. Gradually add the confectioners' sugar, then add the Kahlúa and vanilla extract, and beat until blended. Scrape down the sides of the bowl. Increase the speed to high and beat until the buttercream is creamy, about 2 minutes.

assemble the cookies

6. Spoon about ¾ teaspoon of the buttercream onto the center of the bottom of half of the cookies. Top each with another cookie, right side up, and press the cookies together lightly until the filling spreads evenly to about ¹⁄₁₆ inch from the edges. Serve, or refrigerate. Bring to room temperature before serving.

STORE IN AN AIRTIGHT CONTAINER IN THE REFRIGERATOR FOR UP TO A WEEK.

chocolate espresso sandwich cookies

MAKES ABOUT 32 SANDWICH COOKIES

Judith Sutton—an ultraprofessional writer, editor, recipe developer, and good friend—is responsible for this recipe, and it's a knockout: crispy-chewy chocolate espresso cookies filled with rich chocolate espresso ganache. The cookies are also great plain, without the filling.

chocolate espresso cookies

1 cup all-purpose flour

¼ cup nonalkalized cocoa powder

½ teaspoon baking soda

⅛ teaspoon salt

1¾ teaspoons instant espresso powder, such as Medaglia d'Oro

1½ teaspoons vanilla extract

½ cup (1 stick) unsalted butter, softened

½ cup granulated sugar

½ cup firmly packed dark brown sugar

1 large egg, at room temperature

espresso ganache filling

5 ounces bittersweet chocolate, coarsely chopped

⅓ cup heavy cream

½ teaspoon instant espresso powder, such as Medaglia d'Oro

make the cookies

1. Position two racks near the center of the oven and preheat the oven to 350°F.
2. In a medium bowl, whisk together the flour, cocoa powder, baking soda, and salt until thoroughly blended.
3. In a small cup, combine the espresso powder and vanilla extract and stir with a small rubber spatula until the espresso powder is dissolved.
4. In the bowl of an electric mixer, using the paddle attachment, beat the butter at medium speed until creamy, about 30 seconds. Add both sugars and continue beating until the mixture is light in texture and color, 2 to 3 minutes. Scrape down the sides of the bowl. Beat in the egg until well blended. Beat in the espresso mixture. At low speed, beat in the flour mixture in three additions, scraping down the side of the bowl after each addition.
5. Drop the dough by slightly rounded teaspoonfuls onto ungreased baking sheets, leaving about 1½ inches between them. Bake, two sheets at a time, for 7 to 9 minutes, until the edges of the cookies are very lightly browned but the centers are still slightly soft; switch the positions of the baking sheets halfway through the baking time for even browning. (For crisp cookies, bake for 8 to 10 minutes, until the centers are no longer soft.)
6. Cool the cookies on the baking sheets on a wire rack for 1 to 2 minutes, then, using a metal spatula, transfer the cookies to the rack to cool completely.

make the filling

7. Place the chocolate in the bowl of a food processor and process until finely chopped. In a small saucepan, combine the cream and espresso powder and bring to a boil, stirring to dissolve the espresso powder. With the motor

running, add the hot cream mixture to the chopped chocolate and process for 25 to 30 seconds, or until completely smooth, stopping to scrape down the side of the bowl once or twice if necessary.

8. Scrape the ganache into a medium bowl. Let stand at room temperature until just slightly set and spreadable, about 30 minutes.

assemble the cookies

9. Spread a gently rounded teaspoonful of the ganache filling onto the bottom of half the cookies. Top with the remaining cookies, right side up, and very gently press each sandwich together. Let sit at room temperature for about 30 minutes to set the ganache.

STORE IN AN AIRTIGHT CONTAINER AT ROOM TEMPERATURE FOR UP TO 3 DAYS.

Cookie Bite **Instant coffee can be used in place of the espresso powder, but the flavor will not be as intense.**

french macaroons

MAKES **20 SANDWICH COOKIES**

These luxurious cookies—light, nutty meringue rounds sandwiched together by rich buttercream—are ubiquitous in France and Switzerland. Piping perfect macaroons takes some practice, and baking them takes a bit of finesse: they are baked at a high temperature, but with the door propped open with a wooden spoon. They inevitably stick to the parchment paper and must be "steamed" off as soon as they come out of the oven, a tricky little maneuver that actually works like a charm. Don't make these on a humid day; meringue does not like humidity.

almond macaroons

1¼ cups whole or slivered blanched almonds

2 cups confectioners' sugar, divided

4 large egg whites, at room temperature

⅛ teaspoon cream of tartar

1 teaspoon vanilla extract

filling

Basic Buttercream (page 362)

special equipment

Pastry bag fitted with a ½-inch plain tip (such as Ateco #6)

make the macaroons

1. Position a rack in the center of the oven and preheat the oven to 425°F. Line an insulated baking sheet with parchment paper (or stack two baking sheets on top of each other).

2. In the bowl of a food processor, combine the almonds and ½ cup of the confectioners' sugar and process until the almonds are finely ground, 30 to 45 seconds. Add the remaining 1½ cups confectioners' sugar and pulse until blended.

3. In the bowl of an electric mixer, using the whisk attachment, beat the egg whites at medium-high speed until foamy. Add the cream of tartar and beat until soft peaks form. Increase the speed to high and beat until the whites are stiff but not dry. Using a large rubber spatula, fold in the almond mixture one-third at a time (the batter will deflate quite a bit—this is normal). Fold in the vanilla extract.

4. Scrape the mixture into a pastry bag fitted with a ½-inch plain tip. Lift one corner of the parchment paper and pipe a dab of meringue onto the baking sheet, to hold down the parchment paper. Repeat with the remaining corners. Pipe out 1¼-inch-wide mounds of batter onto the baking sheet, spacing them 1 inch apart.

5. Place the macaroons in the oven and use a wooden spoon to prop the door slightly open. Bake for 10 to 12 minutes, until the macaroons are smooth and shiny and an even light brown (the color of coffee ice cream). Lift the baking sheet of macaroons off the bottom baking sheet, if using two sheets,

and take it to the sink. Lift up one corner of the parchment paper and pour about ½ cup of cold water between the paper and the baking sheet, tilting the pan so that the water then runs off into the sink. This will produce steam, which will loosen the macaroons from the paper. Place the baking sheet on a cooling rack and let cool for 5 minutes.

6. Using a metal spatula, gently remove the macaroons from the parchment paper (they will still stick a bit) and place them on the rack to cool completely. Repeat with the remaining batter.

7. Make the buttercream according to the directions on page 362.

assemble the macaroons

8. Using a small offset metal spatula, spread about a rounded tablespoon of the buttercream on the bottom of a macaroon. Top with another macaroon, right side up, to form a sandwich. Repeat with the remaining macaroons and buttercream.

Hazelnut Macaroons: Substitute toasted and skinned hazelnuts for the almonds, and use Hazelnut Buttercream (page 363).

Pistachio Macaroons: Replace ¼ cup of the almonds with shelled unsalted pistachio nuts. Add a few drops of green food coloring to the macaroon base, until it is a pastel green color. Use Pistachio Buttercream (page 363).

Raspberry Macaroons: Add a few drops of red food coloring to the macaroon base, until it is a pastel pink color. Use Raspberry Buttercream (page 363).

STORE IN AN AIRTIGHT CONTAINER IN A COOL, DRY PLACE FOR UP TO 3 DAYS.

chocolate macaroon sandwiches

MAKES **ABOUT 20 SANDWICH COOKIES**

These cookies deliver a blast of chocolate flavor without too much richness. The macaroons are chewy and moist, and the chocolate buttercream is silky, light, and delicious. It does take some practice to pipe evenly shaped macaroons, but even if yours don't look perfect, they will taste like perfection.

chocolate macaroons

1¼ cups blanched whole or slivered almonds

2 cups confectioners' sugar, divided

¼ cup nonalkalized cocoa powder

4 large egg whites, at room temperature

1 teaspoon vanilla extract

filling

Chocolate Buttercream (page 363)

special equipment

Pastry bag fitted with a ½-inch plain tip (such as Ateco #6)

make the chocolate macaroons

1. Position a rack in the center of the oven and preheat the oven to 425°F. Line an insulated baking sheet with parchment paper (or stack two baking sheets on top of each other).

2. In the bowl of a food processor, combine the almonds and ½ cup of the confectioners' sugar and process until the almonds are finely ground, 30 to 45 seconds. Add the remaining 1½ cups confectioners' sugar and the cocoa powder and pulse until blended.

3. In the bowl of an electric mixer, using the whisk attachment, beat the egg whites at medium-high speed until soft peaks form. Increase the speed to high and beat until the whites are stiff but not dry. Using a large rubber spatula, fold in the almond mixture one-third at a time (the batter will deflate quite a bit—this is normal). Fold in the vanilla extract, then fold the mixture a few more times to eliminate some of the air.

4. Scrape the mixture into a pastry bag fitted with a ½-inch plain tip. Lift one corner of the parchment paper and pipe a dab of meringue onto the baking sheet, to hold down the parchment paper. Repeat with the remaining corners. Pipe out 1¼-inch-wide domes of batter onto the sheet, spacing them 1 inch apart.

5. Place the macaroons in the oven and use a wooden spoon to prop the door open slightly. Bake for 9 to 12 minutes, until the macaroons are smooth and shiny. Lift the baking sheet of macaroons off the bottom baking sheet, if using two sheets, and take it to the sink. Lift up one corner of the parchment paper and pour about ½ cup of cold water between the paper and the baking sheet, tilting the pan so that the water then runs off into the sink. This will produce steam, which will loosen the macaroons from the paper. Place the baking sheet on a cooling rack and let cool for 5 minutes.

6. Using a metal spatula, gently remove the macaroons from the parchment paper (they will still stick a bit) and place them on the rack to cool completely. Repeat with the remaining batter.

7. Make the buttercream according to the directions on page 363.

assemble the macaroons

8. Using a small offset metal spatula, spread about a rounded tablespoon of the buttercream on the bottom of a macaroon. Top with another macaroon, right side up, to form a sandwich. Repeat with the remaining macaroons and buttercream.

STORE IN AN AIRTIGHT CONTAINER IN A COOL, DRY PLACE FOR UP TO 3 DAYS.

symphonies

MAKES **ABOUT 28 SANDWICH COOKIES**

This recipe comes from Biagio Settapani, owner of Pasticceria Bruno and Bruno Bakery in New York. Biagio is one of the most warm-hearted people I've ever met, and everything he bakes is imbued with that warmth. These cookies, which he sells at his bakeries, are flavored with a combination of chocolate, almond, and cinnamon. You must line the baking sheets with parchment, and brush the underside of the parchment with water, as directed, to remove the cookies from the paper. Don't try to skip this step or, as Biagio says, you'll have a *piccolo* disaster on your hands.

almond meringues

1⅓ cups blanched whole or slivered almonds

⅔ cup plus 1 tablespoon granulated sugar, divided

¼ teaspoon ground cinnamon

4 large egg whites, at room temperature

⅔ cup sliced unblanched almonds

chocolate filling

3 ounces bittersweet chocolate, coarsely chopped

½ teaspoon solid vegetable shortening

special equipment

Large pastry bag fitted with a medium plain tip (such as Ateco #4)

make the meringues

1. Position a rack in the center of the oven and preheat the oven to 375°F. Line two baking sheets with parchment paper.

2. Place the almonds, 1 tablespoon of the sugar, and the cinnamon in the bowl of a food processor and process until finely ground, about 45 seconds.

3. In the bowl of an electric mixer, using the whisk attachment, beat the egg whites at medium speed until frothy. Increase the speed to medium-high and gradually add the remaining ⅔ cup sugar. Increase the speed to high and beat until the whites form stiff, shiny peaks. Using a large rubber spatula, gently fold in the ground almond mixture.

4. Scrape the mixture into a large pastry bag fitted with a medium plain tip. Pipe the batter onto the prepared baking sheets into 1¼-inch-diameter mounds (the cookies will not spread, so you can pipe them close to one another). Sprinkle some sliced almonds on each mound.

5. Bake the cookies, one sheet at a time, for 8 to 10 minutes, until the almonds are toasted and the cookies are golden brown around the edges; the cookies will still be soft to the touch. Carefully turn the parchment paper, with the cookies sticking to it, upside down on a work surface and brush it lightly with cold water, without splashing the cookies. Let stand until you are able to pull the cookies easily off the paper, about 1 minute. If they stick, repeat the brushing process until they release. Cool the cookies completely on a wire rack.

fill the cookies

6. In the top of a double boiler over barely simmering water, melt the chocolate, stirring occasionally until smooth. Add the vegetable shortening and stir until melted.

7. Spoon about ½ teaspoon of the melted chocolate onto the bottom of a meringue cookie. Place another cookie on top, right side up, to create a sandwich cookie. Repeat with the remaining cookies and chocolate. Refrigerate the cookies for 10 minutes, or just until the chocolate is set.

STORE IN AN AIRTIGHT CONTAINER AT ROOM TEMPERATURE FOR UP TO 2 DAYS, BUT THESE ARE BEST THE DAY THEY ARE MADE.

toasted almond crunch cookies

MAKES **ABOUT 24 SANDWICH COOKIES**

This is modeled after the time-honored "flavor system" of the Good Humor Toasted Almond Bar. It is also a miniaturized version of one of my favorite French cakes, the dacquoise. It's really more a petit four than a cookie, but it looks like a cookie and is so wonderfully delicious that I had to include it here. Part of its appeal is the unexpected combination of textures: melty meringue, silky buttercream, and, sprinkled inside, crunchy almond praline.

almond meringues

½ cup slivered almonds

1 tablespoon cornstarch

⅔ cup granulated sugar, divided

3 large egg whites, at room temperature

filling

Almond Buttercream (page 363)

almond praline

½ cup granulated sugar

¼ cup water

½ cup slivered almonds, toasted

special equipment

Large pastry bag fitted with a ¼-inch plain tip (such as Ateco #2)

make the meringues

1. Position two racks near the center of the oven and preheat the oven to 200°F. Line two large baking sheets with parchment paper.

2. Place the almonds, cornstarch, and ⅓ cup of the sugar in the bowl of a food processor and process until the nuts are finely ground, about 30 seconds. Set aside.

3. In the bowl of an electric mixer, using the whisk attachment, beat the egg whites on high speed until soft peaks form. Add the remaining ⅓ cup sugar and beat until the whites are firm and glossy. Using a rubber spatula, gently fold in the ground almond mixture in two additions.

4. Scrape the meringue into a large pastry bag fitted with a ¼-inch plain tip. Pipe the meringue onto the lined baking sheets into 1½-inch disks, spiraling from the outside of each disk into the center and leaving about ½ inch between the meringues (you should be able to fit 24 on each sheet). Bake the meringues for 1 to 1½ hours, until dry and firm to the touch. Cool the meringues on the baking sheets on wire racks.

make the filling

5. Prepare the buttercream according to the directions on page 363; set aside.

make the praline

6. Lightly oil a jellyroll pan. In a small heavy saucepan, combine the sugar and water and cook over medium heat, stirring constantly, until the sugar dissolves. Increase the heat to high and continue to cook, without stirring, occasionally brushing down the sides of the pan with a wet pastry brush, for

4 to 6 minutes, or until the syrup caramelizes and turns amber brown. Immediately remove the pan from the heat and stir in the almonds. Pour the caramel mixture onto the prepared pan and set it on a wire rack to cool for 30 minutes, or until hardened.

7. Transfer the praline to a cutting board and, using a large knife, coarsely chop it. Put the pieces in a food processor and process until finely ground, about 30 seconds. (This recipe makes quite a bit more praline than you will need for the cookies, but it is difficult to make less than this amount; store the extra praline in an airtight container and use it as an ice cream topping.)

assemble the cookies

8. Using a small offset metal spatula, spread about 1 teaspoon of the buttercream onto the top of a meringue and sprinkle with some of the praline. Top with another meringue, flat side up, and spread a layer of the buttercream over the top. Sprinkle with more praline. Repeat with the remaining meringues, buttercream, and praline.

STORE IN AN AIRTIGHT CONTAINER AT ROOM TEMPERATURE FOR UP TO 2 DAYS, BUT THESE ARE BEST THE DAY THEY ARE MADE.

stroopwafels

MAKES ABOUT 14 LARGE SANDWICH COOKIES

A Dutch favorite, these are large, thin wafer cookies subtly flavored with cinnamon and filled with caramel. They are big for a purpose: they are traditionally laid over a cup of hot coffee, the idea being to soften up the caramel, keep the coffee hot, and enjoy cookie and beverage together. You'll need a pizzelle iron to make these.

wafer cookies

1¾ cups all-purpose flour

2 teaspoons baking powder

1 teaspoon ground cinnamon

½ teaspoon salt

3 large eggs

¾ cup granulated sugar

½ cup (1 stick) unsalted butter, melted and cooled

1 tablespoon vanilla extract

caramel filling

1 cup granulated sugar

¼ cup water

4 tablespoons (½ stick) unsalted butter, cut into tablespoons

3 tablespoons heavy cream

special equipment

Pizzelle iron (to make 3½-inch rounds)

make the wafers

1. In a medium bowl, whisk together the flour, baking powder, cinnamon, and salt until well blended. Set aside.
2. In the bowl of an electric mixer, using the paddle attachment, beat the eggs at medium-high speed until blended. Gradually add the sugar and continue to beat until light, about 2 minutes. Beat in the butter and vanilla extract. At low speed, add the flour mixture, mixing just until combined.
3. Preheat a pizzelle iron according to the manufacturer's instructions, and spray it lightly with nonstick cooking spray. Spoon a rounded tablespoon of batter into the center of each pizzelle mold. Close the lid and cook according to the manufacturer's instructions (about 45 seconds). Using a spatula, transfer the wafers to a wire rack to cool. Repeat with the remaining batter.

make the filling

4. In a small heavy saucepan, combine the sugar and water and cook over medium heat, stirring constantly, until the sugar is dissolved. Stop stirring, increase the heat to high, and cook until the syrup caramelizes and turns a deep amber color (wash down the sides of the pan occasionally with a wet pastry brush during cooking to prevent crystallization). Immediately remove the pan from the heat and carefully add the butter and cream (the mixture will bubble up). Stir until the mixture stops bubbling, the butter is melted, and the mixture is smooth.

assemble the cookies

5. Spoon about 2½ teaspoons of the caramel filling onto the bottom of a wafer. Quickly top with another wafer, pressing down gently to form a sandwich. Repeat with the remaining wafers and filling.

Chocolate Stroopwafels: Reduce the amount of flour in the cookies to 1⅓ cups and add ¼ cup nonalkalized cocoa powder, sifted, along with the flour.

STORE IN AN AIRTIGHT CONTAINER AT ROOM TEMPERATURE FOR UP TO 3 DAYS.

decorator cookies

Here you'll find recipes for holidays and festive occasions such as weddings, or to use as hostess gifts or extra-special bake sale items. As such, they require more sophisticated decorating techniques than most of the cookies in this book. Kids love to decorate too, though, so many of these can be adapted to, shall we say, less sophisticated techniques.

In this chapter, you'll find drop-dead elegance and pure whimsy, side by side. Under elegance, I call your attention to Chocolate Almond Polka Dot Hearts. Once you discover transfer sheets, there will be no limit to the decorations you can apply to a cookie's surface. Springerle cookies have an Old World class and distinction that will never go out of style, and the detail found in the stamps never fails to impress. As for whimsy, there are pigs and lambs and chili peppers. Sanding sugar applied to the lamb cookies mimics that animals' coats, and the Chili Peppers, cut in the shape of a pepper, are chili-hot. But there is no rule that says you must use a particular cutter or decoration for a certain cookie. Have fun with the recipes in this chapter: mix and match, improvise—that's the whole idea.

crispy pear chips

MAKES **60 CHIPS**

Fruit chips often appear on stylish, decorative desserts served in top restaurants. I've included these intensely flavorful chips in the decorative cookie chapter, because their function is mainly as a garnish—they add visual interest, as well as a chewy texture and a burst of flavor. Use them as an accompaniment to your own desserts, artfully arranged on a dollop of whipped cream or ice cream on a pear crisp, for example. They are also a great low-fat snack, and they are very easy to make. The fruit is thinly sliced on a mandoline (available at kitchenware and gourmet shops), poached in a sugar syrup, and then dried in a warm oven. A mandoline (or the less expensive and equally efficient plastic Japanese vegetable slicer, known as a Benriner) is really a requirement for making these chips, which must be paper-thin.

2 cups water

1 cup granulated sugar

1 cinnamon stick

2 ripe but firm Bosc pears

special equipment

Mandoline or plastic Japanese vegetable slicer

Two silicone baking mats (see Sources, page 376)

1. Position two racks near the center of the oven and preheat the oven to 200°F. Line two baking sheets with silicone baking mats.
2. In a large skillet, combine the water, sugar, and cinnamon stick and cook over medium-high heat, stirring constantly, until the sugar is dissolved and the syrup comes to a boil. Reduce the heat to low.
3. Using a mandoline or Japanese vegetable slicer, slice the pears lengthwise (don't worry about the peel, core, and seeds) as thin as possible (they should be almost translucent). Immediately transfer the slices to the skillet, and cook over low heat for 5 minutes. Remove the skillet from the heat and let cool for 10 minutes.
4. Line a plate with paper towels. Transfer a few of the pear slices to the plate and blot them with another paper towel, wiping away as much of the excess syrup as possible. Arrange the blotted slices on the lined baking sheets, leaving little space between them. Repeat with the remaining slices.
5. Bake the slices for 1 hour, or until dried and almost crisp (they will crisp more as they cool). Transfer the chips to a wire rack and cool completely.

STORE **IN AN AIRTIGHT CONTAINER AT ROOM TEMPERATURE IN A COOL, DRY PLACE FOR UP TO 2 WEEKS.**

classic springerle

MAKES **ABOUT TWELVE 6-INCH COOKIES OR THIRTY-SIX 2½-INCH COOKIES**

For hundreds of years Europeans have maintained the "springerle tradition," collecting special molds and plaques and spending hours in the kitchen making the very dramatic, impressive anise-flavored cookies. The word "springerle" means "little horse" in a German dialect; the tradition may have begun with the cookies being shaped into the animal forms. The dough is pressed into molds, dried at room temperature to set the designs, and then baked. The cookies can then be painted with food coloring. Springerle dough contains no fat (except for the small amount in the eggs), so it produces a dry cookie; that dryness is great for holding the designs, which can be very intricate. These cookies can be made well ahead and actually improve with age. They also freeze well.

dough

4 cups all-purpose flour

1 teaspoon baking powder

½ teaspoon salt

4 large eggs, at room temperature

1 cup granulated sugar

1 cup confectioners' sugar

1 teaspoon finely grated lemon zest

1 teaspoon anise extract

decoration

¼ to ⅓ cup vodka

Edible luster dust in various colors (see Sources, page 376)

special equipment

One wooden springerle plaque (mold) with multiple designs or several smaller individual springerle plaques

Several small fine paintbrushes (such as #1 or #2; unused)

make the dough

1. Line two baking sheets with parchment paper. Sift together the flour, baking powder, and salt into a medium bowl. Set aside.

2. In the bowl of an electric mixer, using the whisk attachment, beat the eggs at medium-high speed until light and fluffy, about 2 minutes. Gradually add the granulated sugar and continue to beat until the batter falls in thick ribbons when the whisk is lifted, about 4 minutes. Reduce the speed to medium and beat in the confectioners' sugar, lemon zest, and anise extract. At low speed, add the flour mixture in three additions, mixing just until combined. Scrape the dough out onto a work surface and knead it a few times, until it is smooth. Shape the dough into a rough 7-inch square.

shape the cookies

3. On a lightly floured surface, using a rolling pin, roll the dough out into a 3/16-inch-thick rectangle or square, depending on the size of your mold or molds, dusting the surface of the dough lightly with flour to prevent sticking. Sprinkle the dough lightly and evenly with flour, to prevent the mold(s) from sticking to the dough. Press a wooden springerle mold (or molds) carved side down as firmly as possible into the dough. Remove the mold(s) and, using a large knife or pizza cutter, cut apart the cookies. Arrange them on the prepared baking sheets, spacing them ½ inch apart. Reroll the dough scraps and press and cut out more cookies until all the dough is used. Let the cookies dry on the baking sheets, uncovered, at room temperature for at least 8 hours (or up to 24 hours).

bake the cookies

4. Position two racks near the center of the oven and preheat the oven to 300°F.

5. Bake the cookies for 16 to 22 minutes (baking time will depend on the size of the cookies), switching the position of the sheets halfway through baking, until they are almost firm but not colored. Transfer the cookies to wire racks and cool completely.

decorate the cookies

6. Using a pastry brush, sweep off any flour from the cookies. Pour 1 tablespoon of vodka into a small cup for each of the colors you will be using. Add about ½ teaspoon of the edible luster dust to each cup and stir to mix. Paint the springerle cookies as you like. Let the "paint" dry completely, about 5 minutes.

STORE IN AN AIRTIGHT CONTAINER AT ROOM TEMPERATURE FOR UP TO A MONTH.

stained glass cookies

MAKES **ABOUT 36 COOKIES**

The "stained glass" in these unusual, striking cookies comes from ground hard candy; when the cookies are baked, the candy melts, then hardens as the cookies cool. These make wonderful Christmas tree ornaments and a colorful and festive addition to any cookie tray.

12 ounces assorted sour ball candies

Basic Decorative Cookie Dough (page 357)

special equipment

3-inch cookie cutters in assorted shapes

Small aspic cutters in various shapes or a large plain pastry tip (such as Ateco #6 or #8)

1. Position a rack in the center of the oven and preheat the oven to 350°F. Line two baking sheets with aluminum foil and lightly grease the foil.
2. Separate the sour balls by color, and place each color in a resealable plastic bag. Seal each bag and, using a rolling pin or the flat side of a meat pounder, coarsely crush the candy.
3. Prepare and roll out the cookie dough according to the directions on page 357. Use 3-inch cookie cutters to cut out shapes from the rolled dough. Using small aspic cutters in various shapes or the small opening of a large plain pastry tip, cut out and remove smaller shapes from each cookie (these small pieces of dough can be gathered together and rerolled).
4. Arrange the cookies 1 inch apart on the prepared baking sheets. Fill each cut-out shape with crushed candy. If you want to make ornaments out of the cookies, use a skewer to make a small hole in the top of each one. Bake the cookies, one sheet at a time, for 8 to 10 minutes, until the candy is melted and the cookies are very lightly golden around the edges. Let the cookies cool completely on the baking sheets on a wire rack, then gently peel the cookies off the foil.

STORE **IN AN AIRTIGHT CONTAINER AT ROOM TEMPERATURE FOR UP TO A WEEK.**

lemon lamb cookies

MAKES **26 LARGE COOKIES**

The sanding sugar sprinkled on the icing covering these lamb-shaped cookies creates a wool-like fuzziness that is very appealing and unusual. The cookies are delicious too, with a low-key lemon flavor in both the cookie dough and the icing.

lemon cookies

Lemon-Scented Decorative Cookie Dough (page 357)

icing

Double batch of Decorator's Icing (page 361)

¼ teaspoon lemon extract

White sanding sugar for sprinkling

special equipment

4½-inch-long by 2¾-inch-wide (at its widest point) lamb-shaped cookie cutter

#6 round paintbrush (unused)

Pastry bag fitted with a coupler and narrow writing tip (such as Ateco #1)

make the cookies

1. Make and roll out the cookie dough as directed on page 357. Use a 4½-inch-long by 2¾-inch-wide lamb-shaped cookie cutter to cut out cookies. Bake the cookies as directed and allow to cool.

ice the cookies

2. Make a double batch of the icing as directed on page 361. Stir in the lemon extract. Transfer half of the icing to another bowl, cover the surface of the icing with plastic wrap, and set aside (this is the icing you will use to pipe designs on the iced cookies). Add warm water a few drops at a time to the remaining icing until it does not leave a trail when it drops from a spoon and its consistency is slightly thicker than corn syrup. Dip a #6 round paintbrush into this icing and gently dab it onto the surface of one of the lamb cookies, letting the icing gently drop onto the cookie without actually brushing it on, working with one section at a time and leaving the nose of the lamb uniced, until the cookie is iced. Immediately sprinkle the entire cookie with white sanding sugar. Tip off the excess sugar. Place the cookie on a baking sheet and set aside. Repeat with the remaining lambs. Let dry in a cool place for at least 2 hours.

3. Add warm water a few drops at a time to the reserved icing until it is thin enough to pipe a straight line smoothly and does not form peaks when a spoon is dipped into it. Fill a pastry bag fitted with a coupler and a #1 writing tip with the icing. Carefully pipe a line of icing outlining the icing on a lamb cookie, then pipe a filigree pattern inside the outline to represent wool. Repeat with the remaining lambs. Let the icing dry completely, about 12 hours.

STORE **IN AN AIRTIGHT CONTAINER AT ROOM TEMPERATURE FOR UP TO A WEEK.**

chocolate gingerbread people

MAKES **ABOUT 64 COOKIES**

Making gingerbread people is the perfect parent-child baking project. Kids love it, every step of the way: the forming of the dough, the cookie cutting, the decorating, the biting off of the heads. Gingerbread cookies are a holiday tradition that can only be improved by the addition of chocolate. I've used cocoa powder, which doesn't overpower the gingerbread flavor. Seek out Muscovado sugar instead of standard dark brown sugar for this recipe. Muscovado is a dark cane sugar with a fine, moist texture and a lingering molasses flavor. It is now available in many supermarkets.

chocolate gingerbread dough

2¾ cups bleached all-purpose flour

½ cup nonalkalized cocoa powder, sifted

1 tablespoon ground ginger

1½ teaspoons ground cinnamon

½ teaspoon ground cloves

¼ teaspoon freshly grated nutmeg

½ teaspoon salt

1 cup (2 sticks) unsalted butter, softened

¾ cup firmly packed Muscovado or dark brown sugar

¾ cup granulated sugar

1 large egg

2 tablespoons hot water

1 tablespoon unsulphured (mild) molasses

1 teaspoon baking soda

make the dough

1. In a large bowl, whisk together the flour, cocoa powder, ginger, cinnamon, cloves, nutmeg, and salt until well blended. Set aside.

2. In the bowl of an electric mixer, using the paddle attachment, beat the butter and sugars at medium speed until light in texture and color, about 3 minutes. Beat in the egg.

3. In a small bowl, stir together the hot water, molasses, and baking soda, until the baking soda is dissolved. At low speed, gradually add the baking soda mixture to the butter mixture. Increase the speed to medium and mix until blended. At low speed, add the dry ingredients in several additions, mixing just until combined. Scrape the dough onto a work surface and shape it into a disk. Wrap it in plastic wrap and refrigerate for at least 2 hours, until firm (or up to 3 days).

cut and bake the cookies

4. Position a rack in the center of the oven and preheat the oven to 350°F. Grease two baking sheets.

5. Divide the chilled dough into quarters. Rewrap and refrigerate three of the quarters. On a lightly floured work surface, roll out the remaining dough to a thickness of ⅛ inch, lightly flouring the dough and work surface as needed. Using a 2¾-inch people-shaped cookie cutter, cut out as many cookies as possible from the dough. Carefully transfer the cookies to one of

decoration

Decorator's Icing (page 361)

Paste food coloring in assorted colors (see Sources, page 376)

White sanding sugar (optional)

special equipment

Assorted 2¾-inch cookie cutters

Parchment paper cones (see page 42)

the prepared baking sheets. Gather the scraps of dough together into a ball, and flatten into a disk, wrap in plastic wrap, and refrigerate until firm enough to roll, about 30 minutes; reroll the scraps one time only to make more cookies.

6. Bake the cookies, one sheet at a time, until the tops are set, 8 to 10 minutes. Cool the cookies on the baking sheet on a wire rack for 2 minutes, then transfer the cookies to the rack to cool completely. Repeat with the remaining dough.

decorate the cookies

7. Prepare the Decorator's Icing as directed on page 361. Divide the icing among as many small bowls as you desire for different colors. Cover the icing in each bowl with plastic wrap so it doesn't dry out. Add paste color to each bowl, as desired, on the tip of a toothpick, then add warm water, a few drops at a time, to the icing until it is thin enough to pipe a straight line smoothly and does not form peaks when a spoon is dipped into it. Transfer the icings to parchment paper cones and decorate the cookies as desired. While the icing is still wet, sprinkle it with sanding sugar, if desired. Let the icing dry completely, about 4 hours.

STORE IN AN AIRTIGHT CONTAINER AT ROOM TEMPERATURE FOR UP TO 1 MONTH.

chocolate peppermint polka dot pigs

MAKES ABOUT 17 LARGE COOKIES

The pig, like the frog, is the object of much collecting activity. My sister-in-law, Helen Bellas, has been collecting pig paraphernalia for years. (Her license plate says "OINK.") Helen's obsession inspired me to create this whimsical—but tasty—pig-shaped cookie. It combines the flavors of dark chocolate, white chocolate, and cool peppermint, and is perfect for any time of the year. The cookie is quite easy to make, and only requires a trip to the cake decorating store to find a large pig-shaped cookie cutter.

chocolate peppermint dough

1½ cups all-purpose flour

½ cup Dutch-processed cocoa powder

¼ teaspoon salt

¾ cup (1½ sticks) unsalted butter, softened

¾ cup granulated sugar

1 large egg

1 teaspoon vanilla extract

¼ teaspoon peppermint extract

white chocolate polka dots

4 ounces good-quality white chocolate

1 teaspoon solid vegetable shortening

Pink paste food coloring (see Sources, page 376)

special equipment

4½-inch-long by 2½-inch-wide pig-shaped cookie cutter

Parchment paper cone (see page 42)

make the dough

1. Sift together the flour, cocoa powder, and salt into a medium bowl. Set aside.

2. In the bowl of an electric mixer, using the paddle attachment, beat the butter at medium speed until creamy, about 30 seconds. Gradually add the sugar and beat until light and fluffy, about 2 minutes. Reduce the speed to low and add the egg, mixing well and scraping down the sides of the bowl as necessary. Mix in the vanilla and peppermint extracts. Add the flour mixture in three additions, mixing just until blended. Scrape the dough out onto a work surface and divide it in half. Shape each piece into a disk, wrap in plastic wrap, and refrigerate for at least 2 hours, until firm.

cut and bake the cookies

3. Position a rack in the center of the oven and preheat the oven to 325°F. Line two baking sheets with parchment paper.

4. Place one of the dough disks on a very lightly floured work surface. Sprinkle it lightly with flour and, using a rolling pin, roll it out to a thickness of 3/16 inch. Using a 4½-inch-long by 2½-inch-wide pig-shaped cookie cutter, cut out as many cookies as possible and arrange them ½ inch apart on the prepared baking sheets. Gather up the scraps, reroll them, and cut out more cookies. Bake the cookies, one sheet at a time, for 7 to 9 minutes, until they no longer look wet; they should still be soft to the touch–do not overbake. Transfer the cookies to a wire rack and cool completely.

apply the white chocolate polka dots

5. In the top of a double boiler over barely simmering water, heat the white chocolate and shortening, stirring frequently, until melted and smooth. Remove the pan from the heat. Using a toothpick, add a small amount of the pink paste food coloring and stir until the chocolate is an even pastel pink.

6. Fill a small parchment cone with the melted chocolate. Pipe polka dots, randomly and in assorted sizes, onto each pig. Pipe a small dot for an eye on each one. Refrigerate the pigs until the chocolate is set, about 30 minutes.

STORE IN AN AIRTIGHT CONTAINER AT ROOM TEMPERATURE FOR UP TO A WEEK.

chocolate almond polka dot hearts

MAKES 32 COOKIES

This is one of those "how did you do that?" recipes. You, too, can be the envy of the bake sale stalwarts with this cookie—a striking, heart-shaped almond cookie with a vibrant polka dot pattern imprinted in its chocolate coating. The polka dots are easily applied with a transfer sheet, an acetate sheet with a pattern imprinted on it in cocoa butter. Transfer sheets give cookies (and other desserts as well) a professional look. They're available in many patterns, including hearts, stars, and gold flecks, and messages like Happy Birthday. Although these cookies are intended for Valentine's Day, you can consider this an all-purpose holiday special occasion recipe, using different cutters and transfer sheets as appropriate.

almond shortbread hearts

¾ cup slivered almonds, toasted

½ cup cake flour (not self-rising)

1¾ cups all-purpose flour

¼ teaspoon salt

1¼ cups (2½ sticks) unsalted butter, softened

¾ cup granulated sugar

1 teaspoon vanilla extract

¼ teaspoon almond extract

chocolate polka-dot coating

18 ounces bittersweet couverture chocolate (see Sources, page 376)

special equipment

Six 9¾-by-14¼-inch polka dot transfer sheets (available by mail-order from New York Cake and Baking Distributors; see Sources, page 379)

3-inch heart-shaped cookie cutter

make the dough

1. Place the almonds and cake flour in the bowl of a food processor and process until the almonds are finely ground, about 1 minute. Set aside.
2. Sift together the all-purpose flour and salt into a medium bowl. Set aside.
3. In the bowl of an electric mixer, using the paddle attachment, beat the butter at medium-high speed until creamy, about 30 seconds. Gradually add the sugar and beat until light in texture and color, about 2 minutes. Scrape down the sides of the bowl and beat in the vanilla and almond extracts. At low speed, add the nut mixture, mixing until blended. Add the flour mixture and mix until just combined. Scrape the dough out onto a work surface and divide in half. Shape it into two disks, wrap each disk in plastic wrap, and refrigerate until firm enough to roll, about 1 hour.

cut and bake the cookies

4. Position a rack in the center of the oven and preheat the oven to 350°F. Line two baking sheets with parchment paper.
5. Remove one of the dough disks from the refrigerator. On a lightly floured work surface, using a rolling pin, roll the dough out to a thickness of 3/16 inch, sprinkling the dough lightly with flour as needed to prevent sticking. Using a 3-inch heart-shaped cookie cutter, cut out as many cookies from the dough as possible. Carefully transfer the cookies to the prepared sheets,

spacing them 1 inch apart. Gather up the scraps, shape into a disk, wrap in plastic, and refrigerate until firm enough to roll, about 20 minutes. Repeat the rolling and cutting with the remaining dough and scraps until all the dough is used.

6. Bake the cookies, one sheet at a time, for 15 to 18 minutes, until pale golden brown around the edges. Transfer the cookies to a wire rack and cool completely.

apply the polka dot coating

7. Cut the polka dot transfer sheets into thirty-two 3½-inch squares (the squares don't need to be perfect).

8. Temper the chocolate according to the directions on page 366.

9. Place a cookie upside down on a wire rack. Using a small offset metal spatula, spread a thin, even layer of tempered chocolate over the cookie, spreading it right up to the edges. Immediately press the pattern side of a transfer sheet square onto the chocolate, pressing gently but firmly so that the sheet touches the chocolate all over the surface of the cookie. Transfer the cookie (with its transfer sheet attached) to another wire rack, chocolate side up. Repeat the coating process with the remaining cookies. Allow the cookies to set at room temperature for 2 hours. (If your kitchen is warm, refrigerate the cookies for 1 hour instead.)

10. Gently peel the transfer sheet off each cookie. Serve the cookies chocolate side up.

STORE IN AN AIRTIGHT CONTAINER AT ROOM TEMPERATURE FOR UP TO 5 DAYS.

chili peppers

MAKES **18 LARGE COOKIES**

Adding chili pepper to sweets became popular in the late '80s, riding the wave of the Southwestern food craze. The first bite of these cayenne pepper–fueled cookies is pleasantly sweet and somewhat mild, but just as you take your second bite, the pepper hits you WHAM! right in the back of the throat. Hard-core pepper enthusiasts will probably want to increase the amount of cayenne. Cornmeal gives these hot cookies a nice coarse texture. If decorating is not your forte, skip the icing and just dust the cookies with confectioners' sugar.

cookies

1½ cups all-purpose flour

¼ cup yellow cornmeal

¾ teaspoon baking powder

¼ teaspoon cayenne pepper

⅛ teaspoon salt

½ cup (1 stick) unsalted butter, softened

½ cup granulated sugar

1 large egg

1 teaspoon vanilla extract

decoration

Decorator's Icing (page 361)

Hunter or moss green, kelly green, and Christmas red paste food coloring (see Sources, page 376)

special equipment

6-inch-long by 2-inch-wide (at its widest point) chili pepper cookie cutter

#6 round paintbrush (unused)

Parchment paper cone (see page 42)

make the cookies

1. Position a rack in the center of the oven and preheat the oven to 350°F. Line two baking sheets with parchment paper or foil.
2. In a medium bowl, whisk together the flour, cornmeal, baking powder, cayenne pepper, and salt. Set aside.
3. In the bowl of an electric mixer, using the paddle attachment, beat the butter at medium speed until creamy, about 30 seconds. Gradually add the sugar and beat at medium-high speed until well blended and light, about 3 minutes. Beat in the egg and vanilla extract until smooth, scraping down the sides of the bowl as necessary. At low speed, add the flour mixture one-third at a time, beating just until blended. Scrape the dough out on a work surface and shape it into a disk.
4. Sprinkle the work surface and dough lightly with flour and roll the dough out to a thickness of ⅛ inch. Using a 6-inch-long by 2-inch-wide chili pepper–shaped cookie cutter, cut out as many cookies as possible from the dough. Gather up the scraps, wrap in plastic wrap, and chill for 15 minutes before rerolling and cutting more cookies. Arrange the cookies ½ inch apart on the prepared baking sheets. Bake the cookies, one sheet at a time, for 10 to 12 minutes, until they are just beginning to turn golden brown around the edges of the stem end and are slightly firm to the touch. Transfer the cookies to wire racks and cool completely.

decorate the cookies

5. Prepare the icing as directed on page 361. Transfer about ¼ cup of the icing to a small bowl. Add warm water ½ teaspoon at a time to the icing until it

is thin enough to pipe a straight line smoothly and does not form peaks when a spoon is dipped into it. Dip a toothpick into the hunter or moss green paste food coloring and stir it into the icing until it is dark green. Cover the surface of the icing with plastic wrap and set aside.

6. Transfer about one-quarter of the remaining icing to a small bowl. Add warm water a teaspoon at a time until the icing does not leave a trail when it drops from a spoon and its consistency is slightly thicker than corn syrup. Dip a toothpick into the kelly green paste food coloring and stir it into the icing until it is bright green. Cover the surface of the icing with plastic wrap and set aside.

7. Add warm water ½ teaspoon at a time to the remaining icing until the icing does not leave a trail when it drops from a spoon and its consistency is slightly thicker than corn syrup. Dip a toothpick into the Christmas red paste food coloring and stir it into the icing until it is bright red. Cover the surface of the icing with plastic wrap and set aside.

8. Dip a #6 round paintbrush into the bright green icing and gently dab it onto the stem of a pepper cookie, letting the icing gently drop onto the cookie without actually brushing it on. Continue to dab the icing onto the stem area, forming two points that will protrude into the red area of the pepper. Set the cookie aside to dry, and ice the stems of the remaining cookies. Let the icing dry at room temperature for at least 2 hours before proceeding.

9. Dip the paintbrush into the red icing and gently dab it onto the uniced area of a cookie, one section at a time, until the entire cookie is iced. Set the cookie aside to dry, and repeat with the remaining cookies. Let the icing dry for at least 6 hours before piping on the outline.

10. Scrape the dark green icing into a parchment cone. Pipe a thin line around the edges of a cookie, outlining the outside and the points of the stem area separately. Repeat with the remaining cookies. Let the cookies dry for at least 6 hours.

STORE IN AN AIRTIGHT CONTAINER AT ROOM TEMPERATURE FOR UP TO A WEEK.

snowflakes

MAKES **24 COOKIES**

These highly decorative cookies make beautiful Christmas tree ornaments, holiday decorations, terrific accents to a cookie tray, or hostess gifts. Making the sugar cookie base is easy. Icing the cookies can be a challenge, but, like decorating a gingerbread house, is an engaging holiday ritual. If one way for you to cope with the holidays is to lose yourself for a few hours in a project, this is a good one. Important: silver and pearl dragees should be used only for decorative cookies, to be used to adorn a Christmas tree, for example, not for cookies intended for consumption. Decorate each snowflake differently, as Mother Nature does. To hang a snowflake as an ornament, loop a thin ribbon through the hole in one of the points.

Basic Decorative Cookie Dough (page 357)

Double batch of Decorator's Icing (page 361)

White sanding sugar for sprinkling

Silver or pearl dragees (if cookies are for decorative use only)

special equipment

4½-inch snowflake-shaped cookie cutter

⅝-inch petal-shaped aspic cutter

Plastic drinking straw

#6 round paintbrush (unused)

Pastry bag fitted with coupler and narrow writing tip (such as Ateco #2)

make the cookies

1. Make and roll out the cookie dough as directed on page 357. Use a 4½-inch snowflake-shaped cookie cutter to cut out the cookies. Using a ⅝-inch petal-shaped aspic cutter, cut out shapes from the interior of each snowflake (or leave some without cutouts, if you want). If you plan to hang the snowflakes as ornaments, use a straw to cut out a hole on one of the points of each snowflake. Bake the cookies as directed and allow to cool.

ice the cookies

2. Make a double batch of the icing as directed on page 361. Transfer one-third of the icing to another bowl. Cover the surface of the icing with plastic wrap and set aside (this is the icing you will use to pipe designs on the iced cookies). Add warm water a few drops at a time to the remaining icing until it does not leave a trail when it drops from a spoon and its consistency is slightly thicker than corn syrup. Dip a #6 round paintbrush into the icing and gently dab it onto the surface of one of the snowflake's points, letting the icing gently drop onto the cookie without actually brushing it on. Continue to dab the icing onto the cookie, working with one section at a time, until the entire cookie is iced. Place the cookie on a baking sheet and set aside. Repeat with the remaining snowflakes. Let dry in a cool place for at least 2 hours.

3. Add warm water a few drops at a time to the reserved icing until it is thin enough to pipe a straight line smoothly and does not form peaks when a

spoon is dipped into it. Fill a pastry bag fitted with a coupler and a #2 writing tip with the icing. Pipe small dots along the edges of a snowflake at ⅛-inch intervals. Do the same along the edges of the cutouts. Decorate the interior of the snowflake as you like, with dots, lines, and flourishes, or a filigree pattern. If the snowflake is to be solely decorative, pipe a few larger dots of icing on it and, using tweezers, arrange a dragee in the center of each one. While the icing is still wet, sprinkle the cookie with sanding sugar, tipping off the excess. Repeat with the remaining snowflakes. Let the icing dry completely, about 12 hours.

STORE IN AN AIRTIGHT CONTAINER AT ROOM TEMPERATURE FOR UP TO 2 WEEKS.

pink plaid valentine hearts

MAKES **28 LARGE COOKIES**

These sleek yet sentimental cookies are the ideal Valentine Day's gift. Decorating them with the icing takes some practice, but once you get going, it's almost addictive. The pattern is deceptively complicated; the only requirement is that you can pipe a straight line. Once they've set, you can wrap these eye-catching cookies individually in clear cellophane (available at cake decorating supply stores) and tie each one with a hot pink ribbon.

Basic Decorative Cookie Dough (page 357)

Double batch of Decorator's Icing (page 361)

Pastel pink and deep pink or fuchsia red paste food coloring (see Sources, page 376)

special equipment

3½-inch heart-shaped cookie cutter

#6 round paintbrush (unused)

Two parchment paper cones (see page 42)

make the cookies

1. Make and roll out the cookie dough as directed on page 357. Use a 3½-inch heart-shaped cookie cutter to cut out the cookies. Bake as directed and allow to cool.

ice the cookies

2. Make a double batch of the icing as directed on page 361. Transfer one-third of the icing to a medium bowl and cover surface of the icing with plastic wrap. Transfer half of the remaining icing to another bowl, cover, and set aside. Tint the remaining icing pale pink by stirring in a small amount of the pastel pink food coloring, using a toothpick, until it is pale pink. Stir in warm water a few drops at a time until the icing does not leave a trail when it drops from a spoon and its consistency is slightly thicker than corn syrup. Dip a #6 round paintbrush into the icing and gently dab it onto the surface of one of the hearts, letting the icing gently drop onto the cookie without actually brushing it on. Continue to dab the icing onto the cookie, working with one section at a time, until the entire cookie is iced. Place the cookie on a baking sheet and set aside. Repeat with the remaining cookies. Let dry in a cool place for at least 2 hours.

3. Add warm water a few drops at a time to one of the reserved bowls of icing until it is thin enough to pipe a straight line smoothly and no longer forms peaks. Fill a parchment cone with the icing; set aside. Tint the remaining icing hot pink with deep pink or fuchsia red coloring, using a toothpick; it will take a generous amount of paste color to get the right color. Transfer this icing to another parchment cone.

4. Using scissors, snip a tiny hole at the tip of each parchment cone. Pipe horizontal and vertical lines of the white icing over one of the cookies, using the photo in the insert as a guide. Pipe horizontal and vertical lines of the hot pink icing over the cookie, again using the photo as a guide. Pipe small dots of white icing at the intersections of the hot pink lines. Repeat with the remaining cookies. Let the cookies stand for at least 2 hours at room temperature, until the icing is completely set.

STORE IN AN AIRTIGHT CONTAINER AT ROOM TEMPERATURE FOR UP TO A WEEK.

wedding cake cookies

MAKES **20 LARGE COOKIES**

Think of these as miniature one-dimensional wedding cakes. Artfully decorated, the cookies make great shower or wedding favors. Not-so-artfully decorated, they're still great fun. They can be personalized by adding the names of the bride and groom on the bottom tier, or with visual touches that capture their personalities. If your flower-piping skills are shaky, you can purchase premade royal icing flowers at a cake decorating store and apply them to the cookies (after the surface icing has dried) with a dab of royal icing. Making these cookies is a fun preshower group project for devoted friends of the bride, or groom, for that matter.

Basic Decorative Cookie Dough (page 357)

Double batch of Decorator's Icing (page 361)

Ivory, pink, and leaf green paste food coloring (see Sources, page 376)

special equipment

4½-inch-high by 4½-inch-wide (at its base) three-tiered wedding cake cookie cutter (available at cake decorating stores; see Sources, page 376)

#6 round paintbrush (unused)

Parchment paper cone (see page 42)

Pastry bag fitted with coupler and a small rose tip (such as Ateco #101)

Pastry bag fitted with coupler and small leaf tip (such as Ateco #67)

make the cookies

1. Make and roll out the cookie dough as directed on page 357. Use a 4½-inch-high, 4½-inch-wide (at its base) three-tiered wedding cake cookie cutter to cut out the cookies. Bake the cookies as directed and allow to cool.

ice the cookies

2. Make a double batch of the icing as directed on page 361. Transfer half of the icing to another bowl. Add a small amount of ivory paste food coloring, on the tip of a toothpick, to the icing, to turn it a pale ivory; stir the icing well to blend the color evenly. Transfer about one-third of the ivory icing to a small bowl (this is the icing you will use for piping lines on the cookies). Cover the surface of both ivory icings with plastic wrap and set aside. Transfer half of the remaining uncolored icing to another bowl. Add a tiny amount of pink paste food coloring to one bowl to turn the icing a pale pink, stirring to blend. Add a tiny amount of leaf green paste food coloring to the other bowl to turn it a pale leaf green. Cover the surface of both icings with plastic wrap and set aside.

3. Add warm water a few drops at a time to the larger amount of ivory icing until it does not leave a trail when it drops from a spoon and its consistency is slightly thicker than corn syrup (it should be soft, but not runny, or it will be too transparent to cover the cookies and may separate as it dries). Dip a #6 round paintbrush into the icing and gently dab it onto the surface of one of the cookies, letting the icing gently drop onto the surface of the cookie without actually brushing it on. Continue to dab the icing onto the cookie, working with one section at a time, until the entire cookie is iced. Place the cookie on a baking sheet. Repeat with the remaining cookies, and set aside to dry in a cool place for at least 2 hours.

4. One at a time, add warm water a few drops at a time to the pink, green, and reserved ivory icings just to thin them enough so that they form soft, not stiff, peaks when a spoon is lifted out of the icings. Fill a pastry bag fitted with a coupler and a rose tip with the pink icing. Fill a pastry bag fitted with a coupler and a leaf tip with the leaf green icing. Fill a parchment paper cone with the ivory-colored icing.

5. Using the parchment cone, pipe a fluted line of ivory icing around the edges of a cookie, outlining it. Then pipe fluted lines to separate the tiers. Pipe fluted swags on each tier, each swag beginning and ending at the fluted line above the tier. Now pipe sweet peas where the swags meet along each tier: Position the pastry bag of pink icing with the tip where you want the flower at a 45-degree angle, with the wide end of the tip down. Gently squeeze the bag and, as the icing flows out, raise the tube about ⅛ inch above the surface. Hold that position briefly, then lower the tube to the position in which you started. Release the pressure and pull the bag away. Move the bag so that it is positioned just to the left of the point at which you started the first petal, angle the tip slightly to the left, and repeat the procedure to make a second petal. Then position the bag just to the right of the point at which you started the first petal, angle the tip slightly to the right, and repeat the procedure to make a third petal. Repeat to form sweet peas where the swags meet, and wherever else you want them on the cookie. To make leaves, position the bag with the green icing on one side of a flower. Hold the bag at a 45-degree angle to the surface and gently squeeze it while moving it away from the flower, bringing it to a point as you relax the pressure on the bag. Repeat to form a leaf on the other side of the flower. Repeat the process for all the flowers. Repeat with the remaining cookies. If you want, use the ivory icing remaining in the parchment cone to pipe detailed decorations such as dots and flourishes in the empty spaces on each cookie. Let the cookies dry completely at room temperature, at least 6 hours.

STORE IN AN AIRTIGHT CONTAINER AT ROOM TEMPERATURE FOR UP TO A WEEK.

wicked witch candy cottage

MAKES **ONE 5¼ BY 6-INCH BY 8-INCH-HIGH COTTAGE PLUS A SMALL CAT COTTAGE**

In the Brothers Grimm fairy tale "Hansel and Gretel," the wicked witch lived in an enchanted candy cottage in the woods. She lured little boys and girls to the house, fattened them up with candy, and then ate them. Though her motive was morbid, decorating a house with candy was a stroke of genius on the part of the witch (or her contractor), one kids can readily identify with. The structure for my gingerbread house (which comes with a small cat cottage) is very simple; even a beginner can manage it. The time-consuming part (and the stuff of memories) is the decoration, which can be as simple or elaborate as you, or your helpers, like. I recruited my talented artist sister, Kathleen Bartoletti, to help design and decorate my cottage. We spent an entire day eating high-octane candy and executing design concepts for the house. Important: This dough is very sturdy, a necessity for constructing a gingerbread house, meaning it is too hard for cookies.

gingerbread dough

5½ cups unbleached all-purpose flour

1 teaspoon baking soda

¼ teaspoon baking powder

1 tablespoon ground ginger

1 tablespoon ground cinnamon

1 teaspoon ground cloves

1 teaspoon ground nutmeg

½ teaspoon salt

1 cup solid vegetable shortening

1 cup granulated sugar

1⅓ cups unsulphured (mild) molasses

1 large egg

1 teaspoon vanilla extract

candy window glass

3 ounces peppermint candies (the translucent kind, which are

make the dough

1. Sift together the flour, baking soda, baking powder, ginger, cinnamon, cloves, nutmeg, and salt into a large bowl. Set aside.

2. In the bowl of an electric mixer, using the paddle attachment, beat the shortening and sugar at medium-high speed until well blended, about 2 minutes. Add the molasses, egg, and vanilla extract and beat until well blended, about 2 minutes. If your mixer has a splatter shield, attach it now. At low speed, add the dry ingredients in four additions, mixing just until blended. Scrape the dough out onto a work surface and knead it gently a few times, until smooth. Divide the dough into quarters and shape into disks. Wrap each disk in plastic wrap and chill for at least 1 hour, until firm (or up to 2 weeks).

prepare the candy window glass

3. Place the candies (unwrapped) in a large sealable plastic bag and seal the bag. Using a meat mallet, finely crush the candies. Set aside.

cut out and bake the pattern pieces

4. Copy the pattern pieces on pages 329 through 332 onto manila folder-weight paper and cut them out. (Note: Templates are at 90%.) Label each piece.

5. Position a rack in the center of the oven and preheat the oven to 325°F.

the same color as menthol cough drops, not the pink and white kind) or lemon hard candies

assembly

Double batch of Decorator's Icing (page 361)*

Paste food coloring in forest green, mint green, black, and other assorted shades, as desired (see Sources, page 376)

decoration

Assorted jelly beans

Sugar ice cream cones (for trees)

Large silver or gold dragées

Nonpareils

Candy spearmint leaves

Chocolate-covered raisins

Unblanched almonds

Jawbreakers

Peppermint sticks

Malt balls

Licorice

Gumdrops

Small pebble-shaped candies (for cobblestone path)

Pretzel sticks or candy bars (for optional fence)

Rock candy (to place around trees)

Kosher salt (for snow)

***Note:** You will need to make the two batches of icing separately.

6. Cut a piece of aluminum foil the size of a baking sheet. Place the foil on a work surface and place one of the dough disks on it. Place a piece of plastic wrap over the dough and roll it out evenly to a thickness of 3⁄16 inch. Remove the plastic wrap. Place as many of the pattern pieces as will fit on the dough, leaving at least ½ inch between the pieces (the dough pieces will remain in place on the foil during baking). Using a small sharp knife, cut the dough around the pattern pieces, being careful not to cut through the foil. Remove the pattern pieces from the dough. Remove all the dough scraps from between the pattern pieces and save to reroll. Carefully slide the sheet of foil onto a baking sheet. Repeat the process until you have cut out all the required pieces. Brush the area of foil inside the window openings with shortening.

7. Bake the gingerbread, one sheet at a time, for 5 minutes. Remove the baking sheets from the oven and fill the window openings with a thin layer of the crushed candies. Bake for another 10 to 15 minutes, or until the dough feels firm to the touch. Carefully slide the foil off the baking sheet and onto a completely flat surface to cool (not onto a wire rack).

8. When the pieces are cool, carefully peel them off the foil. Store the gingerbread in an airtight container in a cool, dry place until ready to use (up to 2 weeks at room temperature; or freeze for up to 3 months).

make the icing

9. Make the first batch of icing according to the directions on page 361; ideally, the icing should be made just prior to using. The icing must be stiff enough to use as "cement" for attaching the walls and roof of the structure. Keep a piece of plastic wrap pressed directly on the surface of icing while you are using it to prevent drying out. If not using all of the icing immediately, store in an airtight container in the refrigerator for up to 1 week.

assemble the witch's cottage

10. Cover the cardboard, plywood, or Foamcore base with foil, attaching it with tape to the underside of the base. Half-fill a pastry bag fitted with a medium star tip with icing. Have a heavy can ready. Hold the COTTAGE FRONT

special equipment

20-inch square cake board, plywood board, or Foamcore (for the base)

Pastry bag fitted with a medium star tip (such as Ateco #4)

Pastry bag fitted with a coupler and a small plain tip (such as Ateco #2)

Pastry bag fitted with a coupler and a small leaf tip (such as Ateco #67)

piece in one hand and, with your other hand, pipe a thick line of icing (the icing should be difficult to pipe) along the inside bottom and side edges (but not the angled roof area). Place the piece upright a few inches from the center of the base, so the cottage will be centered, leaning it against the can for support. Hold a COTTAGE SIDE piece in one hand and pipe a thick line of icing along the inside bottom edge and the outside side edges. Join the side piece to the front piece on the base at a right angle, pressing to attach. At this point, the structure will support itself. Remove the can and repeat with the remaining side piece. Holding the COTTAGE BACK piece in one hand, pipe a thick line of icing along the inside bottom and side edges. Join this piece to the two side pieces. Press the edges of all four sides of the building together to form perfect right angles. Allow the structure to dry for at least 30 minutes before attaching the roof.

11. Pipe a very thick line of icing along the slanted top edges of the COTTAGE FRONT and BACK pieces. Hold a ROOF piece in one hand and pipe a thick line of icing along the top inside edge. Gently press the ROOF piece onto the house. Repeat with the other ROOF piece, pressing the top edges together at the crest of the roof. You may need to hold the roof pieces in place for a few minutes until the icing hardens a little so it stays securely in place. Let the roof dry for at least 1 hour before attaching the chimney.

12. Pipe a line of icing around the inside bottom and outside sides of the two CHIMNEY SIDE pieces. Pipe a line of icing around the inside sides and angled bottom edges of the CHIMNEY BACK and FRONT pieces. Place the CHIMNEY FRONT piece on the roof peak, slightly off center toward the back of the cottage. Attach both CHIMNEY SIDE pieces to the CHIMNEY FRONT so that the icing on the bottom edges touches the roof. Attach the CHIMNEY BACK piece to the sides, pressing it gently into place. Let the chimney dry for at least 30 minutes before adding any decorations.

assemble the black cat cottage

13. Add more icing to the pastry bag if necessary. Decide where you want to position the black cat cottage. Have a small can ready. Hold the CAT COTTAGE FRONT piece in one hand and, with your other hand, pipe a thick line of icing along the inside bottom and side edges (but not the angled roof area). Place the piece upright in the position you want it, leaning it against the can for support. Hold a CAT COTTAGE SIDE piece in one hand and pipe a thick line of icing along the inside bottom edge and the

outside side edges. Join the side piece to the front piece on the base at a right angle, pressing to attach. At this point, the structure will support itself. Remove the can and repeat with the remaining side piece. Holding the CAT COTTAGE BACK piece in one hand, pipe a thick line of icing along the inside bottom and side edges. Join this piece to the two side pieces. Press the edges of all four sides of the building together to form perfect right angles. Allow the structure to dry for at least 15 minutes before attaching the roof.

14. Pipe a very thick line of icing along the slanted top edges of the CAT COTTAGE SIDE pieces. Hold a CAT COTTAGE ROOF piece in one hand and pipe a thick line of icing along the top inside edge. Gently press the ROOF piece onto the house. Repeat with the other ROOF piece, pressing the top edges together at the crest of the roof. You may need to hold the roof pieces in place for a few minutes until the icing hardens a little so it stays securely in place. Let the roof dry for at least 1 hour before attaching any decorations.

Home construction tips

- The gingerbread dough can be refrigerated for up to 1 month.
- Find a good old-fashioned candy shop or a mail-order site with a big selection of candies.
- Don't be overwhelmed by the scope of the project. Start early, and remember that the construction and decorating can be done in stages over a long period of time. Make it a family or social event.
- To color the icing, use paste food colorings and add tiny amounts on the tip of a toothpick until you get the right color.
- Instead of using the crushed candies, you can make the windows by attaching a piece of sheet gelatin to the inside of each window openings; use icing to secure them.
- The candy cottage can be personalized by adding family names (including pets) to pieces of gingerbread and attaching them to the front of the cottage

decorate the cottages

15. Make the second batch of the icing as directed on page 361, adding a teaspoon or two of water to thin it slightly. Fill a pastry bag fitted with a small plain tip with the icing. Organize all your decorating candies and accessories so that they are within easy reach. Using the icing as glue, begin attaching candy to the sides, back, and front of each cottage. Refer to the photo in the insert as a guide, or create your own design. Decorate the shutters with the thinned icing (and/or candy, if you want) and attach them on the sides of all windows. For trees, color a small amount of icing with a mixture of forest green and mint green coloring and scrape it into a small pastry bag fitted with a small leaf tip. Invert the sugar cones, and pipe leaves over the cones, covering them completely. Garnish the trees with small candies or star-shaped decors. Attach the trees to the base with icing. Decorate the witch, Hansel and Gretel, and black cat figures with colored icings and candies. Attach them to the base with icing. Use small pebble-shaped candies to make a cobblestone path up to the cottage door, gluing each one in place with icing. When you have decorated the cottages, pour kosher salt onto the base, all around the cottages, to represent snow.

STORE IN COOL, DRY PLACE; THE COTTAGE WILL KEEP INDEFINITELY.

Cookie Bite **Before pouring molasses into a measuring cup, spray the cup lightly with nonstick cooking spray. It will pour much more easily, leaving the cup clean.**

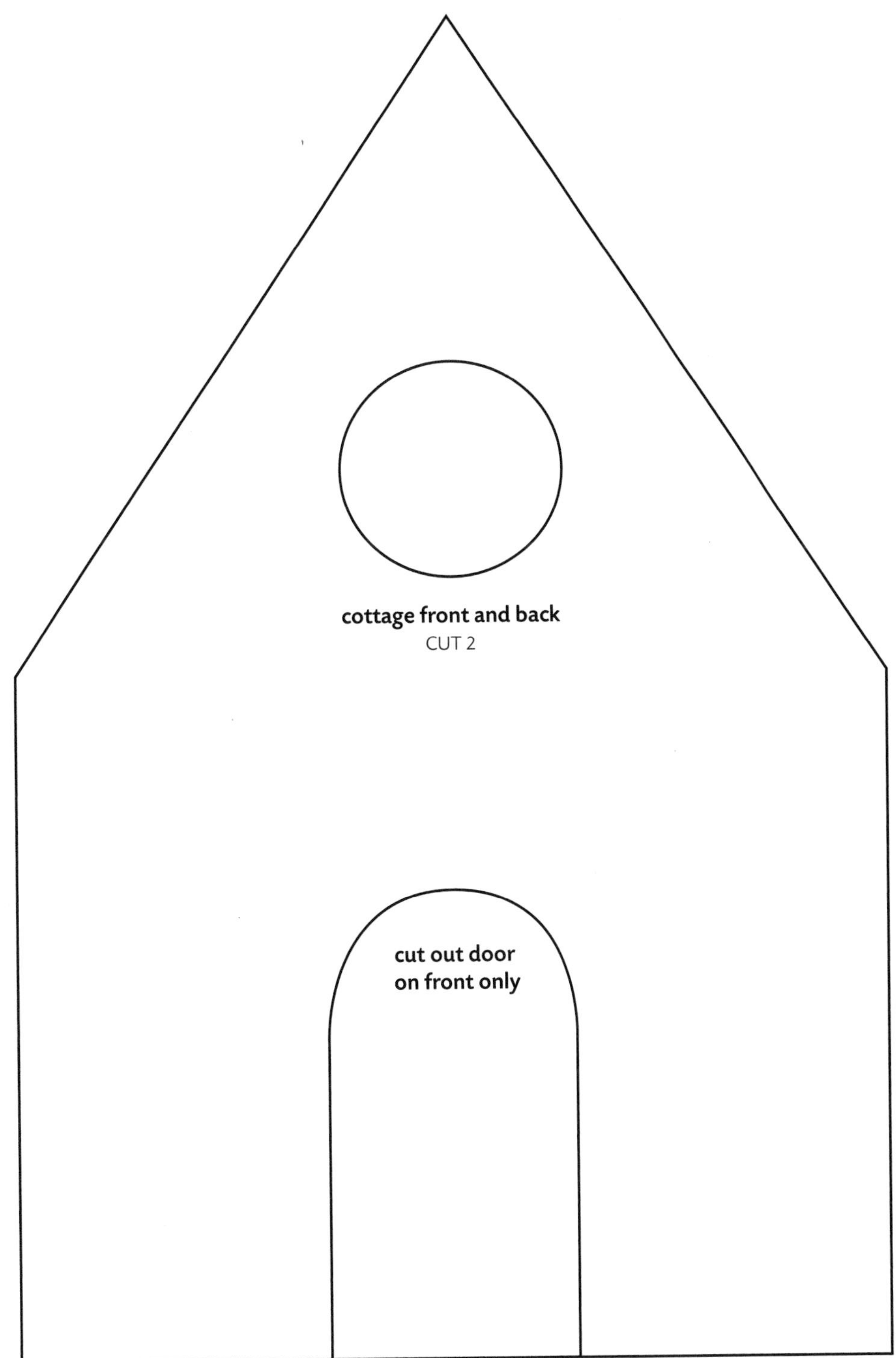
cottage front and back
CUT 2
cut out door
on front only

cottage roof
CUT 2

wicked witch
CUT 1
witch's broom
CUT 1
Hansel
& Gretel
CUT 2
cottage side
CUT 2
bottom

black
cat
CUT 1
cat cottage front
CUT 1
cat cottage back
CUT 1
cat cottage roof
CUT 2
chimney side
CUT 2
chimney
front and back
CUT 2
cat cottage side
CUT 2
heart decoration
CUT 1
front shutters
CUT 1
OF EACH
side shutters
CUT 8

savory cookies and crackers

I couldn't resist this opportunity to present the savory side of the cookie. These are cookies sans sugar, but with wonderfully unexpected aromatic flavors. In this chapter, you'll find some of my favorite biscuit-style hors d'oeuvres. Nothing sets the tone for a great dinner party like finger food with gusto, and that's what I've included in these recipes. Savory cookies and crackers also make great accompaniments to soup or other light suppers, great picnic or brunch fare, irresistible snacks for long car trips—name the occasion, and one of these will fit.

Scan the recipes and you'll find crackers, crisps, rusks, puffs, and shortbreads that are vibrant with flavors such as rosemary, garlic, curry, sesame, pepper, dill, jalapeño, Brie, feta, or blue cheese. Use your creative juices to come up with your own flavor combinations. Many of these doughs can be prepared in advance and frozen. When unexpected (or expected) guests wander in, just turn on the oven, slice, and bake. *Voilà:* instant hors d'oeuvres.

black and white sesame crisps

MAKES **48 CRACKERS**

This recipe comes from Lisa Cole, a cooking school classmate and friend. Lisa is the owner of Inspired Catering in Hartford, Connecticut, and these crispy triangles are a caterer's dream, for reasons that we civilians can also respect: they're striking in appearance, delicious, and the quickest crackers around. They're great with smoked salmon or goat cheese. Wonton skins, black sesame seeds, and toasted sesame oil are available at health food stores and Asian groceries.

¼ cup water

1 teaspoon toasted sesame oil

2 tablespoons white sesame seeds

2 tablespoons black sesame seeds

24 wonton skins

Kosher salt for sprinkling

1. Position a rack in the center of the oven and preheat the oven to 375°F.
2. In a small bowl, stir together the water and sesame oil with a fork (they will not blend completely). In another small bowl, combine the white and black sesame seeds.
3. Place a wonton skin on a work surface and, using a pastry brush, brush it lightly with the sesame oil mixture. Sprinkle it generously with the sesame seeds. Using a large sharp knife, cut the square diagonally in half to make two triangles. Arrange the triangles on an ungreased baking sheet and sprinkle them lightly with kosher salt. Repeat with the remaining ingredients.
4. Bake the crackers, one sheet at a time, for 7 to 10 minutes, until lightly browned around the edges and crisp. Transfer the crackers to a wire rack and cool completely.

STORE **IN AN AIRTIGHT CONTAINER AT ROOM TEMPERATURE FOR UP TO 2 WEEKS.**

rosemary cheese crisps

MAKES ABOUT 48 CRACKERS

Rosemary mingles well with the two cheeses in these flaky, buttery, and all-around wonderful crackers, which are simply fabulous warm out of the oven. They're great as an hors d'oeuvre or snack, as are the sun-dried tomato and goat cheese variations that follow.

1½ cups all-purpose flour

½ cup grated white Cheddar cheese

¼ cup plus 2 tablespoons finely grated Parmesan cheese, divided

2 teaspoons finely chopped fresh rosemary

1 teaspoon salt

⅛ teaspoon freshly ground black pepper

9 tablespoons cold unsalted butter, cut into ¼-inch pieces

¼ cup sour cream

2 teaspoons extra-virgin olive oil

1 large egg yolk

special equipment

1¾-inch scalloped round cookie cutter

1. Place the flour, Cheddar cheese, 2 tablespoons of the Parmesan cheese, the rosemary, salt, and pepper in the bowl of a food processor and pulse until combined. Scatter the butter pieces over the flour mixture and pulse until the mixture resembles coarse meal. Add the sour cream, olive oil, and egg yolk and pulse just until blended. Turn the dough out onto a work surface and shape it into a disk. Wrap the disk in plastic wrap and refrigerate for at least 2 hours until firm (or up to 2 days).
2. Position a rack in the center of the oven and preheat the oven to 375°F.
3. Place the chilled dough on a lightly floured work surface and, using a rolling pin, roll it out to a thickness of ⅛ inch, sprinkling it with flour as necessary to prevent sticking. Using a 1¾-inch scalloped round cookie cutter, cut out as many rounds as possible from the dough and arrange them ½ inch apart on ungreased baking sheets. Reroll the scraps and cut out more crackers until all the dough is used. Sprinkle a small amount of the remaining ¼ cup Parmesan cheese on top of each cracker.
4. Bake the crackers, one sheet at a time, for 13 to 16 minutes, until light golden brown. Transfer the crackers to a wire rack and cool completely.

Sun-Dried Tomato Cheese Crisps: Omit the rosemary and add 3 tablespoons chopped sun-dried tomatoes (packed in oil, drained) and 2 tablespoons chopped fresh basil along with the sour cream.

Goat Cheese and Herb Crisps: Substitute ⅓ cup firmly packed soft goat cheese for the Cheddar cheese. Add 1 tablespoon finely chopped fresh chives and substitute 2 teaspoons finely chopped fresh herbs of your choice (such as parsley, thyme, or basil) for the rosemary.

STORE IN AN AIRTIGHT CONTAINER AT ROOM TEMPERATURE FOR UP TO 3 DAYS.

curried brie rounds

MAKES **ABOUT 30 CRACKERS**

Brie may be a familiar taste at the cocktail hour, but curry is something of an unexpected guest. The dough for this unusual buttery, rich nibble is put together in minutes, but it must be chilled for at least 3 hours before slicing and baking; however, it can be made ahead and frozen for up to a month. Just slice the frozen dough and bake for 25 to 28 minutes. Serve these savory pastry rounds warm on their own or cold with tart green apple slices or ultrathin slices of honey ham.

1 cup all-purpose flour

½ cup pecan halves, toasted

½ teaspoon salt

Pinch of freshly ground black pepper

1 teaspoon Madras curry powder

5 tablespoons unsalted butter, cut into ½-inch cubes and frozen

3 ounces Brie cheese, chilled, rind removed, and cut into ½-inch cubes

1. In the bowl of a food processor, combine the flour, pecans, salt, pepper, and curry powder and process until the pecans are finely ground, about 30 seconds. Scatter the frozen butter pieces over the flour and pulse until the mixture resembles coarse meal. Scatter the Brie over the mixture and process until the dough just begins to come together, about 15 seconds.

2. Scrape the dough out onto a work surface and shape it into a 7½-inch log about 1½ inches in diameter. Wrap the dough in plastic wrap and refrigerate for at least 3 hours, until firm (or up to 3 days).

3. Position a rack in the center of the oven and preheat the oven to 325°F. Line a baking sheet with parchment paper or foil.

4. Slice the chilled dough log into 3/16-inch-thick slices and arrange them 1 inch apart on the prepared baking sheet. Bake for 22 to 25 minutes, until just lightly golden brown around the edges. Transfer the rounds to a wire rack and serve warm or cool completely.

STORE **IN AN AIRTIGHT CONTAINER AT ROOM TEMPERATURE FOR UP TO A DAY, OR REFRIGERATE FOR UP TO A WEEK; BRING TO ROOM TEMPERATURE BEFORE SERVING.**

pine nut parmesan shortbread

MAKES **12 WEDGES**

Here's another superb recipe from dessert expert Lisa Yockelson, who also excels at savory baking—she knows that man (or woman) does not live by dessert alone. Buttery, with a cayenne kick, these aromatic cookies make a great hors d'oeuvre. Wonderful warm, when the flavors really shine and the texture is particularly seductive, they are also delicious at room temperature particularly with a paper-thin slice of prosciutto on top of each one.

1 cup all-purpose flour

¼ teaspoon baking powder

¾ teaspoon sweet paprika

¼ teaspoon salt, preferably fine sea salt

⅛ teaspoon cayenne pepper, or to taste

½ cup (1 stick) unsalted butter, softened

2 teaspoons chopped fresh thyme

⅓ cup finely grated Parmesan cheese

2½ tablespoons pine nuts

1. Position a rack in the center of the oven and preheat the oven to 350°F. Have an 8-inch fluted tart pan with a removable bottom at hand.
2. Sift together the flour, baking powder, paprika, salt, and cayenne pepper into a medium bowl. Whisk to combine, and set aside.
3. In the bowl of an electric mixer, using the paddle attachment, beat the butter at low speed for 3 to 4 minutes, until creamy. Beat in the thyme and Parmesan cheese. Add the sifted flour mixture in two additions, beating just until blended.
4. Transfer the dough (it will be crumbly) to the tart pan and lightly press it into an even smooth round with your fingertips. Scatter the pine nuts over the shortbread, then pat them into the dough. Prick the shortbread at 1-inch intervals with the tines of a fork.
5. Bake the shortbread for 30 to 35 minutes, or until a very pale golden brown. Let the shortbread cool in the pan on a rack for 15 minutes, then carefully remove the outer rim of the pan. With a long sharp knife, cut the still-warm shortbread into 12 wedges. Serve barely warm, or cool completely.

STORE **IN AN AIRTIGHT CONTAINER AT ROOM TEMPERATURE FOR UP TO 3 DAYS.**

buttermilk dill crackers

MAKES **ABOUT 64 CRACKERS**

This is a very dense cracker, made with oats and bread flour and flavored with dill and onion. These are delicious topped with thinly sliced smoked salmon and a dab of crème fraiche. They're also great with tuna salad or chicken salad, and they'll stand up to any dip you can concoct.

1 cup old-fashioned rolled oats

2¼ cups bread flour

1 teaspoon salt

½ teaspoon baking soda

⅓ cup solid vegetable shortening

2 tablespoons unsalted butter, softened

2 tablespoons granulated sugar

2 tablespoons finely chopped fresh dill

2 tablespoons finely minced red onion

1 cup buttermilk

Water for brushing

1¾ teaspoons kosher salt, for sprinkling

1. Position two racks near the center of the oven and preheat the oven to 325°F. Line two baking sheets with parchment paper or aluminum foil.
2. In a medium bowl, combine the oats, bread flour, salt, and baking soda. Set aside.
3. In the bowl of an electric mixer, using the paddle attachment, beat the shortening, butter, and sugar at medium-high speed until blended, about 1 minute. Beat in the dill and red onion until blended. At low speed, add the dry ingredients in two additions, alternating them with the buttermilk. The dough will be sticky.
4. Scrape the dough out onto a lightly floured work surface and divide it in half. Shape each piece into a 4-inch square.
5. Sprinkle one of the squares lightly with flour, and, using a rolling pin, roll it out into a very thin 10½ by 14½-inch rectangle, sprinkling it with additional flour as necessary to prevent sticking. Using a pizza cutter, trim the edges of the rectangle so that they are even (the rectangle should now measure roughly 10 by 14 inches). Carefully roll the dough up on the rolling pin and transfer it to one of the prepared baking sheets. Prick the dough all over with a fork at 1-inch intervals. Using a pastry brush, brush off any flour from the dough. Brush the dough lightly all over with water. Sprinkle with half of the kosher salt. Using a pizza cutter or paring knife, score the dough (do not cut all the way through) into 32 rectangles (8 on a long side by 4 on a short side). Repeat with the remaining dough.
6. Bake the crackers, two sheets at a time, for 26 to 32 minutes, switching the position of the racks halfway through baking, until lightly browned (do not underbake, or the crackers will not be crisp). Cut the crackers apart at the scored lines while still warm. Let the crackers cool completely on the baking sheets.

STORE **IN AN AIRTIGHT CONTAINER AT ROOM TEMPERATURE FOR UP TO 2 WEEKS.**

rosemary garlic breadsticks

MAKES **24 BREADSTICKS**

Made with pizza dough, these breadsticks, or *grissini,* as the Italians call them, have a chewy-crisp texture. The trick in shaping them is not to dust the work surface with flour; flour would eliminate traction, making the dough slip and consequently difficult to roll. The possible add-ins for these breadsticks are endless. I've included a few of my favorites, but you could sprinkle them with sesame, poppy, or fennel seeds after brushing them with the egg wash.

dough

1 tablespoon plus 2 teaspoons olive oil, divided

1 tablespoon cold water

2 teaspoons finely minced garlic

⅔ cup warm water (105° to 115°F)

½ teaspoon active dry yeast

1¾ cups all-purpose flour

1 tablespoon finely chopped fresh rosemary

1 teaspoon salt

¼ teaspoon freshly ground black pepper

Cornmeal for sprinkling

1 large egg, lightly beaten with 1 teaspoon water for egg wash

make the dough

1. Combine 1 tablespoon of the oil, the cold water, and the garlic in a small saucepan and cook over medium heat until the water has evaporated and the garlic is tender, about 3 minutes. Drain the oil from the pan and set the garlic aside to cool.

2. Put the warm water in a small cup and sprinkle the yeast over it. Let stand for 5 minutes, or until the yeast is creamy. Stir until the yeast dissolves.

3. In the bowl of a food processor, combine the all-purpose flour, rosemary, salt, and pepper and pulse a few times to mix. Add the yeast mixture and garlic and pulse until the dough forms a ball. Scrape the dough out onto a lightly floured work surface and knead, adding a little more flour if necessary, until smooth and elastic, about 5 minutes.

4. Coat a large bowl with the remaining 2 teaspoons olive oil. Place the dough in the bowl, turning it to oil all sides. Cover with plastic wrap, place in a warm, draft-free place, and let rise until doubled in bulk, about 1½ hours.

form and bake the breadsticks

5. Sprinkle two jellyroll pans with cornmeal. Divide the dough into 4 equal pieces. Divide each piece into 6 equal pieces, to make a total of 24 pieces. Cover the dough pieces loosely with plastic wrap and let rest for 10 minutes (this will make the dough easier to roll).

6. Roll one of the dough pieces into a thin rope about 10 inches long and place it crosswise on one of the prepared jellyroll pans. Repeat with the remaining dough, placing 12 breadsticks on each pan and spacing them about 1 inch apart. Let the breadsticks rise at room temperature for about 30 minutes, until they are slightly puffed.

7. Position two racks near the center of the oven and preheat the oven to 375°F.

8. Brush the tops and sides of the breadsticks with the egg wash. Bake for 15 to 18 minutes, switching the position of the pans halfway through baking, until they are golden brown at the tips and crisp. Set the pans on wire racks and cool the breadsticks completely.

Cheddar Black Pepper Breadsticks: Omit the garlic and rosemary. Increase the amount of black pepper to ½ teaspoon and add ½ cup shredded white Cheddar cheese to the food processor with the flour in Step 3.

Tomato Parmesan Breadsticks: Omit the garlic and rosemary. Add ⅓ cup finely grated Parmesan cheese and ¼ cup chopped sun-dried tomatoes (packed in oil, drained, and blotted with a paper towel) to the food processor with the yeast mixture in Step 3.

Lemon Fennel Breadsticks: Omit the garlic and rosemary. Add 2 teaspoons finely grated lemon zest and 2 teaspoons crushed fennel seeds to the food processor with the flour in Step 3.

STORE **IN AN AIRTIGHT CONTAINER AT ROOM TEMPERATURE FOR UP TO A WEEK.**

jalapeño jack rusks

MAKES **36 RUSKS**

The ingredient list may look long, but these rusks are easy to throw together. Like savory biscotti, they are extremely crisp, and full of jalapeño flavor, with a boost from chili powder and onion. They're perfect cocktail food, unusual and unexpected. Serve them as hors d'oeuvres with melted Manchego or Monterey Jack cheese and a tomato slice on top of each one, and your cocktail hour may never end. They would also make a nice addition to the bread basket for a Tex-Mex or Nuevo Latino meal.

6 tablespoons (¾ stick) unsalted butter, divided, 4 tablespoons softened

½ cup chopped onions

2 tablespoons finely chopped jalapeño pepper

1¾ cups all-purpose flour

1 teaspoon baking powder

1 teaspoon salt

¼ teaspoon freshly ground black pepper

2 teaspoons chili powder

½ cup plus 2 tablespoons finely grated Parmesan cheese, divided

½ cup shredded Monterey Jack cheese

2 large eggs

1 tablespoon Worcestershire sauce

⅛ teaspoon Tabasco sauce

¼ cup whole milk

1. Position two racks near the center of the oven and preheat the oven to 325°F. Line two baking sheets with parchment paper or foil.
2. In a small skillet, melt 2 tablespoons of the butter over medium heat. Add the onions and jalapeño pepper and cook, stirring frequently, until the onions are translucent, about 2 minutes. Remove the pan from the heat and cool completely.
3. In a medium bowl, whisk together the flour, baking powder, salt, pepper, and chili powder. Set aside.
4. In the bowl of an electric mixer, using the paddle attachment, beat the remaining 4 tablespoons butter, ½ cup of the Parmesan cheese, and the Monterey Jack at medium speed until blended. Beat in the eggs one at a time, beating well after each addition. At low speed, add the Worcestershire sauce, Tabasco sauce, cooled onion mixture, and milk, beating until blended. Add the flour mixture, mixing just until blended.
5. Scrape the dough out onto a lightly floured work surface and gather it into a disk. Divide the dough in half. Shape each piece into a 12-inch log, sprinkling the dough lightly with flour as necessary to prevent sticking. Transfer both logs to one of the prepared baking sheets, spacing them about 3 inches apart (the logs will spread). With the heel of your hand, flatten the logs slightly, until they are 1¾ to 2 inches wide. Sprinkle the logs with the remaining 2 tablespoons Parmesan cheese.
6. Place the baking sheet on the upper oven rack and bake for 35 minutes, or until the logs just start to brown lightly. Set the baking sheet on a wire rack and cool for 10 minutes. Reduce the oven temperature to 300°F.

7. Slide a pancake turner under each log to loosen it from the parchment paper or foil. Carefully transfer the logs to a cutting surface. Line the baking sheet with clean parchment paper or foil. Using a serrated knife, cut the logs on the diagonal into ½-inch slices. Arrange the slices cut side down on the two baking sheets, spacing them ½ inch apart. Bake for an additional 20 to 25 minutes, switching the position of the baking sheets halfway through baking, until the rusks are dry and beginning to color around the edges. Transfer them to wire racks and cool completely.

STORE IN AN AIRTIGHT CONTAINER AT ROOM TEMPERATURE FOR UP TO A WEEK.

black olive and feta cheese rusks

MAKES **ABOUT 36 RUSKS**

These biscotti-like crackers may seem more Italian in origin, but they're the perfect medium to carry these full-blooded, dance-on-the-table Greek flavors—onion, feta cheese, and lots of Kalamata olive bits. Serve with a dry white wine such as Sauvignon Blanc or Orvieto.

dough

6 tablespoons (3/4 stick) unsalted butter, divided, 4 tablespoons softened

1/2 cup chopped onions

1 3/4 cups all-purpose flour

1 teaspoon baking powder

1/2 teaspoon dried oregano

1/2 teaspoon salt

1/4 teaspoon freshly ground black pepper

1/2 cup finely grated Parmesan cheese

1/2 cup crumbled feta cheese

2 large eggs

3/4 cup pitted Kalamata olives, finely chopped

1/4 cup whole milk

1 large egg, lightly beaten with 1 teaspoon water for egg wash

1. Position two racks near the center of the oven and preheat the oven to 325°F. Line two baking sheets with parchment paper or foil.
2. In a small skillet, melt 2 tablespoons of the butter over medium heat. Add the onions and cook, stirring frequently, until translucent, about 2 minutes. Remove the pan from the heat and cool completely.
3. In a medium bowl, whisk together the flour, baking powder, oregano, salt, and pepper. Set aside.
4. In the bowl of an electric mixer, using the paddle attachment, beat the remaining 4 tablespoons butter, the Parmesan cheese, and feta cheese at medium speed until blended. Beat in the eggs one at a time, beating well after each addition. At low speed, add the cooled onion mixture, olives, and milk, beating until blended. Add the flour mixture, mixing just until blended.
5. Scrape the dough out onto a lightly floured work surface and gather it into a disk. Divide the dough in half. Shape each piece into a 12-inch log, sprinkling the dough lightly with flour as necessary to prevent sticking. Transfer both the logs to one of the prepared baking sheets, spacing them about 3 inches apart (the logs will spread). With the heel of your hand, flatten the logs slightly, until they are 1 3/4 to 2 inches wide. Brush the top and sides of each log with the egg wash.
6. Place the baking sheet on the upper oven rack and bake for 35 minutes, or until the logs just start to brown lightly. Set the baking sheet on a wire rack and cool for 10 minutes. Reduce the oven temperature to 300°F.
7. Slide a pancake turner under each log to loosen it from the parchment paper or foil. Carefully transfer the logs to a cutting surface. Line the baking sheet with clean parchment paper or foil. Using a serrated knife, cut the

logs on the diagonal into ½-inch slices. Arrange the slices cut side down on the two baking sheets, spacing them ½-inch apart. Bake for an additional 18 to 22 minutes, switching the position of the baking sheets halfway through baking, until the rusks are dry and beginning to color around the edges. Transfer them to wire racks and cool completely.

STORE IN AN AIRTIGHT CONTAINER AT ROOM TEMPERATURE FOR UP TO A WEEK.

Cookie Bite **To pit olives, place each one on a cutting board and gently crush it with the flat side of a large sharp knife. Carefully pop out the pit with your fingers.**

blue cheese pear rolls

MAKES **32 SAVORY COOKIES**

When I first tasted rugelach, I fell instantly in love with their signature cream cheese dough. It's an easy dough to work with and very tender, with a slight tang that is perfect for carrying grown-up flavors. I knew it could be put to savory use, and here you find exhibits one and two. The blue cheese version and the caramelized onion and thyme variation that follows are very *haut* hors d'oeuvres, with a depth of flavor that is all the more vivid and tantalizing when they are served warm. Any good blue cheese, such as Danish blue, works well here.

blue cheese pear filling

½ cup chopped (¼-inch pieces) dried pears

¼ cup apple juice

2 tablespoons unsalted butter, melted

½ cup chopped toasted walnuts

1 cup (about 3 ounces) crumbled blue cheese

Freshly ground black pepper

cream cheese dough

¾ cup (1½ sticks) unsalted butter, softened

6 ounces cream cheese, softened

1 teaspoon granulated sugar

½ teaspoon salt

1½ cups all-purpose flour

1 large egg, lightly beaten with 1 teaspoon water for egg wash

soak the pears for the filling

1. In a small bowl, combine the pears and apple juice. Let stand at room temperature for at least 1 hour (or up to 8 hours).

make the dough

2. In the bowl of an electric mixer, using the paddle attachment, beat the butter, cream cheese, sugar, and salt at medium speed until smooth, about 1 minute. At low speed, add the flour, mixing just until the dough comes together. Scrape the dough out onto a work surface and shape it into a ball. Divide the dough into 4 equal pieces and shape each piece into a disk. Wrap each disk in plastic wrap and refrigerate for at least 1 hour until firm (or up to 3 days).

assemble and bake the rolls

3. Position a rack in the center of the oven and preheat the oven to 375°F. Line a baking sheet with parchment paper or foil.

4. Drain the chopped pears and set aside. Remove one of the dough disks from the refrigerator and place it on a lightly floured work surface. Roll it into a 9-inch circle. Brush the dough lightly with 1½ teaspoons melted butter. Leaving a ¾-inch border all around the edges, spread 2 tablespoons of the pears, 2 tablespoons of the walnuts, and ¼ cup of the blue cheese evenly over the dough. Press the filling gently into the dough. Season with a few grinds of black pepper. Using a large sharp knife, cut the round evenly into 8 wedges. Starting at the outer edge, roll up each triangle towards the point in the center. Arrange the rolls point side down on the prepared baking sheet, spacing them 1 inch apart. Brush the top of each roll with egg wash.

5. Bake the rolls for 18 to 20 minutes, until lightly browned. Transfer the rolls to a wire rack and cool completely. Repeat the process with the remaining dough and filling.

Caramelized Onion Thyme Rolls: Omit the dried pears, walnuts, and blue cheese. Prepare the dough as directed. To make the filling, melt 3 tablespoons unsalted butter in a large skillet over medium heat. Add 2½ cups chopped onions and cook, stirring frequently, until they are softened, about 5 minutes. Add 2 teaspoons fresh thyme leaves and continue to cook until the onions begin to caramelize and turn brown, about 8 minutes more. Add salt and freshly ground black pepper to taste, and cool the filling completely. Spread about ¼ cup of the filling over each buttered dough round and proceed as directed.

STORE IN AN AIRTIGHT CONTAINER AT ROOM TEMPERATURE FOR UP TO 2 DAYS, BUT THESE ARE BEST THE DAY THEY ARE MADE.

savory cheese palmiers

MAKES **ABOUT 22 SAVORY COOKIES**

It's hard to imagine palmiers without that sweet crunch, but once you've tried this combination of robust cheeses and puff pastry, you'll never look back. It's a true indulgence that makes for a really good, knock-their-socks-off cocktail snack or brunch item, particularly served slightly warm. The palmiers can be baked up to a month in advance and frozen. To defrost, heat the unthawed palmiers in a preheated 350°F oven for about 5 minutes.

dough

½ recipe Really Rapid Puff Pastry (page 358; freeze the remaining half for another use)

filling

⅓ cup finely grated Parmesan cheese

½ cup shredded Swiss Gruyère cheese

½ teaspoon salt

⅛ teaspoon freshly ground black pepper

Pinch of cayenne pepper

1 large egg, lightly beaten with 1 teaspoon water for egg wash

make the dough

1. Prepare the puff pastry according to the directions on page 358.

make the filling

2. In a medium bowl, combine the cheeses, salt, black pepper, and cayenne pepper.

assemble the palmiers

3. Using a floured rolling pin, roll the dough into a 12 by 13-inch rectangle. Brush the surface of the dough all over with egg wash (cover the remaining egg wash and refrigerate for later use). Sprinkle the filling evenly over the dough, pressing it into the dough with your hands. Fold each 13-inch side two-thirds of the way in toward the center (see page 245), then fold each side in again so that the folded edges meet at the center. Fold the dough over again from the center, forming six layers of dough. Cut the dough crosswise in half, to make two 6½-inch-long strips. Wrap each strip well in plastic wrap. Place the dough on a tray and refrigerate at least 1 hour, until firm (or up to 2 days).

4. Position a rack in the center of the oven and preheat the oven to 375°F.

5. Remove one strip of dough from the refrigerator and unwrap it. Trim off the ends if they are uneven. Using a large sharp knife, cut the dough into ½-inch slices, cutting only as many slices as will fit on one baking sheet and arranging them cut side down on the ungreased baking sheet, spacing them 2½ inches apart. Rewrap the uncut portion of dough and refrigerate until needed. Using a pastry brush, brush some of the reserved egg wash over the top of each cookie.

6. Bake the cookies for 12 minutes, until the bottoms are brown. Remove the sheet from the oven and turn each palmier over. Bake them for another 8 to 12 minutes, until they are golden brown on both sides. Transfer the palmiers to a wire rack and cool completely. Repeat the process with the remaining dough.

   Goat Cheese and Chive Palmiers: For the filling, combine 4 ounces (generous ½ cup) soft goat cheese, ¼ cup finely grated Parmesan cheese, ¼ cup chopped fresh chives, and ¼ teaspoon salt in a medium bowl. Stir briskly until no large clumps of goat cheese remain. Proceed as directed in Step 3.

STORE IN AN AIRTIGHT CONTAINER IN THE REFRIGERATOR FOR UP TO 3 DAYS, OR FREEZE FOR UP TO A MONTH.

pizza puffs

MAKES **ABOUT 38 PUFFS**

Mastering my simple puff pastry recipe will pay off in many ways, as evidenced by these flaky, flavorful cheese hors d'oeuvres. The pastry can be made ahead, of course, and frozen for up to a month. After that, putting the puffs together is very easy and quick—fill them, brush with garlic-infused olive oil, top with cherry tomato halves, and bake. They are best served right out of the oven, with a chilled, crisp white wine such as Pinot Grigio and a bowl of Italian olives.

dough

½ recipe Really Rapid Puff Pastry (page 358; freeze the remaining half for another use)

topping

3 tablespoons extra-virgin olive oil

1 teaspoon finely minced garlic

½ cup finely grated Parmesan cheese, divided

⅓ cup shredded Fontina cheese

19 cherry tomatoes, cut in half

Kosher salt and freshly ground black pepper

Small fresh basil leaves for garnish

special equipment

1¾-inch fluted cookie cutter

make the dough

1. Prepare the puff pastry according to the directions on page 358.

assemble and bake the puffs

2. Position a rack in the center of the oven and preheat the oven to 350°F. Line two baking sheets with parchment paper or foil.
3. In a small bowl, combine the olive oil and garlic; set aside.
4. Place the dough on a lightly floured work surface and roll it into an 10 by 11-inch rectangle. Sprinkle half of the rectangle with ¼ cup of the Parmesan cheese and all of the Fontina cheese. Fold the half without the cheese over the half with the cheese and press the edges to seal. Roll the dough out to a thickness of 3/16 inch. Using a 1¾-inch fluted cookie cutter, cut out as many rounds from the dough as possible and arrange them ½ inch apart on the prepared baking sheets.
5. Brush each round lightly with the garlic-infused oil (reserve the remaining oil). Sprinkle the rounds with the remaining Parmesan cheese. Top each with a cherry tomato half, cut side up. Press the tomato down firmly into the dough so that it doesn't slide off during baking. Sprinkle each round with salt and a grind of pepper. Bake for 20 to 25 minutes, until the rounds are golden brown around the edges and on the bottom.
6. Place the baking sheet on a wire rack and brush each tomato with garlic oil to give it a shine. Garnish each puff with a small basil leaf, and serve immediately.

STORE **IN AN AIRTIGHT CONTAINER AT ROOM TEMPERATURE FOR UP TO 4 HOURS IF NECESSARY, BUT THESE ARE BEST SHORTLY AFTER THEY ARE MADE.**

basic recipes

• sweet pastry crust #1 • sweet pastry crust #2 • brown sugar crust #1 • brown sugar crust #2 • basic decorative cookie dough • really rapid puff pastry • basic sugar glaze • decorator's icing • basic buttercream • praline paste • pistachio paste • almost-foolproof tempered chocolate • apricot orange filling • prune filling • sour cherry filling •

These are the building blocks—dough, crust, or filling—for some of the recipes in this book, and the accessories—icing, glaze, or frosting—for many others. Use these basic recipes to create variations of the cookies in this book (sandwiching together a rolled cookie with a flavored buttercream, for example) or to embellish simpler cookies (glazing a drop or refrigerator cookie).

There are recipes for four basic pastry crusts: a brown sugar version, a buttery versatile one, and a richer variation of each. There are also a number of fruit fillings, sugar glazes in several flavors, nut pastes, and a basic cookie dough that can accept myriad forms of decoration. You'll also find a wonderful buttercream recipe that's silken and flavorful, with lots of variations. Puff pastry may seem like something you only order in a bakeshop, but I urge you to try my Really Rapid Puff Pastry. You will find endless ways to use it, including savory preparations. See the Pizza Puffs and Savory Cheese Palmiers in Savory Cookies and Crackers for just a few ways to use puff pastry for hors d'ouevres.

sweet pastry crust #1

MAKES **ONE 9 BY 13-INCH CRUST**

This simple, buttery crust is mixed up in an electric mixer, then patted directly into the baking pan.

1¼ cups all-purpose flour

¼ teaspoon salt

½ cup (1 stick) unsalted butter, softened

⅓ cup granulated sugar

½ teaspoon finely grated lemon zest

½ teaspoon vanilla extract

1. Position a rack in the center of the oven and preheat the oven to 350°F. Grease the bottom and sides of a 9 by 13-inch baking pan.
2. In a small bowl, whisk together the flour and salt; set aside.
3. In the bowl of an electric mixer, using the paddle attachment, beat the butter and sugar at medium speed until combined, about 1 minute. Beat in the lemon zest and vanilla extract until combined. At low speed, add the flour mixture and mix just until the mixture is crumbly, 10 to 15 seconds.
4. Pat the dough evenly into the bottom of the prepared pan. Prick the dough well with a fork. Bake the crust for 15 to 18 minutes, until golden brown around the edges (or as directed in the recipe). Transfer the pan to a wire rack to cool while you prepare the topping.

sweet pastry crust #2

MAKES **ONE 9-INCH SQUARE CRUST**

This buttery, tender crust makes a wonderful base for many bar cookies. Because of the egg, it's just a bit richer than Sweet Pastry Crust #1 (page 353). It's mixed up quickly in the food processor and then patted into the pan; no chilling or rolling necessary.

1⅓ cups all-purpose flour

⅓ cup granulated sugar

¼ teaspoon salt

½ cup (1 stick) cold unsalted butter, cut into ½-inch cubes

1 large egg yolk

2 teaspoons cold water

¾ teaspoon vanilla extract

1. Position a rack in the center of the oven and preheat the oven to 350°F. Grease the bottom and sides of a 9-inch square baking pan.
2. Place the flour, sugar, and salt in the bowl of a food processor and process until blended. Scatter the butter pieces over the flour mixture and process until the mixture resembles coarse meal, about 6 seconds.
3. In a small bowl or cup, whisk together the egg yolk, water, and vanilla extract. With the food processor running, add the yolk mixture through the feed tube and process just until the dough begins to come together in large clumps, 15 to 20 seconds.
4. Scrape the dough into the prepared pan and, using your fingers, pat it evenly into the bottom of the pan. Bake the crust until golden, 20 to 25 minutes (or as directed in the recipe). Transfer the pan to a wire rack to cool while you prepare the topping.

brown sugar crust #1

MAKES **ONE 9 BY 13-INCH CRUST**

Brown sugar lends a deep caramel flavor to this tender butter crust. The dough is mixed just until crumbly, then patted into the pan.

1¼ cups all-purpose flour

½ teaspoon salt

½ cup (1 stick) unsalted butter, softened

½ cup firmly packed light brown sugar

1. Position a rack in the center of the oven and preheat the oven to 350°F. Grease the bottom and sides of a 9 by 13-inch baking pan.
2. In a small bowl, stir together the flour and salt; set aside.
3. In the bowl of an electric mixer, using the paddle attachment, beat the butter and brown sugar at medium speed until combined, about 1 minute. At low speed, add the flour mixture and mix just until crumbly.
4. Pat the dough evenly into the bottom of the prepared pan. Prick the dough well with a fork. Bake the crust for 16 to 20 minutes, until golden brown around the edges (or as directed in the recipe). Transfer the pan to a wire rack to cool while you prepare the topping.

Brown Sugar Ginger Crust: Add 2 tablespoons chopped crystallized ginger and ⅛ teaspoon ground cardamon with the flour in Step 3.

brown sugar crust #2

MAKES **ONE 9 BY 13-INCH CRUST**

The addition of an egg makes this crust slightly richer than Brown Sugar Crust #1 (page 355), but it's just as easy to make. The dough is mixed in the food processor, and then patted into the baking pan.

1½ cups all-purpose flour

⅔ cup firmly packed light brown sugar

¼ teaspoon salt

11 tablespoons cold unsalted butter, cut into ½-inch cubes

1 large egg

1 teaspoon finely grated lemon zest

½ teaspoon vanilla extract

1. Position a rack in the center of the oven and preheat the oven to 350°F. Grease the bottom and sides of a 9 by 13-inch baking pan.
2. Place the flour, brown sugar, and salt in the bowl of a food processor and pulse a few times to blend. Scatter the butter cubes over the flour mixture and process until the mixture resembles coarse meal, with a few pea-sized pieces of butter, about 6 seconds.
3. In a small bowl, whisk together the egg, lemon zest, and vanilla extract until blended. Add the egg mixture to the food processor and process for a few seconds, just until the dough is blended but still crumbly. (Do not allow the dough to form a ball around the blade, or the crust will be tough.)
4. Turn the dough out into the prepared pan. With floured fingertips, press the dough evenly into the bottom of the pan (reflour your fingertips as necessary). Bake the crust for 20 to 22 minutes, until golden brown (or as directed in the recipe). Transfer the pan to a wire rack to cool while you prepare the topping.

basic decorative cookie dough

MAKES **ABOUT THIRTY-SIX 3-INCH COOKIES**

This is a wonderful dough for cut-out cookies. It's easy to work with, holds its shape beautifully, and has a delicate orange-kissed vanilla flavor that goes nicely with just about any icing or filling.

3¼ cups all-purpose flour

¼ teaspoon salt

1¼ cups (2½ sticks) unsalted butter, softened

1 cup granulated sugar

1 large egg

1 large egg yolk

1 tablespoon vanilla extract

1 teaspoon finely grated orange zest

1. In a medium bowl, whisk together the flour and salt; set aside.
2. In the bowl of an electric mixer, using the paddle attachment, beat the butter and sugar at medium-high speed until light and creamy, about 2 minutes. Add the egg, egg yolk, vanilla extract, and orange zest and mix until well blended. Reduce the speed to low and add the flour mixture one-third at a time, mixing just until combined. Turn the dough out onto a work surface and divide it into 4 pieces. Shape each piece into a disk, wrap well in plastic wrap, and refrigerate for at least 30 minutes, until firm (or up to 2 days).
3. Position a rack in the center of the oven and preheat the oven to 350°F. Line two baking sheets with parchment paper.
4. On a lightly floured work surface, roll one of the dough disks out to a thickness of ⅛ inch. Using cookie cutters, cut the dough into shapes (save the scraps for rerolling). Using a metal spatula, transfer the cookies to the prepared baking sheet, spacing them ½ inch apart. Bake, one sheet at a time, for 10 to 15 minutes, until pale golden brown (baking time will vary depending on the size and shape of the cookies). Transfer the cookies to a cooling rack and cool completely. Repeat with the remaining dough.

   Lemon-Scented Decorative Cookie Dough: Reduce the vanilla extract to 1 teaspoon, and substitute 2 teaspoons finely grated lemon zest for orange zest.

STORE, **WELL WRAPPED IN PLASTIC, IN THE REFRIGERATOR FOR UP TO 3 DAYS, OR FREEZE FOR UP TO 1 MONTH; COOKIES CAN BE STORED IN AN AIRTIGHT CONTAINER AT ROOM TEMPERATURE FOR UP TO A WEEK OR FROZEN FOR UP TO 1 MONTH.**

really rapid puff pastry

MAKES **2 POUNDS 2 OUNCES**

A form of puff pastry may have been in use as early as the fourteenth century, but most food historians credit its modern incarnation to a nineteenth-century French chef, Claude Gellée, who was experimenting with a new kind of cake to cheer up his ailing father. Perfect puff pastry is buttery, flaky, and rich. A great flavor carrier, and wonderfully melty-chewy in the mouth, it is an essential component of many desserts. It can be tricky to make, but this recipe is almost foolproof—and really quick. The dough is made like a piecrust, and then folded several times, like classic puff pastry dough. Whether or not you've ever made puff pastry, I urge you to try this easy recipe. It's great for savory hors d'oeuvres as well as for cookies and other sweets.

1¾ cups bread flour

1⅓ cups cake flour (not self-rising)

1 teaspoon salt

2 cups (4 sticks) cold unsalted butter, cut into ½-inch cubes

½ cup plus 1 tablespoon ice water

1. In the bowl of an electric mixer, using the paddle attachment, combine the bread flour, cake flour, and salt at low speed. If your mixer has a splatter shield attachment, attach it. Add the butter pieces one-third at a time, mixing for just a few seconds. The mixture will be very crumbly, with large pieces of butter in it. Continuing to mix at low speed, add the ice water, and mix just until the dough starts to come together (there should still be large pieces of butter in it).

2. Scrape the dough out onto a floured work surface and, with a rolling pin, pound and pat it into a rough rectangle. Roll the dough out into an 8 by 16-inch rectangle, dusting it with flour as needed. Turn the dough if necessary so a short side is closest to you. Brush off any excess flour from the dough with a pastry brush. Fold the bottom third of the dough up over the center, then fold the top third over, as if you were folding a business letter; there will now be three layers of dough. Rotate the dough 90 degrees, so that the open sides are at the top and bottom, and roll the dough out again to an 8 by 16-inch rectangle. Fold it again into three layers. The dough has now been "turned" twice. Wrap the dough well in plastic wrap and refrigerate for 30 minutes.

3. Remove the dough from the refrigerator and place it so that an open end is closest to you. Roll and fold the dough as before, to make two more turns. The dough is now ready to use, or it can be stored for future use.

STORE, WELL WRAPPED IN PLASTIC WRAP, IN THE REFRIGERATOR FOR UP TO 3 DAYS, OR FREEZE FOR UP TO 1 MONTH.

Cookie Bite Because cake flour comes in a box, measuring it can be a challenge. To avoid waste, lay out a piece of waxed paper and place a measuring cup on top. Spoon the flour into the cup, overfilling it. Level the top with a knife, and set aside. Bring two opposite sides of the waxed paper together, and pour the flour back into the box.

basic sugar glaze

MAKES ½ CUP

This silky-smooth, thick glaze should be spread on hot cookies, right out of the oven. It hardens into a thin, lusciously sweet coating, the perfect final touch. The lemon glaze has the most intense flavor, so use it to perk up cookies made with a simple dough, not when it would be competing with other strong flavors.

1 cup confectioners' sugar, sifted

1 tablespoon unsalted butter, softened

3 tablespoons heavy cream

1 teaspoon vanilla extract

Pinch of salt

In the bowl of an electric mixer, using the paddle attachment, beat the confectioners' sugar, butter, heavy cream, vanilla extract, and salt at medium speed just until combined, about 30 seconds. Cover the surface of the glaze with plastic wrap and set aside at room temperature until ready to use.

Lemon Glaze: Omit the vanilla extract and add 1 teaspoon finely grated lemon zest to the glaze.

Almond Glaze: Add ¼ teaspoon almond extract to the glaze.

STORE **IN AN AIRTIGHT CONTAINER IN THE REFRIGERATOR FOR UP TO 3 DAYS; BRING TO ROOM TEMPERATURE BEFORE USING.**

decorator's icing

MAKES **ABOUT 2½ CUPS**

Also known as royal icing, this classic icing is perfect for decorating cookies because it spreads and pipes easily and eventually hardens to a beautiful matte glaze. It holds color well and can take a lot of food coloring, but always use paste coloring—too much liquid will eventually cause the icing to break down and separate. Avoid using the icing on humid days, as it will not dry very well. While working, keep the bowl of icing covered with a damp paper towel or plastic wrap to prevent drying. Store any unused icing in an airtight container. This recipe can be doubled.

3 tablespoons meringue powder (available from New York Cake and Baking Distributors; see Sources, page 379)

6 tablespoons warm water

One 1-pound box confectioners' sugar

In the bowl of an electric mixer, using the whisk attachment, beat the meringue powder, water, and confectioners' sugar at medium-low speed until the icing forms stiff peaks, about 7 minutes. Thin the icing to the consistency you want by adding a little warm water, a few drops at a time.

STORE **IN AN AIRTIGHT CONTAINER AT ROOM TEMPERATURE FOR UP TO 2 WEEKS; WHEN READY TO USE, STIR THE ICING TO RESTORE ITS ORIGINAL CONSISTENCY.**

basic buttercream

MAKES 2 CUPS

This is a French-style buttercream, which, despite the amount of butter it contains, is light and silky, and extremely versatile. I like this version because it uses whole eggs, so you won't find yourself with any leftover yolks or whites.

¾ cup granulated sugar

¼ cup water

2 large eggs, at room temperature

Pinch of salt

14 tablespoons (1¾ sticks) unsalted butter, softened

½ plump vanilla bean or 1 teaspoon vanilla extract

1. In a small heavy saucepan, combine the sugar and water and cook over medium heat, stirring constantly and occasionally brushing down the sides of the pan with a wet pastry brush, until the sugar dissolves. Remove the pan from the heat and attach a candy thermometer to the side of the pan.
2. In the bowl of a heavy-duty electric mixer, using the whisk attachment, begin to beat the eggs at medium speed.
3. Meanwhile, place the sugar syrup over high heat and cook, without stirring, until it reaches 238°F on the candy thermometer. Immediately remove the pan from the heat and, with the mixer off, pour about ¼ cup of the hot syrup over the beaten eggs. Beat at high speed until blended, about 10 seconds. Turn the mixer off and add another ¼ cup syrup, then beat at high speed for another 10 seconds. Repeat this process until all of the syrup is used.
4. Using a rubber spatula, scrape down the sides of the bowl, and continue to beat at medium-high speed until the mixture is completely cool, about 5 minutes. Beat in the salt.
5. Meanwhile, if you are using the vanilla bean, split the bean lengthwise in half with a paring knife. Use the knife to scrape out the small seeds, and put them in a small bowl.
6. At medium speed, beat the softened butter 1 tablespoon at a time into the egg mixture. Add the vanilla seeds or vanilla extract, increase the speed to medium-high, and beat until the buttercream is smooth and shiny, about 4 minutes.

Almond Buttercream: Substitute ¼ teaspoon almond extract for the vanilla extract.

Chocolate Buttercream: Omit the vanilla extract. Beat 2½ ounces extra bittersweet or bittersweet chocolate, melted and cooled, into the finished buttercream.

Hazelnut Buttercream: Beat ¼ cup praline paste (page 364, or see Sources, page 376) and 1 tablespoon Frangelico liqueur into the finished buttercream.

Pistachio Buttercream: Beat ¼ cup Pistachio Paste (page 365) and 2 to 3 drops of green food coloring into the finished buttercream.

Raspberry Buttercream: Beat ¼ cup seedless raspberry jam, 1 tablespoon Chambord (black raspberry liqueur) or kirsch (optional), ½ teaspoon finely grated lemon zest, and 3 to 4 drops of red food coloring into the finished buttercream.

STORE IN AN AIRTIGHT CONTAINER IN THE REFRIGERATOR FOR UP TO 3 DAYS, OR FREEZE FOR UP TO 2 MONTHS; BRING TO ROOM TEMPERATURE AND STIR BEFORE USING.

praline paste

MAKES **1 GENEROUS CUP**

Prepared praline paste is available in gourmet shops and by mail-order, but it's easy to make your own. The combination of caramelized almonds, hazelnuts, and fragrant hazelnut oil makes a flavorful addition to cookie doughs or fillings.

½ cup blanched whole or slivered almonds

½ cup skinned hazelnuts

¾ cup granulated sugar

3 tablespoons water

1 tablespoon hazelnut or vegetable oil

1. Position a rack in the center of the oven and preheat the oven to 350°F.
2. Spread the almonds and hazelnuts on a baking sheet and toast in the oven for 8 to 12 minutes, shaking the pan once or twice, until golden and fragrant. Let the nuts cool completely on the baking sheet.
3. Brush another baking sheet lightly with vegetable oil. Combine the sugar and water in a medium-sized heavy saucepan and bring to a boil over medium-high heat, stirring to dissolve the sugar and occasionally brushing down the sides of the pan with a wet pastry brush. Continue to cook, without stirring, until the mixture turns a light caramel color, 3 to 5 minutes. Remove the pan from the heat and stir in the toasted almonds and hazelnuts. Return the pan to the heat and cook, stirring, until the nuts are completely coated with the caramel and it deepens to an amber color. Immediately pour the caramelized nut mixture onto the oiled baking sheet. Allow the praline to cool for 30 minutes, or until hard.
4. Using a large knife, coarsely chop the praline. Place in a food processor and process for about a minute, until it is the consistency of sand. Add the oil and process for another 30 seconds, or until it becomes a paste.

STORE **IN AN AIRTIGHT CONTAINER IN THE REFRIGERATOR FOR UP TO 1 WEEK.**

pistachio paste

MAKES **ABOUT 1⅔ CUPS**

More of a moist, crumbly nut mixture than a smooth paste, pistachio paste adds just-out-of-the-shell pistachio flavor to buttercreams and other cookie fillings. You can use it to make homemade pistachio ice cream too.

1¼ cups shelled unsalted pistachio nuts

¾ cup granulated sugar

2 tablespoons water

2 tablespoons vegetable oil

1. Position a rack in the center of the oven and preheat the oven to 350°F.
2. Spread the pistachio nuts on a baking sheet and toast in the oven for 5 to 7 minutes, shaking the pan once or twice, until fragrant. Let the nuts cool completely on the baking sheet.
3. Brush another baking sheet lightly with vegetable oil. Combine the sugar and water in a medium-sized heavy saucepan and bring to a boil over medium-high heat, stirring to dissolve the sugar and occasionally brushing down the sides of the pan with a wet pastry brush. Continue to cook, without stirring, until the mixture turns a medium caramel color, 3 to 5 minutes. Remove the pan from the heat and stir in the toasted pistachios. Return the pan to the heat and cook, stirring, until the nuts are completely coated with the caramel and it deepens to an amber color. Immediately pour the caramelized nut mixture onto the oiled baking sheet, separating the nuts a bit with a wooden spoon so they are not mounted. Allow the pistachio praline to cool for 30 minutes, or until hard.
4. Using a large knife, coarsely chop the praline. Place in a food processor and process for about a minute, until it is the consistency of sand. Add the vegetable oil and process for about 30 seconds longer, until blended.

STORE **IN AN AIRTIGHT CONTAINER IN THE REFRIGERATOR FOR UP TO 1 WEEK.**

almost-foolproof tempered chocolate

The only time you need to temper chocolate is when the chocolate for your cookie, candy, or dessert needs a glossy shine. In the case of cookies, it is usually a coating (as in Chocolate Almond Polka Dot Hearts, page 314). Tempering does make a huge difference—it makes the chocolate lustrous, brilliant, and professional looking, without any streaking. Many competent home bakers quake at the notion of tempering chocolate. While it is time-consuming, the procedure is actually quite simple.

Tempering is the process of heating chocolate to between 110° and 120°F, in order to melt out stable and unstable cocoa butter crystals, then cooling it to between 80° and 84°F, at which temperature the stable crystals can reform, but unstable ones can't. The chocolate is then heated to between 84° and 91°F, to give it a workable consistency, and maintained at that temperature while being used.

Because they contain milk solids, milk and white chocolates are a bit harder to temper than dark. As food editor of *Chocolatier* magazine, I've tested and observed lots of ways to temper chocolate. Of all of those methods, this is my favorite. Though perhaps not the quickest way, I think it is the easiest and most foolproof. Melt and temper more chocolate than you think you will need; any extra chocolate can be cooled and reused.

special equipment

Heating pad (such as the type used for backaches)

Good-quality digital or mercury chocolate thermometer (with a gauge that goes from 80° to 130°F)

1. Wrap the heating pad in plastic wrap to protect it from chocolate stains, and set the control dial to the lowest setting.

2. Set aside a large chunk of the chocolate (about 2½ inches square) you are tempering (this chocolate must be in good temper to start, shiny and without any white streaks). Chop the remaining chocolate and place it in a medium or large bowl, depending on how much chocolate you are working with. Set the bowl over a saucepan of hot but not quite simmering water (the water should not touch the bottom of the bowl) and heat, stirring occasionally, until the chocolate is melted and reaches a temperature of between 110° and 120°F. Turn off the heat.

3. Remove the bowl from the saucepan and add reserved chocolate chunk to the melted chocolate. Let the chocolate cool, stirring frequently, until it reaches 82° to 84°F for dark chocolate or 80° to 82°F for milk or white chocolate. Remove the unmelted portion of chocolate.

4. Return the bowl to its place over the saucepan (the heat should still be off) and let sit until the temperature of the chocolate rises to between 86° and 91°F for dark chocolate or 84° to 87°F for milk or white chocolate. Be careful not to allow the chocolate to go above the maximum temperatures. Maintain that temperature range while working with the chocolate by keeping the bowl on the wrapped heating pad.

Cookie Bite **To test whether or not chocolate is properly tempered, spoon a small amount onto a plate and refrigerate for 3 minutes. If the chocolate is glossy, it is "in temper."**

apricot orange filling

MAKES **ABOUT 1 CUP**

Freshly squeezed orange and lemon juices brighten the flavor of dried apricots in this sweet-tart filling. Slightly thicker and more flavorful than preserves, it makes a wonderful filling for Bakery-Style Hamantaschen (page 260). For best results, use California dried apricots.

4 ounces (about 2/3 cup) dried apricots

1/3 cup freshly squeezed orange juice

1½ tablespoons freshly squeezed lemon juice

3 tablespoons granulated sugar

1/3 cup golden raisins

1/3 cup walnuts, chopped

1. In a medium saucepan, combine the apricots, orange juice, lemon juice, sugar, and raisins. Bring to a gentle boil over medium heat, stirring just until the sugar is dissolved. Reduce the heat to low and simmer until the apricots are softened, about 12 minutes. Remove the pan from the heat and cool completely.

2. Scrape the filling into a food processor and pulse until almost smooth. Transfer to a bowl and stir in the walnuts.

STORE **IN AN AIRTIGHT CONTAINER IN THE REFRIGERATOR FOR UP TO 3 DAYS.**

prune filling

MAKES **ABOUT 1 CUP**

One taste of this filling can turn even the most die-hard prune hater into an admirer. It is accented with orange marmalade, lemon juice, and cinnamon, with finely chopped almonds for a little crunch.

9 ounces (about 1¼ cups) pitted prunes, coarsely chopped

¼ cup orange marmalade

1 tablespoon granulated sugar

½ teaspoon finely grated orange zest

2 tablespoons freshly squeezed lemon juice

¼ teaspoon ground cinnamon

⅓ cup finely chopped blanched whole or slivered almonds

1. In a medium saucepan, combine the prunes, marmalade, sugar, orange zest, lemon juice, and cinnamon. Cook over medium-low heat, stirring constantly, until the liquid is absorbed, about 5 minutes.
2. Transfer the filling to the bowl of a food processor and process until the prunes are finely chopped, about 20 seconds. Transfer the filling to a medium bowl and stir in the almonds. Let the filling cool completely.

STORE **IN AN AIRTIGHT CONTAINER IN THE REFRIGERATOR FOR UP TO 3 DAYS.**

sour cherry filling

MAKES **1 SCANT CUP**

Dried sour cherries, now available in many supermarkets, produce an intense, tart filling, perfect for Bakery-Style Hamantaschen (page 260) or Sour Cherry Pockets (page 264). A little red food coloring brightens the color.

1 cup dried sour cherries*

1 cup water

½ cup granulated sugar

½ teaspoon finely grated lemon zest

1 tablespoon kirsch (optional)

3 to 4 drops red food coloring

*__Note:__ If you are using the filling for Hamantaschen, increase the cherries to 1¼ cups.

1. In a small saucepan, combine the cherries and water. Let stand for 1 hour, or until the cherries are softened.
2. Bring the mixture to a boil, then reduce the heat to low, cover the pan, and simmer for 20 minutes, or until the cherries are very soft. Check the mixture occasionally during cooking to make sure the liquid has not evaporated completely; if it has, add a tablespoon or two as needed. Drain off any remaining liquid and transfer the cherries to a food processor.
3. Add the sugar, lemon zest, and kirsch, if using. Process until the cherries are finely chopped and the filling is no longer chunky, about 30 seconds. Transfer the mixture to a small bowl and stir in the red food coloring. Let the filling cool completely.

STORE **IN AN AIRTIGHT CONTAINER IN THE REFRIGERATOR FOR UP TO 3 DAYS.**

Cookies for Every Occasion

Quick and Easy

Black and White Sesame Crisps
Chocolate Peanut Magic Bars
Coconut Macaroons
Dark Victory Brownies
Flosso Bars
Lemon Cornmeal Cookies
Melting Moments
Vanilla-Scented Shortbread
Tropical Shortbread Bars
White Chocolate Macadamia Cookie Bark

Afternoon Tea

Caramelized Pecan–Orange Biscotti
Chocolate Cranberry Spice Cookies
Chocolate-Dipped Almond Crescents
Chocolate-Dipped Earl Grey Shortbread Wedges
Financiers
Glazed Lemon–Poppy Seed Hearts
Hermits
Lemon Curd Bites
Linzer Hearts
Madeleines
Melting Moments
Party Dates
Pirouettes
Pistachio Biscotti
Pistachio Shortbread Rounds
Raspberry Almond Squares
Raspberry Almond Tea Cakes
Tangerine Kumquat Rounds

The Coffee Hour

Almond Anise Biscotti
Almond Java Rounds
Caramelized Pecan–Orange Biscotti
Chocolate Almond Biscotti
Chocolate Almond Gems
Chocolate Espresso Shortbread
Chocolate Walnut Bars

Cinnamon Doughnut Holes
Hazelnut Biscotti
Toasted Almond Crunch Cookies

For Kids/With Kids

Chocolate Peanut Butter Spirals
Chocolate Pecan Thumbprints
Chocolate Peppermint Polka Dot Pigs
Chocolate Sandwich Cookies
Cinnamon Animal Crackers
Classic Peanut Butter Cookies
Colossal Peanut Butter Cookies
Hermits
New York Black and White Cookies
Peanut Butter Surprise Brownies
Peanut Butter Chocolate Chunk Cookies
Stained Glass Cookies
Triple Chocolate Devil Drops
White Chocolate–Macadamia Cookie Bark
Whoopie Pies

For Grown-Ups

Almond Anise Biscotti
Brandy Snaps
Cats' Tongues
Chinese Almond Cookies
Chocolate Chip Rum-Raisin Cookies
Chocolate-Dipped Earl Grey Shortbread Wedges
Chocolate Drizzled Toasted Coconut Cookies
Glazed Rosemary-Lemon Butter Cookies
Kourabiedes
Lemon Cornmeal Cookies
Lusty Lemon Bars
Pfeffernüsse
Rum-Raisin Sandwich Cookies
White Chocolate Eggnog Bars

Nuts about Nuts

Caramel Almond Squares
Chocolate Macadamia Peanut Butter Chip Cookies
Chocolate Peanut Butter Surprise Bars
Chocolate Peanut Magic Bars
Classic Pine Nut Macaroons

Crunchy Peanut Bars
Deluxe Bittersweet Chocolate Pecan Brownies
Fruit and Nut Bars
Milk Chocolate Macadamia Nut Cookies
Peanut Butter Chocolate Chunk Cookies
Pecan Tassies
Turtle Bars

Picnic Fare

Blueberry Crumble Bars
Brooklyn Heights Brownies
Chocolate Marble Chunk Cookies
Cornmeal Lime Shortbread
Fruit and Nut Bars
Honey-Roasted Peanut Cookies
Milk Chocolate Macadamia Nut Cookies
Oatmeal Raisin Cookies
Orange Cream Bars
Raspberry Almond Squares
Raspberry-Filled Shortbread Fingers
Soft-Baked Chocolate Chunk Cookies
White Chocolate Chip Fudge Cookies
White Chocolate–Macadamia Cookie Bark

Over-the-Top Chocolate

Brooklyn Heights Brownies
Chocolate Chocolate Chip Cookies
Chocolate Crackles
Chocolate Espresso Cheesecake Bars
Chocolate Hazelnut Truffle Bars
Cookie Shop Chocolate Chip Cookies
Dark Victory Brownies
Deluxe Bittersweet Chocolate Pecan Brownies
Double Chocolate Brownies
Double Chocolate Pecan Biscotti
Midnight Brownies
Monster Fudge Nut Cookies
White Chocolate Chip Fudge Cookies

Ship Well

Alsatian Christmas Cookies
Amy-oes
Apple Spice Oatmeal Cookies

Banana-Oatmeal Chocolate Chip Cookies
Brooklyn Heights Brownies
Classic Springerle Cookies
Cookie Shop Chocolate Chip Cookies
Crunchy Peanut Bars
Fruit and Nut Bars
Hermits
Mandelbrot
Oatmeal Raisin Cookies
White Chocolate Sour Cherry Cookies

Holidays

Alsatian Christmas Cookies
Brandied Eggnog Cookies
Chocolate Almond Shortbread Hearts
Classic Gingerbread Cookies
Classic Pine Nut Macaroons
Glazed Lemon–Poppy Seed Hearts
Molasses Spice Cookies
Pink Plaid Valentine Hearts
Russian Tea Cakes
Snowflakes
Stained Glass Cookies
White Chocolate Eggnog Bars
Wicked Witch Candy Cottage

Bake Sale Bonanza

Caramel Coconut Brownies
Caramelized Pecan–Orange Biscotti
Chocolate Almond Biscotti
Chocolate Almond Polka Dot Hearts
Chocolate-Drizzled Toasted Coconut Cookies
Chocolate Espresso Cheesecake Bars
Chocolate Pistachio Checkerboard Cookies
Gianduja Chocolate Chunk Cookies
Lattice-Topped Linzer Bars
Lemon Lamb Cookies
Linzer Hearts
Lusty Lemon Bars
Milk Chocolate Macadamia Nut Cookies
Monster Fudge Nut Cookies
New York Black and White Cookies

Palmiers
Pink Plaid Valentine Hearts
Soft-Baked Chocolate Chunk Cookies
Sour Cream Apple Crumble Bars
Triple-Ginger Pecan Biscotti
Whoopie Pies

Showstoppers

Brooklyn Heights Brownies
Chili Peppers
Chocolate Almond Shortbread Hearts
Chocolate Gingerbread People
Chocolate Peppermint Polka Dot Pigs
Lemon Lamb Cookies
Pink Plaid Valentine Hearts
Snowflakes
Stained Glass Cookies
Wedding Cake Cookies
Wicked Witch Candy Cottage

Tish's Personal Favorites

Brooklyn Heights Brownies
Caramel Almond Tiger Cookies
Caramel Coconut Brownies
Chocolate Espresso Cheesecake Bars
Chocolate Hazelnut Truffle Bars
Chocolate Macadamia Peanut Butter Chip Cookies
Chocolate Toffee Brownie Bites
Colossal Peanut Butter Cookies
Ginger Quakes
Glazed Hazelnut Jam Sandwiches
Honey-Roasted Peanut Cookies
Orange Almond Madeleines
Orange Cream Bars
Rum-Raisin Sandwich Cookies
Sour Cream Apple Crumble Bars
Triple-Ginger Pecan Biscotti
White Chocolate Key Lime Bars

Sources

The A. L. Bazzini Company

200 Food Center Drive
Hunts Point Market
Bronx, NY 10474
(800) 228-0172; (718) 842-8644
Website: bazzininuts.com

Roasted nuts, seeds, nuts in the shell, dried fruits, and nut butters; catalog available

American Spoon Foods

P.O. Box 566
Petoskey, MI 49770
(800) 222-5886; (616) 347-9030
Website: spoon.com

Dried fruit, including sour cherries and cranberries, nuts, and preserves; catalog available

The Baker's Catalogue

P.O. Box 876
Norwich, VT 05055-0876
(800) 827-6836
Website: kingarthurflour.com

Baking ingredients and equipment, including specialty flours, decorating sugars, candied fruit, bakeware, utensils, molds (including springerle molds), cookie cutters, the Microplane Zester, baker's ammonia, and a terra-cotta bear

Bridge Kitchenware Corporation

214 East 52nd Street
New York, NY 10022
(800) 274-3435; (212) 838-6746
Website: bridgekitchenware.com

General bakeware and cookie cutters; $3 for catalog, refundable with first purchase

A Cook's Wares

211 37th Street
Beaver Falls, PA 15010
(412) 846–9490
Website: cookswares.com

General bakeware, cookie cutters, chocolate, and extracts

Dairy Fresh Chocolate

57 Salem Street
Boston, MA 02113
(800) 336–5536; (617) 742–2639

Callebaut, Lindt, Peter's, and Valrhona chocolates

DeChoix Specialty Foods

58–25 52nd Avenue
Woodside, NY 11377
(800) 834–6881; (718) 507–8080
Website: dechoix.com

Chocolate, fruit purées and pastes, and nuts and nut products

Easy Leaf Products

6001 Santa Monica Boulevard
Los Angeles, CA 90038
(800) 569–5323; (213) 469–0856
Website: easyleaf.com

23-karat edible patent gold leaf

Gourmail

126A Pleasant Valley #401
Methuen, MA 01844
(800) 366–5900, ext. 96
Website: gourmail.com

Valrhona, Callebaut, and Cocoa Barry chocolate

The House on the Hill

P.O. Box 7003
Villa Park, IL 60181
(630) 969–2624
Website: houseonthehill.net

Cookie molds and cutters; catalog available

J. B. Prince Company

36 East 31st Street, 11th Floor
New York, NY 10016
(212) 683–3553
Website: jbprince.com

Professional-grade bakeware, silicone baking mats, and cookie cutters

Katagiri & Company

224 East 59th Street
New York, NY 10022
(212) 755–3566
Website: katagiri.com

Japanese specialty food, including green tea powder

KitchenAid Home Appliances

P.O. Box 218
St. Joseph, MI 49085
(800) 541–6390
Website: kitchenaid.com

Electric mixers and food processors; catalog available

Kitchen Glamor

39049 Webb Court
Westland, MI 48302
(800) 641–1252
Website: kitchenglamor.com

Cookware, decorative sugars, paste colors, and cookie cutters and molds; catalog available

La Cuisine

323 Cameron Street
Alexandria, VA 22314-3219
(800) 521–1176; (703) 836–4435
Website: lacuisineus.com

General bakeware, as well as cookie cutters and springerle molds, nut pastes, meringue powder, coarse sugar, dragees, and other cookie-making and decorating supplies; catalog available

Martha By Mail

(800) 950–7130
Website: marthabymail.com

Cookie cutters; catalog available

New York Cake and Baking Distributors

56 West 22nd Street
New York, NY 10010
(800) 94–CAKE–9; (212) 675–CAKE
Website: nycake.com

General bakeware, decorating supplies (including a large selection of paste food colorings), cookie cutters, acetate transfer sheets, and chocolate

Penzey's Spices

P.O. Box 933
Muskego, WI 53150
(800) 741–7787
Website: penzeys.com

Spices, herbs, and extracts; catalog available

Sur la Table

Pike Place Farmers Market
84 Pine Street
Seattle, WA 98101
(800) 243–0852
Website: surlatable.com

General bakeware, cookie cutters, and springerle molds and plaques; catalog available

Sweet Celebrations

7009 Washington Avenue South
Edina, MN 55439
(800) 328–6722
Website: sweetc.com

Baking equipment and ingredients, including cookie cutters and molds, decorating sugars, and the Microplane Zester; catalog available

Tropical Nut & Fruit

P.O. Box 7507
1100 Continental Boulevard
Charlotte, NC 28273
(800) 438–4470; 704–588–0400
Website: tropicalnutandfruit.com

Chocolate, dried fruits, and nuts

Williams-Sonoma

100 North Point Street
San Francisco, CA 94133
(800) 541–2233
Website: williams-sonoma.com

General bakeware and cookie cutters; catalog available

Wilton Industries

2240 West 75 Street
Woodridge, IL 60517-0750
(800) 994–5866
Website: wilton.com

Pastry bags and tips, cookie cutters, meringue powder, flower nails, and a wide selection of other cookie making and decorating ingredients and equipment; catalog available

Index

A

B

Q

R

S

T

U

V

W

Y

Z

Metric Conversion Guide

length

TO CONVERT	MULTIPLY BY
Inches into millimeters	25.4
Inches into centimeters	2.54
Millimeters into inches	0.03937
Centimeters into inches	0.3937
Meters into inches	39.3701

volume

TO CONVERT	MULTIPLY BY
Quarts into liters	0.946
Pints into liters	0.473
Quarts into milliliters	946
Milliliters into ounces	0.0338
Liters into quarts	1.05625
Milliliters into pints	0.0021125
Liters into pints	2.1125
Liters into ounces	33.8

weight

TO CONVERT	MULTIPLY BY
Ounces into grams	28.35
Grams into ounces	0.03527
Kilograms into pounds	2.2046

to convert fahrenheit to celsius

SUBTRACT 32, THEN MULTIPLY THIS NUMBER BY 5/9

For example: 350°F − 32 = 318 × 5/9 = 176.6°C

to convert celsius to fahrenheit

MULTIPLY BY 9, DIVIDE THIS NUMBER BY 5, THEN ADD 32

For example: 180°C × 9/5 = 324 + 32 = 356°F

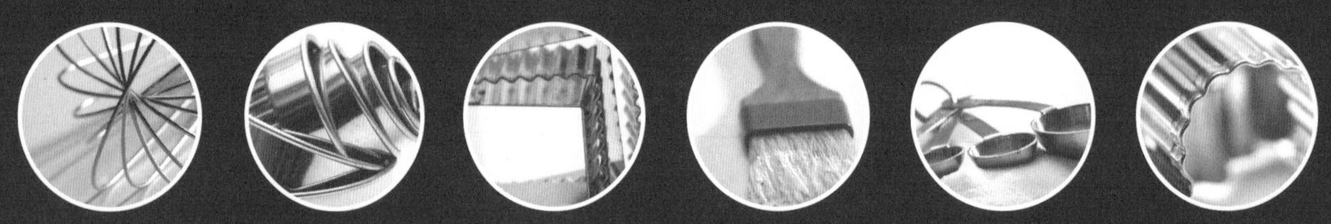